Leading the Reference Renaissance

Today's Ideas for Tomorrow's Cutting-Edge Services

Edited by Marie L. Radford

Neal-Schuman Publishers, Inc.

New York   London

Published by Neal-Schuman Publishers, Inc.
100 William St., Suite 2004
New York, NY 10038
http://www.neal-schuman.com

Printed and bound in the United States of America.

The paper used in this publication meets the minimum requirements of American National Standard for Information Sciences—Permanence of Paper for Printed Library Materials, ANSI Z39.48-1992.

Library of Congress Cataloging-in-Publication Data

Leading the reference renaissance : today's ideas for tomorrow's cutting-edge services / edited by Marie L. Radford.
    p. cm.
    The papers in this volume resulted from presentations at the second Reference Renaissance: Current and Future Trends Conference in 2010.
    Includes bibliographical references and index.
    ISBN 978-1-55570-771-2
    1. Reference services (Libraries)—United States. 2. Electronic reference services (Libraries)—United States. 3. Internet in library reference services—United States. 4. Reference services (Libraries)—Forecasting. I. Radford, Marie L., editor of compilation.

Z711.L44 2012
025.5'2—dc23
                                        2011041992

*This book is dedicated to all the leaders
of the Reference Renaissance—
the reference librarians, staff, and administrators
who are visioning and creating the future.*

Contents

List of Tables
and Figures

Tables

Figures

Acknowledgments

I would like to thank everyone who contributed to the development of this book and to the planning and success of the Reference Renaissance 2010: Current and Future Trends Conference, the second of its kind that followed the incredible 2008 inaugural event. In particular, I would like to thank the conference Chair, Brenda K. Bailey-Hainer, then President and CEO, and Justine Schaffner, then Library Services Consultant, both from Bibliographical Center for Research (BCR), Colorado. Without their efforts neither the first nor second conference would have taken place, and thus this volume would not exist.

I also extend thanks to the members of the conference planning committee, especially those who served as chapter reviewers and consultants for this book: Wayne Bivens-Tatum, Princeton University; Kay Cassell, Rutgers, the State University of New Jersey; Melissa Gold, Millersville College, Pennsylvania; Nancy Huling, University of Washington; M. Kathleen Kern, University of Illinois at Urbana-Champaign; Vince Mariner, Ask PA; Julie Strange, Maryland AskUsNow!; Amy VanScoy, North Carolina State University Libraries; and Lynn Westbrook, University of Texas, Austin.

In addition, special recognition goes to the major Reference Renaissance Conference sponsors, BCR, RUSA, and Tutor.com, and to these other sponsors: Compendium Library Service, OCLC, Reference Universe (Paratext), Serial Solutions, and the University of Denver.

I deeply appreciate the contribution of each of the presenters, and attendees, who provided an exciting conference in terms of their forward-looking vision, dedication, and enthusiasm for the Reference Renaissance, including new exciting programs such as Petcha Kucha sessions and Lightning Talks.

A debt of gratitude is also due to Neal-Schuman Publishers, in particular to Charles Harmon, Director of Publishing, and to the members of the editorial staff. I also am grateful for the editing assistance and enthusiasm of Vicky Weber, Ripon College, Wisconsin, a Rutgers University RiSE (Research in Science and Engineering) scholar.

I am ever thankful for the love, gentle encouragement, and ever sage advice of my husband, Gary P. Radford, PhD, and to Meg K. Radford, my daughter, for her editing assistance and support.

Introduction

Marie L. Radford

According to gaming visionary Jane McGonigal, "We can make any future we can imagine" (http://www.ted.com/talks/jane_mcgonigal_gaming_can_make_a_better_world.html). She was talking about the potential for creativity in the multiplayer gaming world, but I believe this idea to be as true for reference services as well.

Leading the Reference Renaissance: Today's Ideas for Tomorrow's Cutting-Edge Services seeks to push our collective imaginations, to make a contribution to visioning for reference futures by highlighting both intriguing research and exciting innovations that are now taking place in reference service throughout the United States.

None of the authors of the chapters are content to be passive in this rapidly morphing reference environment, but rather strive to be among the field's top innovators. That choice to lead rarely makes work easy, and there are always naysayers and doubters who ridicule those on the forefront of new approaches and service models. Part of the reference renaissance has to do with our attitudes, the way in which we view and approach challenges, obstacles, and opportunities that are presented to the profession, reference service, and to ourselves. The chapter authors here are activists who say "not dead yet" to those who proclaim that reference is becoming moribund. They are infusing new energy and enthusiasm into public service for all types of libraries.

This volume offers undeniable evidence that the reference renaissance continues. It extends the work of the first *Reference Renaissance: Current and Future Trends* volume, edited by Dave Lankes and myself and published by Neal-Schuman in 2010. That book presented the updated proceedings of the first Reference Renaissance Conference; it was well-received and generated a sustained interest that provided some of the impetus for the second Reference Renaissance: Current and Future Trends Conference in 2010.

Conference speakers presented papers, panels, and workshops that analyzed issues, and identified and described reference practices that extended service boundaries and questioned traditional assumptions. They also advanced collaborative, organizational, and technological systems, proposed standards and new assessment methods, and/or suggested innovative approaches that revealed an exciting and unfolding reference future. After the conference, I put out a call for papers for all conference presentations and then sent out all submissions for blind review to a team of expert reviewers.

This new collection highlights bold explorations of the revolutionary changes in technology, e-reference tools, and in our basic conceptualizations of what reference service encompasses. It sets out to capture the most exciting and innovative initiatives in the revitalized reference movement, and features these fully juried chapters that are divided into three parts: Visionary Thinkers on the User Experience and the Future; Revelations from Reference Research; and Reference in Action—Innovative Initiatives Forging the Future.

In Part I, Andrew Walsh provides his provocative thoughts and issues challenges to implement mobile reference in "Setting Reference Free: Reference Services for the Mobile Age," in which he reveals applications such as Quick Response (QR) Codes and Augmented Reality (AR), which are becoming more widespread in use, especially in the United Kingdom and at his home institution, the University of Huddersfield. Next, I put forth an essay that introduces some ideas about the technologies and other forces that are impacting reference futures, and my take on how it will unfold in the near and not-so-near future. Then avant-garde thinkers Steven J. Bell, Wayne Bivens-Tatum, and James LaRue provide three essays on the reference User Experience (UX) which is becoming more and more a focus for libraries. Recently I learned that one of my former students, Stephen Francoeur of the Newman Library of Baruch College in New York City, was given a new title, "User Experience Librarian," in this urban academic library setting with a heavily used reference and instruction program. Our chapters make for interesting reading in defining this new way to rethink user services. Jean Costello, who blogs as the Radical Patron, provides a view from a disenfranchised user, one who urges librarians to stop reinventing the wheel and to reconnect with traditional strengths of value-added service to users who may have become jaded and perplexed by the overabundance of information that is not vetted by professionals.

Part II offers eight chapters that feature analysis and literature reviews in reference research. They are grouped under the three topic areas of Virtual Reference Encounters and Instruction Initiatives; Meeting Challenges through Evolving Service Models and Staff Development; and Assessment—Using Data to Inform the Future. These present research-based reports and thought-provoking essays. Results from studies of emerging technologies such as web conferencing and the impact of generational differences on virtual reference service (VRS) are presented, as well as discussions on how best to teach problem solving in this environment. In addition, research in new staffing models involving student led-VR and an investigation of the traditional and emerging roles for reference librarians are included. One researcher looks at a comparison of stressors in academic versus public librarians and another compares results from numerous studies of e-mail VR. All of these research chapters take on different research questions, methods of analysis, and theoretical approaches that offer exciting findings that are well-grounded in data.

Part III features 15 "reports from the field" that are grouped under the four topic areas of Implementing Intriguing Initiatives and Extending Outreach; Collaborative Solutions and Successes; Assessing Reference and Tracking User Behavior; and Virtual Tools and Attitude Adjustments to Improve Service. Chapters focus on innovative service models including the following: embedded librarians, mobile reference through cooperative texting (SMS), roving reference, outreach initiatives and challenges from academic librarians, and reorganization and consolidation of service points. In addition, authors look at technological advances that impact reference service, such as how LibGuides are helping to improve VR, how Wikipedia should be used, novel and improved web-based assessment techniques for tracking user behavior and e-resource use, and more.

Updating the information presented at the second Reference Renaissance Conference, these chapters investigate and report all aspects of reference in a broad range of contexts including academic and public libraries, consortia, and collaboratives. Not only do they capture the current state-of-the-art, but they also give us a glimpse of the road ahead to the trends and ideas that are forging the reference future. It is not enough to just dream about the future; we all need to take action to make our dreams become reality. Each of us has to take responsibility to stand up and take on the mantle of change agent. You are invited to learn from these authors, and to be inspired to join them as leaders of the reference renaissance.

## PART I

VISIONARY THINKERS ON THE USER EXPERIENCE AND THE FUTURE

Setting Reference Free: Reference Services for the Mobile Age

Andrew Walsh

Introduction

This essay focuses on mobile services and how they relate to the reference service. In it I cover some things that are moving into the mainstream, such as short message service (SMS) text messaging or social networking services, and some emerging technologies, such as Quick Response (QR) codes and location-based services, and one or two that may be a bit more speculative or cutting edge that may well not make an impact, but are worth thinking about. I also give you three specific challenges.

Before I write about anything else, I have a clear message to give you. TURN ON YOUR MOBILE PHONES. When I go to training events, conferences, briefings, etc., the first thing we are told is to turn off our mobiles. As you read this, I want you to think a little bit about the devices that you most likely have in your pocket or on your desk. You may have a smartphone which can do all sorts of amazing things. My phone knows where I am through Global Positioning System (GPS) (or triangulation of the mobile phone signal if GPS is turned off or unavailable); connects me instantly to friends and colleagues all over the world through e-mail, Facebook, and Twitter; effortlessly links me to the sea of information that is the Internet, which increasingly includes serious research databases; acts as a gaming device; electronic-book reader; a way of watching or listening to television or radio programs; an educational tool for my young children; a music player; a camera, a camcorder, a Dictaphone, a satellite navigation system (SatNav) and more. The fact that if I forget to knock the sound off it occasionally gives an irritating ring tone is almost incidental. I want you to remember what incredibly powerful devices so many of you are carrying around in your pockets or bags every day. It is terrible asking people to ignore this power, in your libraries, in your teaching, in your everyday work.

Sorry. Little rant over and, before I move on any further, I thought I would have a little diversion to tell you a little about where I come from. I work at the University of Huddersfield, which is in Yorkshire, the North of England. A midsized U.K. university, we have just over 23,000 students, of which around 3,000 are postgraduates (http://www2.hud.ac.uk/about/facts/index.php). Some of you may recognize the chancellor of our university, the actor Patrick Stewart, who is a local lad and really helps out at the university a great amount.

We have, as a joint computing and library service, a fairly simple and perhaps vague-sounding aim: "to deliver an inspiring information environment for the digital age."

3

This mission works together with a set of objectives that go into a little more detail, mentioning things like "delivering accessible, reliable and innovative digital technologies" and "building information skills for life" (http://www2.hud.ac.uk/cls/aboutus/aim.php).

The way these aims and objectives, however, are reflected in our everyday work, is by having a certain element of freedom to innovate, to constantly improve services, and though we do not have much money, we do have enough freedom to "hit above our weight" in many ways. So, for instance, my colleague, Dave Pattern, was one of *Library Journal*'s "movers and shakers" last year, and the only English one. Just to name a few concrete things: we have a fantastic library catalog (http://webcat.hud.ac.uk/), we were the first U.K. university to subscribe to Summon (http://library.hud.ac.uk/summon), we have been investigating mobile technologies over the past year or so (e.g., Walsh 2010a,b), and we have recently found a firm link between the use of library resources and academic achievement (White & Stone, 2010).

So, getting back to mobile things, I alluded before to the fact that most of you probably have mobile phones, though this essay is also relevant about mobile learning in general. So I now ask you to think about more than phones (e.g., iPods, handheld game machines, and digital cameras). I have guessed that you probably have a mobile phone and I am willing to bet that most of your library users do as well.

Looking at the last figures from the recent Pew Internet report on mobile access (Smith, 2010), 59 percent of American adults have accessed the web wirelessly, which includes 40 percent accessing some aspect of the web from their mobile phones. Their figures also show that 82 percent of adults own a cell phone. I believe that those figures are going to continue to increase, especially in terms of the uses that people are adopting for their mobile phones. You can see this in younger users: nine out of ten 18- to 29-year-olds own a cell phone; 95 percent of these use text messaging, and a massive 65 percent access the Internet from their phone.

The Morgan Stanley (2009) mobile Internet report notes, "The mobile Internet is ramping faster than desktop Internet did, and we believe more users may connect to the Internet via mobile devices than desktop PCs within 5 years." Thinking about libraries in particular, just to reinforce this point, one of the Association of College and Research Library's (ACRL) top ten trends in academic libraries for 2010 was that "Explosive growth of mobile devices and applications will drive new services" (ACRL Research Planning and Review Committee, 2010).

Mainstream Mobile Technology

So, practically everyone has a cell phone, which means that practically everyone can text either free as part of a contract, or for a few cents a message. This leads to another question: Is your library using text messaging to talk to your users or allowing questions to be texted to its reference service? If not, WHY NOT? There is not a vast difference in the length of time text messaging has been available to the masses and e-mail has been easily available. I am thinking of the World Wide Web making the Internet widely accessible. Does your library put an e-mail address out there for people to get in touch, but not a number to text to? Texting is OLD technology, mature technology. This is not last year's technology—it is not even last decade's! So, this is my first challenge to you: If your library does not accept SMS to your reference service, it should start doing so now!

You can sign up to a commercial service, get a web-based text messaging portal, ask a tame IT expert to create a web portal of your own, use your e-mail system to send free text messages (if you know the carrier), or even stick a cheap pay-as-you-go cell phone with a few dollars' worth of credit on it in your main reference desk drawer. It does not have to be complicated. It can be as simple as you want, but just do it. It is such a simple, cheap technology that practically all of your users are familiar with. So use it.

Facebook (http://www.facebook.com/) and Twitter (http://www.twitter.com/) are two incredibly widespread platforms now, but what you may not have realized is that these, especially Twitter, really come into their own on mobile platforms. Facebook, in many countries, is now even becoming accessible for free on phones that do not normally have Internet access included in their package. Has your library got a presence on these platforms? If not, why not? They have the massive advantage of being free! If I want a question answered I will often turn to Twitter to ask a network of friends and colleagues, so why not allow your users to get on their phones and Tweet a question to @yourlibrary? These applications now also have the ability to tag updates with a location, which has implications I'll come to later on.

Podcasting and screencasting are mainstream now, but have you thought of quick-and-dirty screencasts to answer inquiries? I sometimes take a few minutes to create a quick screencast to demonstrate something and e-mail it in response to a query. If I put that video on YouTube (http://www.youtube.com/) it can be delivered in a mobile-friendly format for people to watch wherever they wish.

Instant podcasts using mobile phones are also fantastically easy to do, and in library use instruction I demonstrate Audioboo (http://audioboo.fm/). These podcasts can be great both for people who have a learning style that suits listening more than reading or doing and for those users who may not have English as a first language. It can be really helpful for those people to go back and listen to your answer a few times and really work out what you meant.

Emerging Mobile Technologies

On to emerging technologies—that is, ones that are nudging against popular awareness, that may well become mainstream in the near future, or may die and wither away! There are two things I want to talk about here: QR codes and location-aware or location-based services. QR codes have pottered about the edge of mass awareness for a while now. They are seriously popular in Japan because the mobile network providers install a QR reader on all phones. Everywhere else they seem on the verge of mass adoption because the increase in smartphones makes them easy to use, and importantly, their application is easy to install.

QR codes are matrix codes, like a 2-D square version of a bar code. Whereas a bar code just runs horizontally, a QR code runs vertically as well, so it can embed much more data into a small space. They were developed by a company called Denso Wave in Japan, who wanted a method to help them track vehicle components. They released this code they had developed as an international standard, free for everyone to use. Because of this there is a large range of free QR readers for mobile phones, so they work on practically any camera phone. Importantly for us, they are also free to make. They are fantastic for linking to context-appropriate help around your library. What are your top reference inquiries?

- "How do I use the photocopier?" Embed a "how-to" video into a code placed on your copiers.
- "Where are the travel books?" Put a set of subjects with QR codes around the library with small audio tours embedded in them to guide people straight there.
- Do people get confused using the catalogs in remote corners of the library? Embed the phone number of your reference desk into a code next to each catalog.

If you can work out what your common questions are and where they originate in the library, you can embed virtual or remote help where your users need it, instead of them having to pluck up courage to come to a physical desk. If you give printed guides out at your reference desk, embed further help into those handouts in the form of videos, quizzes, podcasts, useful webpages, sections of electronic books, and much more than you could ever hope to cover in a sheet or two of paper. All through a small, free-to-generate, blocky code that is maybe an inch square.

However, there are definite barriers to using QR codes. The two key barriers are unfamiliarity and the fact that users have to choose to install an application. It seems as if both of these things are improving, though. I increasingly see QR codes in the wild, and a recent Mashable story (Van Grove, 2010) suggests that applications such as SCVNGR (http://www.scvngr.com/) and stickybits (http://www.stickybits.com/) that include the ability to scan QR codes will provide a back-door route for QR codes to break into the mainstream.

My next emerging mobile technology is "location-aware" services, which are nicely illustrated by applications such as Gowalla (http://gowalla.com/) and Foursquare (https://foursquare.com/). These applications run on location-aware smartphones, allowing you to "check in" to locations. They offer rewards for doing so, such as points, badges, virtual items to pick up and exchange, and "mayorships" (for the person checked into a location the most times) depending on the application. These rewards are sometimes turned into "real-world" rewards, such as discounts or free products from retailers.

Importantly, there is a social networking aspect to them. As well as communicating your location via third-party networks such as Twitter, you can set up networks of friends in these applications, bringing an element of both competition and socializing into them. They also allow you to leave "tips" about a location for others to view. Why not use this idea to put your library's common questions and answers up for the world to see? Or contact details for your virtual or mobile reference service? Incidentally, you can tell a service such as Foursquare that you manage a location and set up more information and rewards for customers. I wonder how much extra traffic your location may get if the "mayor" of your library gets their fines written off?

Existing social networks are also coming into this location-aware space, with Twitter and Facebook allowing you to "geolocate" updates. I will come back to these type of applications later.

These are the fun, free, and social sides of these applications and there are plenty of other location-aware, mobile-friendly platforms around. Commercial platforms are available that deliver campus information and bring in elements of these location-aware services, or if you have the time and talent, they can be developed in-house.

Huddersfield is developing such a service over the coming academic year, based on the same type of reward systems in Foursquare and Gowalla. It will be called Lemon Tree and is being produced by a fantastic creative local outfit called Running in the Halls (http://www.rith.co.uk/). It will be focused around our library, and have the same sort of social networking, the same sort of competition around points and badges as these other applications, but will offer those rewards for activities such as checking out a book, leaving a book review, watching a video on our webpages, and more. We are hoping for good things out of this, not just a way of engaging with current nonusers of the library services, but as a way of educating our users so they know more about how the library works. We do not want to sit at the reference desk telling our users how to put print credit onto their accounts—we want them to know already because they have gained the "print master" badge in Lemon Tree.

More Speculative Mobile Technologies

Next up is something a bit more speculative, namely augmented reality (AR) applications. These are a sensible step up from QR codes and location-aware applications, and there are already many AR applications around. These applications put a layer of virtual reality over the physical world, or "augment" physical reality. In science fiction this would be done through an implant straight into your brain, or perhaps through special contact lenses. At its most primitive in fiction it may be through a pair of special glasses that projects an additional layer of information onto the lens.

Until recently you may have said we were a long way off from this being a practical technology. But think a little more about what is needed for AR to work. You need a device that is connected to the Internet to pull the virtual layer of information to you. You need a device that knows where it is and which direction it is facing. You need a device that has a decent bit of processing power so it can make sense of this information. You need a device that has a camera on it so it can see where it is and a decent display so it can lay the virtual information over top of the "real-world" display. So, what you really need is the sort of device that is a top-end smartphone or any iPad at the moment, but what industry experts are telling us will be the norm for all of us to be carrying in a few years' time. I am told that, by 2015, most phones will be smartphones, with basic models less available (IDC, 2011).

So, the technology is around and getting more commonplace. There are even videos on YouTube showing how AR works. There are custom AR applications around that have been developed as research projects, including for libraries, but the problem with using them inside buildings is that you need to find alternatives to GPS to locate the user. This can be done by mapping Wi-Fi or Bluetooth signal strength from several aerials triangulating the users' position, or using markers (like the QR codes described earlier). Can you imagine applications like this helping your users navigate your library? Can you picture a "librarian" tag appearing throughout your library's AR application, ready for the user to click on and go straight through to sending you a question by text, or instant messenger, or any other method you want to make available to them?

This is really speculative, but there are already freely available generic AR apps around. One of the early pioneers of AR on smartphones is Layar (http://www.layar .com/), which is available on Android and iPhone platforms, superimposing virtual information on the real world as seen through the phone's camera.

These sort of AR applications mean you do not need to create AR applications or even virtual layers yourself; you can use the sort of location-aware social networks described earlier that will automatically appear in "layars" other people have created. Why not take advantage of this technology for common reference questions? Set up your library on Foursquare or Gowalla and add tips. Tweet commonly asked questions and attach your location. When users point their smartphones at your library using one of these AR browsers, they will see the information displayed before they even enter the building. Even better, they will see your library, with information about it, even if they did not know you were there.

AR is already here and we have no idea what it will turn into over the next few years. So, my second challenge to you is this: Be radical. Think of how AR could change your reference service and do something about it now. If you do not, by the time you think about it others will be dominating the space and you will have NO control.

Information Literacy

I believe that mobile technology changes the relationships you have with your users. It changes the relationships they have with information. It changes what it means to be information literate. I am only going to focus on this aspect briefly, but it is important to the way you will have to deal with people at your reference desks, at the other end of the phone, by e-mail, from now on.

Recommending a fantastic reference work to answer a question may be great for the user in your library, or if it is online, great for the user at a fixed desktop. But what use is it to the user who is sitting on a bus staring at a tiny screen? If you look something up yourself and provide the answer, is it at all helpful if the patron cannot write it down because she is walking through a crowd on her way to work?

Forget things like what the official Information Literacy standards say because how will you ever hope to measure them for the mobile learner? Lists of attributes or standards someone must meet are all well and good, but perhaps relational models are more appropriate here, like the different "lenses" that may apply when people look for information (Edwards, 2006). Different lenses apply at different times, so perhaps we need to think about what a "mobile" lens may look like. According to Murphy (2010):

> There are differences in information-seeking behaviours beyond simply reading news on your mobile. What you first use to search often depends on convenience—and the easiest route is often dictated by your mobile technology habits. You can easily grab an answer from Google or Wikipedia using a mobile web browser or application. Text messaging is even easier, and it's become endemic with mobile phones. You can text a friend or ChaCha for a quick answer. Then there's social networking. (p. 14)

In my mind, for a mobile user, being information literate might mean knowing the right application to use, or the right person to message from their social networking community, or how to well phrase a question in 140 characters to get a meaningful answer via Twitter. If you do not accept this and help users to find that right, trustworthy application, or teach them how to define their question properly so they can ask it in 140 characters, you will be holding them back from becoming information literate *in this environment*. And remember, this is the environment that will be the norm for information searching before long.

Mobile technologies change how people interact, not just with one another, but with the world of information. This technology changes their environment. Do not expect them to act the same way as in the old environment.

Summing Up

This all brings me to my third and final challenge. I have written a little about how we may use mobile phones in our work, but I bet that many of you have "No mobile phones" signs around your libraries. Do not try to deprive your users of these fantastic tools. Instead take a look around your libraries and see if you can change any "No mobiles" signs to "Mobiles welcome—but please switch them to silent."

References

ACRL Research Planning and Review Committee. (2010). Top ten trends in academic libraries: A review of the current literature. *College & Research Libraries News, 71*(7), 286–292.

Edwards, S. (2006). *Panning for gold: Information literacy and the net lenses model*. Adelaide, Australia: Auslib Press.

IDC. 2011. *IDC Worldwide Quarterly Mobile Phone Tracker*, March 29. Framington, MA: IDC.

Morgan Stanley. (2009). *Mobile Internet Report*. Retrieved on July 9, 2011, from http://www.morganstanley.com/institutional/techresearch/mobile_internet_report122009.html.

Murphy, J. (2010). Using mobile devices for research: Smartphones, databases, and libraries. *Online*, May/June, 14–18.

Smith, A. (2010). *Mobile Access 2010. Pew Internet & American Life Project*. Retrieved on July 9, 2011, from http://www.pewinternet.org/Reports/2010/Mobile-Access-2010.aspx.

Van Grove, J. (2010). Why QR codes are poised to hit the mainstream. Retrieved on July 9, 2011, from http://mashable.com/2010/07/20/qr-codes-mainstream/.

Walsh, A. (2010a). Mobile phone services and UK higher education students, what do they want from the library? *Library and Information Research, 34*(106), 22–36. Retrieved on July 9, 2011, from http://eprints.hud.ac.uk/7758/.

Walsh, A. (2010b). QR codes—using mobile phones to deliver library instruction and help at the point of need. *Journal of Information Literacy, 3*(1), 55–65. Retrieved on July 9, 2011, from http://eprints.hud.ac.uk/7759/.

White, S., & Stone, G. (2010). Maximising use of library resources at the University of Huddersfield. *Serials, 23*(2), 83–90. Retrieved on July 9, 2011, from http://eprints.hud.ac.uk/7811/.

Envisioning and Creating Reference Futures

Marie L. Radford

Introduction

I'm about to engage in some risky business—making a few predictions about the future of reference. Predictions are always risky, but also fun, so why not choose to live right on the edge rather than playing it safe? I will explore the rapidly changing nature of reference as an ever-increasing array of information technologies are joining and morphing with traditional reference modes of service delivery to become vibrant hybrids, to demand new staffing models, and to bring into focus possibilities that were hitherto unimagined. The unimagined suddenly has become reality. Indeed, it is apparent that technology and societal developments are driving us, enticing us, even forcing us to take reference service to the next level (or else?). I begin with a discussion of the dynamic reference landscape and then I take some educated guesses, extrapolating from today's trends, to speculate on the reference futures on the horizon. I also highlight some important issues impacting reference futures including need for increased collaboration, impact of social networking technology and especially mobile technology.

It is not difficult to predict that change—swift, unrelenting technological change—is the number-one force impacting reference service today and for the foreseeable future. Networked digital devices are setting a breakneck pace for change, governed by Moore's Law, a bold prediction made in 1965 by Intel cofounder Gordon Moore. He said that microchip miniaturization would lead to a doubling of computing power approximately every year (Moore, 1965). Incredibly, he was right. So far, anyway!

All technology changes. All that is commonly used today will soon be replaced by something new (think cell phone, iPad2). That something else will be faster, smarter, cheaper, more durable, more capable, better, and, of course, "way cooler." Within the coming years, the nascent field of nanotechnology will continue to push the limits of speed, capacity, and miniaturization beyond anything we can imagine. Our present reality holds the challenge of adapting to:

- new systems,
- developing products, and mergers of competitors (like H.W. Wilson and EBSCO),
- emerging formats,
- novel virtual environments,
- increasing diversity in the types of users, and
- growing and competing demands on our services.

Libraries are in transition from a time when information was scarce and precious to today when information is vast, readily available, and mostly free (Connaway, Dickey, &

Radford, 2011). In this transition time, libraries are vying for information seekers' attention and must re-engineer to accommodate users' work flows and habits (Connaway, Radford, & Williams, 2009). According to Sadeh (2008), the time is now to think more carefully about the User Experience (UX) in libraries and to figure out how to best adapt future services to changing user needs.

Challenges and Realities

It is impossible to talk about the future without recognizing that this is a time of economic challenge and increased stressors and constraints on human and fiscal resources. Funds are insufficient to purchase needed resources and many libraries have been asked to make deep cuts in their budgets, which were already lean. Libraries are being asked to "do more with less" and to cope with frozen positions and staff shortages. Although libraries are experiencing decreasing support, the economic downturn has resulted in many libraries having increasing demand. Out-of-work citizens find that the library is the only place that they can have free access to computers and Wi-Fi, access, which they need to fill out online applications and investigate job leads. Parents with limited budgets are mining library DVD and audiobook collections for free movies and quality literature on CD for their children, as well as for themselves. All over the country, public libraries are seeing rising gate count and reference activity. According to latest available statistics from the Association of Research Libraries (ARL), academic libraries are also seeing large increases in interlibrary loan requests and instruction counts (Kyrillidou & Morris, 2011). Students enjoy collaborative work and are crowding library spaces, particularly in the late evening. To cope with these demanding times, new service models are being considered as these challenges drive us toward more collaborative and cooperative solutions.

Tomorrow's Reference 'Scape

Reflect a moment. If you were asked to write about the challenges and opportunities for reference service excellence in the future, what realities or possibilities would you consider? Which ones would you believe to be significant enough to write about? We can see foreshadowing of the future in the trends of today, similar to looking down a road. As we travel along the road, the more we can make out what is in the distance as it gets closer. We can get a glimpse of the future by examining things that are just occurring now, by what is just beyond sight, on the horizon, and by paying attention to the preferences of our service users and potential users, especially the younger ones. We are fortunate to have an abundance of opportunities presented by the large Millennial (1979–1994) and younger iGeneration (born since 1995) populations, who have a decided proclivity for online and networked systems. We need to find out more about these generations of users who have different information-seeking preferences and communication behaviors than their older cohorts (Connaway & Radford, 2011).

We sometimes already have the disoriented feeling that things are morphing, moving so rapidly that we are seeing today by way of a rearview mirror. We know that change is accelerating—but we can perhaps see some inkling of the future, some glimpses just around the bend ahead?

Two important documents, both released by the Association for College and Research Libraries (ACRL), contain important trend information for library futurists to consider.

One of these is the ACRL Top Ten Trends for 2010 (Connaway et al., 2010). Another is *Futures Thinking for Academic Librarians: Higher Education in 2025* (Staley & Malenfant, 2010), which predicts that there will be a rise of the nontraditional student (e.g., part-time, minorities, older, diverse in culture and language). It also forecasts that our service modes will merge and we will move seamlessly among hybrid e-mail, chat, instant messaging (IM), text messaging, phone, face-to-face (FtF), and new modalities of delivery yet to come.

I see two major changes ahead for all reference modes, and I owe thanks to Dave Lankes of Syracuse University for getting me to think about this idea. The two major changes are as follows:

1. What we do
2. The way we do it

I see every aspect of reference service changing, sooner than we think, and perhaps drastically, and I believe this will be for the better. I see a major departure from the old business as usual that is driven by user preferences for communication and changes in their information-seeking behaviors. The service models that we continue to embrace were working in the 1960s, 1970s, even throughout the 1980s and 1990s. But now as we are firmly in the twenty-first century, it is obvious that we need to rethink many of our outmoded ideas and ways of doing reference.

So, taking the longer view, what do I think the future holds for reference? More collaboration and cooperation between all types of libraries and librarians is being driven by the faltering economy, which is obliging many libraries to try creative staffing solutions as well as technology innovations. Ahead will be an exciting time of growth, exploration, and opportunity. One benefit of technology that we are just beginning to harness is the advances in social media, which will allow us to engage in increased reference consultation with one another in a way that will be seamless to our users.

The old tradition of one person-per-hour on the desk, whether physical or virtual, will fall by the wayside. I have called this the "Lone Ranger" mind-set (Radford, 2008) which we have brought with us from the Carnegie Library's reference desk staffing models (in which one person was strategically positioned to monitor the library stacks while providing assistance) into the virtual reference (VR) arena. Another prediction that I will make is that social media technology will soon be used to dispel the feeling that we are alone with queries when we are offering reference assistance. I am envisioning that a new application for libraries will be developed that will be similar to Twitter or collaborative social question and answer (SQA) systems like Yahoo! Answers. It will be used for difficult or esoteric subject questions, perhaps "crowd sourcing" reference librarians and lay subject experts across America, or across the world. This collaboration will result in better service to users and more satisfaction for librarians with specialized expertise. It will require librarians to rebrand from "visit a library" to "ask a librarian" and to have an easily searchable platform for local information that reduces the now significant time these questions take.

At the Reference Renaissance 2010 conference, Ahniwa Ferrari, Washington State Library, said, "Without cooperation, hours are limited," and noted that it is time to leverage resources where it makes sense while retaining local autonomy and authenticity. Radical Patron blogger Jean Costello observed that "Library staff members are bogged down with the basics—creating and re-creating the same wheels." I envision librarians shedding the routine work and being more continually engaged in professional endeavors of the highest intellectual order, to design and deploy user-centered solutions.

To make this happen sooner rather than later, I have been promoting the idea of "intergenerational collaboration" (Radford, 2008). This idea is in response to hearing that some libraries are experiencing wars between librarians from different age groups, as our institutions now have as many as four or five generations of staff on their rosters. This type of mentoring involves pairing up more mature staff to mentor younger staff and vice versa. Younger staff members are more facile with mobile communication technology and social networking. The mature staff members are more experienced. They are facile in print resources and also in service excellence and community and local institutional knowledge. These pairings will unleash creativity and increase understanding and the skill base for all. If there are no younger librarians on your staff (a sorry reality for some libraries with frozen positions), harness the energy and knowledge of student workers and part-timers, volunteers, or MLIS interns if a library school is nearby. These young people can assist by helping out with your library's social media presence (e.g., starting and/or helping to update a Facebook page, designing tweets for programs, marketing campaigns, etc.). Think of the possibilities!

Impact of E-resources and Killer Apps

Regarding e-resources, there is evidence in today's trends that e-journals and e-books will continue to flourish and will enable us to offer on-demand parsing and repurposing information (e.g., delivering book chapters to desktops, retrieving or printing relevant sections of e-journal text, manipulating data or parameters on charts). This evolution of text will forever and irretrievably change the nature of collection development and document access. I predict that soon we will have one-stop shopping for scholarly databases, with an interface as easy as Google Scholar, and I see this as less than ten years away. Delivery of content to users' desktops and mobile devices (phones and tablets) will dominate as e-text becomes ubiquitous, for fiction as well as nonfiction. User demand will also push us to more personalized interfaces (e.g., designed for novice or expert searchers) and personalized librarians (e.g., firmly embedded in online courses). Librarian avatars will be commonplace and they will be designed to look like the library user, whose personalized profile will be accessible through new web protocols. Research is investigating avatar-based interactive training that suggests that users have a preference for interacting with people who look like them—and that they learn more (DeMara et al., 2008).

Librarians will continue to be needed by our users, despite advances in search engines, which, luckily, still leave much to be desired and will for some time. My current research, yet unpublished, has shown that ready-reference type queries are still being received at the rate of about 30 percent for VR live chat and IM transcripts randomly selected from 2010. Which new technologies will continue to impact reference work? The two most important of these will be the web and mobile technology. As Web 2.0 technologies mature, they are already being left behind by the rapid adoption of Web 3.0

and Web 4.0 and beyond. These technologies will have many applications for librarians, including improved service to underserved populations such as English-language learners. Sophisticated translation software is being developed that will enable English-speaking librarians to provide VR to Spanish-speaking users as the software translates the text in real time.

The killer application for the next ten years and beyond will certainly be mobile and wireless services. I am totally sure of this, but I am not sure of exactly how these will be used in libraries. Our young people are leading in finding new ways to use mobile phones. Already people are using their cell phones at the reference desk to take pictures of computer screens to capture citation and call number that they can then carry off into the stacks and also keep for later reference. Capitalizing on this use of phones, an academic library consortium in Illinois, CARLI, has created a mobile version of their online catalog with a "text me this call number" widget. Students can click on a button to have a call number plus citation texted to them. Then they go to the library and show their phones to the reference librarian, asking, "Can you tell me where this is located?" More and more of these innovative uses of cell phones are emerging as 3G, or third-generation, phones are appearing. These phones include video on demand that is pushed to your cell phone. The 4G, or fourth-generation, phones connect to several wireless technologies and move transparently between them with more morphing and merging of a vast array of mobile applications.

One indication that this trend is continuing is the large number of mobile phones being produced with keyboards. Another trend is toward purchase of smartphones. According to Pew Internet & American Life Project (2011), 83 percent of adults now have a cell phone and 42 percent of them have a smartphone, which is 35 percent of all U.S. adults. This percentage, I predict, will continue to grow rapidly, and soon there will be no dumb phones, only smartphones with built-in or touch keyboards. I strongly agree with Andrew Walsh, who writes elsewhere in this book about Augmented Reality (AR), which is another technology that will soon find its way into library services. AR merges the virtual and real worlds (one common application is the yellow line that appears on televised football fields so the viewer can see where the first down and distance measurements are). In the library, AR can create a path to help a user find an item or can provide detailed information about special collections, programs, etc. Again, this is a technology that is under development. I believe it will be increasingly important, but exactly how is yet to be imagined or realized.

In addition, the Quick Response (QR) code, a square bar code, can be an easy way to push library websites and online services (like VR), or video content (tutorials, screencasts) through the cell phone or iPad camera. This technology is already heavily used in Japan, and is now increasingly seen in the United States. These now strange-looking codes are quickly becoming ubiquitous. They are easy to create and easy to use once a bar code reader application is downloaded to your cell phone or iPad. People are putting them on business cards to link to full résumés or webpages. I have heard that some libraries are putting QR codes on print books that are on display. The QR code launches a book review or link to author information or recommender sites. These books are the first to be checked out. Again, here is a technology that is emerging, and our imaginations will discover more uses.

Conclusion

The future holds unique opportunities for librarians willing to take some risks. To play it safe by sticking our heads in the reference stacks is not an option. Darwin (1859) declared that organisms either adapt to changing environmental conditions or they will perish. The challenge for all of us is to take on a new attitude that embraces the need to adapt rather than to hold on to what the previous definitions of library, librarian, and reference service have been and to take on dual roles—both as change agents and as managers of incremental change. The top skill we need going forward will be the ability to thrive with change, not just to sit back and watch (or fret), or worse, to pooh-pooh new initiatives and young (or not so young) colleagues with bold ideas. Ultimately, creating the reference future is in our hands, on the front lines, every day, in the quality of the service we provide today and imagine for tomorrow, in our openness to renaissance and metamorphosis, and in the decisions we make.

References

Connaway, L. S., Dickey, T. J., & Radford, M. L. (2011). "If it is too inconvenient I'm not going after it": Convenience as a critical factor in information-seeking behaviors. *Library & Information Science Research, 33*, 179–190.

Connaway, L. S., Downing, K., Du, Y., Goda, D., Jackson, M. L., Johnson, R., Lewis, J. S., & Salisbury, L. (2010). 2010 top ten trends in academic libraries: A review of the current literature. *C&RL News, 71*(6), 286–292.

Connaway, L. S., & Radford, M. L. (2011). *Seeking synchronicity: Revelations and recommendations for virtual reference.* Dublin, OH: OCLC Research.

Connaway, L. S., Radford, M. L., & Williams, J. D. (2009). Engaging Net Gen students in virtual reference: Reinventing services to meet their information behaviors and communication preferences. In D. M. Mueller (Ed.), *Pushing the edge: Explore, extend, engage: Proceedings of the Fourteenth National Conference of the Association of College and Research Libraries, March 12–15, 2009, Seattle, Washington* (pp. 10–27). Chicago: Association of College and Research Libraries. Retrieved on July 13, 2011, from http://www.oclc.org/research/publications/archive/2009/connaway-acrl-2009.pdf.

Darwin, C. R. (1859). *On the origin of species by means of natural selection, or the preservation of favoured races in the struggle for life.* London: John Murray.

DeMara, R. F., Gonzalez, A. J., Hung, V., Leon-Barth, C., Dookhoo, R. A., Jones, S., Johnson, A., Leigh, J., Renambot, L. , Lee, S., & Carlson, G. (2008). Towards interactive training with an avatar-based human-computer interface. *Interservice/Industry Training, Simulation, and Education Conference (I/ITSEC) 2008. Paper No. 8054.* Retrieved on July 13, 2011, from http://www.evl.uic.edu/aej/papers/avatar08.pdf.

Kyrillidou, M., & Morris, S. (Comp. & Eds.). (2011). *ARL Statistics 2008–2009.* Washington, DC: Association of Research Libraries.

Moore, G. E. (1965). Cramming more components into integrated circuits. *Electronics, 38*(8), 82–85.

Pew Internet & American Life Project. (2011, July). Retrieved on July 13, 2011, from http://www.pewinternet.org/Reports/2011/Smartphones.aspx.

Radford, M. L. (2008). A personal choice: Reference service excellence. *Reference and User's Services Quarterly, 48*(2), 108–115.

Sadeh, T. (2008). User experience in the library: A case study. *New Library World, 109*(1/2).

Staley, D. J., & Malenfant, K. J. (2010). *Futures thinking for academic librarians: Higher education in 2025.* Retrieved on July 13, 2011, from http://www.ala.org/ala/mgrps/divs/acrl/issues/value/futures2025.pdf.

The Reference User Experience: It's Up to You to Design It

Steven J. Bell

There are two ways to explain the User Experience (UX) concept to an individual or group. The first and more traditional approach involves sharing its definition. For example, UX is the quality of experience a person has while interacting with a specific design. Sitting in a task chair, driving an automobile, or dining on fine cuisine all involve connecting with a product or service that was the outcome of an intentional design process. The presentation of the definition could be followed by a description of some iconic providers of great user experiences, such as Apple Computer or Nordstrom. These descriptions can emphasize how a user experience is designed, implemented, and evaluated. Between the definition and practical examples, a reasonably good understanding of UX is anticipated.

The second method would directly immerse the individual or group in a user experience so that he or she becomes a part of that experience. Users learn to know it by experiencing it. The desired outcome is to enable someone to better understand what it means to deliver or be on the receiving end of a great user experience. One such technique I use involves sharing a 30-second video from the scene at the Pike Place Fish Market in Seattle (http://www.pikeplacemarket.org/). Most individuals immediately recognize the market. What they may have not previously noticed is the size of the crowd, the depth of the engagement, the way the employees work the crowd, and the techniques used to generate excitement. It is quite a scene and unlike any other fish market in the world. The video makes it clear that a great UX is thoughtfully planned and well executed. One word used to describe it could be "staged." But there are some important lessons to be learned from this and other UX videos.

Understanding the "Wow" Experience

The type of UX delivered at the fish market is sometimes described as a "wow" experience. The goal is to create something unique, exciting, and memorable; it should actually wow a person. In that, the fish market succeeds exceedingly well, even though all the market fundamentally offers is a mundane transaction. Wow is more than just good customer service and quality product. Those are important, but just as Disneyland is more than a theme park and Las Vegas is more than a resort town, a wow experience exceeds expectations and leaves those consuming it desiring to repeat the experience. Though it is difficult to concretely state what constitutes a wow UX, the Retail Council of Canada conducts an occasional survey, last completed in 2009, that seeks to understand what defines a positive retail shopping experience. Thousands of shoppers complete the survey. They are asked questions about their interactions with store personnel: did someone smile at them, was eye contact made, did sales clerks demonstrate expert knowledge of the product line, and was the service fast and efficient? In analyzing the results of the survey, the Verde Group, which along with the Wharton School conducts the survey, identifies a set of key components of the wow experience. The five core activities that contribute to the wow UX are as follows:

1. Customer engagement—creating some emotional connection
2. Executional excellence—thorough knowledge of products and services
3. Brand experience—customers identify with a recognized brand
4. Expedited service—streamlined service that is fast and efficient
5. Problem recovery—problems are resolved quickly and without hassle

What about the reference transaction? If performed well it should deliver one or more of the wow experience qualities. Executional excellence would certainly be evident; referrals to the appropriate resources along with guidance in their use are a must. Expediency is important as well. Community members want quick, efficient service. The challenge, and where most reference services could fall short, is in putting it all together. According to the retail survey report, there are more than 20 different dimensions of a great UX. A single wow experience is typically composed of multiple elements of the experience, not just any single dimension. That makes it difficult to achieve, and explains why many retail transactions may be good but are certainly not up to UX standards.

Reference Service Need Not Wow . . . But . . .
Reference librarians may argue, and I might agree, that the reference transaction need not offer the mix of qualities that add up to a wow experience. Community members seek out reference assistance to obtain answers to their questions, or to get general research advice or assistance with a specific assignment. In most cases, giving them what they want to solve their immediate problem while completing the transaction in a satisfactory style should suffice. Why bother to wow a student challenged by a research assignment or a senior citizen wanting to learn how to build a ship in a bottle? Just complete the transactions and get those community members on their way.

Fair enough, but in an age when community members are able to get information from many non-library sources, from social networks to social Q&A "ask-a-"services, to search engines, why should they bother to seek out reference services? What is it that differentiates the library reference transaction? What would encourage or stimulate community members to tell their friends what a great experience they had at the library? Probably not a routine, mundane transaction devoid of any emotional connection. If library workers want to tip the scales in their favor, it will help to contemplate the design of a better public services experience.

To succeed as an experience, a reference transaction need not replicate the fish market experience But to succeed as a UX, reference service transactions can *differ* from the fish market experience. UX experts advise against simply copying another organization's experience. Reference librarians need to design an experience unique to what they do for the community. But what would it look like, and how would it work?

In designing the reference UX it's important to keep in mind that most community members have low initial expectations for receiving library services. When interviewed about their research experiences by researchers working with Project Information Literacy (Lessons Learned: How College Students Seek Information in the Digital Age; http://projectinfolit.org/pdfs/PIL_Fall2009_finalv_YR1_12_2009v2.pdf), college students had rather shocking things to say about conducting research that requires library resources. Typical adjectives used by students to describe their library research experience included stress, anxiety, terror, and even nausea. These findings suggest that to delight or wow community members library workers need only to exceed the low expectations that community members already have for an anticipated bad experience.

Designing the Reference UX

Three outcomes in particular would lead to a great reference UX:

1. Be different.
2. Achieve memorableness.
3. Create loyalty.

When it comes to doing research and finding information our community members have multiple options. To them, all the resources and services may seem the same; information obtained from one source is as good as any other. Therefore it is important to establish, so they can realize it, how our reference services are different. Whether it's the quality of the resources, the expertise of the personnel, or the personal attention delivered, it must be unique from other information sources. Great experiences are also memorable. If reference librarians can go beyond the mundane it would be a start toward a memorable experience that community members will desire to enjoy again. Of the three desired outcomes loyalty is perhaps most important. When a community member is loyal, he or she not only returns to the library again and again, but tells friends about the great library experience. Word-of-mouth advertising is the Holy Grail of library marketing.

Achieving these three outcomes requires multiple strategies, and UX experts offer a variety of recommendations for ways to implement them. Joseph Michelli is an acknowledged expert in the UX field. He has authored books about the UX at the Pike Place Fish Market (Michelli, 2004) and Starbucks (Michelli, 2006), and explains how these organizations design and implement their unique blend of UX. In his book about the Ritz-Carlton chain, *The New Gold Standard: 5 Leadership Principles for Creating a Legendary Customer Experience Courtesy of the Ritz-Carlton Hotel Company*, Michelli (2008) offers a suite of strategies based on the excellent UX delivered at these hotels. It offers a good model for a reference service to emulate. Here are seven strategies most applicable to reference and public service units:

1. Start with core values.
2. Personalize to create meaning.
3. Meet the users' needs.
4. Anticipate the users' needs.
5. Motivate and empower staff.
6. Create emotional connections.
7. Aim for totality.

A great UX starts in the staff room. Michelli and other UX experts point to the importance of people coming together to identify their core library values, and then committing to making those values an integral part of their daily operations. How might this work? Take, for example, two important core values, building relationships and creating trust. One reason our libraries may be experiencing a decline in the use of reference service is a lack of trust. Many individuals regard their own social networks as a more trusted source. When asked to identify who they perceive as a trusted source, today's students point to "someone like me." Teachers or parents are other often named trusted sources. It's rarely a librarian. Committing to a core value of relationship building could help library workers to improve the degree to which community members perceive them as trusted sources.

One way to start building relationships is to focus more on personalization in delivering reference services. How often do reference librarians begin a transaction with "Hi, my name is... And you are... ?" More typically, library workers prefer to remain anonymous at service points. Establishing a relationship with someone who is an unknown is unlikely. A stronger commitment to personalization will help to enhance the library reference experience. Some of the best relationships between reference librarians and community members develop off the desk, often in instruction sessions. Some libraries see a drop in reference desk transaction statistics owing to community members who go directly to a librarian with whom they have an established relationship. Library workers can benefit from examining how these relationships develop, and understanding how to replicate those conditions in other service venues.

Research about UX has shown that meaning is perhaps the most important thing that people derive from their experiences. While meaning is a vague concept, we do know that when experiences are meaningful they are lasting and they motivate individuals to want to experience them again. When individuals are asked to compare the meaning derived from a significant purchase of a tangible consumer good, such as a car, with the meaning derived from an intangible experience, such as a concert or vacation, the majority pointed to the intangible experience as the most meaningful one. This is why every reference service transaction should have some personalization built into it in order to deliver some added value of meaning to the recipient.

A critical component of building relationships and delivering meaning is knowing and understanding the needs of the user community. The good news is that more librarians are taking action to do both. More library workers are taking the time to study our user community members, both through observation and through conversation that is designed to know and understand how the facility and resources are being used. What we need to avoid is making judgments and decisions based on our assumptions about what the users want and need. For example, a reference librarian may believe that every student needs to be well versed in Boolean search logic. While that may be desirable, attempting to drill it into students without really understanding their search behaviors may be problematic. We can do better than just meeting the needs of community members. Since library workers often know the type of work the community members do, such as an often-encountered student assignment, they should be able to develop reference services that anticipate research needs. There are good examples of how to do this. Many academic and public libraries create library research guides designed for specific course assignments and community projects.

One of the lessons learned from studying the Ritz-Carlton Hotel (Michelli, 2008) is that UX is not left to chance. When some employees "get it" and others do not, the likely result is an inconsistent and uneven experience. To ensure that service is consistent in its delivery, every staff member must know and internalize the chain's core values. The Ritz-Carlton motivates and empowers its hotel workers to deliver a unique and meaningful experience. In addition to written guidelines, there are regular staff development meetings that reinforce the importance of delivering on the core values. Employees are also empowered to quickly resolve guest problems and fix what is broken. There is no need to send e-mails to supervisors and colleagues to report minor issues or to gripe about frustrations in dealing with them. Every staff member knows he or she must take personal responsibility for solving the issue. The hotel management even offers a pool of funds that workers can draw from to solve guest problems (e.g., for relocating an unsatisfied guest to a more expensive room).

When people are asked why their experiences are meaningful or what differentiates an experience from a mere transaction or even from good customer service, the response often points to the presence or delivery of some emotional connection between themselves and those serving them. That is, something about a particular experience creates a strong feeling or bond between an individual and the experience he or she is having. People will often point to a unique relationship or repeatedly receiving special treatment as a source of the emotional connection. Reference librarians may think their work would hardly be the stuff of emotional connections, but it is not uncommon, for example, that alumni report strong feelings for the college library. For many, it is more so the space than the library workers that accounts for the emotional connection, but in some cases it is about more than sacred space. Striving for emotional connections will contribute to the building of relationships that foster loyalty in community members.

Any of these strategies can contribute to an improved public service and reference UX. Reference librarians should think about how integrating these into their work could help to make a difference for community members. However, it is important to remember that any one strategy is less effective when performed in isolation. When it comes to designing a better library UX, it is best to think in terms of totality. Taking the holistic UX perspective means that every library touch point, any physical or virtual space where the user connects with the library, should offer a thoughtful, well-designed user experience. Offering a reference desk UX is desirable, but if the user then has difficulty finding a book in the stacks or locating a staff member to help find the book, then his or her general impression of the library may be that it offers an overall bad experience, no matter how good the initial experience was. That's why keeping totality in mind, when developing a library UX, is so critical to the process. Achieving totality, as one might imagine, is difficult, and for most organizations it represents a significant challenge. It may be best to see totality as a long-term goal, with UX design for reference services or other units as the more immediate goal.

What Will You Design?

Many of the ideas discussed in this chapter are put into practice in commercial, for-profit operations, such as retail stores and hotels. Because they often are associated with business, some library workers may find them off-putting and inappropriate for the library because it is not a business. It is easy to become cynical about ideas such as UX, and to be skeptical that such concepts have a place in the world of the library worker. The point is not to turn the library into a business, but to thoughtfully borrow some ideas from business that could help libraries to design a better UX. The first step may be to introduce the concept of UX to public services workers. Videos and readings will be useful in this educational stage. Unfortunately few libraries have yet to design a library experience for their community members. When more libraries design and implement experiences for their community members, we will all have more examples to share and replicate. Perhaps you and your colleagues will be pioneers of reference service and library UX. I hope I have inspired you to think more about how your users experience your library and to take action to make this better in small or large, but meaningful, ways. It is, after all, up to you to design their UX.

References

Michelli, J. A. (2004). *Why fish fly: Lessons for creating a vital and energized workplace from the world famous Pike Place Fish Market*. New York: Hyperion.

Michelli, J. A. (2006). *The Starbucks experience: 5 principles for turning ordinary into extraordinary*. New York: McGraw-Hill.

Michelli, J. A. (2008). *The new gold standard: 5 leadership principles for creating a legendary customer experience courtesy of the Ritz-Carlton Hotel Company*. New York: McGraw-Hill.

We Are the User: Imagination, Sympathy, and the User Experience

Wayne Bivens-Tatum

When given the topic "the user experience," I assumed there must be an entire discipline and literature devoted to it. Being a well-trained reference librarian with all the resources of a large research library at my disposal, I naturally turned to Wikipedia, where I discovered that there are some excellent principles in the User Experience (UX) literature. I will tell you why you can ignore them. In a brief history of UX design, I discovered that the UX literature consists of many complicated elements: information architecture, industrial design, interaction design, human-computer interaction, etc. (Baskinger, 2010). If I could master all those, I might give up librarianship for something more lucrative. From a conference presentation I discovered that there are also numerous research methods for UX design: eye tracking, data mining, ethnographic studies, intercept surveys, A/B testing, etc. (Rohrer, 2009). Perhaps I could do some benchmarking and message board mining in my usability lab... if I had a usability lab.

In another study, a UX team "adopted the Rapid Iterative Testing and Evaluation (RITE) to achieve success by taking advantage of its three main facets: an easily modifiable prototype, faster, more frequent feedback, and a design that evolved over time" (Douglass & Hylton, 2010). This is fascinating stuff.

Then I figured there must be some library literature on the subject as well. Surely, I thought, some enterprising librarians in need of tenure had written a "how we dunit good" article on the "user experience." Indeed, there was. A UX case study in a library summed up several studies on what library users want. It seems they want "familiar and easily learned discovery interfaces" that provide a range of quality resources electronically (Sadeh, 2008, p. 8).

Modifiable design, easy interfaces, good resources... I'm glad I had studies to tell me this. This is not difficult stuff. We do not have to master the UX literature and we do not have to feel bad that our best efforts of UX research are going to be pretty primitive compared to what, say, major software companies do. I'm not saying do not do any studies or talk to users or track eye movements or whatever it is you're doing now. I'm just saying that users don't have problems because we aren't doing enough user experience studies. The problems result from a failure of moral reasoning on our part. Because of our failure of moral reasoning, we even get the easy stuff wrong.

We sometimes act as if library users are some exotic species difficult to understand, necessitating expensive research teams most of us will never get doing time-consuming studies most of us don't have staff for. We should just remember that We Are the User. We are library users, too, but we are so familiar with our libraries that we overlook the flaws, work-arounds, and frustrations. We are so snug in our systems and habits that we forget what it is like not to be so comfortable with our libraries, and we forget we have forgotten. Snug can make you smug.

Inspired by political philosopher and economist Amartya Sen's (2009) recent work in *The Idea of Justice*, I have been reconsidering Adam Smith's *The Theory of Moral Sentiments* (1976), the ethics companion to *The Wealth of Nations* (1976), and even less read and understood. In his *The Theory of Moral Sentiments*, Smith (1976) argues that our moral understanding and actions are based on sentiment, especially sympathy and imagination. We naturally feel sympathy at the pain and distress of others, and are able to imagine ourselves in their place. Smith writes:

> How selfish soever man may be supposed, there are evidently some principles in his nature, which interest him in the fortunes of others, and render their happiness necessary to him, though he derives nothing from it, except the pleasure of seeing it. Of this kind is pity or compassion, [basically, sympathy] the emotion we feel for the misery of others, when we either see it, or are made to conceive it in a very lively manner. That we often derive sorrow from the sorrows of others, is a matter of fact too obvious to require any instances to prove it; for this sentiment, like all the other original passions of human nature, is by no means confined to the virtuous or the humane.... The greatest ruffian, the most hardened violator of the laws of society, is not altogether without it. (p. 9)

And, one might add, the most jaded reference librarian. We can sympathize with others because of our capacity for imagination.

> As we have no immediate experience of what other men feel, we can form no idea of the manner in which they are affected, but by conceiving what we ourselves should feel in the like situation. Though our brother is on the rack, as long as we ourselves are at our ease, our senses will never inform us of what he suffers. They never did, and never can, carry us beyond our own person, and it is by the imagination only that we can form any conception of what are his sensations. Neither can that faculty help us to this any other way, than by representing to us what would be our own, if we were in his case. It is the impressions of our own senses only, not those of his, which our imaginations copy. By the imagination, we place ourselves in his situation. (Smith, 1976, p. 9)

By imagination we can place ourselves in the situation of library users. Creating positive user experiences is not that difficult if we just have some imagination and sympathy. How many studies do we need to tell us people like ease, familiarity, simplicity, and quality, and in that order? By all means talk to library users and study how they use the library. But do we need more studies to solve this problem, or more imagination and sympathy? This is not something we should be overwhelmed by. Nor is it something we should feel inadequate to address, if we haven't mastered the UX literature. With studies we get principles, but without imagination and sympathy those principles will take us only so far. We need to break out of our complacency and imagine ourselves in the place of the library user.

If we did, what would we think about a guide to history resources at a college library website I visited recently? (I will not give the name of the college to spare them embarrassment, but I am sure you can find similar examples.) The "guide" was ten screens long, an alphabetical list divided into such useless categories as "subscription databases" and "indexes," which turned out also to be subscription databases. It was a big block of text with no attempt to prioritize or guide, and the library had numerous "guides" just like this one. It turns out "African-American History" has almost identical resources to just plain "History," but adding more subject guides made their "guides" page a mass block of text, which was possibly the goal.

Imagination? Sympathy? The guide might as well be in Chinese. I imagine students would feel the way I do looking at the Shanghai University Libraries website (http:// www.lib.shu.edu.cn/). Go check out that website, think about how it makes you feel, and then take a fresh look at your own library website. Contrast that with a typical LibGuide (http://demo.libguides.com/) or with search boxes like Primo (http://www.exlibrisgroup .com/category/PrimoOverview) or Summon (http://www.serialssolutions.com/discovery/ summon/) prominently displayed on library websites. Or, as an experiment, go to the website of the Staatsbibliothek Bayerische, the Bavarian State Library (http://www .bsb-muenchen.de/index.php). There is no need to read the language. You will know where to search, and you will immediately know what "Suche" means. It is easy to understand why a well-designed LibGuide or a single search box is more user friendly than ten screens of dense prose, and this understanding does not require an expensive research team or extensive studies or an immersion in the UX literature. It just takes some imagination and sympathy. Users want simplicity, ease of use, and quality resources. Well, guess what? So do I. Personal interactions are not a big part of UX studies, but they are a big part of reference, either in person or virtually. Go near a reference desk, and you will occasionally see the Serious Librarian. A great example is the representative photograph in the entry for "Librarians" in the *Occupational Outlook Handbook* (U.S. Bureau of Labor Statistics, 2010): very stern and professional, eyes fixed on the computer monitor, scowl firmly in place. As a library user, would any of you want to approach this librarian to ask a question? If you wandered into that library, would you see welcoming curiosity or indifferent hostility? Imagination? Sympathy? Scowling librarians staring at computer monitors might as well be making obscene gestures to the library users. Watch some of your own reference librarians from afar, and try to think about what library users might see.

Making things better for library users is not that difficult, if we just shake ourselves out of our complacency, forget what it is like to be a librarian, and remember what it is like to be a normal person again. It is a matter of moral reasoning as much as anything else: imagination and sympathy. What would we want if we were in the place of the user? What can we do to make that happen? The choices are often easy, even if acting on them is sometimes hard.

References

Baskinger, M. (2010, June). From industrial design to user experience: The heritage and evolving role of experience-driven design. *UX Magazine*. Retrieved on July 13, 2011, from http://www .uxmag.com/design/from-industrial-design-to-user-experience.

Douglass, R., & Hylton, K. (2010). Get it RITE: Rapid Iterative Testing and Evaluation (RITE). *User Experience Magazine*, 9(1). Retrieved on July 13, 2011, from http://www.upassoc.org/ upa_publications/user_experience/past_issues/2010-1.html.

Rohrer, C. (2009). *User experience research methods in 3D: What to use when and how to know you're right.* Presentation at BayCHI, SF chapter of ACM SIGCHI, Palo, Alto, CA. January 13. Retrieved on July 3, 2011, from http://www.xdstrategy.com/wp-content/uploads/User_Research_and_Desirability_BayCHI2009-Final-public.pdf.

Sadeh, T. (2008). User experience in the library: A case study. *New Library World, 109*(1/2).

Sen, A. (2009). *The idea of justice.* Cambridge, MA: Belknap Press of Harvard University Press.

Smith, A. (1976). *The theory of moral sentiments.* Oxford, Oxfordshire: Clarendon Press.

U.S. Bureau of Labor Statistics. (2010). Librarians. *Occupational Outlook Handbook, 2010–11 Edition.* Retrieved on July 3, 2011, from http://www.bls.gov/oco/ocos068.htm.

The User Experience and the Librarian: Now You See 'Em, Now You Don't

James LaRue

O ver the past four years, I have been involved in three public elections. The first two were attempts to increase our public library district's mill levy. Both failed. The third was to defeat a round of statewide initiatives to sharply curtail public sector funding and expenditures. These measures were defeated.

A consequence of these experiences is that I have become far more aware as a public library director of the context of support, of why people do or do not vote to fund public institutions. One aspect of that context is the detectable presence of librarians. As professionals, we exist along a spectrum of visibility. At one end are the invisible designers and maintainers of service delivery systems; at the other, more obvious and visible providers. That spectrum of visibility has three broad dimensions. (My remarks in this chapter are intended to explicate the chart shown in Figure I.1.)

Figure I.1. The Reference User Experience: A 3-D View		
The 1st two dimensions of the user experience are customer service and staff competence. The 3rd dimension spans a continuum or context of library and librarian visibility.		
Invisible		Visible
Servant who waits Thoughtful design Institutionally focused	⇐ General Characteristics ⇒	Leader who acts Skin in the game Community focused

Facility – Secluded
Self-service
  Interesting spaces
  Browse-able / easily
   navigable
  Systems that are simple
Technology
  Integrated resources
	⇐ In House ⇒	Facility – Central
		Staff
		  Available (friendly, polite,
		   responsive)
		  Knowledgeable
		  Deep reference interview
		Technology
		  Troubleshooter
		  Demonstrator/Teacher

Privacy / Anonymity Background Assumed	⇐ In Community ⇒	Customer Relations Management Seat at the table Declared
Source: http://www.jlarue.com/userexperience.pdf.		

Under *General Characteristics* I would describe the "invisible librarian" as possessing the psychology of the servant who waits. The invisible librarian creates systems that respond reliably, that fulfill a mission, but only when activated from outside. An example here is the cataloger, who creates metadata, or the IT librarian who manages the Integrated Library System. These systems are poised to receive the request and then serve up the data.

The visible librarian is the leader who acts, actively seeking out and anticipating service needs. An example might be the reference librarian who attends Chamber of Commerce meetings, and volunteers to put together a demonstration of ReferenceUSA to help local leaders better gather business intelligence. Under this dimension, "invisible librarians" may see themselves as more institutionally focused. "Visible librarians" are more community focused.

The distinction between these two does not imply that one is more valuable than the other. We need intelligently designed and managed systems. We also need alert extroverts who push our products and investigate emerging needs.

A second dimension of visibility is reflected by how we orient ourselves in-house, meaning within our facilities. Again, the invisible librarian is focused on the design and management of our assets. For physical space, this is about creating inviting spaces whose functions are self-demonstrating. It is also about creating service systems that are genuinely easy to use. Public librarians who adopt self-check systems, for instance, must rethink rules and procedures that once required staff intervention.

With computer systems, our resources remain divided: one search for our catalog, another for periodicals, yet another for local digital resources, and so on. A librarian may be invisible, but still desperately need to make it possible for our users to find things. If such systems are well-designed, the patron seldom needs to seek additional assistance, and indeed may not recognize the thought that went into the information infrastructure. But if the systems are poorly designed, users blame the library. The visible librarian is focused on the fundamental relationship of the reference interview, a one-on-one interaction. Here, the success of the user is directly related to the quality of customer service. Regarding technology, the visible librarian is both trainer and troubleshooter, overcoming system confusion through personal intervention.

The third dimension concerns librarian visibility in the *community*. The invisible librarian values the confidentiality or anonymity of a service transaction (whether information searches or circulation records). Such librarians tend to operate in the background of a community as discreet responders to inquiries. Again, as long as the library is well-funded and well-operating, the library and the librarian are simply assumed by the community to be there. They require no additional attention or respect, until the withdrawal of their services is threatened.

On the other side of the spectrum, visible librarians take a more active role in managing their relations with customers. This might be in the form of surveys, phone calls, e-mails, lunches, or other follow-up communications. The visible librarian, rather than waiting for an invitation, seeks a "seat at the table," the opportunity to be where things are happening.

This approach, rather than about assuming significance and support, is about the declaration and demonstration of value. Online Computer Library Center's (OCLC)

From Awareness to Funding: A Study of Library Support in America (2008) found that one of the key determinants of fiscal support for libraries was the belief that one's local librarian is a passionate advocate for lifelong learning. While there is plenty of work for librarians at either side of the visibility spectrum, making our contribution a little more obvious may also be the path to making it sustainable.

Reference

Online Computer Library Center (OCLC). (2008). *From awareness to funding: A study of library support in America*. Retrieved on July 13, 2011, from http://www.oclc.org/reports/funding/default.htm.

Thoughts on Twenty-First-Century Library Services from a Disenfranchised User

Jean Costello

I write about reference from a patron's perspective to offer insights that might inform library practice. Having spent time with librarians at the Reference Renaissance 2010 Conference, my sense is there is not much I can add to enrich librarians' deep understanding for the art and science of reference. Instead, what I thought might be helpful is to share my observations as a patron attending a library conference. I would also like to describe some circumstances that have diminished my reference experiences as a user, as well as to reveal my vision of new and exciting opportunities for librarianship.

When people ask me how the conference was, I will tell them it has been the highlight of my advocacy experience; being with you all has been really fun, illuminating, and energizing. I so appreciate the hospitality and assistance of the folks from Bibliographical Center for Research, CO (BCR); Brenda Bailey-Hainer and Justine Shaffner, who have made me feel welcome and have helped connect me with attendees from around the country, Canada, and England. What has been most striking is how good it is to see library folk unburdened by the need to continually demonstrate value. I follow libraries closely through the mainstream media, including *Library Journal*, library blogs, *The Chronicle of Higher Education*, and also periodically through scholarly journal articles. These sources reveal how much time and energy "justifying your existence" takes away from more meaningful work.

I have also been surprised to find how seldom reference service is discussed in most of the sources I follow. It is as though the reasons I used to visit libraries—to expand or deepen my engagement with the world through the art and knowledge of various generations, cultures, or scholarly disciplines—are no longer of interest to the library community. This correlates with how, over the past 15 years, libraries have been increasingly less equipped to meet my needs.

I live in Massachusetts, and public libraries there are small and independent and have their hands full providing services to constituents with more basic needs than mine. Even though there are 26 public or academic libraries within a ten-mile radius of my home, there is no fluid way for me to access services from them. Frankly, navigating their individual access policies, websites, and database interfaces feels like a game of Chutes and Ladders. The effort required to obtain service is almost always greater than my desire for it, so I turn to other sources. I realize this situation is particularly acute in Massachusetts, though it is also true that systemic barriers to service exist throughout our library ecosystem.

What a dilemma! I am here because I am a strong and persistent library advocate—and yet at this point I am also pretty much a disenfranchised nonuser. How can that be? Are libraries ready to let a patron like me go? I truly hope not, for when I think about my information needs, librarians seem uniquely qualified to service them. Moreover, these needs cannot easily be met by technology or for-profit firms and therefore positioning libraries to meet them would be a good institutional survival strategy.

I need better information-filtering strategies. I am perpetually awash in information, and no matter how many times I adjust my filters, they never seem to hold for long. Identifying trusted sources and authenticating information is also a challenge, for my sensibilities and sensors are rooted in an age of strong and independent journalism, less "creative" government, and more transparent scholarly practices. These days, it is just too hard to know which sources to trust given the disintegration of our journalistic enterprises, a government that believes it is okay to broadcast fake TV news reports as a supposed means of informing the public, and widespread concealed industry influence in research and peer review.

Librarians can help. I know that you have heard this before, but it bears saying over and over again. A century ago in this country, your profession set itself to the challenge of making the world's information accessible and serviceable. It was wildly successful in this endeavor. Libraries earned the reputation as trusted information sources. They created data systems whose quality was widely acknowledged, and schemas were copied liberally as the information age unfolded.

Though the times have changed, the need for serviceable information may be even greater now than it was decades ago. Information is no longer scarce, but officials and institutions worthy of public trust are, libraries excepted. How we need a profession dedicated to sorting it all out, to laying tracks for more navigable informational journeys in pursuit of knowledge. We need better systems for discovery and contextualization that easily connect patrons with material, without regard for profit or influence. We need a trusted profession to help influence and establish new standards of authority. And we continue to need strong local institutions to help people use information in meaningful ways, to enrich their own lives and those of their communities. We have the talent and resources to do this now. What is missing is the vision and the will, and I call on librarians to cease mourning that patrons no longer need you as we once did. Take pride in your role of facilitating our independence and set about the work of this new age—rooted in durable core values but conducted on new terrain with new tools.

My hope is that you take up this challenge to add more widespread value in the ways I have just described. Your influence and impact can be enormous. If you do so, I hope that more of the public will see the passion, talent, and commitment I have had the opportunity to see these past few days. It's inspiring.

PART II

REVELATIONS FROM REFERENCE RESEARCH

Virtual Reference Encounters and Instruction Initiatives

CHAPTER 1

Chattin' 'bout My Generation: Comparing Virtual Reference Use of Millennials to Older Adults

Marie L. Radford and
Lynn Silipigni Connaway

Overview

This chapter provides an overview of a research project that studied generational differences in the attitudes toward and use of virtual reference (VR), and the information-seeking and communication behaviors of members of the Millennial generation (Prensky, 2001) when compared to older adults. It reports findings from the *Seeking Synchronicity: Evaluating Virtual Reference Services from User, Non-User, and Librarian Perspectives* (Radford & Connaway, 2005–2008) grant project funded by the Institute of Museum and Library Services (IMLS), Rutgers University, and Online Computer Library Center (OCLC). Results shed light on how people of different ages make decisions to use VR, what their preferred modes of communication are, what they like and dislike about VR, and how these services can be made more attractive to nonusers, who can be seen as potential users. Research-based recommendations with key implications for sustainability and growth of consortial VR, library use instruction, and marketing are suggested.

Introduction

What, if any, generational differences can be seen in the way people currently approach their information needs, including their use of virtual reference services (VRS), and online resources? Is there such a thing as a Digital Native as advocated by Prensky (2006)? How can librarians design better online and face-to-face (FtF) reference services and pathways to e-resources to engage the younger population, who seem to be radically different from previous generations, especially in their information-seeking behaviors and proclivities? The findings from the *Seeking Synchronicity: Evaluating Virtual Reference Services from User, Non-User, and Librarian Perspectives* project (Radford & Connaway,

2005–2008) provides some interesting answers to these questions and also uncovers areas for future investigation.

This chapter focuses on *Seeking Synchronicity* results from three phases of data collection and analysis: focus group interviews, online surveys, and interviews with users and nonusers of live chat VRS. It is to be noted that VRS nonusers had never used live chat VR, but were nearly always users of physical libraries. Results from all phases of the project's data collection revealed differences in information seeking from younger people who are members of the Millennial generation (Prensky, 2001), in comparison to older adults (see also Connaway & Radford, 2011; Connaway & Radford, 2010; Connaway, Radford, Dickey, Williams, & Confer, 2008; Radford & Connaway, 2010; Radford & Connaway, 2007).

Who Are the Millennials?

In this chapter, the Millennial generation refers to the large cohort of approximately 75 million people in America who were born between 1979 and 1994. They have been given a variety of different names, such as Gen Y or Net Gen (Tapscott, 1998). Results from research reported here reveals that Millennials approach technology, information seeking, libraries, librarians, print, and e-resources differently from members of older generations. According to Prensky (2006), the Millennial generation is the first cohort of "digital natives." Their ability to have continual access to web-based information and social networking sites is taken for granted by them, but was not available to those growing up before the web existed (Salaway, Katz, Caruso, Kvavik, & Nelson, 2006). The Millennial's world can be seen as an "infosphere" where there is a lack of boundaries between work, home, recreation, and study (Thomas & McDonald, 2005; Fox, Anderson, & Rainie, 2005).

Although there are differences in individuals, when studied as a cohort, certain patterns emerge. Perhaps because of today's milieu of the availability of a wide variety of choices in music, entertainment, and consumer culture, the Millennials have demonstrated that they prefer more choice/selectivity in interfaces, flexibility/convenience, and personalization. Their perception and use of libraries is influenced by some of their generational traits, in that they tend to be impatient, like to learn by experimenting through trial and error, and are highly focused on results (Hallam & Partridge, 2006; McHale, 2005; Oblinger & Oblinger, 2005, 2006). Connaway and colleagues (2008) report that college and university students are likely to turn to Google and other web sources and browsers as their first choice to get their information. These sources are "go-to" selections because they are seen as convenient and easy to use, and they deliver results quickly. Millennials also use the library for electronic databases and journals, but avoid using the catalog or physical building (Connaway et al., 2008).

Librarians are largely viewed in negative ways by Millennials (Radford, 2006b; Radford & Connaway, 2007; Connaway et al., 2008). Agosto and Hughes-Hassell (2005) investigated attitudes of urban teens who "reported frustration with . . . aspects of library service such as strict rules, unpleasant staff, lack of culturally relevant materials, dreary physical spaces, and limited access to technology" (p. 161). *Seeking Synchronicity* results support these findings, indicating that the younger generation favors the independence of online access, the interactivity of social media, the flexibility and anonymity of VRS that can be accessed anywhere at any time (Radford & Connaway, 2007).

An additional phase of research from *Seeking Synchronicity* involved transcript analysis of 850 live chat sessions that were selected randomly during 2004 to 2006 from a body of more than 500,000 QuestionPoint (OCLC, 2011) and 24/7 (QuestionPoint, n.d.) live chat sessions. Close qualitative investigation uncovered behavioral differences in the synchronous chat environment between Millennials and older adults and in librarian interactions with the different user groups. This analysis further found that Millennials use more chat language and texting shortcuts than older adults. They are, perhaps surprisingly, also more deferential to librarians, using polite language (such as please and thank you) more often than older adults and tend to end abruptly, leaving the interaction without a closing statement (such as thank you or good-bye) more frequently (see Radford & Connaway, 2005–2008, and Radford, Radford, Connaway, & DeAngelis, 2011).

These behaviors were found to be more prevalent among the youngest members of the Millennial generation, who are referred to here as "screenagers" (Rushkoff, 1996), because they have an insatiable appetite for screens, moving text, and images. Across all the different phases and methods of data collection in *Seeking Synchronicity*, the screenagers were consistent in stating that they prefer independent means of finding information—doing it themselves using the web, or choosing to ask friends, rather than librarians. They also are not confident that librarians have the subject knowledge needed to answer their questions. Their preferred modes of communication are mobile and digital: texting, cell phones, and instant messaging (IM). These individuals report that their primary use of IM is for socializing purposes, so using live chat for homework or reference help may seem inappropriate to them.

What Millennials Told Us in Focus Group Interviews

Early in the *Seeking Synchronicity* project, a series of eight focus groups were held with a variety of user and nonuser groups in different parts of the eastern United States. It is of interest to note that from the start of the project, the idea was not to research screenagers or Millennials at all, just VRS users and nonusers. However, after the first focus group with screenagers, the results were so dissimilar from those with older adults that the decision was made to expand the number of groups with teens who were nonusers of VRS from one focus group interview to three. These focus group interviews were conducted with the youngest members of the Millennial generation in urban, sub-urban, and rural locations in three eastern states. Local public and school librarians assisted in recruiting the participants, who were each given a $25 gift card for a book-store chain. Audio recordings were made of the focus group interviews, which were then transcribed verbatim and analyzed qualitatively following the constant comparative method (Glaser, 1965). Results among and within focus groups were compared and a number of themes emerged from this data analysis (Radford & Connaway, 2007).

These results were quite unexpected. These teens, who were 12 to 18 years old at the time, revealed startlingly different findings from the focus group interviews with older adults. They revealed unusual patterns of information seeking and use, plus a much greater reluctance to ask librarians for reference assistance. They told us that they use Google and other search engines to browse the web, ask friends, and generally attempt to find needed information themselves. A typical attitude regarding librarians was exemplified by this remark from one young focus group member: "I've just never thought they any [*sic*] useful. I'd rather do it on my own."

Google is highly trusted and seen as much easier and more convenient than library subscription-based databases. Another participant said: "Yeah, 'cause I wouldn't really trust my librarian. I trust Google." This screenager revealed a confidence in his or her ability to distinguish accurate information in searches: "Um, like, I find something on Google and there's enough information on it and it seems logical, I'll just go with it." Although the majority carried cell phones, these respondents also said they never used telephone reference for homework help, and were totally unaware that libraries offer this mode of service: "The library has a phone?" one teen inquired with an amazed look on her face. There was consensus in one focus group that they would *never* e-mail a librarian with a question.

When probed about why they would not use e-mail or live-chat VRS, the Millennials said that they were not aware that the service existed. Others felt that their question would not be taken seriously by the librarians:

> Plus I think the IMing kind of gives it a cold feeling to it like, you know. They really don't care. They're just doing their job. When you can actually sit and talk to someone face-to-face you kind of can see if they care or not, you know. If they don't care, you're like 'Well, you're not going to help me very much anyway' and you can move on. But [in] the IM, you can keep trying to ask the same person the same question like over and over. And if they don't care, they're just going to keep ignoring you.

One worried that the librarian was not capable of multitasking: "A librarian's trying to do like 15 of those conversations at once they're going to mix up replies."

These young people also had privacy and security issues that were revealed in each focus group, without any prompting. When asked whether they would consider using live-chat VR to ask for help from librarians, one teen replied: "I don't usually like to talk to like people I don't know on the Internet," and another revealed being fearful of online interactions with an anonymous person: "I'm not going to go get tutored on the Internet by somebody who I personally don't know who might be some psycho serial killer out there when I could get personal help from my home and people in my community" (see also Radford & Connaway, 2007). This fear was something we had not anticipated as a reason why some young people would be reluctant to try VRS.

These issues revealed generational differences that are important for librarians to understand, especially in VR and FtF encounters with young people who may need to be freed from their anxiety about the safety and quality across different types of reference services.

Online Surveys with VRS Users and Nonusers

Web-based surveys were conducted with 137 VRS users (including 49 Millennials and 88 older adults) and 184 VRS nonusers (including 122 Millennials and 62 older adults). Online surveys contained Likert-style questions as well as open-ended questions and were developed based on results from the focus group interviews and transcript analysis, in addition to a review of the literature, and previous research conducted by the authors (see Radford, 2006a). Because of the unexpected and intriguing results from the Millennial focus group interviews, we decided to make an effort to have a substantial number from this generation in the online survey respondents. Participants were recruited through a variety of methods, including use of electronic discussion lists, social networking sites (Facebook ads), paper flyers posted at two universities, via school and public librarians, and by word of mouth. Participants were given $25 for taking the survey. Results were analyzed by quantitative as well as qualitative methods, including the constant comparative method (Glaser, 1965) and the critical incident technique (Flanagan, 1954).

As seen earlier, one theme that emerged from the focus group interviews was that FtF interactions were seen as intimidating. So in the surveys, people were asked directly about intimidation. The results were interesting. Nearly half of older adults (47 percent of 88) and three-quarters of the Millennial VRS users (76 percent of 88) found chat to be the least intimidating mode of reference. One Millennial VRS user said: "Yes. It [VRS] makes the librarians easier to approach and you can find out while you are still connected whether their advice yields the results you are looking for." Millennial nonusers who had never used live-chat VR responded that e-mail was the least intimidating mode of reference service for them.

Connected to the Millennials' reluctance to chat with strangers was the finding that a personal recommendation was much more important to younger VRS users, who reported that they were willing to use VRS when it was recommended by a trusted friend, librarian, or teacher. They also were found to be more likely to recommend VRS than older adult respondents. One Millennial VRS user said: "I'd absolutely recommend this service to everyone." When they receive courteous, friendly service, and are provided with needed information, they tell their friends. They also tell their friends if they have a negative experience with a librarian or problems with the technology.

A larger majority of the Millennial nonuser online survey respondents stated that remote access to information is important compared to the adult VRS nonuser respondents. The Millennial VRS nonuser online survey participants valued librarian friendliness and politeness more than the older adult VRS nonusers. In addition, more Millennials than older adults believed that the library is convenient (see also Connaway, Dickey, & Radford, 2011). Nonusers thought they would try VRS if they could receive information quickly and around the clock, as one Millennial nonuser said: "If it is available 24/7, I'll try it."

Telephone Interviews with VRS Users and Nonusers

Following the online surveys, telephone interviews were held with 107 VRS nonusers (including 73 Millennials and 34 older adults) and 76 VRS users (including 21 Millennials and 54 older adults). Telephone interviews built upon the results of the previous phases and included more open-ended questions than the online surveys. These were recorded by the team of interviewers, who captured as many direct quotes as possible in the process. As was the case with the online surveys, we decided to make an effort to have a substantial number of telephone interviews with members of the Millennial generation. Participants were recruited through a variety of methods as was done for the online surveys and were given $30 for taking the survey. Results were analyzed by qualitative methods, including the constant comparative method (Glaser, 1965) and the critical incident technique (Flanagan, 1954).

When asked why they did not use the service, Millennial interviewees, like those in the online survey population, responded that they were unaware that it existed. One nonuser said: "I think I am unfamiliar with it.... I stray away from the unknown, I guess."

In addition, 45 percent (33) of the Millennials and 38 percent (12) of the older adults mentioned the Internet as an alternative to the library and 28 percent (20) of the Millennials said they used the Internet for "personal convenience." In particular, Google was mentioned by 15 percent (11) of Millennials and 3 percent (2) of older adults. As an example, one older adult nonuser replied: "I don't know how to access computer library service. When I need to look something up I use Google."

Reflecting the Millennials' high level of comfort in the IM environment, 35 percent (43) of 122 Millennials and 53 percent (33) of 62 older adult nonusers agreed with the statement, "Chat reference might be too complicated." Perhaps not surprisingly, of older adult nonusers 35 percent (22) were more anxious that their typing was not adequate compared to 16 percent (19) of the Millennials, who seemed to be much more relaxed about typing speed and accuracy.

When asked what might convince them to ask for help from VRS, convenience again was mentioned, including 24/7 access to librarians. Thirty percent (32) of all respondents cited immediate answers and 17 percent (18) appreciated having home access.

Commonalities in Generation Responses from Online Survey and Telephone Interviews

Results from focus groups, telephone interviews, and online surveys reveal that differences in communication and information-seeking behaviors were found between the Millennials and older adults. A personal relationship with a librarian was more important to Millennials, who also valued recommendations from friends, the librarians' positive attitude toward them, and politeness in interpersonal communications more than did older adults. Showing a reluctance to experiment with unknown technology, a greater number of older adults than Millennials believed that chat reference would be too complicated; therefore, they chose not to use it.

Both users and nonusers considered convenience to be a major factor when choosing how to get their information (see also Connaway & Dickey, 2010; Connaway et al., 2011; JISC, 2010). Most of the respondents from all age cohorts preferred to interface with friendly librarians and to develop ongoing relationships with them. Although most preferred FtF reference services and believed the library is convenient, some said using online sources are more convenient than physical library materials because of their ability to access e-sources from any location.

Many of the nonusers did not believe a librarian could help them or did not know that VRS was available. Both Millennials and older adults were satisfied with other information sources; therefore, they believed that they did not need to use VRS. Human resources, such as family, friends, teachers, and colleagues, were identified as prime information sources. The web was identified as an alternative to the library and was used for "personal convenience." The nonusers might use VRS if it were available 24/7 and if they could receive information quickly and without much effort on their part.

As noted previously, both the VRS nonuser online survey respondents and telephone interview participants were not using live chat services because they were simply unaware that they existed. The nonuser online survey respondents also reported that they did not choose VRS because they were concerned that the questions might annoy the librarian, they did not believe the librarian could help them, and they were satisfied with other sources of information. However, a larger percentage of Millennials than older adults were more concerned that their questions might be annoying, and some worried about "bothering" the librarians. A Millennial nonuser said in reference to a FtF encounter: "The librarian I asked seemed too occupied with other matters to pay any attention to my question, and she made me feel stupid and intrusive for even asking her such a thing." One older adult nonuser revealed a different point of view in saying the following:

> I do not see myself using chat reference services because in the absence of having a reference librarian help me locate an appropriate or required source, I have friends in the LIS discipline with exemplary reference/research skills who could help me. Additionally, because I am in research, I have cultivated my own knowledge base of where/how to track down information. The only time I could ever imagine using chat reference is if I were incapacitated or unable to physically be in a library or if I were unable to reach one of my LIS colleagues. Otherwise, I see myself as a self-sufficient researcher who relies on her own social network and knowledge to locate reference material.

When asked, nonusers thought they might try VRS if they could get information quickly at any time of the day or night. The VRS nonuser telephone interview participants, including greater proportions of Millennials, said they did not choose VRS because they used the web. Some specifically mentioned using Google, including a much greater proportion of Millennials. Both cohorts did not use VRS because of satisfaction with other information sources (e.g., family, friends, colleagues, teachers, the web). One Millennial said: "I choose to go FtF because I'm not lazy, and I can get a more accurate answer FtF, not on chat reference. And I can be there to get the books I want, and not waste a librarian's time on the computer." Another asked: "Why use VRS when phone, face-to-face, or even e-mail could be more convenient?"

When asked to describe a critical incident focusing on a successful reference experience, VRS nonusers who participated in online surveys and telephone interviews most often said that they valued accuracy, correct answers, convenience, and delivery of the information. These respondents also highly valued librarians who are knowledgeable, have a positive attitude, and good communication skills. Millennials value convenience and online access to sources and services, and friendly librarians, and tend to be more concerned that the questions may be annoying to the librarian. Older adults were more worried than Millennials that chat may be too complicated and that their typing skills are not adequate to participate in chat.

Recommendations and Future Research Directions

Based on these findings, a number of strategies can be used to encourage Millennials to use VRS. It is important to engage in creative marketing that promotes a range of options and emphasizes convenience and time-saving factors. Marketing all the various ways that users can gain access to expert librarian help will allow users to feel that they are being met where, when, and how they wish. Another benefit may be to remind people of traditional services, like telephone reference, that now can be rebranded as mobile access to the library when users are on the go. Librarians need to reassure potential users that there are multiple ways of reaching professional help and that "multi-asking" is possible.

During FtF encounters and information literacy sessions, it is suggested that librarians demonstrate VRS and recommend its use. It is important not to assume that users of any age know how to use chat reference or that it is available. This approach can be used in public library programs for older adults. People who have not yet tried the service can be intimidated by live chat reference and may choose other modes just based on this lack of familiarity with VRS. A quick demonstration can open the possibility for someone who is a nonuser to become an avid user. This research showed that regardless of age, the large majority of users enjoyed live chat reference and said that they were highly likely to be repeat clients.

It is essential to keep in mind a basic professional value that excellent service should be extended to all users, regardless of age level. An impatient high school teen posing a homework question to a VRS in June becomes a college freshman asking a research question in September. If screenagers are treated well, taken seriously, and given consistent help and encouragement, they will return and they will spread the word to their friends. The Millennials value personalization, so a greeting that uses their first name, if possible, is a good strategy for building rapport. For sustainability and growth of VRS, repeat customers who speak highly of the service and spread the word through viral marketing are essential.

Looking to the future, additional research must observe use patterns in a range of generations to further explore whether age is a primary factor in information-seeking behaviors, or if it is but one of many factors, including context and situation that contribute to how people get information. Are there Digital Natives and Digital Immigrants (Prensky, 2001), or are there instead other ways to characterize differences in how people adopt and use information technology? White (2008), for example, offers a different model, one that contrasts the behaviors of Digital Residents (who have an ongoing, developing presence online) to that of Digital Visitors (who log on to the virtual environment to perform a specific task or to acquire specific information, and then log off).

Additional research is recommended to study the roles of social networking, mobile technology, and text messaging in information seeking as it would help us better understand how people get their information and why they make these choices. short message service (SMS) reference is becoming more widespread, although it appears to be misunderstood by many professionals who think that users want it to be purely synchronous, although research findings dispute this idea (Pearce, Collard, & Whatley, 2010).

The *Seeking Synchronicity* project is in the process of analyzing a new set of more than 550 QuestionPoint live chat transcripts and Qwidget sessions selected randomly from 2010. Qwidget is QuestionPoint's IM widget which is similar to IM in format and was added in 2008 (Introducing Qwidget, 2008). Generational differences are being tracked so that a longitudinal comparison can be made between the first sample from 2004–2006 and the new sample drawn from 2010. The goal will be to see whether the communication and information-seeking behaviors of both cohorts have changed, and if so, how.

Although there is much discussion about the technology-immersed Millennials, there is insufficient evidence to support assumptions about their actual behaviors and preferences. As suggested by the term screenager, the younger generation may be comfortable interacting with video games, searching the web, and texting on cell phones, but this does not necessarily equate to them being more technologically astute than older individuals.

Many of the Millennials who participated in this study are confident in their abilities to find and evaluate information. However, their interactions with VR librarians do not support their confidence, as young people often need help with basic searching strategy and evaluation of accuracy or authority. This finding was supported by Pew Internet and American Life Project research which asserted that "Adolescents have been called 'digital natives,' but data suggests that they are both comfortable with new technologies, and yet not always as technically savvy as we collectively believe them to be" (Lenhart, Ling, Campbell, & Purcell, 2010, n.p.). There is a need to continue to investigate and compare the information-seeking and communication behaviors of individuals, with age being one variable of study. Others include the individuals' familiarity and exposure to different types of technology, as well as their socioeconomic and educational levels, as exemplified by the work of Agosto and Hughes-Hassell (2005). Longitudinal studies also will help to discern whether individuals choose and continue to use technologies and services that are familiar and comfortable to them instead of the newest technologies and services available to them.

The Millennials are attracting a great deal of attention from scholarly researchers, as well as from corporations who are interested in marketing services and products to them. It is indisputable that each member of this generation is a unique individual with a different background, including access to and knowledge of technology, who may or may not reflect the cohort's tendencies. However, there is no doubt that differing patterns emerge when empirical data are analyzed by age. Here this research has focused on investigating Millennial information-seeking preferences and communication behaviors, especially those that have impact on potential use of library reference services. Learning more about these preferences enables librarians and VR system designers to confront a critical challenge. This challenge is to figure out how to better serve these members of the younger generation, whose predilections for finding and using information resources and services seem to be so technologically driven and so dissimilar from previous generations of library users.

References

Agosto, D. E., & Hughes-Hassell, S. (2005). People, places, and questions: An investigation of the everyday life information-seeking behaviors of urban young adults. *Library and Information Science Research*, 27(2), 141–163.

Connaway, L. S. & Dickey, T. J. (2010). *Towards a profile of the researcher of today: The digital information seeker: Report of findings from selected OCLC, RIN, and JISC user behavior projects.* Retrieved July 13, 2011, from http://www.jisc.ac.uk/media/documents/publications/reports/2010/digitalinformationseekerreport.pdf.

Connaway, L. S., Dickey, T. J., & Radford, M. L. (2011). "If it's too inconvenient I'm not going after it": Convenience as a critical factor in information-seeking behaviors. *Library & Information Science Research*, 33(3), 179–190.

Connaway, L. S., & Radford, M. L. (2010). Virtual reference service quality: Critical components for adults and the net-generation. *Libri, 60*(2), 165–180.

Connaway, L. S., & Radford, M. L. (2011). *Seeking synchronicity: Revelations and recommendations for virtual reference.* Dublin, OH: OCLC Research. Retrieved July 13, 2011, from http://www.oclc.org/reports/synchronicity/default.htm.

Connaway, L. S., Radford, M. L., Dickey, T. J., Williams, J. D., & Confer, P. C. (2008). Sense-making and synchronicity: Information-seeking behaviors of Millennials and baby boomers. *Libri, 58*(2), 123–135.

Flanagan, J. C. (1954). The critical incident technique. *Psychological Bulletin, 51*(4), 327–359.

Fox, S., Anderson, J., & Rainie, L. (2005). *The future of the Internet.* Pew Internet and American Life Project. Retrieved July 13, 2011, from http://www.pewinternet.org/pdfs/PIP_Future_of_Internet.pdf.

Glaser, B. G. (1965). The constant comparative method of qualitative analysis. *Social Problems, 12*(4), 436–445.

Hallam, G., & Partridge, H. (2006). Evidence-based practice: Whose responsibility is it anyway? *Evidence Based Library and Information Practice, 1*(3), 88–94.

Introducing Qwidget, the Question Point Widget. (2008). Retrieved on July 13, 2011, from http://questionpoint.blogs.com/questionpoint_247_referen/2008/01/introducing-qwi.html.

JISC. (2010, March). *Digital information seekers: How academic libraries can support the use of digital resources.* Retrieved July 13, 2011, from http://www.jisc.ac.uk/publications/briefingpapers/2010/bpdigitalinfoseekerv1.aspx.

Lenhart, A., Ling, R., Campbell, S., & Purcell, K. (2010). *Teens and mobile phones.* New York: Pew Internet and American Life Project. Retrieved July 13, 2011, from http://pewinternet.org/topics/Teens.aspx.

McHale, T. (2005). Portrait of a digital native: Are digital-age students fundamentally different from the rest of us? *Technology & Learning, 26*(2), 33–34.

Oblinger, D. G., & Oblinger, J. L. (Eds.). (2005). *Educating the Net generation.* Educause. Retrieved July 13, 2011, from http://www.educause.edu/content.asp?PAGE_ID=5989&bhcp=1.

Oblinger, D. G., & Oblinger, J. L. (2006). Is it age or IT: First steps toward understanding the Net generation. *CSLA Journal, 29*(2), 8–16.

OCLC (Online Computer Library Center). (2011). *QuestionPoint: 24/7 reference services.* Retrieved July 13, 2011, from http://wiki.questionpoint.org/w/page/13839418/24-7-Coop-FAQs.

Pearce, A., Collard, S., & Whatley, K. (2010). SMS reference: Myths, markers, and modalities. *Reference Services Review, 38*(2), 250–263.

Prensky, M. (2001). Digital natives, digital immigrants, Part 1. *On the Horizon, 9*(5), 1–6. doi:10.1108/10748120110424816.

Prensky, M. (2006). Listen to the natives, *Educational Leadership, 63*(4), 8–13.

QuestionPoint: *24/7 Reference Services.* (n.d.). 24 7 Coop FAQs. Retrieved July 13, 2011, from http://wiki.questionpoint.org/w/page/13839418/24-7-Coop-FAQs.

Radford, M. L. (2006a). Encountering virtual users: A qualitative investigation of interpersonal communication in chat reference. *Journal of the American Society for Information Science and Technology, 57*(8), 1046–1059.

Radford, M. L. (2006b). Investigating interpersonal communication in chat reference: Dealing with impatient users and rude encounters. In R. D. Lankes, E. Abels, M. D. White, & S. N. Haque (Eds.), *The virtual reference desk: Creating a reference future* (pp. 23–46). New York: Neal-Schuman Publishers.

Radford, M. L., & Connaway, L. S. (2005–2008). *Seeking synchronicity: Evaluating virtual reference services from user, non-user, and librarian perspectives.* Retrieved July 13, 2011, from http://www.oclc.org/research/activities/synchronicity/default.htm.

Radford, M. L., & Connaway, L. S. (2007). "Screenagers" and live chat reference: Living up to the promise. *Scan, 26*(1), 31–39.

Radford, M. L., & Connaway, L. S. (2010). *Digital natives meet digital libraries: Discovering their behaviors and preferences for information seeking.* Paper presented at Libraries in the Digital Age (LIDA) 2010, Zadar, Croatia, May 24–28. Retrieved on July 13, 2011, from http://web .ffos.hr/lida/datoteke/lida_2010_proceedings.pdf.

Radford, M. L., Radford, G. P., Connaway, L. S., & DeAngelis, J. A. (2011). On virtual face-work: An ethnography of communication approach to a live chat reference interaction. *The Library Quarterly, 81*(4), 431–453.

Rushkoff, D. (1996). *Playing the future: What we can learn from digital kids.* New York: Harper Collins.

Salaway, G., Katz, R. N., Caruso, J. B., Kvavik, R. B., & Nelson, M. R. (2006). *The ECAR study of undergraduate students and information technology,* 2006. Boulder, CO: Educause.

Tapscott, D. (1998). *Growing up digital: The rise of the Net generation.* New York: McGraw-Hill.

Thomas, C., & McDonald, R. (2005). Millennial net value(s): Disconnects between libraries and the information age mindset. *Florida State University D-Scholarship Repository.* Retrieved July 13, 2011, from http://web.archive.org/web/20060807012805/dscholarship.lib.fsu.edu/cgi/ viewcontent.cgi?article=1008&context=general.

White, D. (2008, April 23). Not "natives" & "immigrants" but "visitors" & "residents." *TALL Blog: Online Education with the University of Oxford.* Retrieved July 13, 2011, from http://tallblog .conted.ox.ac.uk/index.php/2008/07/23/not-natives-immigrants-but-visitors-residents/.

## CHAPTER 2

The Tutorial Dialogue and Problem Solving in Virtual Reference Interactions

Mary Kickham-Samy

Overview

This study examines the natural dialogue that occurred in a small, purposefully selected sample of virtual reference (VR) transcripts in order to identify patterns of discourse that sustained participant engagement and promoted learning. The researcher compared tutoring situations to VR transactions. Both involved a student and a more experienced partner in intense collaboration for the purpose of removing obstacles to learning. Based on activity theory and Vygotsky's (1978) concept of the "zone of proximal development" (ZPD), this study describes the way that participants in VR transactions co-constructed meaningful conversations to solve research problems. The researcher used the interactional sociolinguistic methodology of Erving Goffman (1974, 1981) and John Gumperz (1982) to identify and then analyze how a student and a librarian established common ground and made contextual inferences in preparation for exploring topics and navigating library resources.

Introduction

The Association of College and Research Libraries (ACRL) published a document that defines five standards of competency for an information-literate individual (http://www.ala.org/ala/mgrps/divs/acrl/standards/objectivesinformation.cfm). These standards address the areas of assessing one's information needs, and then, accessing, evaluating, and using this information effectively and ethically. Academic libraries are mandated by ACRL to provide instruction in these areas to all students regardless of whether the student attends class on campus or from a distance. While the library community has demonstrated success in providing remote access to library resources, especially online databases, its success in instructing students in searching, accessing, using, and evaluating the information they find using these tools is less clear.

This study extends the research into the viability of instruction in VR environments. It examines ways that instructional goals and strategies are set, assessed, and reset through natural dialogue. One area of research that sheds light on instructional strategies in VR environments is that of tutoring.

Literature Review

Theoretical Framework

The theoretical framework for this study is activity theory, based largely on the writings of Vygotsky (1978). At the core, activity theory is the notion that consciousness is a reciprocal transformation that takes place when internal cognitive processes engage with the outside world (Wertsch, 1981). Vygotsky conceived of human transformation as the relationship between a stimulus, a response, and a mediating object, a tool. Language is one tool that an individual uses to mediate with the outside world. Through language, the individual engages with society to construct knowledge. Learning takes place when this engagement involves the learners in an activity just outside their current state of development, but within the sphere of their ability to understand, their zone of proximal development (ZPD). Influenced by activity theory, Wells (2002) proposed that education should be essentially a form of "semiotic apprenticeship," in which students engaged with experts within a framework of dialogue.

Tutoring and Virtual Reference

Tutoring and VR services are educational environments in which a student engages in dialogue with a more experienced person to solve an academic problem. With tutoring, one main purpose is to guide the student in understanding specific topics that are troublesome obstacles to further learning (Person, Graesser, Magliano, & Kreuz, 1994). Similarly, with VR, the goal for the academic librarian is to provide help for the student anytime and anywhere the student is blocked from continuing with a research project. In both the tutoring environment and the VR environment, students go to a more expert partner for help when they arrive at an obstacle to their continuing with their studies, when they are blocked from moving forward. Finally, both learning environments focus on problem solving.

One difference between tutoring and VR is the level of student control. In a tutoring environment, the tutor has more control because the tutor often has a copy of the course syllabus and the textbook. The tutor knows the content of the course, the specifics of assignments, and the scope of the tests. This is not true in VR. In a typical VR exchange, the student knows the requirements of the assignment and has background information on the content of the course from class lectures and assigned readings, whereas the librarian has knowledge of databases to search, and expertise in forming search strategies. Together, the two participants combine their knowledge and skills to find a solution to the research problem.

Tutoring as an Instructional Environment

In the 1980s, Benjamin Bloom (1984) and Cohen, Kulik, and Kulik (1982) conducted meta-analyses of research into tutoring, and discovered overwhelming evidence that tutoring was a more successful learning environment than the traditional classroom. In his frequently cited paper, Bloom (1984) reported on the results of two doctoral dissertations that showed that students who learned in tutoring environments outperformed those who learned in group instruction with 30 students. These studies found that students who learned in a one-on-one environment performed better on achievement tests than those who learned in a traditional classroom. The average tutored student scored higher than 98 percent of the students who were in a traditional classroom environment.

Research into tutoring accelerated when educators envisioned the future of education punctuated with cost-effective and efficient computer-mediated tutoring. This enthusiasm for computer programs that mimicked human-to-human tutoring prompted researchers to try to find out how human tutors behaved, so that they might more closely approximate this behavior in the computer-to-human tutoring environments (Fox, 1993; Graesser, Baggett, & Williams, 1996; Litman et al., 2006). This research showed that tutoring was successful because of four components:

1. Sensitivity to individual student needs
2. Natural dialogue patterns
3. Flexibility of the tutor
4. Deep explanations of real-life problems

Sensitivity to Individual Student Needs

In order to better understand how tutoring was sensitive to the individual student, Merrill, Reiser, Merrill, and Landes (1995) examined what tutors did to deter students from making mistakes, and what kind of feedback tutors provided when students did make mistakes. By analyzing transcripts generated from audio-taped tutoring sessions, they found that tutors focused their attention not on a preset script of tutor-initiated questions, but rather on student-initiated questions. Tutors based their decision on how fast to give feedback and what kind of feedback to give on the student's line of reasoning and way of thinking.

Natural Dialogue Patterns

Graesser, Person, and Magliano (1995) observed that most tutoring was conducted by tutors who lacked experience, formal training, and expertise in the subject matter, and despite its counterintuitive nature, these tutors made greater academic gains with students than classroom teachers, who were subject-matter experts, experienced, and professionally trained. From this, they hypothesized that tutoring was successful not because of superior teaching strategies, but rather because of the "conversational dialogue patterns" embedded in this form of interaction (p. 96).

To establish support for their hypothesis, Graesser, Person, and Magliano (1995) videotaped two different naturalistic tutoring environments: 44 tutoring sessions with 25 college students, and 22 sessions with 13 high school students. Using the corpora from these two tutoring environments, they looked for eight factors that that they considered important in successful learning environments. These factors were as follows:

1. Active student learning
2. Sophisticated pedagogical strategies
3. Anchored learning in specific examples and cases
4. Collaborative problem solving and question answering
5. Deep explanatory reasoning
6. Convergence toward shared meaning
7. Feedback, error diagnosis, and remediation
8. Affect and motivation (p. 497)

The results of their study showed that, under "normal" tutoring with typical tutors, the most prominent components were "collaborative problem solving and question answering," "anchored learning in specific examples and cases," and "deep explanatory reasoning." The other five components, notably "sophisticated pedagogical strategies," were either underused or absent (Graesser et al., p. 497).

Fox (1993) researched tutorial dialogues over a seven-year period. Fox video-recorded students and tutors engaged in actual tutorial sessions in order to observe and document naturally occurring conversation as it emerged. She was able to identify three characteristics of tutorial dialogues. First, the tutoring dialogue was embedded in the specific context, or situation. This means that, in addition to the content of the lesson being studied, the participants were aware of other factors, such as knowledge that they were preparing for a test, the amount of time they had for preparation, and the limitations on the length of the session. Second, she found that individual words and phrases within the tutorial dialogue did not have absolute meaning, but derived meaning from the ongoing conversation. Words and phrases acquired meaning as the student and the tutor negotiated the conversation. Third, tutoring was an "interactional achievement" (p. 6). Both participants mutually constructed and negotiated the outcomes of the sessions.

Flexibility of the Tutor

One of the advantages of tutoring over classroom instruction is the flexibility that the tutor has to adjust instruction to the specific needs and competencies of each individual student (Person et al., 1994). For this reason, researchers looked at whether the questions that students asked and answered were in any way a means of assessing a student's competency in a subject. In one study, Person and colleagues (1994) analyzed 44 one-on-one tutoring sessions to find out whether the quantity of questions that students asked was an indicator of their knowledge of the subject. The authors found that the number of questions students asked did not correlate with the students' understanding of the subject as reflected in their scores on examinations and final grades.

The authors also found that students asked many more yes-no questions than long-answer questions, and that few of these questions pointed to gaps in their knowledge. They concluded that students were unable to ask questions that pointed to specific gaps in their knowledge because they were either unable to identify their problems or were inhibited from asking questions that exposed their lack of understanding (Person et al., 1994).

Graesser and Olde (2003) also looked at whether the quantity or the quality of student questions reflected student understanding of the subject matter. The researchers asked 108 college students to read, write, and ask questions about a defective device. By correlating the quantity and the quality of questions asked with scores on a comprehension test of the device, the researchers showed three tendencies. First of all, the number of questions asked had no correlation to an understanding of the device. Second, the students with the most knowledge about the device asked the most constructive and relevant questions. Third, students with the best knowledge of the subject also asked questions involving deep explanatory reasoning, such as why, how, or what-if questions. These two studies, Person and colleagues (1994) and Graesser and Olde (2003), suggest that the instructional practice of asking and answering questions has a limited impact on the success of a tutoring session.

Students ask questions most frequently when they become aware of missing information. However, students are not very good at asking questions, so once they are aware of missing information, students often need help in forming a question. Due to social inhibitions, students sometimes allow politeness to interfere with their learning efficiently (Graesser & McMahen, 1993).

Deep Explanations of Real-Life Problems

Merrill and colleagues (1995) examined what tutors did to deter students from making mistakes, and what kind of feedback tutors provided when students did make mistakes. They found that tutors based their decision on how fast to give feedback and what kind of feedback to give on the student's line of reasoning and way of thinking. Finally, the decision regarding whether feedback was direct or indirect was based on a careful calibration of the costs and benefits of allowing the student to identify errors and correct them.

Finally, tutoring is a successful instructional environment, not because of skillful teaching strategies, but because of intense collaboration between the tutor and the student and the involvement of complex reasoning skills in solving a specific problem. The literature shows that tutoring is successful despite the fact that students are poor at asking questions and the average tutor employs unsophisticated teaching strategies and has little technique. Tutoring is effective because it provides an environment that is sensitive to the needs of the student, follows natural conversational rules, is flexible, and involves the student and the tutor in deep explanations of real-life problems.

The Problem

This study extends the research into the way that natural human dialogue in one-on-one learning environments facilitates the dynamic process of identifying, articulating, and solving problems. By analyzing the interactions of students and librarians in VR environments, the researcher endeavored to identify the teaching and learning strategies of both participants, the librarian and the student. Much of the previous research into one-on-one learning environments focused on the "average" tutor, who had little training and experience in teaching. This study focuses on the teaching strategies and techniques of librarians, who have at least one advanced degree and who are career educators. In previous tutoring studies, the tutor employed or had access to a preset curriculum script. In VR sessions, the librarian does not have access to this information. These differences may have generated a greater interdependency between the participants than in previous studies. This study addresses the following research questions:

- RQ 1: In those transcripts that the researcher examined, what patterns of dialogue emerged and how did these patterns affect the outcome of the sessions?
- RQ 2: In those transcripts that the researcher examined, under what conditions did instruction emerge and student learning take place?

Methodology

Data Source

The source of the data for this study was an archive of transcripts maintained by Question Point (http://www.questionpoint.org/), a product of Online Computer Library Center (OCLC), a library service provider. The transcripts were generated by two types of technology: either chat with sophisticated co-browsing capabilities or simple instant messaging (IM) widgets, a product known as "Qwidget."

Each transcript is divided into three parts: opening information, the body of the transcript, and closing information. The opening information contains nine bits of information: (1) the student's initial query, (2) the student's wait time for a librarian to accept the question, (3) the session length, (4) the language, (5) the student's IP address, (6) the student's browser information, (7) information about co-browsing capability, (8) the librarian's affiliation, and (9) the student's college affiliation. The body of the transcript includes each message the participants send to each other, and the time in minutes and seconds between each message sent. When it is necessary to transfer a call from one librarian to another, the text of the instant messaging between the two librarians is also included in the body of the transcript. The closing information indicates which party closed the session, and the resolution code. The resolution code indicates whether the student's question was answered, whether it needed follow-up by the student's library, or follow-up by the librarian herself. It can also be designated a "lost call" when a disconnection occurs and there is no identifying information for follow-up. Finally, it can be labeled a "test." After the session has been closed, the librarians may also elect to send a note to the student, or a private note to the librarian at the student's home institution, all of which information is contained in the closing information. Other content that may be included in the closing information are follow-up e-mails to the student or, when necessary, follow-up e-mails to subject matter experts. So, the transcripts contain a large amount of information.

Participants
The participants were the librarians and students of the Research Help Now! Michigan Virtual Reference Collaborative (http://researchhelpnow.org/) or the QuestionPoint global service. In other words, they were either Michigan students helped by librarians of the Research Help Now! Michigan Virtual Reference Collaborative or of the Question Point global service, or they were Michigan librarians helping students participating in the QuestionPoint 24/7 service. The librarian/participants were librarians with master's degrees in library science from an American Library Association (ALA)–accredited program. The student/participants were a diverse group of college students of all ages with a wide variety of ethnic, educational, social, and economic backgrounds.

Sampling Procedures
Among the hundreds of transcripts generated by Michigan VR librarians and/or their students during the months of February through April 2010, the researcher selected and archived approximately 80 transcripts that she identified as substantial enough in length and duration to foster a viable learning environment. Next, the researcher read the students' questions that were embedded in the archived transcripts. From among these substantive transcripts, 15 were selected for the study because they involved a complex research question and exhibited potential for student collaboration and learning.

Method of Analysis
The discourse analysis methodology used in this study, interactional sociolinguistics, is based on the work of the anthropologist John Gumperz (1982), and the sociologist

Erving Goffman (1974, 1981). Schiffrin (1994) says that "interactional sociolinguistics views discourse as a social interaction in which the emergent construction and negotiation of meaning is facilitated by the use of language.... Put another way, language and social context co-constitute one another" (p. 134). The researcher chose this methodology because it is based on concepts closely aligned with activity theory. Vygotsky (1978) and his followers recognized the inherent social nature of learning, that it was not a lonely internal process. Learning did not take place independent of outside factors, but rather it took place in a social context. Vygotsky viewed learning as a mutually constructive activity during which the learner engaged with society in a reciprocal manner to co-construct knowledge.

This study utilizes John Gumperz's (1982) work in situated inference, which asserts that conversation is based on what the participants in the conversation are able to infer from the context. He says that conversation "begins with informed guessing based on what we know about the physical setting, the participants and their backgrounds, and how we relate the situation at hand to other known activities" (p. 101). Similar to Vygotsky's notion that knowledge is socially constructed, to Gumperz conversation is constructed through not only the words the participants speak, but also through the inferences one brings to the conversation from the cultural factors and social surroundings.

This study also utilizes Goffman's (1974) "frame analysis" methodology, which he defined as the identification of "basic elements" that organize or explain "human experience" (pp. 10–11). Using frame analysis, the researcher identified an event within human experience, and then asked the question "what is it that's going on here?" (Goffman, 1974, p. 8). In addition, this study employs Goffman's concept of "footing" to identify the mechanisms that participants in VR learning environments used to position and align themselves to facilitate successful interaction. Footing is the establishment of common ground between the participants. It can be argued that Goffman's use of footing was a device that the participants used to remain within what Vygotsky called the zone of proximal development, so that mutual learning and knowledge construction could take place.

There are commonalities between the concepts and methods employed by Vygotsky and the social linguists, Goffman and Gumperz. Vygotsky studied how individuals learned by engaging with society through language and everyday activity. Similarly, Erving Goffman and John Gumperz studied the way that human understanding of everyday interactions was constructed from contextual cues that emerged from human dialogue.

Results

Establishing Common Ground, or Footing
From an in-depth analysis, accomplished through reading and rereading the transcripts, basic, as well as complex, discourse patterns emerged. Among the basic patterns that were found in the data was the establishment of common ground, which Goffman (1974, 1981) referred to as footing. Examples of establishing common ground were displayed in the openings of sessions in the form of a greeting ritual, such as "hi," followed by the student's name, and in closing rituals (see Goffman, 1967; Ross, Nilsen, & Radford,

2009). The librarian also established common ground, by restating the student's question or making reference to it in some way.

The following is an example of establishing common ground when clarifying the student's question. The student's lack of understanding of the word "obsolete" created the potential for confusion. However, without being presumptuous, the librarian maintained common ground and carefully helped the student clarify the question.

> STUDENT A: i just need obsolete websites that have famous revenge quotes.
> LIBRARIAN A: I'm not sure what you mean by obsolete.
> LIBRARIAN A: Obsolete means "out of date."
> LIBRARIAN A: I can probably help you find various websites, though, that would give you some quotes about revenge being obsolete.
> STUDENT A: ok i mean more valuable
> LIBRARIAN A: Might you also mean "reliable" sites?
> STUDENT A: yes

The following is an example of establishing common ground in a closing ritual. In this exchange, the student's problem was solved. Then, both participants expressed appreciation for the other's effort. The process of establishing common ground was lengthy because there was a conscious effort to avoid an abrupt and potentially rude closing.

> STUDENT B: many thanks. i appreciate your time!
> LIBRARIAN B: Great job!
> STUDENT B: Thank you. Have a great evening....
> LIBRARIAN B: You are very welcome.
> STUDENT B: bye
> LIBRARIAN B: You're a great researcher.
> STUDENT B: lol
> LIBRARIAN B: lol

This exchange illustrated a painstaking effort on the part of the librarian and the student to remain connected and end the session using politeness rituals that Goffman would call face-work (see Goffman, 1956, 1967).

The following example illustrates a situation in which the librarian and the student fail to establish common ground. Although it is possible that a technical issue caused the session to end prematurely, it is also possible that the student lost confidence in the librarian's ability to address the problem that the student posed.

> STUDENT C: I am trying to start my research paper... and I don't know where to begin. [...]
> LIBRARIAN C: Have you searched in any of the research databases...?
> STUDENT C: Yes, I have the information I need, I just don't know how to start the paper
> LIBRARIAN C: Okay, let me find a source that might help you understand the different parts of a research paper. Hold please.
> STUDENT C: thank you

LIBRARIAN C: The Owl is a great source. Did you get the page?
STUDENT C: Patron is no longer connected.

Parallel Problem Solving

The next set of examples displays a more complex pattern, one of parallel problem solving. Parallel problem solving takes place when the two participants work to solve more than one problem at one time. Most discourse involves adjacency pairs, where a statement is followed by a relevant response, the most common of which is a question followed by an answer. However, in chat environments, this adjacency-pairs rule is often violated. The participants engage in disjointed discussions.

The next two transactions illustrate parallel problem solving. In the first situation, the librarian and the student worked in tandem to solve one specific problem using four different strategies. In the second example, the librarian and the student negotiated four separate problems, but in the end, they resolved only one.

One Problem, Four Strategies

In the following example, the student asked for a list of best jobs in the 1970s. The librarian took the question at its face value and began a search.

STUDENT B: Where can I find a list of the best jobs in 1970?
LIBRARIAN B: Hi. In the 1970s?—Let me do a search for you. Just a second...

Then, the student provided more information. With this additional information, the librarian realigned strategies and goals with those of the student.

STUDENT B: I'm trying to do a comparison between the best jobs listed in us news & world report for 2010
LIBRARIAN B: So, you want to compare those "best jobs" to best jobs of the 1970s.

This new information required the librarian to reassess the strategy employed and reestablish common ground.

In the next segment of this transaction, the librarian began to reestablish common ground with the student by slowing down and becoming tentative.

LIBRARIAN B: Maybe we should search the US news and world report of the 70s.
STUDENT B: yes exactly. thanks.

The librarian's use of the word "maybe" was a means of establishing common ground with the student. The librarian sought and received confirmation from the student before proceeding.

In the next segment, the librarian decided to search for an article that listed best jobs in the 1970s not only in the *U.S. News & World Report*, but also at a government website. As a teaching strategy, this approach kept the student actively engaged in the whole process.

LIBRARIAN B: [...] I have an idea. Let me send you the URL to the Bureau of Labor Statistics. While you search that, I'll look for an equivalent article in USNews and World Report of the 1970s. [...]
STUDENT B: thanks...great idea

The interaction became more and more complex as the librarian suggested more websites to search. Parallel problem solving emerged.

In the following segment, the numbers next to each line of text signify parallel discussions. The "1"s represent the search at the Bureau of Labor Statistics (BLS), the "2"s represent a search in the *Occupational Outlook Handbook* (*OOH*), and the "3"s represent the search for a specific article in the *U.S. News & World Report*. The librarian and the student seemed quite comfortable engaging in discourse in which the structures were not adjacent to one another; they were disjointed. The discourse was not linear, but rather there were three parallel discussions going on at once.

> LIBRARIAN B: http://www.bls.gov/ [1]
> LIBRARIAN B: There is an Occupational Outlook Handbook for 1970s also. [2]
> STUDENT B: checking it out now. [1]
> LIBRARIAN B: You can try to google that. [2]
> LIBRARIAN B: OK. I'm going to look in magazines.... [3]
> STUDENT B: great thanks [3] googling now [2]

In the continuation of this exchange (see the following exchange), the librarian ran into an obstacle and adjusted the strategy. The two participants began to reestablish common ground and reshape their strategy.

> LIBRARIAN B: Guess what? The US News and World Report is not archived electronically back till 1970s.
> LIBRARIAN B: So I'm going to join your search.
> STUDENT B: bummer. looking at bls now
> [Reestablishing common ground]
> LIBRARIAN B: I'm sure we can find something.
> STUDENT B: crossing fingers
> LIBRARIAN B: Still looking...

In this VR session, the librarian and the student established excellent footing and worked as a team.

> LIBRARIAN B: I found a document. I'll send it to you. [...]
> STUDENT B: thanks
> LIBRARIAN B: [URL]
> STUDENT B: cool
> LIBRARIAN B: Bingo! Look on page 79.
> STUDENT B: you rock!

Eventually, the participants were able to solve the student's research problem.

Four Problems Posed, One Problem Solved

In the next transcript, the student asked for help in narrowing a research topic. From this question, as the dialogue continued, four problems emerged: (1) narrowing a topic, (2) finding information, (3) managing course assignment issues, and (4) student self-efficacy. In the first segment of this transcript, the student had a topic for a paper, but expressed concern about how to identify main ideas. Diverting from the student's stated concern, the librarian introduced a second issue, which was whether or not the student had source material for the paper.

> STUDENT E: I am writing a paper and i need to know what could be some possible body paragraph topics. My thesis is: In troubled times people bail out of commitments [...]
>
> LIBRARIAN D: Have you already researched articles, etc. ... ?

This first segment showed that the librarian and the student began their interaction with two divergent interests. They had not yet established common ground.

In the next segment of the same transaction, the librarian returned to the student's concern about the topic. By suggesting types of troubles, the librarian tried to guide the student in defining what "troubled times" meant. Although concerned about the topic, the student answered the librarian's question about resources.

> LIBRARIAN D: [...] possible topics: divorce, bankruptcy, mortgage defaults ...
>
> STUDENT E: Oh ok I understand now I just thought if I chose those they would be to broad
>
> STUDENT E: I have tryed researching articles ...
>
> LIBRARIAN D: One good resource ... would be "Opposing Viewpoints ... "
>
> STUDENT E: Is that a website?

After the student addressed the librarian's question about sources, the librarian resumed focusing on helping the student find source material. The participants continued to fail to establish common ground.

Deep Explanatory Reasoning Question
In this same transaction, the student asked a deep explanatory reasoning question. This question indicated that the student was grappling with a complex concept involving critical thinking skills.

> STUDENT E: Also if i go to research about these topics what am i really analyzing the reason that made these people leave their commitments?

This question gave the librarian information about why the student was having difficulty.

Course Management Issue
In the third segment of this transaction, the librarian introduced a third problem, a concern about course management issues. The participants were now juggling three problems: narrowing the topic, finding source material, and conforming to constraints related to the requirements of the course.

> LIBRARIAN D: Maybe these ideas are too broad ... I would need to see your assignment to know.
>
> LIBRARIAN D: It's a website on your school's library site ...
>
> LIBRARIAN D: How long a paper is this supposed to be?
>
> LIBRARIAN D: ... maybe you can focus on one area, like marriage, political activity, etc. etc.
>
> STUDENT D: I like the idea of marriage

LIBRARIAN D: Opposing Viewpoints is a great resource because [it has] ... opinion pieces on social issues.

LIBRARIAN D: Within marriage, you could cover, li[vi]ng with parents, delaying having kids ...

After negotiation, the librarian and the student began to establish common ground. The student began to narrow the topic and the librarian began to guide the student in ways to develop it.

Student Self-Efficacy Issue

Just as they were beginning to form common ground, the student introduced a fourth problem: a lack of confidence in the student's writing skills. The librarian attempted to give the student some guidance on this.

STUDENT D: I am not that good of a writer so ...

LIBRARIAN D: When you [are] looking at the articles in Opposing Viewpoints ... try to see ... how those writers organized their materials.

The librarian continued to try to give the student advice on how to write. However, the student returned to focusing on the original goal, which was to identify, narrow, and develop the topic.

LIBRARIAN D: Broadly speaking, when you write, you should ...

STUDENT D: my thesis will relate to why people bail out of marriage

Throughout this session, the librarian tried to negotiate with the student to discuss source material, course management issues, and basic writing skills, but the student remained focused on the topic, and in a gentle way, controlled the session.

Making Contextual Inferences

The next example illustrates how inferences are used to negotiate meaning and solve problems. With inferences, informational statements are left out of the dialogue. This lack of stated information requires the participants to infer meaning from the context in order to communicate successfully. Inferences are a common discourse phenomenon.

After reading the student's question, the librarian identified a database suitable for this student's research, and then proceeded to develop a strategy to guide the student.

STUDENT D: I am doing a career research project. I have already looked in OOH for information on a career as a Medical Administrative Assistant. Where else might I find information about career in the medical field? [...]

LIBRARIAN B: Let me see what databases might help.

LIBRARIAN B: Your college has "Vocational & Career Collection." That is a great database for research into a career. Let me see what you need to access it. Just a second.

STUDENT D: Yes it does, I searched there many times already and really wasn't able to find much. I think I am having some trouble with keywords.

By examining the adjacent pair of sentences, from the information the librarian gave, the student was able to make an important inference. The student realized that the database was actually a good and useful one. This realization caused a reassessment of the problem. The student became aware that the problem was not the resource the student was using, but the ineffective way the student was searching it. The student realized help was needed to identify search terms. In the example above, the student redefined the problem from that of finding sources to that of finding appropriate search terms. The librarian began to realign the discourse to more closely address this problem.

Discussion

Results indicated that problem-solving strategies used in VR environments were established and modified as a product of the natural dialogue that took place between the librarian and the student as they engaged in a problem-solving activity. This analysis also showed that strategy switching took place when new unexpected information was introduced. As the participants engaged in activity and dialogue, they co-constructed a better understanding of the research problem. However, sometimes the new knowledge created disequilibrium and uncertainty. In response, the participants stopped their activity to regain common ground before proceeding with their problem-solving task.

Establishing common ground consisted of a complex series of exchanges between the two participants that involved active and purposeful engagement. The goals that were set and the strategies used to achieve these goals were also a delicate negotiation between the student and the librarian. The librarian tried to influence the student to proceed in one direction. The student was either convinced and followed the librarian, or started to pull in a different direction. Skill in reestablishing common ground was important in bringing transactions to a successful conclusion and making the experience a positive one for the student and the librarian.

When a session involved several layers of problems, the participants carefully negotiated which to address and in what order. When the participants detected that the discussion was moving in an unproductive direction, they redirected their attention from solving the problem to realigning themselves, or establishing a common footing. Once common footing was reestablished, the participants proceeded to implement their modified goals and strategies.

Limitations and Recommendations

There are two main limitations to this study. First, this study lacked triangulation. It consisted of one primary source of data, the archived transcripts of actual virtual reference sessions. Interviews with and surveys of participants need to be done in order to better support the findings. Second, this research was an exploratory study based on a small sample of transcripts. Similar studies in which many transcripts are analyzed need to be conducted to validate this approach and its findings.

The results of this study suggest two broad recommendations. First, librarians should focus attention on the students' contributions to the session in order to identify student concerns and maintain student confidence. The librarian should maintain common ground with the students in order to encourage them to stay connected. One way to maintain common ground is for the librarian to explain why a process or procedure is preferable. When students understand why the librarian is suggesting a solution, they are better able to follow the suggestions and participate in finding a solution to their research problems. Second, the librarian should be alert to student behavior even when it appears to be passive because active learning may be taking place internally. While observing the librarian's search strategies and reading the librarian's explanations, the students are internally processing this new information and forming their own conclusions. They are making important inferences, with which they can find their own best solutions to their research problem. Therefore, VR librarians should be mindful not only of what the students say, but also what they do not say.

Conclusion

In VR transactions, problem solving can be shown to take place within a five-part framework:

1. A student poses a problem and the participants move to establish common ground.
2. Goals are established and strategies are initiated to solve the problem.
3. New information is introduced, and integrated into the framework.
4. The goals and the strategies are reassessed, and common ground is reestablished.
5. New goals and strategies are negotiated, and then, added, deleted, or modified.

For this progression to remain intact and uninterrupted, the participants in the transaction engage in a delicate, sometimes fragile, dialogue that is sustained through a careful sensitivity to the concerns of the other. The progression is broken whenever one of the participants strays from the sphere of understanding of the other. The progression of this framework is maintained through skills in establishing common ground, which is established not only through overt words and phrases within the dialogue, but also through hard-won inferences derived from the context of the interaction.

This framework is consistent with activity theory. Learning takes place within a dynamic relationship between a learner, a tool, and society. In a VR environment, the tools are the library resources and social influence is the librarian. By maintaining common ground with the librarian, the student is able to remain within what Vygotsky (1978) called the zone of proximal development (ZPD). Learning occurs when the learner engages in activity through dialogue with the librarian and manipulation of the research tools of the library.

References

Bloom, B. S. (1984). The 2-sigma problem: The search for methods of group instruction as effective as one-to-one tutoring. *Educational Researcher, 13*(6), 4–16.

Cohen, P. A., Kulik, J. A., & Kulik, C. (1982). Educational outcomes of tutoring: A meta-analysis of findings. *American Educational Research Journal, 19*(2), 237–248.

Fox, B. A. (1993). *The human tutorial dialogue project: Issues in the design of instructional systems.* Hillsdale, NJ: Lawrence Erlbaum.

Goffman, E. (1956). The nature of deference and demeanor. *American Anthropologist, 58*(3), 475–499.

Goffman, E. (1967). *Interaction ritual, essays on face-to-face behavior.* Garden City, NY: Doubleday.

Goffman, E. (1974). *Frame analysis: An essay on the organization of experience.* Boston, MA: Northeastern University Press.

Goffman, E. (1981). *Forms of talk.* Philadelphia: University of Pennsylvania Press.

Graesser, A. C., Baggett, W., & Williams, K. (1996). Question-driven explanatory reasoning. *Applied Cognitive Psychology, 10,* S17–S31.

Graesser, A. C., & McMahen, C. L. (1993). Anomalous information triggers questions when adults solve quantitative problems and comprehend stories. *Journal of Educational Psychology, 85*(1), 136–151.

Graesser, A. C., & Olde, B. A. (2003). How does one know whether a person understands a device? The quality of the questions the person asks when the device breaks down. *Journal of Educational Psychology, 95*(3), 524–536.

Graesser, A. C., Person, N. K., & Magliano, J. P. (1995). Collaborative dialogue patterns in naturalistic one-to-one tutoring. *Applied Cognitive Psychology, 9,* 495–522.

Gumperz, J. J. (1982). *Discourse strategies.* Cambridge, UK: Cambridge University Press.

Litman, D. J., Rose, C. P., Forbes-Riley, K., VanLehn, K., Bhembe, D., & Silliman, S. (2006). Spoken versus typed human and computer dialogue tutoring. *International Journal of Artificial Intelligence in Education, 16,* 145–170.

Merrill, D. C., Reiser, B. J., Merrill, S. K., & Landes, S. (1995). Tutoring: Guided learning by doing. *Cognition and Instruction, 13*(3), 315–372.

Person, N. K., Graesser, A. C., Magliano, J. P., & Kreuz, R. J. (1994). Inferring what the student knows in one-to-one tutoring: The role of student questions and answers. *Learning and Individual Differences, 6*(2), 205–229.

Ross, C. S., Nilsen, K., & Radford, M. L. (2009). *Conducting the reference interview* (2nd ed.) New York: Neal-Schuman.

Schiffrin, D. (1994). *Approaches to discourse.* Malden, MA: Blackwell.

Vygotsky, L. S. (1978). *Mind in society: The development of higher psychological processes.* Cambridge, MA; London: Harvard University Press.

Wells, G. (2002). The role of dialogue in activity theory. *Mind, Culture, and Activity, 9*(1), 43–66.

Wertsch, J. V. (1981). Introduction to "the problems of activity in psychology" by Leont'ev, A. N. In J.V. Wertsch (Ed.), *The concept of activity in Soviet psychology* (pp. 37–40). Armonk, NY: Sharpe.

## CHAPTER 3

Fast and Furious: Using Web Conferencing and Other Tools for Virtual Reference and Instruction

Rebekah Kilzer, Larry Milliken, and Jay Bhatt

Overview

As the number of distance learning students increases across academia, the challenges to offering high-quality library and information services also become more prominent, and problematic. Offering individual reference and research help is straightforward for students physically in the library, but providing the same caliber of service to online or distance students can be challenging.

The Drexel University Libraries are using a suite of tools to provide high-quality, accessible reference, instruction, and research help for our students, both on campus and at a distance. Web-conferencing tools such as Wimba and Adobe Connect Pro, instant messaging (IM), course management systems, and course-related blogs are some of the approaches used to integrate virtual reference (VR) and instruction. The Libraries have taken a proactive approach toward serving distance students by implementing IM reference service available to any student who visits the Libraries' website, select databases, and other service points. Online office hours and appointments are offered using web-conferencing software, enabling students and librarians to interact and hold impromptu discussions at a moment's notice, with few technical barriers. By offering such services using these tools, librarians are successfully trying to reach out and meet the research and information needs of students.

Introduction

For students new to library research, the task of searching for scholarly resources can be daunting. Librarians have long known that the tools and interfaces that libraries currently employ for reference, and autonomous search and retrieval, are not always intuitive. Nor is the overall organizational scheme of library resources easy to understand, especially for beginning students. Librarians providing reference service often need to guide new researchers past these initial hurdles.

Another role of the reference librarian is to provide an introduction to library research at a higher, more intense level. Most academic libraries subscribe to hundreds of article databases, many of which have disparate search interfaces. In addition to straightforward instructions on using database interfaces, using a variety of personalized instruction techniques can reduce library anxiety, especially in first-year students (Van Scoy, 2003).

Understanding basic changes in these interfaces and subsequently providing a relevant instructional approach has become a responsibility of the public services librarian. Entire conferences are dedicated to understanding how the sphere of contemporary reference has changed due to the constantly evolving technological world. Being responsive to these changes, and the changes in higher education, is the responsibility of the academic librarian, and is one way to maintain a close relationship with students, faculty, and other library users.

In addition to traditional students, Drexel University has a long history of distance education, with nearly 5,000 students in online degree programs, mostly at the graduate level. Due to current space limitations and growing on-campus enrollments, students are encouraged to work remotely. Working with students who are accessing library resources and services from outside of the physical building poses a particular challenge when thinking about library instruction and research support. One challenge facing librarians at Drexel today is how to use and implement new technologies to reach out to students for both reference- and instruction-related activities.

Many institutions worldwide use virtual reference services (VRS) employing a variety of new and emerging technologies. Steiner (2010) discusses many technologies including screencasting, screen sharing, creating instructional videos, chat, text transactions, and web conferencing to facilitate and carry out VR. Bedwell, Rodrigues, Duggan, and Orlov (2008) reported high levels of IM use and satisfaction as a VR tool that extends reference services through chat widgets. In the same study, it was also found that the IM widget was the preferred method of acquiring reference assistance (Bedwell et al., 2008). In another research study, it was found that students asked many in-depth research questions through IM reference channels, and that IM is becoming a primary reference service (Maximiek, Rushton, & Brown, 2010).

Technologies such as blogs, wikis, and really simple syndication (RSS) provide means for exchanging information among patrons and librarians. Blogs can be used to provide more specialized information on relevant course-related topics (Zanin-Yost, 2010). Librarian-faculty collaboration in developing course-related blog posts was used to highlight core resources that students would need to complete their assignments and research projects (Bhatt, 2006). Since these blog posts can be integrated within course management systems, students can easily develop awareness of these resources. Xiao (2010) found that library instruction and student learning could be effectively improved by integrating course-specific library resources into course management systems. The approaches used in these studies can inspire students to enhance their awareness of relevant information resources.

Drexel librarians began to explore integrating these technologies in an autonomous, flexible, and supportive environment. This experience of trying, exploring, and implementing various technologies culminated in a unique collaborative learning experience for those involved. This chapter showcases how some of these technologies can be used to enhance reference and instruction services in the respective subject areas.

Reference Services for Distance Students

Drexel offers a wide range of accredited online degree programs for graduate students through Drexel University Online, including hybrid classes featuring both face-to-face and e-learning components. Implementation of technology to support capture, management, and delivery of multimedia presentations provides distance learners with an online representation of the classroom experience including audio, video, and synchronized instructional materials ("Mediasite Technology," 2007).

Betts, Hartman, and Oxholm (2010) reported that current economic and demographic factors will influence future online and blended program enrollments. From a handful of students enrolled in the fall quarter in 2002, Drexel Online enrollments have grown to nearly 5,000 students in 2010 and each online student enrolls in an average of 1.7 courses per term.

Wimba and Adobe Connect Pro Platforms for Reference and Instruction

As the Drexel University Libraries strive to provide online students with the same high-quality support that is provided to on-campus students, increasing use has been made of the web-conferencing packages Wimba (http://www.wimba.com/) and Adobe Connect Pro (http://www.adobe.com/products/adobeconnect.html) as methods of presenting instruction and reference assistance in a rich and engaging format. Both tools allow librarians the flexibility to select the level of interaction appropriate to the particular setting by choosing a combination of screensharing, audio, and video from the librarian with either text or audio/video chat and two-way screensharing from the audience. Both of these platforms also offer additional options for interactivity that could be useful in instructional settings such as easily created polls with instantly displayed results and the ability for the audience to signal that they are (virtually) raising their hands or clapping. These packages are also similar in that they are paid services, although Adobe does offer a free version of Connect with limits on the number of people connected and other limited features. The licensing of these services is managed university-wide by Drexel University's Office of Information Resources and Technology. At Drexel, these tools have primarily been used for synchronous communication, whether for instruction or reference service, although they both can record and archive the web-conferencing sessions so the presentations, and even discussions, can be accessed asynchronously. While there are many similarities between Wimba and Adobe Connect Pro, each tool fits differently into the Libraries' instructional and reference programs. The choice of which tool to use is mostly driven by the circumstance of use and by the unique characteristics of each package. One common reason for choosing one over the other when meeting with a class for an instructional workshop is that the students and faculty may already be using one of these platforms as part of the course and would be familiar with the options. Most often in these cases the tool is Wimba, because it has been available for use at Drexel for the longer time and is widely used by faculty teaching online or hybrid courses. It is especially convenient to continue to use Wimba for these classes because the students will have already overcome one of the biggest hurdles to using Wimba, having to download and install the client software on their computers. This scenario highlights one of the most important issues that librarians face when choosing technologies for communicating with users: that of balancing the need for features that encourage high engagement for students with the need for the tool to be easy to set up and use. One helpful way to think about the relative merits of the technologies often used by librarians to communicate with users can be seen in Figure 3.1, created by Tim Siftar, the Libraries' Information Science and Technology/Education Librarian. This chart plots how each of the technologies compare in terms of ease of use and potential for high engagement. Steinbronn and Merideth (2007) wrote about this kind of engagement, which Drexel views as being "different from simple interaction with technology in that it shifts the focus from thinking about computers in education as a form of a media delivery device to that of a communication tool in an authentic setting for learning" (p. 266).

The usefulness of Wimba at the Drexel University Libraries is realized in structured settings, such as meetings with the students and faculty of a particular course for an instruction session. The Drexel University Health Sciences Libraries are the heaviest users of Wimba in the Drexel organization, primarily in support of online classes in the graduate nursing programs. These are mostly synchronous sessions that meet with several sections of a course at a time. The audience size can grow quite large, with as many as 80 students and up to 4 professors attending the online session. These sessions are archived and the link made available to the students for those who missed the live event and for use as a refresher later in the term. The format for the sessions using Wimba is a live demonstration of library research methods using specialized health sciences databases

Figure 3.1. Chart Showing Relative Ease of Use and Potential for High Engagement of Common Library Communications Technologies

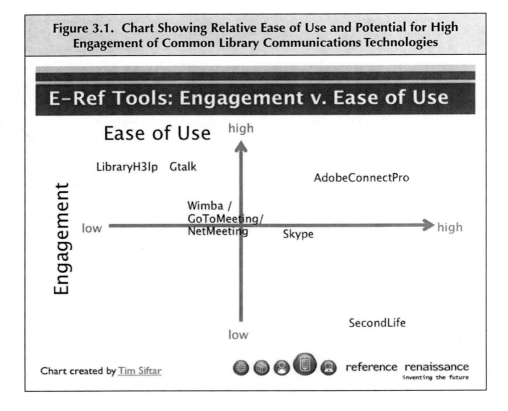

such as CINAHL, PsycINFO, and PubMed. Interaction with students comes from voice/text chat and the "raise hands" feature. Questions and discussions are interactive and students can share specific topics for the librarian to address. Other topics typically covered are selecting research topics, search strategies, and bibliographic management. The Wimba sessions also provide a great marketing opportunity for the availability of point-of-need and one-on-one reference assistance.

The Libraries' use of Adobe Connect Pro is more varied than is the case with Wimba. The difference is largely due to the greater ease of use of Adobe Connect. As long as the audience will be interacting through text chat, and does not need to screenshare or broadcast audio or video to the group, Adobe Connect Pro can be used without students having to install anything on their computer. They can enter a session by just following a link. Even if they do need to share their screen or audio/video chat, the only required element is a small browser plug-in that can be installed without having to restart the session. With this flexibility, Adobe Connect Pro can be used in structured settings, such as scheduled meetings with classes for instruction or with small teams of students working on group projects. It has also been used in semi-structured and ad hoc reference consultation situations.

Over the past year, Larry Milliken, the Humanities/Social Sciences Librarian, has been experimenting with using Adobe Connect Pro in a semi-structured setting, offering virtual office hours twice a week. This is referred to as semi-structured in that while the time for the session is fixed, the participants are not. The service has been marketed on library blogs, on the Humanities and Social Sciences research guides, in both the Freshman Writer's Toolbox, a specialized research guide for the university's Freshman Writing Program, and in library orientation workshops that are presented to sections of English 101. In addition, since spring 2010, this service has been included with the librarian's contact information in many course syllabi in the humanities and social sciences subject areas.

Overall the response to the offering has been small, and this highlights some of the challenges that the trial has faced. Factors limiting the uptake in use to just a trickle of sessions have been the limited number of hours available, the comparatively small sizes of the humanities and social sciences programs at Drexel in general, and the small size of the online programs in those fields. The limited hours, just two hours weekly, are largely due to the difficulty of monitoring an open Adobe Connect session while working on other tasks, as the software only provides a small visual notification that someone has entered the online meeting space. An audible cue would enable the expansion of hours to include whenever a librarian would be routinely at his or her desk. The small potential number of users for this trial is addressed with the expansion of marketing in the Freshman Writing Program classes and would be less of an issue for the larger schools and colleges at the university.

Perhaps the most interesting scenario for using Adobe Connect has been ad hoc reference assistance. In this completely unstructured situation, the librarian has the ability to take a reference transaction from a text-based IM/e-mail (or voice-based phone) interaction and transform it into a screensharing Adobe Connect session. All that needs to be done is to open a meeting space and send the link to the user. Many librarians have used this service model to enhance those reference consultations that involve leading a student or faculty member into an unfamiliar database or to co-browse through search results. When the users enable screensharing from their side, this method can also be useful for troubleshooting technical issues that may be difficult to explain verbally.

When thinking about how ad hoc Adobe Connect reference service can be employed, it is helpful to look at Hensley and Miller's (2010) study of the library usage of distance learners at the University of Illinois–Urbana/Champaign. They found that nearly half of the participants in their survey preferred to communicate with the library by chat or phone, while 18 percent report having actually communicated with the library by e-mail, 15 percent by phone, and 20 percent by chat/IM (Hensley & Miller, 2010, p. 677). Evidence that distance students are using remote reference services shows a great potential for this service model in providing them with more interactive online reference assistance. Another advantage of the flexibility of Adobe Connect is that it can be offered to users regardless of how they contact a librarian. At the Louisiana State University Libraries, Ryan, Daugherty, and Mauldin (2006) analyzed their institution's VR chat transcripts and noted that 23 percent of the chat interactions involved instruction and 15 percent involved in-depth research assistance. These results support what Drexel has noticed anecdotally, which is that the minority of virtual reference transactions fall into areas where the rich interaction of Adobe Connect Pro sessions would be necessary. Most interactions, such as known item queries, policy questions, and directional inquiries, could therefore be handled using whatever medium the patron used to initiate the contact and Adobe Connect Pro sessions could be started if the incoming question is in-depth enough to warrant a screensharing approach. This approach leverages the flexibility of the tool to help fine-tune virtual reference service to the appropriate level of interactivity for each transaction.

IM at Drexel University Libraries
IM was becoming popular as a method for delivering VR in libraries in the early 2000s and the Drexel University Libraries were offering chat reference through four IM protocols through 2006. In 2007, the Libraries began to investigate the usefulness of Meebo (http://www.meebo.com/), a web-based IM service, to streamline the back-end processes for staff. Managing the four IM accounts through Meebo resulted in simpler log-in procedures and offered an opportunity to embed a chat widget into the Libraries' website pages, providing a lower barrier of entry for students wishing to ask a question. The Meebo widget was added to the Libraries' website in January 2008, during the winter quarter, and the number of IM questions has continued to increase since this change (see Figure 3.2).

However, there was some difficulty in managing the work flows on the staff side. In addition to having four accounts to log in to and maintain, only one person could ever be logged in at a time. This limitation required extra communication during shift changes to avoid accidentally disconnecting an IM conversation. Another challenge was that the widget was embedded in the webpage, so if a student was asking a question and clicked a link, he or she would be disconnected from the IM conversation. To get back to the librarian, the student would have to navigate back to the page and restart the dialogue, or simply be "dropped." After some conversations about work flow, the Libraries decided

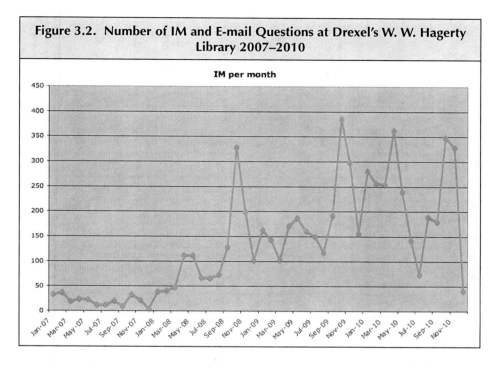

Figure 3.2. Number of IM and E-mail Questions at Drexel's W. W. Hagerty Library 2007–2010

to transition the IM reference service to LibraryH3lp (https://libraryh3lp.com/), which allowed consolidation of various IM accounts into queues, which could be simultaneously monitored by multiple staff at once. LibraryH3lp also offers a "follow-me" widget. This allows the questioner to navigate through the site and keep the IM window open and viewable.

This change was implemented in the winter quarter of 2009 when the Meebo widget was replaced by the LibraryH3lp widget. The IM questions increased from around 632 questions in the fall quarter of 2008 to 844 questions during the fall quarter of 2009 (see Table 3.1).

Before the winter quarter of 2010, the chat widget was replaced with a clickable icon (see Figures 3.3 and 3.4), which communicated whether there was a chat librarian available. This change seems to have resulted in a decrease in IM traffic but has remained fairly steady since then. Fall term is usually the busiest for IM questions, so whether the icon has caused a drop will become clearer over time. As of the writing of this document, IM traffic seems to average about 408 questions per quarter, with significant increases in fall quarters, when new students arrive and library instruction sessions in courses are heaviest.

As the IM traffic at the Drexel University Libraries has increased, the staffing model has also evolved. Originally, reference librarians were monitoring IM traffic during their time at the desk. As more questions came in, this approach was reviewed, and the decision was made to schedule one reference staff person per hour solely for IM from 8:30 a.m. to 5:00 p.m., Monday through Friday. Evening and weekend staff would monitor

Table 3.1. Number of IM Questions at Drexel's W. W. Hagerty Library by Quarter, 2007–2010.

Quarter	IM questions	Quarter	IM questions
Winter 2007*	92	Winter 2009	412
Spring 2007*	62	Spring 2009	522
Summer 2007	44	Summer 2009	463
Fall 2007	62	Fall 2009	844
Winter 2008	131	Winter 2010	795
Spring 2008	294	Spring 2010	747
Summer 2008	270	Summer 2010	446
Fall 2008	632	Fall 2010	720
*Includes raw data			

Figure 3.3. Drexel University Libraries University City Campus Chat Widget

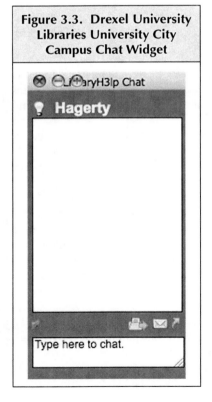

IM from the reference desk, but disable it when too busy. This approach is manageable for traffic, but as demands for librarians' time continue to increase, this approach may need to be further revised for sustainability.

Course Management Systems and Faculty Referrals

Several research studies have recommended integrating library services and resources into course management systems such as Blackboard Vista (Scales, Wolf, Johnson, & Cummings, 2007; Solis & Hampton, 2009; Hensley & Miller, 2010). Course management systems offer librarians several opportunities for increased and meaningful participation in various online courses

Figure 3.4. Drexel University Libraries University City Campus Chat Icon

LIBRARY CHAT is available

(Cox, 2002). These include e-mail consultations, linking book(s) chapters, journal articles, and customized selection of databases for particular classes, announcing new resources to students, and providing access to online tutorials. These studies have shown that while linking a variety of library databases, journal articles, and other sources through course management systems is important, marketing the services to faculty members and students is also crucial. Librarians can work with faculty members and demonstrate how these resources can be integrated while developing the course content. Collaboration among the faculty and librarians is absolutely essential in order to impart information-seeking skills to students in online programs. With efficient integration of library resources, students will spend less time finding them, and more time using them to find the information they need for their projects or term papers (Lenholt, Costello, & Stryker, 2003). Linking to these resources in courses will motivate students to use them rather than simply using free search engines such as Google and Yahoo!

With an increasing number of courses now available online and with more face-to-face courses using course management systems, it has become apparent that librarians need to exploit opportunities for virtually reaching out to students in online classes. Through course-specific integration of customized information resources, distance learners not only become aware of the resources' availability, but also learn how to use them efficiently to locate the information they need to complete their projects or assignments. Students in online programs will need to know how to access articles and databases remotely and, therefore, providing instruction will be very useful for them. Being information aware is the first critical step for students to begin efficient use of these resources in completion of their assignments or research papers (Bhatt, Chandra, & Denick, 2008).

Drexel's College of Engineering has begun to offer several online courses in disciplines such as Computer Science, Electrical and Computer Engineering, Software Engineering, and Engineering Management. Student enrollment now exceeds 250 in online classes, and several faculty members now collaborate with librarians to integrate course content in those courses.

Library resources can be effectively integrated into course management by making mandatory use of an e-reference work. In one course, students are required to use the AccessScience online database and locate background information on a topic related to Infrastructure Engineering and then use one of the databases highlighted on the Course Resource page to find related research papers (see Figure 3.5).

Another way to integrate library resources is to make the librarian a virtual consultant. One example of a course in which a librarian is assigned this role is the Problems in Human Relations course offered by the Engineering Management Department in the College of Engineering. This course requires engineering students to efficiently search business and engineering databases to locate articles on topics such as organizational behavior and leadership. The assignment requires students to complete midterm and final assignments demonstrating how they plan on linking the course material to a real-life situation at work, in their community, volunteer group, nonprofit organization, etc., that represents a "problem in human relations" that needs to be addressed. Since students are required to submit papers supporting their topic from peer-reviewed articles,

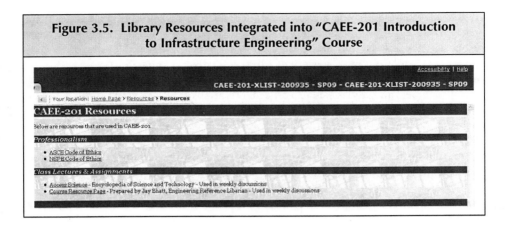

Figure 3.5. Library Resources Integrated into "CAEE-201 Introduction to Infrastructure Engineering" Course

in addition to books and lecture materials, it is important that they become aware of the databases available to them. They will also need to use them efficiently to locate journal articles for their references. The instructor has invited the engineering librarian to be an integrated member of the course team and has published an article that asserts:

> To leverage librarians' expertise during delivery, you can make the librarian an integral player in the delivery of the course. They can be a resource for the students that need library types of things. They can be put right into discussion topics. Some professors set up a discussion topic called "Ask a Librarian." ("In the Field," 2005, p. 4)

The course lectures, video files, and other useful web resources are included in the course page. The librarian is available as a virtual consultant through the "Ask a Librarian" discussion topic to provide responses to questions that students ask (see Figures 3.6 and 3.7). Some students ask about how to find a specific journal article or

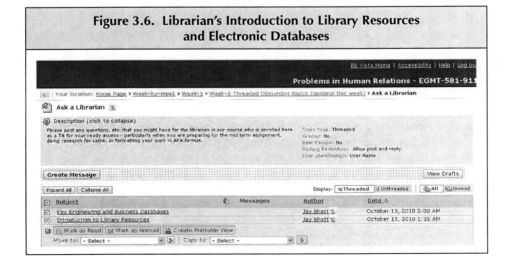

Figure 3.6. Librarian's Introduction to Library Resources and Electronic Databases

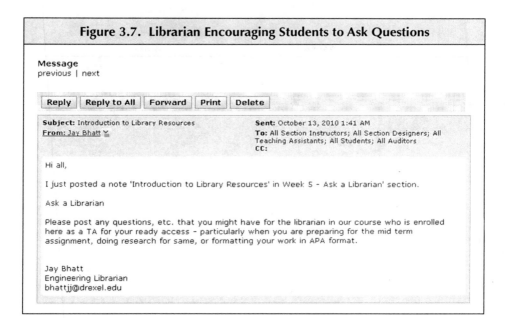

Figure 3.7. Librarian Encouraging Students to Ask Questions

Message
previous | next

Reply | Reply to All | Forward | Print | Delete

Subject: Introduction to Library Resources
From: Jay Bhatt

Sent: October 13, 2010 1:41 AM
To: All Section Instructors; All Section Designers; All Teaching Assistants; All Students; All Auditors
CC:

Hi all,

I just posted a note 'Introduction to Library Resources' in Week 5 - Ask a Librarian' section.

Ask a Librarian

Please post any questions, etc. that you might have for the librarian in our course who is enrolled here as a TA for your ready access - particularly when you are preparing for the mid term assignment, doing research for same, or formatting your work in APA format.

Jay Bhatt
Engineering Librarian
bhattjj@drexel.edu

how to conduct a search in electronic databases to locate peer-reviewed papers on their research topics.

It should be noted, however, that due to a large number of courses now available online, it is practically impossible for librarians to participate individually in each course. A solution could be to create a general online course highlighting important tips on using library resources in the respective subject areas. Any writing-intensive courses, or those requiring research, could have librarian help integrated for students in these courses.

Course-Related Blogs

Several engineering and biomedical engineering courses, including freshman and senior engineering design, require students to actively integrate new information as it is published in scientific literature in their final projects. This focus on keeping current requires students to continuously monitor updated research through databases and web resources. To support this requirement, the engineering librarian has created a blog with entries relevant to assignments given.

The EngLibrary blog provides access to web and electronic resources to help users keep current in engineering-related subject areas (see Figure 3.8). In addition to the resources, class-specific blog items are linked under categories representing the major engineering disciplines. For example, the Introduction to Bioacoustics course is offered in the School of Biomedical Engineering, Science and Health Systems. In this course, students are required to write a research paper referring to the current acoustics-related technologies used in biomedical applications. As interdisciplinary research continues to grow, many students from other departments take courses in areas related to biomedical

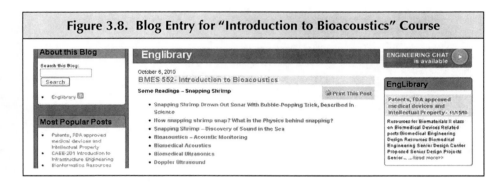

Figure 3.8. Blog Entry for "Introduction to Bioacoustics" Course

engineering. Students need to use print and e-books, handbooks and encyclopedias to develop subject background in related areas. The blog provides links to related subjects and the advanced keyword search in the catalog in order to motivate students to locate items from other related subject areas.

The blog archive is searchable to help users retrieve earlier items. The searching feature is demonstrated during the online instruction sessions because users do not automatically think about searching for older blog posts. As most instructors use the course management system, the link to the course blog is announced to the students through the mail feature of the system. The blog item links are also added in the course management webpage for easy access to the students in the class.

Other Library Blogs

The Engineering Library Instruction blog differs from the EngLibrary blog in that tips are generally provided to show how a particular database can be used. Web of Science is an important database that Drexel faculty members and graduate students use to find cited references to their own papers. In addition, there are other complex features that users will need to learn before they can use this database efficiently. To assist users, the Engineering Library Instruction blog provides tips and links to online tutorials on how to use these features more efficiently (see Figure 3.9).

As new technologies emerge, it is imperative for the library staff to learn and become proficient with them. This knowledge is crucial since they can employ these new tools in teaching information research skills to students. This leadership role has been recognized by the Academic Director of Drexel University Online, who reports, "Library professionals have long been at the forefront of information technology, and they continue to lead the charge in learning with IT" (Hartman, 2009, p. 48). The Drexel Emerging Technologies blog highlights library staff presentations and tips on using new emerging technologies to promote library research skills. For example, this blog highlights an announcement of the Library's staff presentations about the Libraries' purchase of Summon (http://www.serialssolutions.com/discovery/summon/) and how staff members can also learn new features by actively participating during this event. The knowledge gained will help staff in creating virtual presentations to demonstrate new technical features to students in distance learning programs.

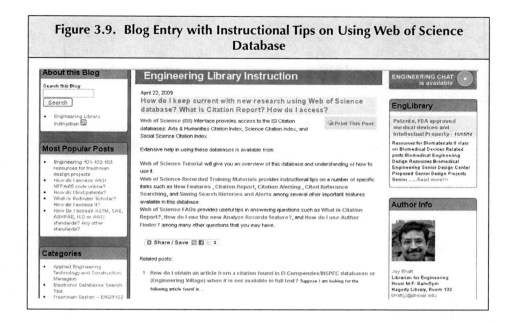

Figure 3.9. Blog Entry with Instructional Tips on Using Web of Science Database

Conclusion

Drexel, like many other institutions of higher education, is a rapidly evolving learning environment. As the size of the student body has increased, with online and distance learners in the fore of the increases, the university's librarians have had to be nimble to adapt to greater demands on their attention. The goal has remained constant: to provide the same high-quality and personalized library assistance to all students regardless of their program or whether their classes are held on campus or online. This commitment has meant that the librarians have had to adopt new strategies to reach out to students who may never set foot on the main campus. To meet the reference and instruction needs of all students, wherever they are, increasingly technology has been involved to make and expand connections between the students and their librarians. The librarians then collaborate with faculty and students to craft learning environments using these technologies. This variety of new technologies gives ample opportunities to students to learn based on their individual learning styles no matter where they are.

In the effort to provide consistent, high-quality reference services and to collaborate effectively with students, Drexel librarians have been very willing to experiment with new technologies and with new uses of existing technologies. The potential usefulness for reference and instructional settings of new tools or methods is evaluated as they become available. Many of these attempts have seen great success. The use of IM technology, embedded throughout the Libraries' web presence, has provided students with easy access to a librarian's assistance in a format that is familiar and comfortable to them. Library content within Blackboard course shells has also been an effective means of reaching both on- and off-campus students. With web-conferencing technologies it has been seen that some formats, such as the structured instruction sessions presented to whole classes and the ad hoc reference and instruction consultations with individual students, are very effective in providing a personal connection. The semi-structured office hours format has not been as successful. Experience using each of these solutions has provided knowledge that can be drawn upon as technologies evolve and as Drexel explores and evaluates new ways to connect with students.

Being successful in reaching out to students who may not physically come into the library can be challenging. It requires willingness to experiment with new technologies and a commitment to provide the same level of service to all students. In reviewing how reference and instruction are provided to the student population, one thing that has been realized is that Drexel librarians view all this as the "normal" way to interact with students. By having students receive reference help from the same subject librarians who support the face-to-face programs, rather than having a distance librarian who performs triage, and by using the same technologies to interact with them as are used to support on-campus students, high-quality personalized help to all students is provided no matter where they are.

References

Bedwell, L., Rodrigues, D., Duggan, L., & Orlov, S. (2008). IM a librarian: Extending virtual reference services through instant messaging and chat widgets. *Partnership: The Canadian Journal of Library and Information Practice and Research, 3*(2), 1–17.

Betts, K., Hartman, K., & Oxholm, C. (2010). Re-examining & repositioning higher education: 20 economic and demographic factors driving online and blended program enrollments. *Journal of Asynchronous Learning Networks, 13*(4), 3–23.

Bhatt, J. (2006). Using RSS to increase user awareness of e-resources in academic libraries. [Web log post]. Retrieved from http://www.higheredblogcon.com/index.php/using-rss-to-increase-user-awareness-of-e-resources-in-academic-libraries/.

Bhatt, J., Chandra, S., & Denick, D. (2008). Using Web 2.0 applications as information awareness tools for science and engineering faculty and students in academic institutions. In S. M. Dhawan, P. R. Goswami, P. K. Jain, T. Asraf, & D. C. Kar (Eds.), *Shaping the future of special libraries* (pp. 635–644). New Delhi, India: Ane Books Pvt. Ltd.

Cox, C. (2002). Becoming part of the course using Blackboard to extend one-shot library instruction. *College & Research Library News, 63*(1), 11–29.

Hartman, K. (2009). From a distance. *American Libraries, 40*(10), 48–51.

Hensley, M. K., & Miller, R. (2010). Listening from a distance: A survey of University of Illinois distance learners and its implications for meaningful instruction. *Journal of Library Administration, 50*(5), 670–683. doi:10.1080/01930826.2010.488946.

In the field: Course quality and instructor workload (pt. 1). (2005). *Distance Education Report, 9*(1), 4–7.

Lenholt, R., Costello, B., & Stryker, J. (2003). Utilizing Blackboard to provide library instruction. Uploading MS word handouts with links to course specific instructions. *Reference Services Review, 31*(3), 211–218. doi:10.1108/00907320310486809.

Maximiek, S., Rushton, E., & Brown, E. (2010). Coding into the great unknown: Analyzing instant messaging session transcripts to identify user behaviors and measure quality of service. *College & Research Libraries, 71*(4), 361–374.

Media..ite technology meets the needs of both students and faculty at Drexel University. (2007). *Distance Learning, 4*(3), 67.

Ryan, J., Daugherty, A., & Mauldin, E. (2006). Exploring the LSU Libraries' virtual reference transcripts. *Electronic Journal of Academic and Special Librarianship, 7*(3). Retrieved from http://southernlibrarianship.icaap.org/content/v07n03/ryan_j01.htm.

Scales, J., Wolf, D., Johnson, C., & Cummings, L. (2007). Courseware and library services: Bridging the gap for distance students. *Library Hi Tech, 25*(1), 147–156. doi:10.1108/07378830710735920.

Solis, J., & Hampton, E. M. (2009). Promoting a comprehensive view of library resources in a course management system. *New Library World, 110*(1/2), 81–91. doi:10.1108/03074800910928603.

Steinbronn, P. E., & Merideth, E. M. (2007). Perceived utility of methods and instructional strategies used in online and face-to-face teaching environments. *Innovative Higher Education, 32*(5), 265–278. doi:10.1007/s10755-007-9058-4.

Steiner, H. (2010). Livening virtual reference with screencasting and screen sharing. *Library Hi Tech News, 4/5*, 9–11. doi:10.1108/07419051011083172.

VanScoy, A. M. (2003). Reducing library anxiety in first-year students. *Reference & User Services Quarterly, 42*(4), 329–341.

Xiao, J. (2010). Integrating information literacy into Blackboard. Librarian-faculty collaboration for successful student learning. *Library Management, 31*(8–9), 654–668. doi:10.1108/01435121011093423.

Zanin-Yost, A. (2010). Library 2.0: Blogs, wikis, and RSS to serve the library. *Library Philosophy and Practice 2010(9)*. Retrieved from http://www.webpages.uidaho.edu/~mbolin/lpp2010.htm.

Meeting Challenges through Evolving Service Models and Staff Development

Inventing the Future by Examining Traditional and Emerging Roles for Reference Librarians

Amy VanScoy

Overview

As reference librarians invent their future, examining the variety of possible roles and constructing their own seems a wise course. Conceptual papers and research studies on these traditional and emerging roles are reviewed in this chapter to articulate the diversity of possible roles, to explore how they might interconnect, and to examine how librarians can use them to shape their work. Most of the discussion has focused on two major roles: *information provider* and *teacher*. There are a number of other roles that have received less attention and deserve a closer look as we move into the future, such as *communicator*, *relationship builder*, *guide/advisor*, *counselor*, or *partner*. This chapter provides a possible framework for a proactive approach to inventing the future.

Introduction

The role of the reference librarian has been a popular topic throughout the history of reference work. Often this discussion of role has been contentious or prescriptive and argued for one role at the expense of others. As reference librarians invent their future, examining the variety of possible roles and constructing their own seems a wise course. Conceptual papers and research studies on these traditional and emerging roles are reviewed to articulate the diversity of possible roles, to explore how they might interconnect, and to examine how librarians can use them to shape their work.

Most of the discussion has focused on two major roles: *information provider* and *teacher*. There are a number of other roles that have received less attention and deserve a closer look as we move into the future, such as *communicator*, *relationship builder*, *guide/advisor*, *counselor*, or *partner*. Research studies on reference librarians provide evidence that these many roles are present in reference work. It is unclear, however, how these roles interconnect and how librarians choose them.

Inventing the future requires reflection and action to shape the direction for change. Examining the diverse roles for reference librarians and reflecting on how they can be used in practice expands options for librarians. This chapter provides a possible framework for a proactive approach to inventing our future.

Relevance to Today's Practice

There are many urgent issues requiring the attention of reference librarians. Taking time to reflect on one's role in the reference interaction may seem like a luxury that hardly rises to the top of a long list of priorities. However, setting aside some time to reflect and be proactive about one's practice has long-term benefits.

As librarians involved in instruction well know, reflective practice is a hallmark of good teaching, and Schön (1983) among other scholars has argued for the importance of reflective practice for all professionals. However, in the demanding environment that is current reference work, librarians must often practice in a reactive manner without thinking deeply about what reference should be. Often new roles are not ones that librarians have chosen deliberately, but are driven by new technologies or budget restrictions. Taking time to reflect on the key roles for reference librarians and to explore how these roles should influence reference work could contribute to improved practice.

Assuming that taking time to reflect on the proper role for reference librarians and letting that role drive one's practice is worthwhile, a synthesis of the literature into a framework for reflection and discussion is a useful tool. Clearly articulating the variety of roles that librarians have played can open up choices for librarians today—choices that librarians can explore and experiment with as they proactively shape their new roles.

Objective

Although "roles of reference librarians" can refer to new and expanded job duties, such as tech support or creation of online tools, this paper focuses on the one-on-one reference interaction itself. Even within this narrow scope, the role of the librarian within the reference interaction has always been open to debate and continues to evolve.

Whether the reference interaction occurs at the traditional reference desk, in a virtual reference (VR) environment, in a virtual world, or during a consultation at a coffee shop, each librarian plays a role with his or her user. What is the nature of this role? What are values and motivations behind these roles? What are roles that have not had a strong voice in the literature? It is challenging to think creatively about new roles for reference librarians, when past roles have not been thoroughly described.

This chapter clearly articulates past and current roles of reference librarians as described in conceptual papers and as reported in research studies in order to expose the variety of perspectives on the topic. Although the literature abounds with essays arguing that reference librarians should play one role or another, there is little theory or research on this topic. With a few notable exceptions, when there is theory, it tends to be isolated and untested. Research studies tend also to be isolated and sporadic. This review may begin to rectify this situation by bringing together a variety of arguments about the role of reference librarians. It complements existing discussions of the changing role of the reference librarian, such as that of Rockman and Watstein (1999), in its focus on the reference interaction itself and its attempt to create a framework that encompasses the past roles for reference librarians in both conceptual papers and research studies.

Much of the debate in the literature has centered on the dichotomous roles of reference librarian as *information provider* or *instructor*, as if these perspectives are the only ones and are mutually exclusive. However, other roles have been addressed in the literature, including *communicator, relationship builder, guide/advisor, counselor*, and *partner*. Although these roles have not been thoroughly defined in the literature, Table 4.1 lists these various roles and defines them in terms of the motivations behind them. Articulating and examining these various perspectives provides a basis for reflection, discussion, and improved practice.

The Information Provider

The role of the *information provider* is one of the major roles addressed in the literature. It is likely motivated by the belief that reference exists to provide answers to users' questions. This role is described by Bunge (1980) as "finding needed information for the user or assisting the user in finding such information" (p. 468). In their textbook chapter, Bunge and Bopp (2001) suggested some examples of activities included in this component of reference service: "the simple provision of an address or telephone number, to tracking down an elusive bibliographic citation, to the identification and delivery of documents about a specific topic" (p. 7) as well as the more in-depth consultation required of "research assistance" (p. 10). Bunge (1980) used the general term "information services" (p. 468); Rothstein (1961) called it "getting information out of books" (p. 13); and Whittaker (1977) referred to this function as "enquiry work" (p. 58). Rieh (1999)

Table 4.1. The Various Roles for Reference Librarians and the Differing Motivations Based on Beliefs about the Goals of Reference

Roles for Reference Librarians	Professional Beliefs Motivating These Roles
The Information Provider	The goal of reference is to provide answers to questions.
The Instructor	The goal of reference is to teach skills in library and information use.
The Communicator	The goal of reference is a flow of accurate information and a human connection between the user and the resources.
The Relationship Builder	The goal of reference is a productive, long-term relationship between librarian and user.
The Guide/Advisor	The goal of reference is to guide and advise users.
The Counselor	The goal of reference is to develop lifelong information users through mentoring or coaching.
The Partner	The goal of reference is a balance of power and expertise between librarian and user.

used the term *information provision*, which seems the best term for a contemporary discussion of this function.

Information provision has been a key function since the beginning of reference scholarship. Green (1876) advocated for librarians providing information, later described by Tyckoson (1997) as "assist[ing] readers in solving their inquiries" (p. 6). Wyer (1930) may be the greatest advocate of answering questions as the main purpose of reference service. His theory of reference focused on levels of service: "conservative," "moderate," and "liberal." The "liberal" level of service, where the librarian completely answers the user's question, was considered by Wyer to be the fullest level of service. He called it "progressive" and "enlightened" (p. 9). Those, like Wyer, who view provision of information as the purpose of reference work value delivering an answer to a user or providing them with a specific source that the user can employ to answer his or her question.

There is evidence in the literature that practicing reference librarians value provision of information as a function of their work. In fact, in all the studies addressing this topic, participants included information provision as a key role. As part of their study of tasks and roles in the reference process, Alafiatayo, Yip, and Blunden-Ellis (1996) surveyed academic reference librarians in the United Kingdom about their "perceptions of their role." They reported that "respondents perceived their role as intermediaries between the inquirers and information resources" (p. 368). Respondents' open-ended comments describing their role involved information provision. The "highest ranked activity" was "answering requests to find source materials" (p. 368). A limitation of this study is that the researchers clearly defined reference service as information provision, and their data collection instrument conveyed this bias. The choices that librarians were given to rank included 12 activities, nearly all information provision-type activities. However, since there is so little research in this area, the results of this study need to be acknowledged.

Other studies emphasize the importance of information provision as a key role for reference librarians. Watson-Boone's (1998) participants seemed to focus on the information provision aspect of their work (pp. 28–32). Some of Gerlich's (2006) participants focused on information provision, as revealed in this representative quote: "helping people find things that they need... in the quickest and most efficient way" (p. 65).

Information provision is also an important role for reference archivists. Duff and Fox (2006) reported "a high level of satisfaction when documents were found quickly and easily, when they were able to find good complete answers, and when the user found the information they needed" (p. 147). When asked to describe a satisfactory reference experience, the authors reported that "all 13 participants chose examples where they provided an answer that satisfied the user" (p. 147). Later the authors stated that "the main cause of archivist dissatisfaction was being unable to find the answer" (p. 148).

Obviously, the role of *information provider* is considered important to reference scholars, as well as to practitioners. However, there are some critics of this role. Wagers (1978) critiqued the "information as an end-product of service" approach, calling it "stultifying" and calling for theory that could "transcend" it (p. 278). Campbell (1992), though neither a scholar nor practitioner of reference, published an influential paper devaluing the information provision function of the work, suggesting that 75 percent of reference transactions could be automated (p. 31). Kuhlthau (2004) saw some value in the information provision role of reference work, noting that helping students with physical access was important, but just not as important as helping them with intellectual access (p. 114). Information provision is an important function of reference service, both in the opinion of scholars and librarians. Yet it is clearly not the only way to conceive of what reference librarians do.

The Instructor

The instruction role of the reference librarian may be motivated by the belief that reference exists to instruct users in library and research skills, so that users can find information on their own. The current climate of information literacy in higher education has highlighted the instruction function of reference work, but it has played an important role throughout the history of reference service. Bunge (1980) defined instruction as "helping users learn the skills they need to find and use library materials" (p. 468). More contemporary definitions extend this definition beyond just instruction in use of resources at the library to information literacy instruction, in general.

Those who advocate for the *instructor* role see their goal as making the user self-sufficient. Vavrek (1968) articulated this value in saying that "service falls short of its capacity when the reference librarian neglects or refuses to extend a device for self-education to the user" (p. 510). Others see instruction as part of the educational mission of a library, especially an academic library. Elmborg (2002), for example, went so far as to argue that "the reference desk can be a powerful teaching station—more powerful, perhaps, than the classroom" (p. 455).

The literature shows evidence that amongst practicing librarians the instruction function is valued. All of the studies include participants specifically noting instruction or the researcher noting that instruction was an important part of their service. Respondents in Alafiatayo and colleagues' (1996) study perceived their role partially as "teaching" (p. 370). Although the reference librarians studied by Watson-Boone (1998) did not specifically talk about teaching in relation to their reference work, she observed that instruction was an important component of their jobs (p. 33). Some of the academic reference librarians in Gerlich's (2006) study described their work as "teaching" (p. 60).

In their interpretation of reference archivists' "orientation," Duff and Fox (2006) reported a strong sense of the participants' role as teachers and the importance of teaching archival users to be independent (pp. 133–135). As mentioned earlier, however, the main source of satisfaction and dissatisfaction in the archivists' narratives related to success and failure in finding answers or specific materials for the user. The authors did not explore why the reference archivists, who claim a teaching orientation, feel satisfaction or dissatisfaction, not about student learning, but about effective question answering.

The Information Provider versus the Instructor

The conflict over whether information provision or instruction is the proper role of reference librarians is perhaps the greatest debate in reference work. The debate seems to have begun with Wyer's (1930) "conservative," "moderate," and "liberal" levels of service. Although Wyer did not place instruction in opposition to a liberal level of service, it seems that his work has been interpreted this way. In his discussion of instruction, Wyer claimed that helping a user to increase his or her knowledge about using the library was "commendable" (p. 279). He simply did not include instruction in his concept of reference. It is this separation of provision from instruction that Wagers (1978) claimed "created an unprofitable distinction" between the functions (p. 272).

A number of scholars have supported the argument that information provision, rather than instruction, is the proper role of reference. Rothstein (1961) essentially saw arguments supporting instruction as excuses not to provide better service (p. 14). McClure (1974) stated that "any person is entitled to receive specific answers to questions involving needs for exact information . . . when people come to the library they do not want to learn about the methods and mechanics of biographic control; they want information" (p. 208). Rugh (1975) claimed that while instruction was important, it should not be considered a component of reference service, but rather something separate (p. 297). After reviewing the literature on the provision/instruction debate, Schiller (1965) concluded that information provision is the primary purpose of reference and that instruction is "not necessarily a reference function" (p. 60). Even Whittaker (1977), who included instruction in his model of reference, acknowledged that "it is not universally accepted that library instruction is part of it [reference]." Despite Whittaker's inclusion of instruction, he classified it under the "library users" section, rather than the "librarians" section, with no explanation for this choice (p. 58).

Rothstein noted in 1955 that debate about levels of service had "dominated the theoretical discussion of the nature and extent of reference work" (p. 42). By 1992, Rettig described the positions as "firmly entrenched" and "inimical" (p. 159). He further described instruction and information provision as "the two cultures of reference librarianship" (p. 158). This is an apt metaphor. Just as people from different cultures can be challenged to understand each other and accept each other's values, librarians from different "cultures" of reference sometimes have difficulty understanding and appreciating each other.

Despite decades of debate, no research has been done to study this conflict in practice. It has remained a purely theoretical debate in the literature. Future research could help to clarify the priority reference librarians place on these two roles and how they might complement each other or interconnect.

Some scholars bemoan the debate between instruction and provision, arguing that it is misguided or unproductive to set information provision and instruction in opposition to each other. Wagers (1978) argued that early reference theory included both instruction and information provision (p. 274), but later theory "bifurcated" the earlier unified theory into an "information dogma" (p. 271) that excluded instruction. He further argued that guidelines separating instruction from reference "prevent integration of significant components of service into a viable theory" (p. 277). He continued: "later theorists . . . in their desire to appear progressive, distorted these early contributions and erected misleading conceptions of effectiveness" (p. 279).

So perhaps the issue is not whether instruction or information provision is better, but whether or not one should separate the two functions. Wagers (1978) argued against separation: "Such a narrowing of scope [to just giving specific information] may be productive if it serves to isolate key factors, but misleading if vital elements are not taken into account. With preliminary investigations which identify the relationships among reference factors, such a focus is presumptuous" (p. 277).

Nielsen (1982) is often cited as an advocate of instruction, but really he advocated for a new role for librarianship to be discussed later in this review. He expressed concern that the role of instructor and the role of information provider would coexist and cause division in the profession and competition for resources. He saw this situation as a problem and argued for a new role. "The present competition between those who advocate the intermediary role and those who advocate the teaching role is unfortunate and unnecessary. It divides the ranks of reference librarians at a time when unity of purpose on behalf of user needs has never been more important" (p. 188).

Clearly the roles of information provider and instructor are important ones for reference librarians. The relative importance of each of these roles, however, is not clear. As previously mentioned in Duff and Fox (2006), for example, individual librarians seemed to value their role as information provider, as well as their role as instructor. In addition to these two key roles, however, other roles are explored in the literature. While they have not been included in the classic information provider/instructor debate, they merit consideration.

The Communicator

A review of the literature demonstrates that the *communicator* may not be a separate role but a skill that overlays other roles. However, it is frequently discussed, and therefore is a possible role to consider. The role of the *communicator* is motivated by the belief that reference exists as the human connection between the user and the resources. A common metaphor for communication is a conduit, and many librarians may see themselves as conduits or channels or intermediaries between the collection and the user. The role of the *communicator* is not clearly defined in the literature. It involves the dynamic between librarian and user, both the actual communication that occurs and the subsequent relationship that develops, discussed in this review as the *relationship builder*. Future research should work to clarify this ambiguity.

Bunge (1999) proposed "communication" as a way of conceiving of reference (p. 15). Although Bunge (1980) did not include the concept in his encyclopedia definition of reference, he later addressed it in an extensive literature review (1984). Radford (1999) took a communications theory perspective and demonstrated the value of "interpersonal aspects," including attitude of the librarian, quality of communication skills, and approachability in the reference encounter (pp. 73–74) as well as the content aspects of information delivery, providing access to information, and subject knowledge. She extended this work in an analysis of interpersonal dimensions in virtual reference (VR) live chat transcripts (Radford, 2006). Radford and Connaway (2009) have more recently developed a content/relationship model of reference work. This model emphasizes the importance of interpersonal dimensions, such as relationship quality, attitude, approachability, and greeting and closing rituals to the success of a reference interaction in traditional as well as virtual environments.

The relative value of the interpersonal dimension in reference service constitutes another important debate in reference work. This debate is not nearly as clearly articulated as the one concerning instruction versus information provision. Some scholars claim that communication or relationships are of key importance; while others set up an explicit or implied dichotomy, such as information provision versus interpersonal aspects. Radford (1999) set her communication approach in opposition to Katz, who she claimed advocated information provision as the sole role for reference librarians. Like Radford, Stover (2004) argued that "answering reference questions accurately is important, but in many ways attitudes, actions, and non-verbal communication are just as important as factual authenticity for quality reference service" (p. 290). Evidence from the field suggests that the interpersonal dimension is valued in the profession. Alafiatayo and colleagues' (1996) respondents described reference work as "a communication process" (p. 370). Gerlich's (2006) participants also mentioned communication (p. 62).

So does the literature suggest that there are two distinct dichotomies: instruction versus information provision and communication/interpersonal relations versus information provision? Or might communication and relational aspects overlay the instruction versus information provision continuum as an additional dimension? Rather than being a separate role, communication may be an aspect to how other roles are performed/executed. Research is needed to understand how all these elements fit together and how they interact in different situations.

The Relationship Builder

Although the *relationship builder* role shares much in common with the *communicator*, there are some differences. Rather than perceiving the reference librarian as a conduit or the human mediator between user and resources, the *relationship builder* takes interpersonal dimensions of the reference interaction a step further. This role may be motivated by the belief that the end goal of the reference interaction is productive, long-term relationships with users. In her study of academic reference service interactions, Radford (1999) argued that there are two goals of the reference encounter: to build relationships with users in addition to helping them satisfy an information need.

In his early discussion of the role of reference librarians, Green (1876) also seemed to support this perspective. Although Tyckoson (1997) interpreted Green's "personal relations" as "promotion of the library," Green's phrase could be interpreted as "developing relationships with library users." Bunge (1984) also focused on the relationship aspects of Green's work, rather than the promotional aspects. Regardless of Green's exact intentions, it is clear that he highlighted the interpersonal aspect of reference work. His metaphor of the reference librarian as a "friendly innkeeper" and advocate of librarians "mingling with users" indicate the importance to Green of librarians working to develop relationships.

To date, studies of reference librarians provide some, but not strong, evidence of the important of the relationship-builder role. In her ethnographic study of reference in an archival environment, Trace (2006) found that development of relationships was a result of "good" reference questions, though whether or not these relationships were a deliberate goal of the service provider is unclear (p. 129). Why is the *relationship builder* role not more frequently mentioned in studies of librarians' roles when there is demonstrated importance of relationship building in reference work? Perhaps it is perceived as a component of the *communicator* role or as an end goal rather than a role. More research is needed to understand how the *relationship-builder* role relates to other roles for reference librarians.

The Guide/Advisor

Another role for the reference librarian is that of *guide* or *advisor*. This role may be motivated by the belief that guiding and advising users in their research is the key role for reference librarians. This role has been mentioned by a number of key reference scholars. Tyckoson (1997) attributed "Aid the reader in the selection of good works" (p. 6) to Green's definition of reference, and it is described by Rothstein (1961) as "guidance in the choice of books" (p. 12). Bunge (1980) defined this function as "users are assisted in choosing library materials appropriate to their educational, informational, or recreational needs" (p. 468). Later he added, "helping to interpret materials so that readers can choose among them according to their interests and needs" (p. 470). Examples of guidance according to Bunge and Bopp (2001) included readers advisory, bibliotherapy, and term-paper counseling. These authors acknowledged that guidance is "not as often discussed in the literature" although they claimed it has been just as significant (p. 11).

Research on reference librarians seems to indicate that they perceive guidance as an important function. Gerlich (2006) reported academic reference librarians using terms such as "guiding," "helping," and "advising" to describe their work (pp. 60–67). She did not probe the meanings of these perceptions, so it is difficult to determine exactly what the librarians meant or how these perceptions related to others expressed by the participants. These librarians see "guiding" and "advising" as a component of what they do; however, there is no evidence in the literature that guidance or aiding in selection is considered a primary or core purpose. In addition, it is unclear whether librarians who express reference work as "guiding" and "advising" are speaking about guiding or advising in selection of sources. One of the reference archivists in Duff and Fox's (2006, p. 134) study mentioned "guiding people to a source," but the authors interpreted this statement as pertaining to instruction.

Bunge and Bopp (2001) described information provision, instruction, and guidance as approaches that a reference librarian may choose from "depending on the needs and goal" of the user (p. 6). Rothstein (1961) viewed "these basic approaches or emphases" as "the three primary colors in the reference work picture...almost every respectable library in the United States and Canada does some of each; almost no two libraries mix the colors in quite the same way" (p. 13). This metaphor of mixing colors to provide the perfect composition of reference service is beneficial because it recognizes some variety in approach to the work and hints at conscious choice in approaching service. However, Rothstein's metaphor is based on Wyer's conservative, moderate, and liberal framework, which is not necessarily adequate for describing the purpose of reference work. Also, Rothstein says that "libraries" mix these colors in certain ways, but libraries are not the entities that are selecting the colors. It may be that librarians "mix" approaches to service, but more research is needed to understand what these colors are and how librarians mix them.

The Counselor

The role of the *counselor* may be similar to that of the *guide* or *advisor*. However, this role may be motivated by a value on mentoring or coaching users as they become accustomed to the information-seeking process. Despite the similarities between *guide* or *advisor*, the assistance described in this role is broader in focus, perhaps dealing with the whole research process or lifelong learning, and it is more in-depth. There is some overlap with instruction or communication, but the focus for this theme is an intense interaction between librarian and user, where the librarian attempts to lead the user to a greater understanding of his or her need.

Drawing on student personnel theory, Maxfield (1954) argued that fact-based reference and instruction do not meet the needs of users and that a counseling approach is required (p. 8). He suggested that this is particularly important for librarians serving undergraduates although he sees evidence of this approach in readers advisory and bibliotherapy (p. 20). He stated that librarians must take into account users' full needs: "There might be significant limitations for undergraduate library users in the conventional reference approach, and that librarianship at the college level possibly should give more careful attention to the student patron *as an individual person*" (p. 8). Later scholars, such as Penland (1970), distilled this approach to a technique, but Maxfield was clearly focused on developing counseling as a core purpose of reference work.

Maxfield's explanation puts the *counselor* role and the *information provider* role in opposition to each other: "The major emphasis in counseling, as already shown, is not upon any information that is to be imparted, but upon aiding of the individual toward self-motivation and self-decision" (p. 19). So while advocates for information provision might not be against counseling values, they would be at odds with the very purpose of counseling librarianship: the focus on development, not information.

Fine (1997) also promoted a *counselor* role for reference librarians. Her major focus lies in using counseling theory and techniques to improve communication and build relationships (p. 90). However, Fine also argues for user development as a goal or at least a positive outcome of the reference interaction: "The growth of one becomes the mutual concern of both" (p. 81).

It may be appropriate to discuss Kuhlthau's (2004) examination of the role of the reference librarian in this section. Although her work focused primarily on users, Kuhlthau applied her finding to the librarian's role, developing five "levels of mediation." The highest level of mediation was termed "Counselor." Kuhlthau's Counselor level focused on helping a user to achieve a greater understanding of the research process: "holistic...over time" (p. 119). This level also has some instruction overtones and may not be a close match to Maxfield's counseling function. However, her deliberate use of the term "Counselor" and her references to holistic and intellectual development suggest more than simply an instructional exchange. She did not view counseling as an alternative or alongside other components but in a hierarchical relationship, with the Counselor level being a superior type of mediation (p. 118).

It is unclear whether practicing reference librarians perceive the intellectual development characteristic as a key role in their work. Alafiatayo and colleagues' (1996) respondents described reference work as "advising, helping, guiding" (p. 370), and Gerlich's (2006) participants used these terms as well. However, as mentioned previously, the intended meaning of these terms is unclear.

The Partner

The *partner* role is inspired by the belief that reference work is a team effort between librarian and user with both bringing areas of knowledge and skill to the interaction.

The role of collaboration or partnership has much in common with the counseling role, but is isolated in this review because of its focus on a balance of power and the emergence of ideas through a synergy between librarian and user. This perspective is a more recent development in thinking about reference work. The literature hints at this theme, but it has not been fully developed. The concept of reference librarianship as a collaborative partnership is not so much a new activity, as a new perspective on existing activities. The perspectives discussed thus far, such as providing answers and instructing users, are somewhat focused on the librarian as agent. The emerging concept of a collaborative partnership between the user and librarian provides a balance of expertise and power.

Nielsen (1982) is among the first to have addressed the need for this new perspective in his call for a new role for reference librarians. He suggested that librarianship should look to human services for inspiration: "Their message calls upon experts of all kinds to rethink their relationships to non-experts, and to work toward the sharing of knowledge rather than its opposite" (p. 188). Rettig (1992) also acknowledged an imbalance of power in the reference transaction. In his critique of both the information provision and instruction approaches to reference, he stated "nor does either culture give due credit to information seekers' and librarians' complementary obligations and roles" (p. 163). He felt that both cultures were "designed to promote a preferred role for reference librarians" (p. 162).

Mabry (2003), who explored the partnership concept, as did Stover (2004), also called for a rethinking of reference librarians' "expert" status. Stover focused on the issue of librarian expertise in what he called a "postmodern approach." He advocated perceiving the user as an expert in his or her own research endeavor. Through listening and dialogue, reference librarians can help users arrive at their own solution. Together, they can create knowledge through the research process, rather than simply finding and delivering existing truths. He stated: "The stance of the librarian as non-expert moves the profession of librarianship away from the technocrat/expert model and back towards its earlier mission of service and human-centered values" (p. 274). As an example of the arrogance of reference librarianship, Stover cites the de-emphasis of social sources of information and browsing, both of which are popular and effective ways for people to get information, in favor of searching (p. 290). Another advocate of this role, Doherty (2005) called for a new approach to reference that puts more control in the hands of the user. He advocated for a "reference dialogue" instead of a "reference interview" (Doherty, 2006, p. 107).

There is some evidence in studies of archival reference that librarians value a balance of power in the reference interaction. Duff and Fox (2006) quoted a participant saying "your role is a guide rather than as an expert" (p. 134). For this participant, a position of expertise was not a goal. Trace (2006) noted the concept of "reciprocity" in reference, which she described as "the constant exchange of information back and forth between the [service provide and user] as both learned from each other" (p. 133). However, among the few studies of reference librarians' perceptions of their work, none reported participants mentioning partnerships, collaboration, sharing, or dialogue as functions of reference work. It is likely that the researchers were not looking for this theme in their data since it is relatively undeveloped.

Both answering the user's question and instructing the user imply an expertise that puts the user in a lower position than the librarian. "Partner" implies that the user and the librarian share an equal position. So this concept of partnership or the reference encounter as a synergistic place where the information need is synthesized is an interesting direction for theoretical discussion to go. It may be that this collaborative partnership concept is not a purpose on its own, but merely a different way to view another role, like counseling. There is enough discussion about this perspective to merit further investigation.

Using Traditional and Emerging Roles to Invent One's Own Future

Examining the current and past roles for reference librarians may be interesting, but then what does today's reference librarian do with this new perspective? Reinventing the role of the reference librarian does not have to mean a complete overhaul of reference work. As demonstrated in this review, there are a variety of roles, including some which have received little attention, to explore. The specific role that a librarian chooses to play may be less important than the deliberate process of examining and articulating this role. Differences in users and environments may require different choices of role to meet user needs. By carefully considering user needs, a librarian can choose the most appropriate role or roles. The only truly wrong choice is practicing without reflection or making an arbitrary, unexamined choice. Specific strategies for reinventing one's future based on role include thinking about some of these possible roles, reflecting about what works for each individual and what does not, and sharing experiences with colleagues and learning from them.

Reflecting on the Role of the Reference Librarian

It is important to take time to think about what is most important in reference work. Using the roles described in this review may be a useful starting point for this self-reflection. Reflection may take the form of asking oneself questions such as:

- Do I value being an expert and providing exact answers that users would need hours to find themselves?
- Do I value teaching users to be independent or to use tools?
- Do I value developing relationships with users?
- Do I value helping them grow as future researchers with the context, secret tips, and enthusiasm they need to be successful?
- Do I play other roles with users that have not been discussed in the literature?

In reflection, one role might emerge as key or predominant in one's practice. Or one might perceive a variety of roles that interact in some way.

Although some organizations dictate the primary role that reference librarians must take, librarians may still find benefit in examining their preferred role. Does the role dictated by the organization match the role or roles valued by the librarian? Answering this question may shed light on conflict or contribute to productive conversations about possible future roles.

Sharing Reflections on Role with Colleagues

As this chapter demonstrates, there are a variety of possible roles for reference librarians. Understanding that librarians approach reference work from different perspectives can provide opportunities for learning and collaboration.

Within a reference department, recognizing the roles that colleagues value can help to turn workplace challenges into opportunities. Sharing differences can be a real asset to a department. In the same way that understanding others' Myers-Briggs type or leadership style can help colleagues understand one another and better communicate, understanding fellow librarians' beliefs about the proper role of reference work can help groups to understand the motivations behind decisions or behind behaviors. Within a department, creating diverse project teams that include librarians with a variety of beliefs about the proper role for reference can help ensure the best-quality services.

Applying Reflections and Discussion to Practice

Once a librarian has reflected on the proper role for reference work, this role should be incorporated into practice. Librarians will likely find that they are already incorporating key roles into their reference practice. Librarians who value the *instructor* role likely already take time to teach users how to find resources on their own, and those who value the *partnership* role likely already leave the reference desk to work alongside users. However, it is easy for outside pressures, habits, or even burnout (which is increasing in likelihood during difficult economic times when staffing shortages occur) to interfere with professionals' ability to act in accordance with the roles they value. It may be useful to actively think about roles that one values as one is practicing reference work. Are constraints such as the arrangement of the service point, the features of the VR software, or the number of librarians staffing the desk having unwanted effects on practice? What changes could be made to ameliorate these conditions and allow librarians to better play their key roles? Discussing roles with colleagues may yield good ideas for solutions to these problems. Clearly articulated roles, both on the part of individual librarians and departments, can help inspire exploration and experimentation for better solutions. This discussion could also contribute to improved communication about the roles of reference librarians to the public.

Conclusion

Reference librarians must continue to reflect on the role that they should play in their interactions with users and be proactive in designing their professional destiny. Will changing roles be shaped by technology or budget constraints, or will they be shaped by what librarians value about reference work? The literature reveals a variety of possible roles for reference librarians. Although *information provider* and *instructor* are the most often discussed, *communicator, relationship builder, guide* or *advisor*, and *partner* are other models that should be explored in more depth. The roles as articulated in this chapter provide a framework and offer a critical challenge for reference librarians to embark on a time of heightened reflection, discussion, and experimentation, as they explore, discover, and create their future.

References

Alafiatayo, B. O., Yip, Y. J., & Blunden-Ellis, J. C. P. (1996). Reference transaction and the nature of the process for general reference assistance. *Library and Information Science Research*, *18*(4), 357–384. doi:10.1016/S0740-8188(96)90005-5.

Bunge, C. A. (1980). Reference services. In *ALA world encyclopedia of library and information services* (pp. 468–474). Chicago, IL: American Library Association.

Bunge, C. A. (1984). Interpersonal dimensions of the reference interview: A historical review of the literature. *Drexel Library Quarterly, 20*(2), 4–23.

Bunge, C. A. (1999). Beliefs, attitudes, and values of the reference librarian. *Reference Librarian, 31*(66), 13–24. doi:10.1300/J120v31n66_05.

Bunge, C. A., & Bopp, R. E. (2001). History and varieties of reference services. In R. E. Bopp & L. C. Smith (Eds.), *Reference and information services: An introduction* (3rd ed., pp. 3–27). Englewood, CO: Libraries Unlimited.

Campbell, J. D. (1992). Shaking the conceptual foundations of reference: A perspective. *Reference Services Review, 20*(4), 29–35. doi:10.1108/eb049164.

Doherty, J. J. (2005). Towards self-reflection in librarianship: What is praxis? *The Progressive Librarian, 26*, 11–17.

Doherty, J. J. (2006). Reference interview or reference dialogue? *Internet Reference Services Quarterly, 11*(3), 97–109. doi:10.1300/J136v11n03_07.

Duff, W., & Fox, A. (2006). "You're a guide rather than an expert": Archival reference from an archivist's point of view. *Journal of the Society of Archivists, 27*(2), 129–153. doi:10.1080/00379810601075943.

Elmborg, J. K. (2002). Teaching at the desk: Toward a reference pedagogy. *portal: Libraries and the Academy, 2*(3), 455–464. doi:10.1353/pla.2002.0050.

Fine, S. (1997). Librarians and the art of helping. *Reference Librarian, 28*(59), 77–91.

Gerlich, B. K. (2006). *Work in motion/assessment at rest: An attitudinal study of academic reference librarians. A case study at mid-size university (MSU A).* (Unpublished doctoral dissertation.) University of Pittsburgh, Pittsburgh, PA.

Green, S. S. (1876). Personal relations between librarians and readers. *Library Journal, 1*(2), 74–81.

Kuhlthau, C. C. (2004). *Seeking meaning: A process approach to library and information services* (2nd ed.). Westport, CT: Libraries Unlimited.

Mabry, C. H. (2003). The reference interview as partnership: An examination of librarian, library user, and social interaction. *Reference Librarian, 40*(83/84), 41–56. doi:10.1300/J120v40n83_05.

Maxfield, D. K. (1954). Counselor librarianship: A new departure. *Occasional Papers, 38*, 1–39.

McClure, C. R. (1974). A reference theory of specific information retrieval. *RQ, 13*(3), 207–212.

Nielsen, B. (1982). Teacher or intermediary: Alternative professional models in the information age. *College and Research Libraries, 43*(3), 183–191.

Penland, P. R. (1970). *Interviewing for counselor and reference librarians.* Pittsburgh, PA: University of Pittsburgh.

Radford, M. L. (1999). *The reference encounter: Interpersonal communication in the academic library.* Chicago, IL: Association of College and Research Libraries.

Radford, M. L. (2006). Encountering virtual users: A qualitative investigation of interpersonal communication in chat reference. *Journal of the American Society for Information Science and Technology, 57*(8), 1046–1059.

Radford, M. L., & Connaway, L. S. (2009, November). *Thriving on theory: A new model for virtual reference encounters.* Paper presented at the American Society for Information Science and Technology 2009 Annual Meeting, Vancouver, British Columbia (Canada). Retrieved June 16, 2011, from http://www.oclc.org/research/activities/synchronicity/ppt/asist09-thriving.ppt.

Rettig, J. (1992). Self-determining information seekers. *RQ, 32*(2), 158–164.

Rieh, S. Y. (1999). Changing reference service environment: Review of perspectives from managers, librarians, and users. *Journal of Academic Librarianship, 25*(3), 178–186. doi:10.1016/S0099-1333(99)80197-9.

Rockman, I. F., & Watstein, S. B. (1999). Reference librarians/educators: Vision of the future. *Reference Librarian, 31*(66), 45–59. doi:10.1300/J120v31n66_06.

Rothstein, S. (1955). *The development of reference services through academic traditions, public library practice, and special librarianship.* Chicago, IL: Association of College and Reference Libraries.

Rothstein, S. (1961). Reference service: The new dimension in librarianship. *College & Research Libraries, 22*(1), 11–18.

Rugh, A. G. (1975). Toward a science of reference work: Basic concepts. *RQ, 14*(4), 293–299.

Schiller, A. R. (1965). Reference service: Instruction or information. *The Library Quarterly, 35*(1), 52–60.

Schön, D. A. (1983). *The reflective practitioner: How professionals think in action.* New York: Basic Books.

Stover, M. (2004). The reference librarian as non-expert: A postmodern approach to expertise. *Reference Librarian, 42*(87/88), 273–300. doi:10.1300/J120v42n87_10.

Trace, C. B. (2006). For love of the game: An ethnographic analysis of archival reference work. *Archives and Manuscripts, 34*(1), 124–143.

Tyckoson, D. (1997). What we do: Reaffirming the founding principles of reference services. *Reference Librarian, 28*(59), 3–13. doi:10.1300/J120v28n59_02.

Vavrek, B. F. (1968). A theory of reference service. *College and Research Libraries, 29*(6), 508–510.

Wagers, R. (1978). American reference theory and the information dogma. *Journal of Library History, 13*(3), 265–281.

Watson-Boone, R. (1998). *Constancy and change in the worklife of research university librarians.* Chicago, IL: Association of College and Research Libraries.

Whittaker, K. (1977). Towards a theory for reference and information service. *Journal of Librarianship, 9*(1), 49–63. doi:10.1177/096100067700900105.

Wyer, J. I. (1930). *Reference work: A textbook for students of library work and librarians.* Chicago, IL: American Library Association.

C H A P T E R   5

Quality and Characteristics of Student-Led Virtual Reference Service: A Two-Year Study

Peter A. Zuber

Overview

During the summer of 2007, reference services at Brigham Young University's Harold B. Lee Library were provided face-to-face from various desks at each library department's locale, a general reference desk on the main floor, and at the periodicals desk. In August of that year, the Science and Maps Department of the library decided to add virtual reference services (VRS) through an instant messaging (IM) widget. This service would be provided primarily by the student assistants hired to work at the reference desk. Having no formal library training, the department relied on their expertise from their major studies and periodic training provided by the reference manager. This chapter describes a study that analyzed the chat logs taken during a two-year period to assess accuracy, quality, and general characteristics of the IM-based, student-led reference service.

Introduction

In August of 2007, the Science and Maps Department of the Harold B. Lee Library at Brigham Young University decided to provide virtual reference services (VRS) through an instant messaging (IM) widget to a focused population of users needing assistance in the disciplines the department supported. It was desirable to place the widget at a location most likely to be discovered by users who were online and on task to complete assignments. These distinctions meant creating a service that was both embedded within the department's resources and available at the point of need. To accomplish this, the widget was placed into each science librarian's subject guide. Subject guides are selector-sponsored websites created for each academic discipline that contain related informational resources, databases, and study helps. Each guide must be discovered, chosen, and navigated to by users from the library's homepage. At the time of the study, no IM interface existed on the library's website. Thus, by virtue of its nested location, the widget provided reference service to the focused population desired and at a time when they were actively engaged and on-task in searching resources.

Student Assistant Profile

In the academic library department under study, university students are typically hired for face-to-face reference at the department's science reference desk under the direction of a staff reference manager. As no formal librarianship degrees are offered by the university, students hired ideally major in fields supported by the library department including physical sciences, life sciences, and engineering. Training is provided in two ways:

1. As new students are hired, subject selectors provide instruction in appropriate databases for each discipline.
2. During the course of the year, more extensive training is provided weekly by the staff reference manager. This training includes reviewing IM transcripts as a group, performing exercises in reference question negotiation, learning best practices for finding answers, doing worksheets on database particulars and potential questions, and participating in challenging games such as "LC Bingo" and a *Jeopardy*-style game focused on procedures, various faculty responsibilities, and library instruction. Typically, experienced students are paired with new hires to provide continual oversight and guidance.

The department's librarians felt that the probability of success using student reference assistants to operate the widgets would be high, given the conditions of vested, interested users and their familiarity with the resources and databases being referenced. In addition, based on previous studies, an assumption was made that the questions posed through the IM service would be similar to those found in face-to-face transactions (Smyth, 2003). Accordingly, for the most part, the answers provided through the widget service came from the student assistants. For this chapter, "student assistants" or "desk" refers to the science reference student assistants answering reference questions, and "users" refers to those asking reference questions.

Literature Review

Depending on its interpretation, VRS might well trace its origins to the 1980s, at least in two implementations—one as an e-mail service initiated and reported by Howard and Jankowski (1986) at the University of Washington Health Sciences Library, and the other as a chat VRS provided by a company called Telebase Systems, which provided chat assistance to users of its "EasyNet" service, a common user interface to database vendors such as Dialog. Users simply typed "SOS" and Telebase staffers could "see which service users were coming in through, what the last search was that they had done, etc. Communication was via chat" (Sloan, 2006, p. 93). Now, close to two and a half decades later, VRS is accepted as any service that leverages any form of digital media to provide reference and consultation services.

There are many studies of VRS, including an examination of competencies needed (Breitbach & DeMars, 2009; Luo, 2007), technical challenges (Stormont, 2007), best practices (Hodges & Meiman, 2009), as well as numerous case studies (Ciacco & Huff, 2007; Davis, 2007; Doan & Ferry, 2006; Kipnis & Kaplan, 2008), including distance learning (off campus) experiences (Meulemans, Carr, & Ly, 2010). DeVoe (2008) suggested that consideration be given to VR tool placement—namely, placing an IM widget at a point of need directs questions to the items specific to the page and the resources being displayed. Point of need was considered an important element of the current study's implementation, not only for advantages of user convenience, but for its "filtering" effect, directing questions germane to the subject to the student reference employee.

Uniqueness of Study

Little research is available on the specific use of students as VRS providers, although one study by Wright and Tu (2010) describes the use of master's-level library and information science students or selected recent graduates of the program to staff a VR service. Where formal training in library science helps offset the lack of extended experience, the program's implementation was founded in six main points:

1. Only library science students were used.
2. Students were selected by a competitive application process.
3. Students must have completed course work in library reference, preferably upper-level courses that include some practical experience.
4. Students had thorough training in the VRS software used.
5. Ongoing training was made available through online links. (Note: It was not clear if this was mandatory.)
6. Supervision was provided by a project coordinator.

In the current study, only items four through six were considered applicable, with item five realized as a combination of subject major experience (life sciences, physical sciences, and engineering) and periodic training by the reference staff manager. This model created a challenging and, as yet, unexplored regime of VRS implementation. Consequently, this study is unique in its use of non-library-trained undergraduate students to provide VRS. However, it was felt that ongoing training and supervision would alleviate concerns about using these students, and once established, the experienced gained by the supervisory staff and overlap of student hires would provide a strong foundation to continue. Given these conditions, additional research raised some questions on the quality and accuracy of the service based on the medium used and the personnel supporting it. For example, although the Reference and User Services Association (RUSA, 2010) has published practical guidelines on VRS practice and implementation, issues still exist in their implementation (notably, the difficulties with the chat medium itself). Several researchers, including Lee (2004) and Woodward (2005) have suggested that this medium creates an interchange that is not conducive to instruction. For example, student impatience, perhaps more expressible in a virtual environment, may create a patron who is less likely to learn. At the same time, librarians may feel constrained to provide information quickly and delay or vacate teaching moments. While Desai and Graves (2008) addressed the issue of the "teachable moment" and how it can be addressed in an online environment, these issues still seemed at play for the current study. Since both players in a given transaction were students, both may experience the same level of impatience. In addition, the student provider of VRS may lack the professional's desire, experience, or aptitude to take advantage of teaching opportunities.

Method

To assess both the nature of an IM reference transaction and the competency of the student as a reference assistant, complete logs of all IM reference transactions from August 2007 to February 2009 were kept. The total number of transcripts analyzed was 1,545 and the total number of student reference assistants assigned to IM was 14. A textual analysis was performed on transcripts covering a period of two academic years, from

August 2007 to February 2009 (excluding the summer of 2008) and transactions were categorized and data extracted using several types of coding and quantitative as well as qualitative methods of analysis. Where some statistics such as number of transactions, transaction time, length, date, etc., are quantitative and easily determined, others are qualitative in nature and require repeated and careful reading and classification, following a coding scheme adapted from the RUSA guidelines (2004). A complete list of these two types of analysis and what criterion was used for each is given in Tables 5.1 and 5.2.

Table 5.1. Data Categories—Quantitative	
Item	**Measure**
When	Date, Time
Number of Transactions	Monthly, Weekly, Hourly
Transaction Duration	Minutes
Dropped Transactions	Desk dropped *User never contacted (+ response time > 30 sec.)*
	User dropped *User contacted but did not respond*
Response Time	Seconds

Table 5.2. Data Categories—Qualitative	
Item	**Measure**
Courteousness *Variant of RUSA Guidelines (2004)*	Initial Greeting *Did the student provide an initial greeting? (Y/N)*
	Delay Explanation *Did the student provide an explanation of a delay if on another task? (Y/N)*
	Confirmation *Did the student confirm that the question was answered? (Y/N)*
Accuracy	Good *Answer complete, issues addressed and answered*
	Satisfactory *Answer incomplete, but provides sufficient direction to complete task*
	Poor *Answer incorrect*
Reference Categories	A compilation of various categories proposed by Katz, (2002), NISO (1997), and Sears (2001)
Reference Effort Required	READ Scale (Gerlich & Berard, 2007)

Quantitative Data

A straightforward computation using descriptive statistics was performed to summarize the quantitative session data, including the number of transactions, response time, and transaction duration. However, "dropped transactions," as defined here, were identified and treated as follows.

It was necessary to specify a minimum 30-second window before a transaction was eligible to be considered a "desk dropped transaction" (meaning the student never answered an IM post from a user). The 30-second buffer was added to eliminate transactions initiated by a user, but quickly disconnected without allowing sufficient time for the reference student to respond. Thus the phrase "user never contacted" means the user was never contacted by the reference desk after 30 seconds or longer. In this case, a "desk dropped transaction" resulted. If the user waited and then responded to the desk contact, even if the contact took longer than 30 seconds to respond, these were not considered dropped transactions.

On average, users were willing to wait almost four minutes without response before disconnecting a call. A maximum allowable time to respond was not specified as it would have excluded some transactions that were completed. The response time statistic was used in this case to qualify how long students took to answer, and a value of "1" was also assigned to a "completed/dropped" category to distinguish from dropped calls in the data spreadsheet. If the transaction was dropped, a "0" was assigned.

Two conditions qualified a "user dropped" scenario. One, if the initial call was answered by the desk, but the user never returned a reply, the call was considered dropped by the user. Since the log specifies the time when the user disconnects their call, calls in this case were disconnected by the user after the desk had responded. Two, if the user dropped within 30 seconds or less before a student responded, the call was considered "user dropped."

Qualitative Data Analysis

Descriptions of how each data category was coded are given below. The author made scoring judgments based on these criteria for each category after reviewing each transaction. To address issues of consistency and quality control, these same data descriptions were provided to two other independent reviewers who performed the same review and scoring on several months of transactions. Scores were compared and, with very few exceptions, scoring was found near identical and consistent. An inter-rater reliability percentage was determined and the consensus agreement ranged between 96 percent and 98 percent.

Courteousness

"Courteousness" was developed as a category after considering the RUSA guidelines (2004). From these guidelines, three conditions were adapted in order to quantify the "Courteousness" statistic.

INITIAL GREETING

The first was a derivation of the "Interest" guideline for remote users found in sections 2.6 and 2.7, and in this implementation was called "Initial Greeting." Therefore, if the student provided an initial greeting such as "Hi, how can I help you?" or "Yes, let me look into that" or even an "Okay" or something similar, a "yes" was awarded for giving an "Initial Greeting." The greeting's intent was to let the user know their question was being considered. The opposite case was the instance where the first response by the student was the answer to the user's question. This normally took a few minutes to provide, and the user was left waiting, wondering if anyone was online. In this case, a "no" was given. Thus two states were possible: Y or N, coded as 1 or 0, respectively.

DELAY EXPLANATION

The second condition was not specifically detailed in the RUSA guidelines (2004) for remote or in-person conditions, but seemed a valuable aspect to monitor, especially in online environments. This condition is called the "Delay Explanation." If, for example, the student was currently involved in another task, replying to the user with "Hi. I'm working on something else right now. Can you wait?" or "Hang on. I'll be right with you," or even "Wait" or something similar, a "yes" was awarded for giving a delay explanation. The intent was to let the user know someone was there and would be helping them soon. This explanation seemed extremely important in online transactions since, unlike in a face-to-face environment, the user has no insight into the current desk activity, or even if a queue has formed, and is left hanging with no response or acknowledgment if the desk is busy. In some cases, if no response was given to the user, dropped transactions would be expected or extremely long response times would result. Two states were possible: Y or N, coded as 1 or 0, respectively.

CONFIRMATION

The third condition was a straightforward application of the RUSA guidelines (2004) "Follow-up" recommendation, narrowed to the online environment as a "Confirmation" by the student that the user's questions were answered. This would take the form of a simple, "Have I answered your questions?" or "Do you need anything else?" or even an "All done?" or something similar. The intent was to give the user a chance to continue if they needed more help. If the student used confirmation questions during the transaction, a "yes" was awarded. If not, a "no" was given. These were coded as 1 or 0, respectively.

Accuracy

Three conditions were evaluated in order to quantify the Accuracy category: Good, Satisfactory, or Incorrect. A value of "Good," scored as a "2" on a scale from 0 to 2, was given if the answer given was not only accurate and complete, but it added value by expanding the question and providing greater insight or addressed related issues. Typically, this response would have included some questioning by the student to the user, delving deeper into the issue being discussed, or adding content that the user may not have known to ask about. It would have provided direction sufficient to not only complete the task, but to understand application and provide guidance for future tasks.

If the answer given provided sufficient direction to complete the task, but did not go beyond to add greater value or completeness, it was considered "Satisfactory" and scored as a "1" on a scale from 0 to 2. The information provided would be accurate, but not considered well rounded or providing more than what the user asked. If the student did not know the answer, but provided a referral to another person or source, the answer was marked satisfactory. If the answer was incorrect, or not known and not referred, it was considered "Poor" and scored as a "0."

Types of Reference Queries

To quantify the kinds of questions being asked, categories used were based on the work by Katz (2002), NISO (1997), and Sears (2001), who provide seven reference question types under three categories. Review of the questions being asked created a classification of each transaction as one of the types listed in Table 5.3 Numbers from 1 to 7 were assigned to each type for coding purposes.

Difficulty and Reference Effort Required

Transactions were also categorized according to their difficulty, using the Reference Effort Assessment Data (READ) scale (Gerlich & Berard, 2007). This scale classifies reference effort into one of six levels, from those requiring the least amount of effort (1) to those requiring the most (6). A brief outline is given in Table 5.4.

From a review of the categories, the expectation was that the student would be able to handle categories 1–2 with minimal instruction, category 3 would require extended experience and training, category 4 could be handled only by the most skilled and adept student, and categories 5–6 should be referred to librarians.

Results and Discussion

Reference Statistics

The reference statistics show a summary of the IM transaction data trends for time of year, day, and time. Table 5.5 shows overall statistics of transactions and duration times.

Table 5.3. Reference Categories

	Coding Value	Type	Description
Reference	1	Ready Reference	Citation questions, using software, journal titles, etc.
	2	Specific Search	Focused searching, need journal articles, specific resources
	3	Research	General informational research questions, getting started, etc.
Policy/Procedural	4	Access	Log-in procedures, access off campus, etc.
	5	Policy	Food, study rooms, music, talking, etc.
Directional	6	Physical Direction	Location of rooms, departments, personnel, physical resources
	7	Website Direction	Location of websites, URLs, etc.

Source: Based on Katz, 2002; NISO, 1997; Sears, 2001.

Table 5.4. READ Scale Summary (Gerlich & Berard, 2007)	
Level	**Requirement**
Level 1	• Answers that require the least amount of effort • No specialized knowledge skills or expertise • No consultation of resources • Less than 5 minutes
Level 2	• Answers given which require more effort • Requires minimal specific knowledge skills or expertise • Answers may need nominal resource consultation
Level 3	• Answers in this category require some effort and time • Consultation of ready-reference resource materials is needed • Minimal instruction of the user may be required • Reference knowledge and skills come into play
Level 4	• Answers or research requests require the consultation of multiple resources • Subject specialists may need to be consulted, more instruction and assistance occurs • Reference knowledge and skills needed • Efforts can be more supportive, or if searching for a finite answer can be difficult to find • Exchanges can be more instruction based as staff teach users more in-depth research skills
Level 5	• More substantial effort and time assisting with research and finding information • Subject specialists need to be consulted • Consultation appointments with individuals might be scheduled • Cooperative efforts between the user and librarian and/or colleagues • Multiple resources used • Research, reference knowledge, and skills needed • Dialogue between the user and librarian may take on a "back and forth question" dimension
Level 6	• The most effort and time expended • Inquiries or requests for information can't be answered on the spot • Staff may be providing in-depth research and services for specific needs of the clients • This category covers some "special library" type research services • Primary (original documents) and secondary resource materials may be used

Table 5.5. Transaction Statistics		
(September 2007–February 2009, excluding summers)		
Total Transactions		= 1545
Average Duration Time	All	= 11 min 45 sec
	Completed	= 13 min 45 sec
	Dropped (User & Desk)	= 6 min

Note the sinusoidal nature of the frequency of transactions in Figure 5.1, where most transactions happened during the peak times of the academic year, during the mid-fall and mid-winter semester months of October and January/February 2009. The study concluded a week into February 2009; hence the month is underrepresented. Transactions peaked at midweek with Wednesday consistently showing as the busiest day (see Figure 5.2). Numbers declined toward the weekend as its natural diversions approached. The desk is closed on Sundays. Time of day showed rising trends toward the afternoons (see Figure 5.3). Classes are preferentially taken during the morning hours. Consequently, the afternoons reveal the most active study period after most

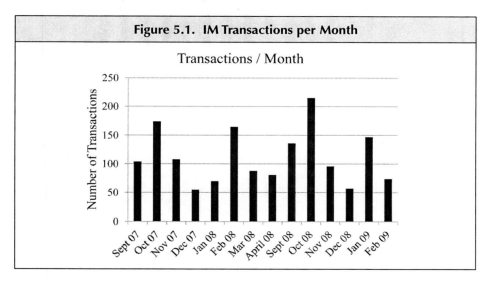

Figure 5.1. IM Transactions per Month

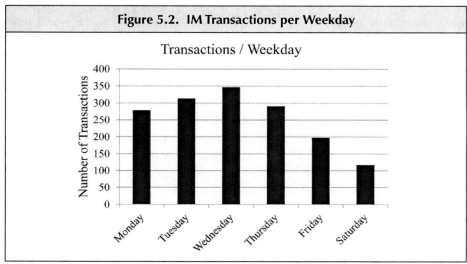

Figure 5.2. IM Transactions per Weekday

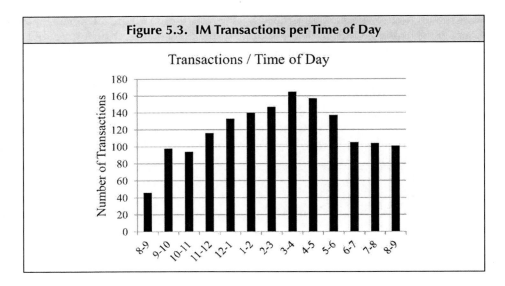

Figure 5.3. IM Transactions per Time of Day

classes are over and students begin their homework. The study shows the lowest numbers in the 8 a.m. to 9 a.m. hour, peaking gradually toward the late afternoon, and moving downward to midmorning activity levels in the evening. These trends seemed reasonable and instructive, especially in considering decisions regarding when to increase or reduce staffing.

Dropped Transactions/Response Times

The dropped transaction results revealed a troubling aspect, that effactully 25 percent of all IM requests went unanswered, either by the desk or the user dropping the request. Although it is not entirely comparative, one might argue that finding this could be likened to ignoring one out of four face-to-face transactions. When the dropped rates are separated by liability as in Table 5.6, desk dropped rates overall are 11 percent to 15 percent for user dropped calls. However, in Figure 5.4, it can be seen that the desk dropped rates are higher than user dropped calls in 9 out of the 14 months. These data provide insight into improvements in responsiveness on the part of the student. It is interesting to note the desk dropped rate appears to lower for each semester during the peak months of October and February 2009, when the greater number of transactions might have suggested a higher drop rate.

Table 5.6. Dropped IM Transactions	
(Percentage of dropped transactions to all requests, September 2007–February 2009)	
Total Dropped Transactions	= 26%
Desk Dropped	= 11%
User Dropped	= 15%

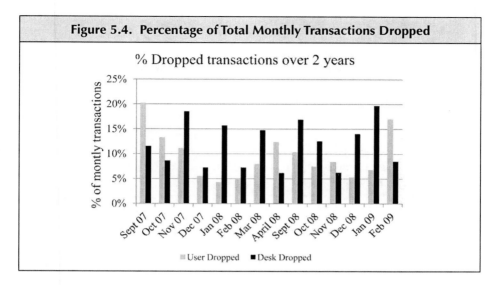

Figure 5.4. Percentage of Total Monthly Transactions Dropped

As shown in Table 5.7, the average response time for a completed call was just under 1 minute (58 seconds). However, desk dropped response time was close to 4 minutes, meaning the user was willing to wait that long before disconnecting and giving up without contact. What could be a reasonable time for the desk to require as its response times for all calls to significantly reduce its drop rate? Three statistics can be used to consider this question.

1. Figure 5.5 shows the percentage of all desk dropped calls by user wait time, slightly more than half of all the desk dropped calls, occurred within a two-minute wait time.
2. From Figure 5.6, the highest number of desk dropped calls occurred between 35 and 70 seconds; with a gradual taper to outliers either willing to wait several minutes, or who might have left their browsers running unattended.
3. Table 5.7 shows user dropped calls having an 83-second average.

Thus, from Figure 5.5, it could be argued that a two-minute time limit would effectually reduce the desk dropped rate by half. From Figure 5.6 and Table 5.7, a more aggressive time limit between 35 to 80 seconds might reduce the desk dropped rate to even lower levels, approaching a near zero limit as the time limit shrinks more aggressively.

Table 5.7. Average Response Times	
Completed Transactions	= 58 seconds
Desk Dropped	= 3.6 minutes (no desk contact, then ended call)
User Dropped	= 83 seconds (desk contact, but user ended call)

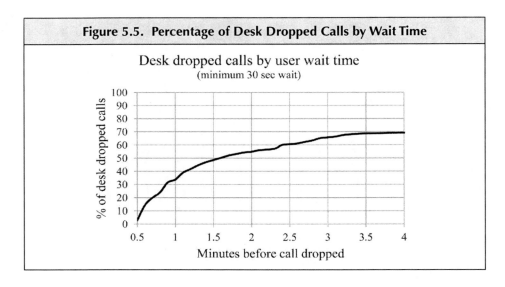

Figure 5.5. Percentage of Desk Dropped Calls by Wait Time

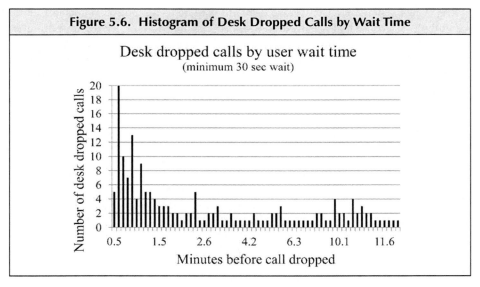

Figure 5.6. Histogram of Desk Dropped Calls by Wait Time

Average response times for user dropped calls were longer than the completed transaction response time by 25 seconds. Since user dropped calls were eventually answered by the desk, it was within the realm of being a completed transaction, but terminated by the user. Since the termination occurred at an 83-second average, and the average response time for completed calls was 58 seconds, does that imply that a greeting (or a delay explanation, depending on the call), given before or at a 58-second time limit might afford a longer window for those users that would have tended to leave the call earlier? The interpretation of this data remains unclear.

Courteousness

The set of courteousness statistics showed initial greetings were relatively high, in the eightieth percentile. Delay explanations, at 11 percent, are effectively dependent on the current conditions when the call was made. Subsequently, they become difficult to evaluate due to this circumstance. However, the follow-up statistic does not have this limitation. At 9 percent, it was quite low and indicates a need for better training of the student in this technique. Ideally, almost all calls could have included follow-up verbiage as recommended in the RUSA (2004) guidelines. See Table 5.8.

Accuracy, Question Type, and Reference Effort

Accuracy for all transactions was reasonably good, scoring in the mid-seventieth percentile for "Good" with 20 percent as satisfactory, creating an effective 93 percent in positive outcomes for all transactions (see Table 5.9). Looking at accuracy over the entire sampling period (see Figure 5.7), there was an important improvement in rating percentage-wise during this time, gaining from 76 percent (1.52 out of a possible 2.0) to 82 percent (1.64

Table 5.8. Courteousness	
Initial Greeting	= 83% of all transactions
Delay Explanations	= 11% (same %, complete or dropped)
Follow-up	= 9%

Table 5.9. Accuracy	
(Average accuracy, all completed transactions)	
Good	= 73%
Satisfactory	= 20%
Poor	= 6.4%

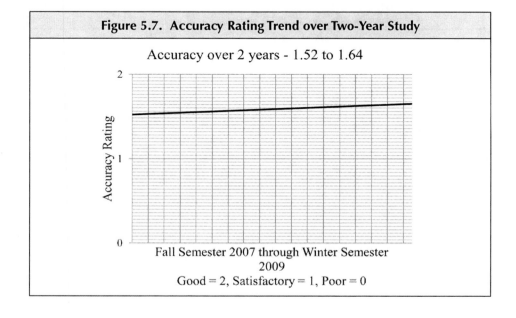

Figure 5.7. Accuracy Rating Trend over Two-Year Study

Accuracy over 2 years - 1.52 to 1.64

Accuracy Rating

Fall Semester 2007 through Winter Semester 2009

Good = 2, Satisfactory = 1, Poor = 0

out of 2.0). Rise could be attributable to experience gained and possible improvement in training techniques. This rise in accuracy over time includes new student hires and experienced students leaving, which typically occurred every eight months.

Ready-reference questions were found to comprise the largest group (see Table 5.10), with research style questions, both general and specific, second and fourth, and access being third. It would make sense that questions regarding site permissions, web access, and off-campus use would be more likely when the user was online and able to use the IM widget. Accordingly, questions dealing with university or library policy or physical directions were the lowest in numbers. Although a higher percentage was expected in website direction through the IM widget, it was surprisingly low at 5 percent.

As shown in Table 5.11, reference effort was focused on rankings of 2 and 3 on the READ scale (Gerlich & Berard, 2007). This analysis would include the ready-reference and research questions, which were among the largest types. Level 1 questions did occur, but typically not through the IM tool. Although a higher value in this category was expected due to the convenience and impersonal nature of the IM medium, and it did

Table 5.10. Reference Categories Percentage

	Coding Value	Type	Percentage of All Transactions
Reference	1	Ready Reference	28%
	2	Specific Search	24%
	3	Research	19%
Policy/Procedural	4	Access	20%
	5	Policy	<1%
Directional	6	Physical Direction	3%
	7	Website Direction	5%

Table 5.11. Reference Effort—READ Scale Percentages

READ Scale	Score
Level 1	9%
Level 2	44%
Level 3	42%
Level 4	4%
Level 5	1%
Level 6	0%

outscore the higher (>3) levels, it effectively realized less than 10 percent of all calls. However, as expected, as the effort required increased, the occurrence of these questions over the IM widget reduced. Does the user perceive a limitation in the IM medium or an inability to efficiently express his or her need through this tool? These are interesting questions for further research.

The challenge of describing a remote reference transaction as a combination of percentages, numbers, and rankings has always been a difficult one. Part of the difficulty lies in appreciating the multifaceted nature of a reference interchange and considering how to accurately represent it in a reasonably quantifiable way. Considering a single element alone, like reference types, is a small peek into a vastly broader world. Linking how that single element interacted within that world with other equally important elements begins to broaden the vision toward a more complete rendering. For this reason, it was felt that merging accuracy ratings, reference types, and reference effort scales together would create at least a three-dimensional rendering of this multidimensional event. To that end, Figures 5.8 and 5.9 are perhaps the most telling of the nature and quality of the student/user reference transaction.

Figure 5.8 shows the students' accuracy as a function of the reference category. Although in all cases, the students showed good accuracy, it is interesting to see the ratio of good to satisfactory scores reduce as the student is questioned in ready-reference areas. Considering that both research categories (specific and research) and the access category scored higher ratios, it could be construed that the student is more familiar with these processes since he or she is experiencing them in his or her own schoolwork.

Figure 5.8. Accuracy Ratings Earned for Different Reference Categories

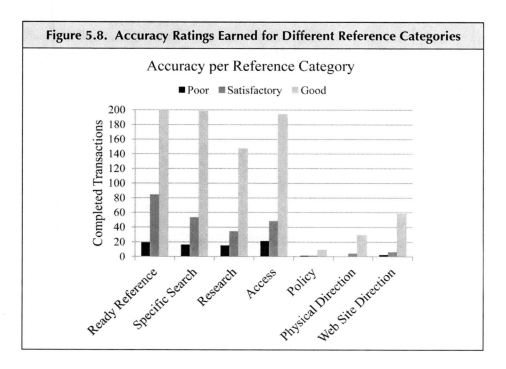

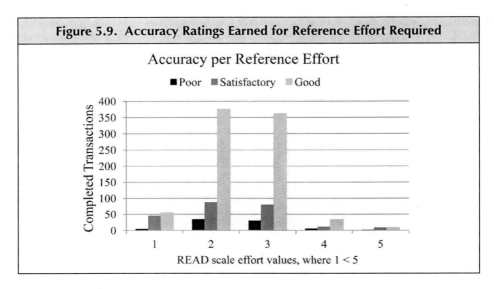

Figure 5.9. Accuracy Ratings Earned for Reference Effort Required

Consequently, the ready-reference score could be an indication that core library knowledge is not as adept and could use some attention. As seen in Figure 5.9, very strong scores in accuracy occur as the questions require greater effort, with the 2 and 3 scale levels scoring almost identically. Again, this result is probably indicative of the student's own experience, but also time spent in training by the department and the reference manager in preparing the students to deal with more specific and involved research questions. It is interesting to note the almost equal ratio of good to satisfactory accuracy at the minimal effort scale of 1. This may be due to a low overall occurrence in this effort category, and some statistical noise may be at play, but coupling that with the accuracy findings for ready reference in Figure 5.8 may be indicative of the need to address clean, effectual answers for the simpler requests.

Limitations

It should be mentioned that this study has limitations. It cannot be generalized to other populations or particular implementations. Results obtained were not compared to typical responses, accuracy, or behaviors of professional librarians at this library, nor were specific groups of student assistants from various disciplines compared. Known metrics for comparative analysis, such as the READ scale (Gerlich & Berard, 2007), or Sears' (2001) categories, were sought and, where applicable, used. However, the interpretation of those metrics and subsequent scoring cannot be considered absolute. IM tools used and statistics gathered will vary with implementation, and with the exception of Figure 5.7, no comparative data for accuracy over time should be assumed or implied.

Conclusion

The analysis given in this chapter was of both the use of the IM tool as a reference medium and the non-library student as a reference worker. Overall, both appear to be successful. To summarize, important findings included the following:

- Ninety-three percent of all completed calls were considered accurately answered, with 73 percent good and 20 percent satisfactory.
- Accuracy improves over time with consistent training and layered experience.
- Approximately 25 percent of all transactions were dropped, either by the desk or the user.
- Desk response time needs attention and training in order to lower dropped transactions.
- Delay explanations can be an important tool when desk traffic is busy.
- Seventy-one percent of all transactions were referenced based, 20 percent access, and the remainder dealt with policy and procedure.
- Eighty-six percent of all transactions had a reference difficulty of Level 2 or 3 on the READ scale.
- Nine percent of all transactions were Level 1 on the READ scale, 5 percent on Level 4 , 1 percent on Level 5, and none were Level 6.

Given attention is paid to the areas mentioned earlier, notably, response time to incoming calls and the need for ongoing training in not only sophisticated, but also simple ready-reference questions, this implementation succeeds. A suggestion for future research would include a focus on response times. Many of the suggestions for time limits derived from these results are simple inferences made from data. Actual limits are unknown, and a study to explore tolerances and best practices would be instructive. In addition, the research suggests that additional training in reference negotiation skills in the IM environment is warranted. Development of a course of study for the non-library trained reference student is encouraged, and to that end, the reference manager is designing his curriculum to support these efforts.

Acknowledgment
The author wishes to thank Andrea Nielsen, one of our brilliant students who helped compile the volumes of data used, and David Layton, our reference manager, whose skill at training and managing our student employees is evidenced by these data.

References

Breitbach, W., & DeMars, J. M. (2009). Enhancing virtual reference: Techniques and technologies to engage users and enrich interaction. *Internet Reference Services Quarterly, 14*(3), 82–91. doi:10.1080/10875300903256571.

Ciacco, R., & Huff, A. (2007). Mission IM-possible: Starting an instant message reference service using Trillian. *Computers in Libraries, 27*(1), 26–31.

Davis, K. (2007). Ask now instant messaging: Innovation in virtual reference. *The Australian Library Journal, 56*(2), 152–174.

Desai, C. M., & Graves, S. J. (2008). Cyberspace or face-to-face: The teachable moment and changing reference mediums. *Reference & User Services Quarterly, 47*(3), 242–255.

DeVoe, K. M. (2008). Chat widgets: Placing your virtual reference services at your user's point(s) of need. *The Reference Librarian, 49*(1), 99–101. doi:10.1080/02763870802103936.

Doan, T., & Ferry, K. (2006). Instant messaging (IM): Providing services and enhancing communication. *Journal of Business & Finance Librarianship, 12*(2), 17–22. doi:10.1300/J109v12n02_03.

Gerlich, B. K., & Berard, G. L. (2007). Introducing the READ scale: Qualitative statistics for academic reference services. *Georgia Library Quarterly, 43*(4), 7–14.

Hodges, A. R., & Meiman, M. (2009). IM is for instant millennials: Developing staffing models and best practices for instant messaging. *Technical Services Quarterly, 26*(3), 199–206. doi:10.1080/07317130802520203.

Howard, E. H., & Jankowski, T. A. (1986). Reference services via electronic mail. *Bulletin of the Medical Library Association, 74*(1), 300–304.

Katz, W. A. (2002). *Introduction to reference work, volume I: Basic information sources* (8th ed.). Boston: McGraw-Hill.

Kipnis, D. G., & Kaplan, G. E. (2008). Analysis and lessons learned instituting an instant messaging reference service at an academic health sciences library: The first year. *Medical Reference Services Quarterly, 27*(1), 33–51. doi:10.1080/02763860802080119.

Lee, I. J. (2004). Do virtual reference librarians dream of digital reference questions? A qualitative and quantitative analysis of email and chat reference. *Australian Academic and Research Libraries, 35*(2), 95–110.

Luo, L. (2007). Chat reference competencies: Identification from a literature review and librarian interviews. *Reference Services Review, 35*(2), 195–209.

Meulemans, Y. N., Carr, A., & Ly, P. (2010). From a distance: Robust reference service via instant messaging. *Journal of Library & Information Services in Distance Learning, 4*(1/2), 3–17. doi:10.1080/15332901003667231.

NISO (National Information Standards Organization). (1997). *Library statistics.* ANSI/NISO Z39.7-1995. Bethesda, MD: NISO Press.

RUSA. (2004). RUSA guidelines: Guidelines for behavioral performance of reference and information service providers. *Reference & User Services Quarterly, 44*(1), 14–17.

RUSA. (2010). RUSA guidelines: Guidelines for implementing and maintaining virtual reference services. *Reference & User Services Quarterly, 50*(1), 92–96.

Sears, J. (2001). Chat reference service: An analysis of one semester's data. *Issues in Science and Technology Librarianship, 32.* Retrieved November 30, 2010, from http://www.istl.org/01-fall/article2.html.

Sloan, B. (2006). Twenty years of virtual reference. *Internet Reference Services Quarterly, 11*(2), 91–95. doi:10.1300/J136v11n02_06.

Smyth, J. (2003). Virtual reference transcript analysis: A few models. *Searcher, 11*(3), 26–30.

Stormont, S. (2007). Looking to connect: Technical challenges that impede the growth of virtual reference. *Reference & User Services Quarterly, 47*(2), 114–119.

Woodward, B. S. (2005). One-on-one instruction: From the reference desk to online chat. *Reference and Users Services Quarterly, 44*(3), 203–209.

Wright, A., & Tu, F. (2010). *Expanding service and enhancing learning: Preliminary report on novel virtual reference collaboration.* In M. L. Radford & R. D. Lankes (Eds.), *Reference Renaissance, Current and Future Trends* (pp. 183–202). New York: Neal-Schuman.

## CHAPTER 6

We Are All Stressed Out! Now What? Looking at Stress in Libraries

Mary Wilkins Jordan

Overview

This chapter looks at the negative effects of stress in the library workplace. It uses the Q Method in an exploratory study to identify some of the most common stressors of public and academic librarians. Based on results, suggestions are made for librarians and libraries to address these stressors and eliminate them.

Introduction

Stress is an increasingly large part of the workplace environment for many librarians. A few studies have been carried out to identify stressors in the profession. However, there has not been a large-scale effort to either identify or address the most common stressors for librarians. In this chapter, some common stressors affecting public and academic librarians are identified. Several suggestions are made on ways to help address some of these stressors, adding a background of literature and methodology discussion to give these ideas on stressors some context.

Looking at Stress in Libraries

The literature is full of information on stress in workplaces of all sorts, including libraries. The pace of change is increasing in all areas of life, and libraries are feeling the stress of keeping up with community demands. One common area of stress is the need to keep up with the technology needs of patrons—called "technostress" (Brillhart, 2004; Huwe, 2005; Gendreau, 2007). The constant accessibility technology gives people, added to the constant need to stay current with the ever-changing technologies librarians need to provide to their communities, can be very stressful in the public library workplace. Lisa Ennis (2005) discusses a study conducted in the mid-1990s that detailed the stress technology causes in libraries. She asserts that some areas of technostress are reducing for librarians, including the reliability of hardware and software, and lack of standardization. But the pace of technological change is continuing to make this a problem in public libraries. Dealing with the ever-increasing amounts of information online is difficult in itself; the converse—explaining to patrons why everything is not available for free online—also provides an area of stress for librarians.

Poor workplace facilities in public libraries can also contribute to the stress felt by librarians, as well as causing injuries at work. Kaehr (2008) looked at repetitive injuries experienced by librarians in the course of their work, including neck injuries, carpal tunnel syndrome, and back injuries. All of these are caused by the repetitive work done by many librarians, the need to be in one place for long stretches of time, or to be moving heavy things around the library, or to make many small repetitive motions such as working on the computer. When stress continues unabated, unrecognized, and untreated, eventually librarians will burn out. Burnout goes beyond just feeling stressed at work every so often, more than handling a limited crisis in the library. "Rather, it is a syndrome of advanced and holistic responses to extended periods of high levels of stress that results in a variety of emotional, physical, and cognitive symptoms" (Caputo, 1991, p. 9). Once a librarian reaches burnout, may symptoms of stress have been overlooked and ignored. Burnout is not a condition that will reverse itself quickly or easily. Librarians experiencing this problem may need professional help to get past it, from an Employee Assistance Program (EAP) or a qualified therapist. Developing strategies to address stress and deal with stressful situations before they spiral into burnout should be the goal of every library organization. Losing a staff member to burnout does not have to happen, but it takes recognition of the problem of stress and a willingness to face the problem directly.

Suggestions abound in the literature for handling stress in libraries. Yucht (2006), a school librarian, incorporated lessons learned in fourth grade to combat stress: Courtesy (think personally), Brains (think productively), and Grins (think positively). Salaz (2006) reported on lessons learned from her mother—a career librarian in an increasingly busy library. She advocates taking time off work regularly, getting involved in committees at work, doing new things, and performing at a high level and enjoying the accolades from coworkers. Spires (2007) recommends reaching out to colleagues for their help at work to help combat workplace stressors. Holcomb (2007) looks at resources to help law librarians deal with the stress they experience at work. One of the specific issues they face is that they will often spend decades in the same workplace; stressful workplaces therefore will build stress levels in the librarians who work there, with no opportunity to relieve it by moving to another organization. She suggests strategies such as getting involved with professional organizations at the local and national level, volunteering for new tasks, and developing good social networks—inside and outside the library.

This discussion is missing an organized, concentrated effort at a high level of the profession to identify some common stressors and to address the problem of stress experienced by librarians. There has not been a focused effort to address the problem of stress across a system of libraries or on a statewide or profession-wide basis. Instead, the problem is treated as an individual one; each individual librarian feeling stress at work is encouraged to take time for deep breathing, to exercise more often, to keep track of time to balance personal and work lives, and to take more breaks (Schatz, 2004; Sheesley, 2001). While these are perfectly valid and certainly helpful suggestions, continuing to treat stress at work as an individual problem, affecting only isolated cases, is not going to help the situation.

Suggesting that individual librarians adjust themselves—without any consideration of organization-wide changes that can be made to help everyone—cannot be the most effective way to reduce stress. Taking a direct approach to acknowledging that stress is a problem for many public and academic librarians, identifying some specific causes of that stress, and developing strategies to reduce or eliminate those stressors, should be a task for every library to address. Conducting research into causes and solutions for workplace stress should be part of the responsibility of state and national library organizations, to help their members to be productive and satisfied in their jobs.

Effects of Workplace Stress

Many problems can arise for employees as a result of workplace stress. Whether physical or mental health problems, or frustration with the workplace, allowing unnecessary stressors to continue causes problems on many different fronts for the affected staff. While it may be impossible to eliminate all stressors for every person at work, making some steps toward their reduction will help staff avoid some of the more negative effects of stress. In a Finnish study, 5 percent of the employees reported being bullied at work; these staff were found to have higher body mass and more chronic disease, and their absentee rate was higher than that of the rest of the staff (Kivimaki, Elovainio, & Vahters, 2000). Taking positive steps to assess these kinds of negative effects can help a library, or other organization, to function more effectively in eliminating these stressors. A study conducted in Holland found that employers did understand that negative effects were occurring at work, but underestimated the effects of these stressors on employees (Houtman et al.,1998).

Negative effects of workplace stress are often seen in the family. In one study of 150 married couples, "both husbands and wives felt that job insecurity stress was negatively related to marital satisfaction, general family functioning, family role clarity, and the number of problems that the family was experiencing" (Larson, Wilson, & Beley, 1994, p. 142). As the economic downturn increasingly intrudes on work life, causing people in all organizations to be concerned for their jobs, this kind of negative stress reaction can be expected to increase. Parents are often seen as being stressed by their particular balancing act in attempting to be successful as both employees and as family members. Warren and Johnson (1995) found that workplaces that actively provided a good organizational structure, supervisor support, and family-oriented benefits had a decreased level of perceived stress for their employee-parents.

Bullying at work, and the accompanying increase in stress, has been found to increase the levels of depression in the victims. There is a clear relationship between bullying and depression, and "the longer the exposure to bullying, the greater the risk of depression" (Kivimaki, Virtanen, Vartia, Vahters, and Keltikangas-Jarvinen, 2003, p. 781). Research by Kivimaki and colleagues (2003) also showed that prolonged bullying increased the risk of cardiovascular disease in its victims, although some of this result may be explained by the increased likelihood of the victim being overweight as well as bullied. Likewise, a study by Nordstrom, Dwyer, Bairey Merz, Shircore, & Dwyer, 2001) found that middle-aged men who identify themselves as stressed at work have an increased likelihood of heart disease. It may seem like an obvious conclusion to draw, that employees who experience stress at work will have an increase in the amount of depression and heart disease. However, connecting these negative health effects to a job in the library may help to make the case that stress is a problem that needs to be addressed instead of dismissed.

Other negative health effects are seen as a result of stress in the workplace, causing even more problems for a person who is suffering from stress. Women experiencing stress at work during their pregnancies are at risk for pregnancy-induced hypertension

(PIH), which puts them and their babies in danger for other prenatal health problems (Landsbergis & Hatch, 1996, p. 348). Workplace stressors can also exacerbate the effects of air pollution on the respiratory health of the stressed staff (Clougherty & Kubzansky, 2009). A study of Chinese female workers even showed a connection between perceived stress in the workplace and an increase in the incidence of dysmenorrhea (painful menses)—the most common gynecological disorder in reproductive-aged women (Wang et al., 2004). Such widespread negative physical effects traced back to stress in the workplace would indicate the severity of the potential problem, and the need for it to be addressed in a clear and direct way.

Method

Q Method has not been used very often in the library and information science (LIS) field yet, but it has the potential to be very useful. It is a blend of quantitative and qualitative strategies for looking at research problems. It has been used in many different fields, however, building on the ideas originally created by William Stephenson (1953), publicized in his book *The Study of Behavior: Q-Technique and Its Methodology* (http://qmethod.org/about). It has been used to look at a variety of subjects, including nursing (Akhtar-Danesh, Baumann, & Cordingley, 2008), policy development (Focht & Hull, 2004), and leadership building for outdoor tour operators (Hutson & Montgomery, 2006). Two books are the most common resources for learning to use Q Method: *Political Subjectivity: Applications of Q Methodology in Political Science* by Brown (1980), and *Q Methodology* by McKeown and Thomas (1988).

The basic idea is a sorting process. The researcher gives all participants identical sets of cards, each with a separate idea relevant to the research hypothesis. The participants sort the entire set of ideas into an ordering of their own preference, from "most" to "least" liked/wanted, depending on the wording of the instructions. This process gives a more accurate state of their opinions than a Likert scale, in which every answer could be rated the same by a participant. With the ranking of a Q Method study, participants must choose their personal interest in the items. Some participants become overly concerned about making their answers "right" during the process, but there is no right or wrong answer. Those items rated as number 2 or 3 may not be very different to the participant, but would be quite different from items ranked in the fifteenth or twenty-fifth positions.

Participants record their answers on answer sheets provided by the researcher. These data are all collected, and at the end of the study the researcher enters them into a Q Method statistical analysis software. There are different software programs available, which can be found at the Q Method website (http://qmethod.org/about). The original program, called PQMethod, is freely available on the Q Method website. It is somewhat clunky to use and interpret the results, especially for those new to the method, but can provide valuable data to users. More information on creating a Q Method study, and using the PQMethod software, is available in Using Q Method to Reveal Social Perspectives in Environmental Research (http://www.seri-us.org/content/primer-q-methodology-available-free-download).

In this chapter, the results of two Q Method studies on stress in libraries are discussed. One study looked at public librarians, and the other looked at academic librarians. Approximately 30 librarians from around the country participated in each study. The public librarians were recruited with a posting to the Publib electronic discussion list (http://lists.webjunction.org/publib/); the academic librarians were recruited through e-mails sent to libraries in different parts of the country, chosen to be geographically different (Arizona, Illinois, South Carolina, Washington, and Massachusetts).

Each group was given a set of stressors, drawn from the literature on stress in libraries and from anecdotal discussions with librarians about stress in their workplaces (see Table 6.1). These stressors were tailored to be specific to the library types, but there was generally a good deal of overlap between the sets. The participants sorted the stressors given to them, in order based on their own view of the impact of the stressors which are affecting them most significantly, ordering them from most stressful to least. Each participant could also provide other information about the stressors they encountered in the workplace. The academic librarian study was done in person, while the public library group sorted their ideas online. The results of each group were entered, separately, into the PQMethod software.

Results

After the Q data were analyzed by the PQMethod software, the stressors identified as most stressful to the participants were calculated by the program. While these may or

Table 6.1. Lists of Stressors Provided to Study Participants	
Academic Librarians	**Public Librarians**
• Budget issues • Difficulties with coworkers • Layoffs—potential or actual • Excessive workload • Issues with students • Issues with management • Salary • Technology you use at work • Workplace culture • Personal control over your time • Shifting schedules • Pressure to be successful • Many deadlines to meet • Issues with academic faculty • Issues with members of the public as patrons • Personal/family issues intruding at work • Building facilities • Lack of recognition for your work • Adapting to changing expectations • Technology you train patrons to use • Lack of time to finish work • Lack of personal space to work (such as a cubicle or desk) • Never taking meal breaks • A lot of interruptions to your work • Issues with collection	• Budget issues • Difficulties with coworkers • Layoffs—potential or actual • Excessive workload • Workload too small • Homeless people in the library • Difficulties with management • Salary • Technology you use at work • Workplace culture • Personal control over your time • Shifting schedules • Pressure to be successful • Many deadlines to meet • Issues with library board • Issues with community groups • Personal/family issues intruding at work • Building facilities • Lack of recognition for your work • Adapting to changing expectations • Technology you train patrons to use • Lack of time to finish work • Lack of personal space to work (such as a cubicle or desk) • Never taking meal breaks • A lot of interruptions to your work

may not be stressful to all librarians, these are likely to affect many academic and public librarians in their workplaces. These studies are serving as a preliminary look at the groups of librarians in different types of libraries, to begin to identify the stressors having the most impact on these librarians. Once some answers are gathered, the important work of figuring out what to do about common stressors can begin.

For the academic librarians, six stressors emerged as significant to the group as a whole:

1. Issues with students
2. Shifting schedules
3. Never taking meal breaks
4. Issues with members of the public
5. Personal control over time
6. Lack of personal space to work

One striking point about these results is that most involve the powerlessness the librarians feel—an inability to make decisions or to affect their workplace as they would want it. This kind of inability to direct the course of a professional workplace is one of the major causes of stress for many people.

The group of public librarians had a set of nine stressors emerge as stressful to the group as a whole:

1. Difficulties with management
2. Salary
3. Issues with library board
4. Personal/family issues
5. Technology you use at work
6. Technology you train patrons to use
7. Lack of personal space in which to work
8. Homeless people in the library
9. Workload too small

Unlike the academic group, there is not such a common thread of ideas running through these stressors. Several involve difficulties with other people: managers, board members, homeless, community groups. Technology is also an issue for this group. Several people made a point of saying they could understand the technology if they had training, but it was not provided or not provided on an ongoing or institution-wide basis. The potential oddity in stressors was the final one: workload too small. People who selected this as a significant stressor seemed ashamed of it in their commentary, and several said they made an effort to hide this from their coworkers, but they felt they did not have enough work to do to justify their jobs.

Discussion

Stress in the workplace can come from many different directions, and libraries are not immune to the negative repercussions. As several participants in this study pointed out, the idea that librarians sit around and read books all day, and work in a pleasant and calm environment, is so contrary to the reality of the librarian experience that this misperception itself causes even more stress. But this issue has not been addressed on a profession-wide basis. Identifying stress as a major problem for librarians has not occurred, so there has been no large-scale effort to pinpoint the major causes of stress and figure out ways to address those stressors.

These studies are intended to be a start in that direction. The identification of these two sets of major stressors for public and academic librarians is a starting point in identifying those stressors most frequently affecting the profession. While the list of stressors is likely to be ever-evolving in response to an ever-changing environment, it is worthwhile to keep working toward defining the problem so steps can be taken to give librarians the tools they need to handle these stressors.

Stress Busters

Addressing stress at an individual level is where most articles on stress begin and end. These are the actions the individual librarian has the most control over in his or her work life. But stopping at this level means stress is considered to be an individual problem, or that only some people are affected by stress, or that it is the responsibility of the stressed person to handle the stress alone. While self-directed action is always good, and taking positive steps toward solving problems can be very helpful for people dealing with stress, it is important to remember that workplace stress rarely affects only one person. Focusing on individual problems may be effective in the short term, but it is important to consider the larger picture of stress so effective strategies can be crafted to help librarians.

Individual Stress Busters

Stress busters can be developed to address the specific stressors faced in an individual library or on a profession-wide basis and some general steps can be taken to help manage stress for all individuals. One of the easiest things to do to keep stress levels in check is to take care of your physical health. People who eat nutritious food to keep their bodies well-fueled are going to be healthier than those who eat out of the vending machines or slam down lunch at their desk. Getting 30 minutes of exercise most days, and combining it with some strength exercise two or three days a week, is a basic recommendation from nearly every health source. (See the Centers for Disease Control [2011] recommendations, http://www.cdc.gov/physicalactivity/everyone/guidelines/index.html). Being physically healthy can help burn off stress, and reduce the negative effects stress can have on the body. Take a walk at lunch. Eat some broccoli and blueberries each day. Take a multivitamin. These and other simple activities can make people healthier and better able to deal with stress.

Just getting outside can help to reduce stress levels and improve health, according to Groenewegen, van den Berg, de Vries, and Verheij (2006), who discuss the value of spending time in nature—what they call green space—to help people's physical and mental state. Several other studies show that people who spend time in nature, engaging in gardening, hiking, or even just being in natural environments helps them to be less stressed and more physically healthy. Building a library garden may be a good way to give people the opportunity to work with some natural items, increase the amount of green space in your library and community, and provide staff and community members with another way to share information about health.

Developing outside interests can also help librarians to ease their workplace stress. Having hobbies outside of work allows people to reduce the importance of problems that happen at work. Ideally, activities that are different from workplace activities will be the ones to take people away from work. If you spend a lot of time at work using the computer or writing documents or reading professional material, it may be wise to choose cooking, biking, or crafts as hobbies that would be very different from work and would take away the pressures you face while doing these work activities.

The idea of building a good work/life balance is not a new one—but a lack of balance is still a major problem and cause for stress in individuals. This is such a problem for workers that the Mayo Clinic has put together information designed to help people to regain (or develop) this balance in their lives, considering it to be a significant health issue (http://www.mayoclinic.com/health/work-life-balance/WL00056). Balancing issues inside and outside work can be very difficult, and it is inevitable that work and life will sometimes spill over into each other and cause problems. Making the effort will pay off in dividends of less stress in each sphere of one's life and more productivity in both.

Developing some good conflict management skills can also help to reduce stress on an individual level. As was seen in the research results, many of the stressors librarians feel come from unsatisfying, difficult, or hostile interactions with other people. In a customer service profession like librarianship, negative interactions with patrons are a regular part of the job—but one that no librarian enjoys. Similarly, in a profession where people may be working together for decades, a certain amount of tension between coworkers is to be expected. But unchecked, or not given appropriate means of expression, what could be mild or temporary tension can become serious stress for those involved, as well as for those who are forced to watch or participate on the periphery.

One of the first steps to take in cooling conflicts of any sort is to remove the emotion from the encounter. It is difficult to do at first; emotions are contagious and negative emotions can cause instant hurt, anger, or fear in people to whom they are aimed. Taking a moment to inhale a deep breath, then let it out, will help to prevent a person from snapping back a response that would only escalate the situation. Reminding oneself to remain calm, to rise above the situation, can help to focus in on the real issue at hand— which can help to solve the problem. At the very least, it should help to wrap up the encounter more quickly than a back-and-forth shouting match would.

Another strategy to take is to confront a problem directly. Instead of attempting to cover up a problem, or a hurt and angry reaction to something a coworker has said, address it in the moment. Acknowledge the problem. Point out something said that was wrong, or impolite, or deliberately hurtful. Unfortunately, there are many passive-aggressive people who do not understand the way to confront a problem; these people will mumble under their breath, hint around at a problem, complain to everyone except the person who should be involved, or refuse to talk at all. They may be started into action when confronted directly and professionally; these people may have fallen into the habit of poking at a problem or at other people but never taking the next important step of solving the problem. Helping them to move forward to create a solution can prevent a small issue from becoming a big, stress-filled problem for everyone.

Developing some alternative strategies for dealing with stress at work can also help to reduce the negative effects stress can have. Instead of rushing to complain to a coworker, who complains about something else, feeding a cycle of unhappiness, consider taking a positive action. Deliberately decide to give this situation less importance in your life. Say something positive to the first two people you see. Instead of rushing to the vending machine and gorging on sugary junk food, step outside and take a few deep breaths. Water the garden, pull some weeds. Walk through the children's department and admire the cute kids looking at books. Look at a funny website. Find a favorite book on the shelf and make plans to take it home (a bubble bath and glass of wine are optional additional activities for later at home, entirely at your own discretion). A once-automatic habit of compounding unhappiness with even more unhappiness can be broken, and a step toward reducing your workplace stress can be made.

Library-Wide Stress Busters

It is a fallacy that only one person is affected by stress in a library. Even a stressor affecting someone on an individual level can affect several other people (such as family issues intruding on work time) at the same time. And stressors originating in the library, such as difficult patrons, problems with managers, or uncertain schedules, will affect most or all people in the library. So looking at stress on a library-wide level will not only help to identify stressors affecting librarians and staff, but figuring out ways to solve or work more effectively with those stressors will help make the entire organization better.

To do this on a formal level, the library should first acknowledge stress exists in the organization. This acknowledgment does not seem like it should be complicated, but being sensitive to overcoming defensiveness about potential problems should help everyone to approach the issue in a productive way, not in a blame-seeking, negative way that would not lead to a good resolution for the organization as a whole. Setting up a formal structure will also help to remove the negative emotions or the stigma from the stress problem, and will allow everyone to proceed in a straightforward way. Establishing a committee, or a group of people from every level and department in the library, gives a set of diverse voices about the problem, to ensure nothing is overlooked in the process.

The committee's first order of business is to set up a research structure. This can be a formal process, which may be important in a larger library, or a more casual one. Collecting stressors affecting those in the library is the first order of business. In a library's research work, the needs of just the individual library can be addressed, so the work can be more focused on the problems faced by the people there.

Research can be very elaborate, or a simple survey. The idea here is to focus on getting feedback from everyone in the library on stressors they encounter in the workplace. Look to staff at all levels, to avoid missing out on important stressors. This is often a very sensitive issue, and people can be either embarrassed by the stress they feel or worried that confessing to problems will lead to negative repercussions. To avoid this problem, whatever method is chosen—and a survey would be the easiest—it should be anonymous, to encourage people to be truthful and provide more complete answers than they may otherwise.

The committee can go through the list of stressors collected, and identify a few most frequently mentioned to address. Then the staff can work together to figure out how to reduce or eliminate them. Getting input from different people, inside and outside the library, may help make this process easier. The point is to address problems, not to sweep them under the rug or to pretend everything is fine. Acknowledgment of a problem does not mean the library is a bad place—every workplace has stressors; instead it means there is a willingness to work to fix the problem, not to let it linger and fester.

Lack of relaxation space, away from the public, is often a problem in libraries. Painting the staff room, putting down a rug, or adding some furniture are great ideas. These do not have to cost much money (always in short supply) but help to brighten up break time or time away from the public desks.

Conflict can be a significant problem in libraries; bringing in a specialist to help build some conflict resolutions skills may help people to feel more confident in their ability to solve problems. The local Chamber of Commerce or a Better Business Bureau may have people who could speak to the library at little or no cost, or the college may have people who work with conflict resolution. It can be more troublesome when the problem is poor management, or the perception of unstable or uncertain managers. Abusive managers are even more problematic. If this is a problem in the library, bringing forward the results of the anonymous survey, along with some constructive ideas the committee has devised to help address those concerns, may help. If the manager in the situation is truly difficult, and unresponsive to positive efforts on the part of the staff (not just complaints—that is not helpful), seeking a third party to assist in reaching a resolution can be helpful. A city human resources office or a university arbitrator may be helpful in letting both sides work out the issues and keep the focus on providing quality library service.

An important part of any plan is developing an evaluation system. Your committee should work out a way to ensure the plan is successful, and that you can check on the progress made. Too often good plans and strategies are developed, with much time and energy and passion—but then there is no effort put into making sure the plan is pushed forward. Make an evaluation part of the planning process, and discuss ways to continue to work on a stressor until the problem is solved to the level of the goal stated in the committee's plan. Starting to address a stressor in the library, and then dropping it midway through the process, signals to everyone that their issues are not important and they are not valued. Likewise, it is not necessary to be tied to one single strategy for solving problems if it does not seem to be working. Be flexible in responding to changing circumstances to ensure the problem is worked through as much as possible. Try a new solution if the first one or two or three do not work. Effort counts here; showing interest in staff this way helps motivate them, and should help to retain them longer and at a higher productivity rate.

Profession-Wide Stress Busters
The library profession has not addressed the issue of stress in the library on a wide-scale basis (http://www.ala.org/). It will be important for the American Library Association (ALA) and other state and national organizations to acknowledge stress as a significant problem in the profession. They can establish research programs to look at stress in different kinds of libraries and different levels of staff, to figure out what stressors are causing the problems for people. Training programs can be established to help people and libraries deal with stress, doing continuing education programs at conferences and establishing groups of trainers who can help libraries work through their stress levels.

Incorporating discussions of stress and stress reduction into library school programs can also help start new professionals on the right foot. By asking students to think about stressful situations and ways to resolve them before encountering them in the workplace, this early training can give new librarians an advantage in dealing with the inevitable stressors they will encounter in libraries.

Conclusion

This exploratory study uses Q Method to investigate some causes of stress for academic and public librarians. Because it has a small number of participants who were not selected randomly, these findings cannot be generalized to larger populations, but do suggest some areas for further research as well as help to develop recommendations. Using Q Method is new in the field, and although it has strengths in combining the quantitative and qualitative streams of information, interpretation of the data could be tricky for some users.

These findings indicate that stress is a real problem for many librarians working in public and academic libraries and that it has a variety of causes. Some basic steps can be taken toward helping professionals to acknowledge the problem and to face up to the responsibility of solving it. By not assigning blame for problems, but instead working toward solutions that benefit everyone, libraries can be happier and better places at which to work.

References

Akhtar-Danesh, N., Baumann, A., & Cordingley, L. (2008). Q-methodology in nursing research: A promising method for the study of subjectivity. *Western Journal of Nursing Research, 30*(6), 759–773.

Brillhart, P. E. (2004). Technostress in the workplace Managing stress in the electronic workplace. *Journal of American Academy of Business, 5*(1/2), 302–307.

Brown, S. R. (1980). *Political subjectivity: Applications of Q methodology in political science.* New Haven, CT: Yale University Press.

Caputo, J. S. (1991). *Stress and burnout in library service.* Phoenix, AZ: Oryx Press.

Centers for Disease Control. (2011). *Physical activity for everyone.* Retrieved June 11, 2011, from http://www.cdc.gov/physicalactivity/everyone/guidelines/index.html.

Clougherty, J. E., & Kubzansky, L. D. (2009). A framework for examining social stress and susceptibility to air pollution in respiratory health. *Environmental Health Perspectives, 117*(9), 1351–1358.

Ennis, L. A. (2005). The evolution of techno stress. *Computers in Libraries, 25*(8), 10–12.

Focht, W., & Hull, J. (2004). Framing policy solutions in a conflicted policy environment: An application of Q methodology to a superfund cleanup. *Oklahoma Policy Studies Review, 5*(1), 30–36.

Gendreau, R. (2007). The new techno culture in the workplace and at home. *Journal of American Academy of Business, 11*(2), 191–196.

Groenewegen, P., van den Berg, A., de Vries, S., & Verheij, R. (2006). Vitamin G: Effects of green space on health, well-being, and social safety. *BMC Public Health, 6,* 149. Retrieved June 10, 2011, from http://www.biomedcentral.com/1471-2458/6/149.

Holcomb, J. (2007). Battling burnout. *Law Library Journal, 99*(3), 669–674.

Houtman, I. L., Goudswaard, A., Dhondt, S., van der Grinten, M.P., Hildebrandt, V. H., & van der Poel, E. G. (1998). Dutch monitor on stress and physical load: Risk factors, consequences, and preventative action. *Occupational and Environmental Medicine, 55*(2), 73–83.

Hutson, G., & Montgomery, D. (2006). How do outdoor leaders feel connected to nature places? A Q-method inquiry. *Australian Journal of Outdoor Education, 10*(2), 29–39.

Huwe, T. K. (2005). Building digital libraries: Running to stand still. *Computers in Libraries, 25*(8), 34–36.

Kaehr, R. (2008). What do meatpackers and librarians have in common? Library related injuries and possible solutions. *Teacher Librarian, 36*(2), 39–42.

Kivimaki, M., Elovainio, M., & Vahters, J. (2000). Workplace bullying and sickness absence in hospital staff. *Occupational and Environmental Medicine, 57*(10), 656–660.

Kivimaki, M., Virtanen, M., Vartia, M., Elovainio, M., Vahtera, J., & Keltikangas-Jarvinen, L. (2003). Workplace bullying and the risk of cardiovascular disease and depression. *Occupational and Environmental Medicine, 60*(10), 779–783.

Landsbergis, P. A., & Hatch, M. C. (1996). Psychosocial work stress and pregnancy-induced hypertension. *Epidemiology, 7*(4), 346–351.

Larson, J. H., Wilson, S. W., & Beley, R. (1994). The impact of job insecurity on marital and family relationships. *Family Relations, 43*(2), 138–143.

McKeown, B., & Thomas, D. (1988). *Q Methodology*. Newbury Park, CA: Sage.

Nordstrom, C. K., Dwyer, K. M., Bairey Merz, C. N., Shircore, A., & Dwyer, J. H. (2001). Work-related stress and early atherosclerosis. *Epidemiology, 12*(2), 180–185.

Salaz, A. (2006). My mama told me, or how two generations of library workers avoid burnout. *OLA Quarterly, 12*(3), 6, 8–9.

Schatz, J. (2004). Taking care of business. *Public Libraries, 43*(3), 138, 140.

Sheesley, D. (2001). Burnout and the academic teaching librarian: An examination of the problem and suggested solutions. *The Journal of Academic Librarianship, 27*(6), 447–451.

Spires, T. (2007). The busy librarian: Prioritizing tenure and dealing with stress for academic library professionals. *Illinois Libraries, 86*(4), 101–108.

Stephenson, W. (1953). *The study of behavior: Q-technique and its methodology*. Chicago: University of Chicago Press.

Wang, L., Wang, X., Wang, W, Chen, C., Ronnennberg, A. G., Guang, W., Huang, A., Fang, Z., Zang, T., Wang, L., & Xu, X. (2004). Stress and dysmenorrhoea: A population based prospective study. *Occupational and Environmental Medicine, 61*(2), 1021–1026.

Warren, J. A., & Johnson, P. J. (1995). The impact of workplace support on work-family role strain. *Family Relations, 44*(2), 163–169.

Yucht, A. (2006). Stress management strategies. *CSLA Journal, 30*(1), 35–36.

Assessment—Using Data to Inform the Future

CHAPTER 7

More Questions Than Answers: Using an Observational Study to Count Reference Activity

Susan Beatty and Claudette Cloutier

Overview

In an effort to determine the nature of the questions being asked at the many library service desks across the University of Calgary, in Alberta, Canada, an observational study of reference desk activity was conducted in fall 2008 and winter 2009. An observer recorded the number, type, and duration of the questions answered by a reference service provider at each service desk for four days per term during reference service hours. Based on the data analyzed after each set of observations, the vast majority of the librarian's time spent at the reference desk is spent on reference questions (more than 90 percent) with most reference conversations concluding in under 5 minutes (more than 90 percent). The branch libraries with integrated service desks, offering a combination of reference, technical support, and circulation, spent more time proportionately on non-reference activities. These results will be used to redesign the reference service models at the University of Calgary.

Introduction

Current trends in reference statistics in academic libraries are downward and have been for at least a decade (Kyrillidou, 2008). Librarians and administrators are querying the activity at reference desks and considering alternative service delivery models given this downward trend. In 2008, Libraries and Cultural Resources (LCR) at the University of Calgary, aware of the trend, struck a task group to determine the nature of the activity at the many reference service desks across the university. The task group conducted a reference desk observational study in fall 2008 and winter 2009. The study was conducted partly to inform the current understanding of reference desk activity and partly to inform decision making surrounding the planning for a new library, the Taylor Family

Digital Library, under construction in 2008 and due to open in 2011. The study's results were examined and compared by type of service model.

Some commonalities were uncovered and confirmed among the service units and models and, more interestingly, some differences were also found. This quantitative study does not illuminate the nature of the reference questions. It is not known if the complexity of the questions being asked at the reference desk has changed, or if there is a correlation between expertise and response time. The quality of the interactions was also not examined. Therefore, it is not known if the answers were correct, useful, or complete. This chapter will discuss the results of the survey, and the similarities and differences in the results, and speculate on possible considerations for future planning for academic library desk service.

The University of Calgary

The University of Calgary is a midsized research university with approximately 30,000 students and a full-time faculty of about 1,600. The University Library is a unit within LCR, which is constituted by the main library and four branch libraries (health sciences, business, law, and geoscience), Archives and Special Collections, The Nickle Arts Museum, The Military Museums, and the University Press.

In 2008, there were 13 reference service points in LCR. The desk in the main library, known as the Information Commons Service Desk, provides integrated reference and technical support services. Reference is provided seven days a week during fall and winter terms by librarians and paraprofessional staff, and technical support is provided by a combination of technical experts and student assistants. Reference service at all other points is offered five days a week by a similar mix of librarians and paraprofessionals, plus student assistants. While the staffing models are similar, the service delivery models are somewhat different according to the type of unit.

There were three types of service models in 2008. The Information Commons offered one-stop service where technical staff members provide technical support and reference staff members provide reference service. At the branches, three of the four locations had a reference desk separate from circulation delivery and one branch offered all services from one desk. Finally, the special service units, such as fine arts, visual resources, and special collections and archives, offered mixed services (circulation, reference/technology support, and collection mediation) from a single service desk. Prior to the observational survey, there was an awareness of the variety of staffing and service models throughout the organization, but no comparative data on the nature of service delivery was available.

Literature Review

Reference statistics have long been a measure of the level of activity in an academic library. Many academic libraries collect these statistics and submit them to various national reporting organizations that track the changing landscape. The data collected is intended to show the level of activity of reference services, which in turn is a measure of the significance of the service within the organization. Libraries use a variety of methods for gathering these statistics from sampling reference questions during specific times of the year, to keeping track of daily statistics, to hybrid models (Philips, 2005). The definitions that are used to define types of reference transactions also vary widely (De

Groote, Hitchcock, & McGowan, 2007; Henry & Neville, 2008; Meserve, Belanger, Bowlby, & Rosenblum, 2009; Ryan, 2008; Bracke et al.,2007; Warner, 2001). Most of these studies focus on the quantitative analysis of reference transactions; however, some models focus on qualitative analysis (Kuruppu, 2007; Mosely, 2007; Norlin, 2000).

In the past decade, a downward trend in reference statistics collected by academic libraries has been widely reported (Applegate, 2008; Banks & Pracht, 2008; Budd, 2009; De Groote et al., 2007; Kyrillidou, 2008; Philips, 2005). While there has been a drop in the number of reference questions asked at reference desks, it is suggested that this drop has been offset by a corresponding increase in the depth and difficulty of questions asked (Tenopir, 1998) and an increase in the number of participants in library instruction sessions (Kyrillidou, 2008). In 2008, the library at the University of Calgary needed to develop a better understanding of the types of questions being asked at the reference service desks to inform practice.

Methodology

In early 2008 the Reference Task Group, formed to administer a study about the collection of reference statistics within LCRs, was tasked with identifying a process leading to a better understanding of the nature of the services offered at the various reference service points in the University of Calgary libraries.

The task group focused on identifying the type of study to undertake. There were numerous discussions on how best to assess reference services given limited resources (time and staff) and which data collection methods should be used (Cullen & Gray, 1995; Halperin, 1974, 1978). The goal became to collect some data which would help in determining the nature of future staffing at service desks. Ultimately, the group focused on collecting data on the numbers and types of questions asked at 11 reference service desks and the time of day, duration, and frequency of these interactions. While the quantitative data could not be the sole determinant in planning for future service delivery, a benchmark was needed from which to work.

The group decided on a methodology that appeared deceptively simple. A form for data collection was created that would allow observers to collect data by hour of day and time taken to complete for the types of questions that we identified as being most frequently asked at the reference desk (see Figure 7.1, pp. 128–129).

For the purposes of the study, the following definitions for question types were used, as modified from De Groote and colleagues (2007):

- Directional: Questions regarding the location of services, policies, collections, and materials contained in the building or at the university.
- Reference: Questions that involve the use of one or more resources.
- Technology: Questions that concern the use of hardware (including audiovisual resources) and/or software applications. Examples include printing (troubleshooting, taking money for printing), general computer troubleshooting, use of MS Office products, uploading and transferring of files, audiovisual equipment and materials use, such as setting up users with a film, etc.
- Referral: Questions where the individual answering the question has referred the client to another person or service point. It may also include cases where the

Figure 7.1. Reference Question Sampling Form

Reference Question Sampling Form   Date: _____

(Circle one below.)

Sample Time Period (1 sheet per hour!): _____ AM PM

Please fill in back side of sheet also!

Name of Observer: _____

(Please indicate if self-observing.)

	< 5 min	6–15 min	16–30 min	31–60 min	> 60 min
Directional					
Reference					
Technology					
Referral					
Circulation					
Other					

Question Type Definitions

Directional: Questions regarding the location of services, policies, collections, and materials contained in the building or university.

Reference: Questions that involve the use of one or more resources.

Technology: Questions that concern the use of hardware (including AV resources) and/or software applications. Examples include: printing (troubleshooting, taking money for printing), general computer troubleshooting, use of MS Office Products, FTPing files, AV equipment and materials use (such as setting up users with a film, etc).

Referral: Questions where the individual answering the question has referred the client to another person or service point. It may also include cases where the person answering the initial question has called for a replacement at the desk and has moved off desk to answer the question in depth (moving the question into the realm of consultation).

Circulation: To be used at desks where circulation functions are also performed by staff on the desk.

Other: Questions that do not seem to fit any of the above categories.

Note: Questions may change during the course of a transaction. If the question changes from one category to another, each type of question will be indicated in the appropriate category along with the time spent in each category. For example, if a question is first recorded as a directional question and then becomes a reference question, it would be recorded first as a directional question then as a reference question. A reference question will be recorded as one question as long as the question is centered on one theme (subject/topic). If an additional question is asked that is on an entirely different topic, then this would be recorded as a new transaction.

(Continued)

Figure 7.1. Reference Question Sampling Form *(Continued)*

Reference Question Sampling Form   Date: _____

(Circle one below.)
Sample Time Period (1 sheet per hour!): _____ AM PM

Please fill in back side of sheet also!

Name of Observer: _____
(Please indicate if self-observing.)

Day of the Week	Month	Term	Service Location
☐ Monday ☐ Tuesday ☐ Wednesday ☐ Thursday ☐ Friday ☐ Saturday ☐ Sunday	☐ January ☐ February ☐ March ☐ April ☐ May ☐ June ☐ July ☐ August ☐ September ☐ October ☐ November ☐ December	☐ Summer ☐ Fall ☐ Winter ☐ Spring	☐ Information Commons ☐ IC Navigator ☐ Health Sciences ☐ Business ☐ Gallagher ☐ Law ☐ Nickle Arts Museum ☐ Archives and Special Collections and CAA ☐ Visual Resources Centre ☐ Fine Arts ☐ MADGIC

Notes:

person answering the initial question has called for a replacement at the desk and has moved off the desk to answer the question in-depth (moving the question into the realm of consultation).

- Circulation: To be used at integrated service desks where circulation activities are also performed by staff on the desk who answer reference questions. (This category was added for the winter 2009 observation.)
- Other: Questions that do not seem to fit any of the other categories.

Early on in the investigation it was recognized that the survey could not be generalizable given the variation in activity throughout the organization. While not statistically robust, the authors believed that this quantitative survey could still provide us with a snapshot of our existing situation and level of service (Kuruppu, 2007). A data collection schedule was developed based on the number of days each service point offered reference services (five or seven days per week). Four dates, from 16 representative sample days, during fall (September to December) 2008 and winter (January to April) 2009 terms were preselected for each service unit. The dates were selected to reflect known levels of activity during the beginning of term, reading week, midterm, and at the end of term. The survey would be conducted by a number of observers, each scheduled to observe for two hours at a time, on different days according to the pre-set schedule. Observation was one-on-one; while there may be more than one person on the desk, the observer would focus on the actions of a single person only. There was no attempt to get a complete measure of all activity, as this was deemed too onerous for an observer at a busy desk. The survey was manageable and doable with the available resources.

Once the data collection form and study methodology were finalized, the group set about recruiting volunteers. Individuals were not asked to self-record, as it is clear in the literature that this can lead to inaccuracy (Cullen & Gray, 1995; Warner, 2001). Recruiting volunteers from a limited number of staff to observe the reference service hours at the 11 desks was a challenge. Once volunteers were recruited, information sessions were held for staff and volunteers to enlighten them about the study and the process. It was important to inform staff of the goals of the study and to ensure them that service quality assessment was not one of the goals. It was also important to clarify to observers their ethical responsibilities regarding the study. For example, all observations were to be kept confidential. Observers should not make personal comments or discuss with others the interactions occurring at the desk. While this may seem obvious, it is important to clarify expectations for all, the observed as well as the observers.

Those observed would also include the people who would come to the desk for service, and it was important to ensure that these people were also aware that a survey was taking place. Signs were posted at each service desk with information that a survey was taking place. The purpose of the survey was described and it was emphasized that all information from observation was to be kept confidential. People were also offered the opportunity to refuse to be observed. Contact information was provided and it was also noted that the survey had been approved by the university's ethics board. No one refused to be observed and no one was contacted by participants for further information about the survey.

Although the data collection form was reviewed and tested at one location prior to implementation of the study, many requests were made for clarification on the process, as well as terminology, during the first round of data collection. For example, circulation was not originally included as a question type on the form, but it became apparent that reference staff at some of the reference service desks provided this function. As a result, the data collection form used during the fall observation period was updated for the winter observation period to include this question type.

Interest in volunteering to observe waned during the winter term. In the end, for the winter study it was necessary to ask some of the reference desk staff to self-observe. While maintaining neutrality, accuracy, and reliability became a possible problem in data collection, the study was completed. When fall and winter results were compared it was determined that the two sets were very consistent. The self-observation did not appear to have had a negative effect on data collection. It is possible that this result is so because participation in the study during the fall helped familiarize staff and observers with the parameters of data collection.

Finally, while it was known that the data would need to be tabulated, the authors had not grasped the amount of time that would be needed to both tabulate and chart the data. Fortunately, one of the service units was able to free up a staff member for data tabulation and analysis.

This reference study was the first to involve all of the reference units of LCR. The authors learned that a study of this magnitude has many facets. The study's design was successful in involving as many of the reference staff and service units as possible, in creating a common understanding of terminology, and in gathering data that reflected the unique and common activities throughout the organization. It was learned that pretesting, while integral to the development of the research process, can never be perfect, and that the important thing is to be flexible and manage the process so that the project is completed.

Data Analysis
While each location's data for fall and winter were tabulated separately, branch and special services data were also combined for each term to present an overview of activity by type of service. Each unit received its cumulated data on questions by weekday, by hour, by time of day, type of question by duration, and total questions by duration. Aggregated data for branches and the special services were also compared with data from the Information Commons reference service desk, giving a more complete view of activity across LCR by service type.

Figures 7.2, 7.3, and 7.4 show data from the winter study. The first observation is that the majority of questions (no matter the type or the location) are completed in less than five minutes. While great differences might have been expected between the service types in duration, in fact this was not found to be the case. The confirmation of the vast proportion of interactions being of short duration called into question the need for librarians to be on the desk. The research team wondered if short duration meant less complex questions.

The reference activity and time taken to complete the question was then looked at more closely. It was noted that in the Information Commons 73 percent of the reference

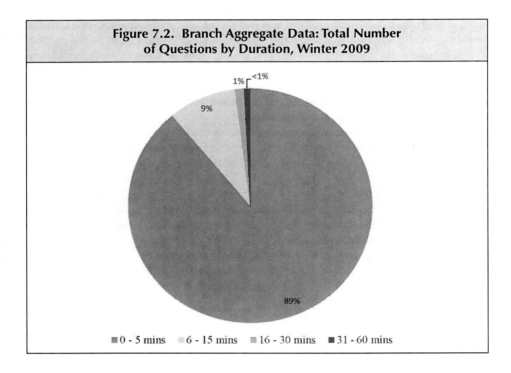

Figure 7.2. Branch Aggregate Data: Total Number of Questions by Duration, Winter 2009

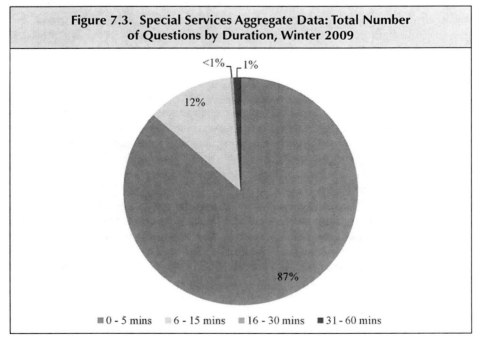

Figure 7.3. Special Services Aggregate Data: Total Number of Questions by Duration, Winter 2009

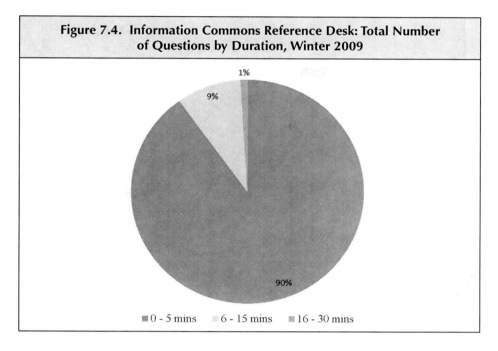

Figure 7.4. Information Commons Reference Desk: Total Number of Questions by Duration, Winter 2009

1%

9%

90%

■ 0 - 5 mins   6 - 15 mins   ■ 16 - 30 mins

questions were completed in less than five minutes, while for the special services, 52 per-cent of the pure reference questions were completed in less than five minutes, and in the branches 67 percent were completed in less than five minutes. Other types of questions were overwhelmingly answered in less than five minutes. Further studies are needed to determine the factors related to amount of time taken to complete. It may be that more complex questions may be received at the special service and branch locations because of their more specialized collections and services. It could also be that with more time available more time is taken to answer questions. That is, the level of activity in a busy location versus a less busy location may determine the length of time of a reference interaction. Or, is the time taken to complete related to staff competency? What does this mean in terms of staffing and resources? These questions and more come to mind as changes in our service models are considered.

The researchers became curious about the patterns of activity that the data revealed. The comparative aggregate data for special services, branches, and the Information Commons showed three different patterns of activity, reflecting three different service models (see Figure 7.5).

When looking at the data for the Information Commons service desk, it appears as if staff time is taken up primarily in answering information-related questions (directional, reference, and referral) while technology support and circulation activity are less frequent. This finding makes sense, as the observation of the technology service staff was separated from that of the reference service staff. As the data were examined, through this separate observation, it was possible to get a view of activity of a "pure" reference service provider over time. This result was an unintended consequence, but in

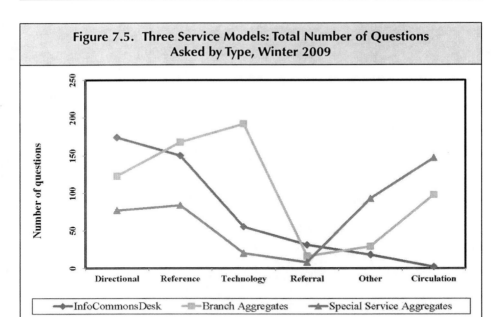

Figure 7.5. Three Service Models: Total Number of Questions Asked by Type, Winter 2009

the end a very important one. The aggregate data from the specialized service desks revealed that the majority of desk activity is spent on circulation and other more unique activities, including the mediation of resources, setup of primary resource, or setup of audiovisual equipment and resources. Information-related activities tend to be less frequent at these service points. Finally, examination of the aggregate data from the library branches indicated that questions regarding other functions that come to the desk, including printing support and circulation, can take time away from the reference function that one would normally expect to see at a special library branch.

If one were to consider that the data reflect the nature of the activities of a single staff member on three different types of service desks, then one can begin to see how adding services results in the competition for staff time. This observation raises many issues for managers surrounding staffing levels, training, staff competencies, and level and quality of service outcomes. There is a movement toward more integration of service at a single service desk in academic libraries (Bracke et al., 2007; Bracke, Chinnaswamy, & Kline, 2008). While this model may make sense from many points of view, it is important for managers and administrators to consider how to meet the competing service demands at an integrated desk, and to develop the appropriate service model and staffing levels. Will a triage model work, with a handoff at point of contact to the technical expert or the media expert or the reference expert, for example? Or will there be an expectation of a wide range of competencies residing within each staff member so that any service request can be met at any time? What are the other alternatives, opportunities, and implications?

The University of Calgary is just beginning to examine these questions. One can see from the three data sets examined that each model has its implications when it comes to the delivery of service. The representation of the nature of activity of these three models was an unexpected result of the survey. It leads to more questions related to the need to determine the quality of service and perhaps more specifically on the nature of the delivery of reference service as affected by service models.

Lessons Learned

This study was an ambitious undertaking. The goal to be inclusive and observe all types of service desks that provide reference was met. Reference was defined in its broadest sense and a wealth of information related to the types of questions and the nature of the activity at the reference desks was discovered. Desks in the main library and branches, special service desks, and primary service desks as well as the desk at The Nickle Arts Museum were observed. Through this study, the reference service staff across LCR was able to observe activities other than their own. It became as much a staff training opportunity as it did a research project, with staff becoming more aware of the broad range of activities within our organization. Prior to the study the definition of reference service varied across LCR, and after the study a common language and understanding surrounding reference activities was obtained. This will help in future planning and assessment.

By conducting the study with available staff it was possible to control costs. Staff time commitment was significant, however, and, as was discovered, commitments waned as time went on and other responsibilities took precedence. The researchers were able to be flexible and revise the study tabulation criteria and methods of data collection as the study went along, with little, if any, detrimental effect to the results. The initial testing could have improved using a larger variety of locations. The tabulation process could have also been improved by testing the tabulation and considering more carefully just what would be done with the data once collected. We were lucky to have someone on staff that could tabulate the data and create an analysis which met the research analysis needs, again with no cost except for staff time.

It is worthwhile to note that a project like this does need many hands. Project leaders and overseers are needed to keep track of the project, answer questions, ensure that everyone is on track, and keep in constant communication with all interested parties. This is no small task, and the amount of time needed can be surprising to those involved.

Where Do We Go from Here?

In the end, some baseline data has been collected about how much time it takes to answer questions and the variety of activities that occur at the reference service desks. The analysis leads to more questions. What were the questions at the desk? What is the difference between a question that takes less than five minutes to complete and one that takes more than five minutes to complete? Is there a correlation between staff competency and time taken to answer a question? If so, what are the competencies librarians should be aiming for as managers? There is much more to uncover.

Planning is currently underway to implement appropriate models for reference service delivery across a multifaceted information organization. Across LCR, reference is moving to more integrated, single-service desks, staffed by a mix of librarians and paraprofessionals. In the new Taylor Family Digital Library (TFDL), which opened in fall

2011, an additional step is being taken. Librarians have been moved off face-to-face desk service at the single-service desk. Using the data and conclusions from the study to inform its recommendations, a reference work group recommended that the new reference model for the single-service desk at TFDL replace librarians on the desk with librarians who are on call to provide reference service. Librarians will be situated near the desk, but not in a public area, and will be available to respond to complex reference questions. New reference service standards for all service points (including branch libraries) within LCR have also been recommended. As new delivery models are launched, it will be necessary to have appropriate tools for acquiring data and for assessing it. New tools and continued assessment will lead to a more interactive and integrated management of resources and service delivery.

Conclusion

The reference desk observation study was a first step to identifying more in-depth questions related to service delivery. Some assumptions and beliefs were confirmed, but the need to continue to investigate the reference service was also confirmed. What is the best service delivery model for reference? Likely there is no one model. However, as the move is made to integrated desk service it is clear that this model offers an excellent opportunity to examine the interrelationships of user needs and service management and delivery.

References

Applegate, R. (2008). Whose decline? Which academic libraries are "deserted" in terms of reference transactions? *Reference & User Services Quarterly, 48*(2), 176–189.

Banks, J., & Pracht, C. (2008). Reference desk staffing trends: A survey. *Reference & User Services Quarterly, 48*(1), 54–59.

Bracke, M. S, Brewer, M., Huff-Eibl, R., Lee, D. R., Mitchell, R., & Ray, M. (2007). Finding information in a new landscape: Developing new service and staffing models for mediated information services. *College & Research Letters, 68*(3), 248–267.

Bracke, M. S., Chinnaswamy, S., & Kline, E. (2008). Evolution of reference: A new service model for science and engineering libraries. *Issues in Science and Technology Librarianship, 53*(Winter). Retrieved on June 18, 2011, from http://www.istl.org/08-winter/refereed3.html.

Budd, J. M. (2009). Academic library data from the United States: An examination of trends. *LIBRES, 19*(2), 1–21.

Cullen, R., & Gray, A. (1995). A method for taking a reliable statistical sample of reference enquiries in a New Zealand public library system. *Journal of Library Administration, 22*(1), 113–123.

De Groote, S. L., Hitchcock, K., & McGowan, R. (2007). Trends in reference usage statistics in an academic health sciences library. *Journal of the Medical Library Association, 95*(1), 23–30.

Halperin, M. (1974). Reference question sampling. *RQ, 14*(1), 20–23.

Halperin, M. (1978). Cluster sampling reference transactions. *RQ, 17*(4), 328–333.

Henry, D. B., & Neville, T. M. (2008). Testing classification systems for reference questions. *Reference & User Services Quarterly, 47*(4), 364–373.

Kuruppu, P. U. (2007). Evaluation of reference services: A review. *The Journal of Academic Librarianship, 33*(3), 368–381.

Kyrillidou, M. (2008). Reshaping ARL statistics to capture the new environment. *ARL: A Bimonthly Report on Research Library Issues and Actions from ARL, CNI, and SPARC, 256,* 9–11.

Meserve, H. C., Belanger, S. E., Bowlby, J., & Rosenblum, L. (2009). Developing a model for reference research statistics—Applying the "Warner Model" of reference question classification to streamline research services. *Reference & User Services Quarterly, 48*(3), 247–258.

Mosely, P. A. (2007). Assessing user interactions at the desk nearest the front door. *Reference & User Services Quarterly, 47*(2), 159–167.

Norlin, E. (2000). Reference evaluation: A three-step approach—surveys, unobtrusive observations, and focus groups. *College & Research Libraries, 61*(6), 546–553.

Philips, S. M. (2005). The search for accuracy in reference desk statistics. *College & Junior College Libraries, 20*(3), 49–60.

Ryan, S. M. (2008). Reference transaction analysis: The cost-effectiveness of staffing a traditional academic reference desk. *The Journal of Academic Librarianship, 34*(5), 389–399.

Tenopir, C. (1998). Reference use statistics. *Library Journal, 123*(8), 32, 34.

Warner, D. G. (2001). A new classification for reference statistics. *Reference & User Services Quarterly, 41*(1), 51–55.

## CHAPTER 8

Researching E-mail Reference Questions: A Review of the Literature and Implications for Practice

Robin E. Veal

Overview

E-mail reference questions offer a unique opportunity to unobtrusively gain a better understanding of user needs. Descriptive statistics and quantitative methodology were initially used to analyze the data provided in the questions. More recently studies have utilized qualitative and mixed methods analysis to gain an understanding of users' needs, beyond statistical measures. Future research using these questions should include the identification of diverse users' needs and the refinement of the web form, the primary interview tool, in an e-mail reference transaction.

Introduction

E-mail reference is just one part of a virtual reference service (VRS), which can also include chat, instant messaging and texting. E-mail reference is the process by which users send in their questions by e-mail, most commonly through a web form in which they are required to input information in predetermined fields. While answering questions through e-mail has both advantages and disadvantages, one of the chief advantages is the record of the transaction with the user. As Schwartz (2003) stated:

> Because e-mail questions can be so easily saved and analyzed we can begin to understand the nature of reference work in ways never before possible. The types of questions we receive can (and should) be used to inform website design, OPAC interfaces, and the creation of new and innovative services that truly meet our users' needs. (p. 14)

E-mail Reference Question Studies

The e-mail reference question is just one part of the e-mail reference transaction. This transaction consists of the question sent by the user via e-mail, the librarian's response, and any acknowledgment of the response or additional information requested by the user. For the most part this literature review focus on studies of e-mail reference questions, not the librarian's response to the question. The studies in this review utilize quantitative, qualitative, or mixed method methodology in order to answer a research question(s) considered important by these scholars.

Many articles in peer-reviewed publications have focused on e-mail reference questions; however, they did not utilize a specific research methodology and thus are not the focus of this review. For example, earlier articles written on e-mail reference (Howard & Jankowski, 1986; Schilling-Eccles & Harzbecker, 1998) describe how an e-mail reference service was implemented. Articles by Bushallow-Wilbur and DeVinney (1996), Stoffel and Tucker (2004), Vandecreek (2006), Gilbert, Mengxiong, Matoush, and Whitlatch (2006), and Lee (2008) described initiatives that include user surveys to assess user satisfaction with e-mail reference services. An article by Croft and Eichenlaub (2006) described and defined a set of best practices for librarians who participate in e-mail reference. In addition, several articles (Abels & Liebscher, 1994; Abels, 1996; Hahn, 1998; Janes, Hill, & Rolfe, 2001; Nilsen & Ross, 2006; Portree, Evans, Adams, & Doherty, 2008; Shachaf & Horowitz, 2006; Stacy-Bates, 2003) discuss the e-mail reference interview (or lack of interview), in addition to methods to evaluate librarian responses to questions to assess the quality of their e-mail reference services. These studies are not considered to be within the focus of this review.

Quantitative Studies

E-mail reference provides a rich source for analyzing the reference transaction. Many studies have analyzed e-mail reference transactions. Many early studies (Fennewald, 2006; Lederer, 2001; Markgren, Ascher, Crow, & Lougee-Heimer, 2004; Moeller, 2003; Powell & Bradigan, 2001; Sullivan, 2004) used mostly descriptive statistics to get a categorical overview of the type of questions and individuals who were utilizing the e-mail reference service. These studies categorized characteristics of the population, such as student or business person, age, grade level, etc., of those who used the e-mail service. They also classified questions in broad predetermined categories. Some examples of these categories are questions about holdings, verification of citations, database searching advice, and in-depth versus quick-response questions.

One of the first large-scale e-mail reference studies was designed by Carter and Janes (2000); it analyzed 3,022 questions submitted to the Internet Public Library (IPL) during the period January to March of 1999. The source of the question, subjects assigned by the user, and how people identified themselves were presented as a total and percentage of the questions analyzed. The questions asked were classified by fact versus source questions, subject assigned by the staff person answering the question, the procedure by which the question was answered, how long it took to answer, how many questions solicited a "thank-you" message, and how many messages were rejected. Shachaf and Snyder (2007) used quantitative content analysis to quantify the number of messages sent by African American and Caucasian students to the Library's reference service. They found African American students sent more messages than Caucasian students and asked more known-item, topical, and technical questions. In addition, they also reported the writing style used in the e-mail by the two groups. They analyzed the words used in greetings, apologies, and purpose of information need and other criteria and found that writing styles of the two groups did not differ significantly.

Qualitative Studies

Several studies used qualitative content analysis to analyze the themes and patterns in the questions being asked by users (Duff & Johnson, 2001; Jones, Kayongo, & Scofield, 2009; Shachaf, Meho, & Hara, 2007; Westbrook, 2009). Duff and Johnson (2001) applied Denis Grogan's (1992) schema to categorize questions sent to archives. In addition, they used Jahoda and Braunagel's (1980) taxonomy of reference questions to establish what was the user's "want" and what type of information the user "gave" in relation to the information needed. A goal of the study was to determine how individuals describe their information needs in order to make it possible to design better web interfaces. Jones and colleagues (2009) reviewed transcripts of more than 3,000 e-mail reference questions and chat sessions to construct a searchable list of frequently asked questions (FAQs) for their library's webpage. They used a combination of several coding structures developed in the literature for initial coding, but also looked for additional codes to emerge as they analyzed the questions. Shachaf and colleagues (2007) conducted a comparative analysis of e-mail questions from three different countries (Israel, Japan, and Lebanon) to analyze the unique needs of both users and the different work styles of the librarians who answered the questions. Westbrook (2009) used qualitative content analysis, specifically emergent coding, to find trends in e-mail questions the Internet Public Library staff considered "out of scope." The top three expectations and reasons why users needed this information were determined from this analysis.

Mixed Method Studies

Two studies (Mon & Janes, 2007; Schwartz, 2003) were found that utilized mixed methods. Schwartz (2003) categorized questions asked by users by analyzing the phrasing and keywords used in the questions. Based on her analysis of the questions, six categories emerged: statements that were not questions, requests for strictly factual information, a request to provide a specific item, requests for instructions to complete a task, requests for advice on the research process, and requests stating a specific need. She suggests that this type of content analysis, where categories are drawn from the data, as opposed to questions being classified according to a predetermined schema, can better help determine what users really need from libraries. Mon and Janes (2007), in addition to analyzing e-mail reference transactions for a variety of quantitative measures such as speed of answer and response length, also utilized qualitative coding for users' comments and assessments to analyze their e-mail reference experience.

Analysis of Studies of E-mail Reference Questions

A review of the e-mail reference question studies shows that most of the early research in this area has utilized demographic information, descriptive statistics, and some quantitative analysis. Studies by Lederer (2001), Moeller (2003), Schwartz (2003), Sullivan (2004), and Fennewald (2006) all used descriptive data to describe service users, what general categories of questions are being asked, and how long it takes to answer questions. While this type of information is helpful, it only scratches the surface of the rich amount of data that is recorded in an e-mail reference transaction. Using more in-depth quantitative analysis, Carter and Janes (2000) found form design not only affected services levels, but was also an important consideration in the analysis of data. Powell and Bradigan (2001) and Sullivan (2004) explored service inequities for e-mail versus in-person or phone reference.

Duff and Johnson (2001) conducted one of the first qualitative analyses of the language in e-mail reference questions to identify user needs. More recent studies (Mon & Janes, 2007; Westbrook, 2009) have used qualitative content analysis to gain a greater understanding of the perceptions their users have of their service to make policy and service recommendations. Shachaf and colleagues (2007) and Shachaf and Snyder (2007) have analyzed e-mail questions for various cultural variables; to identify and help librarians meet the needs of diverse user groups. Jones and colleagues (2009) used a systemic content analysis of e-mail reference questions in the creation of a searchable FAQ service. The recent use of qualitative and mixed method research in the analysis of e-mail reference questions has allowed researchers to more fully tap this rich source of data. While mixed method analyses allows librarians to unobtrusively gain a better understanding of users' needs and perceptions of the library's services, there are limitations. Conducting this type of analysis, usually qualitative in nature, on large amounts of data can be extremely time-intensive, which can pose a dilemma in challenging researchers to find a balance between an efficient but still rich method of analysis.

Table 8.1 summarizes the types of e-mail reference studies, the type of library setting, methodology used, major findings, and implications for library services.

Research Agenda for the Future

Although there is a sizable body of research on the e-mail reference question, an overview of the studies presented in this review reveals that gaps do exist in the literature. More research needs to be conducted into issues of the "unknowns" in e-mail reference. For example, issues such as identifying user needs based on culture or other factors, and assessing whether the response to the question satisfied the user's information need have not been fully studied. Almost all of the articles in this review mention or discuss the lack of a reference interview when answering an e-mail reference question. Therefore, the substitution for the interview, which usually consists of the form the user fills out, also needs more research. In *Introduction to Reference Work in the Digital Age*, Janes (2003) states:

> In an e-mail or Web-form environment, the interview is almost entirely compartmentalized, and thus the pressure is really on getting a solid understanding of the nature of the need from the first encounter, especially given the frequency with which people don't respond to follow-up questions and the necessary time lag involved in getting those responses. (p. 148)

A well-designed web form would seem to be the bridge between efficiency and effectiveness in the e-mail reference interview (Ross, Nilsen, & Radford, 2009). In addition, it could capture key information needed to measure the service's effectiveness. Using various methods to conduct an analysis of e-mail reference questions in order to continuously improve the form, the key interview and service analysis tool should be a priority on the e-mail reference research agenda.

Conclusion

E-mail reference is relatively new, in comparison to traditional reference; therefore the research in this field is still developing. While descriptions of e-mail reference services may be interesting and helpful, applying a specific research methodology to a study gives the findings a level of credibility that sole description does not. Therefore, the key findings of these studies, as presented in Table 8.1, could be used as a more substantial argument for making changes to an e-mail reference service. Some of these key findings are recommendations that librarians need to do the following (*continued p. 146*):

Table 8.1. Summary of Research on E-mail Reference Questions and Implications for Practice

Author	Setting	Methodology	Major Findings	Implications for Library Services
Carter, D & Janes, J. (2000)	Public Library (PL) Online (ONL)	Quantitative (QUAN)	• Users had trouble assigning a subject category to question and what type of resource (a source or fact) was needed to answer the question. • Questions took on average two days to answer and one in five questions received a thank-you reply message.	• E-mail forms should be carefully designed to avoid delays in answering because of wrong categories supplied by the user. • Form design should reflect what is needed for future analysis of data.
Duff & Johnson (2001)	Archive – Land-Based (LB)	Qualitative (QUAL)	• Modified Denis Grogan's schema for categorizing questions based on themes discovered in the data. • Categorized and identified patterns in the words that were used to describe what information was needed.	• Identifying the language used in an e-mail reference question can help libraries develop services based on user's expressed need, instead of perceived needs.
Lederer (2001)	University (UNIV) – LB	QUAN	• Most e-mail questions were sent when in person or phone help was available. • A number of non-affiliates used the service. • Many in-depth questions asked despite warnings that the service does not answer in-depth questions.	• Examining patterns in e-mail reference questions such as number, type of question, who is sending the questions, can help libraries discover unexpected uses of e-mail reference services.
Powell & Bradigan (2001)	UNIV – LB	QUAN	• Found inequities in service, such as librarians spending more time and resources for questions originated through e-mail.	• Libraries need to have consistent polices regarding amount of time and resources provided regardless of how a reference question originates.

(Continued)

Table 8.1. Summary of Research on E-mail Reference Questions and Implications for Practice *(Continued)*

Author	Setting	Methodology	Major Findings	Implications for Library Services
Moeller (2003)	UNIV – LB	QUAN	• More questions were submitted by non-affiliates than affiliates of the university. • More in-depth questions were submitted by non-affiliates. • Librarians provided a response (complete or partial) to questions 73 percent of the time. • The question types were similar to what was asked at physical reference desk.	• E-mail reference can be used by non-affiliated users to either get their questions answered, or get an appropriate referral.
Schwartz (2003)	UNIV – LB	Mixed (MIX)	• More than half of users were graduate students or faculty. • Half of questions received were reference questions. • Question phrasing categories reflected the user populations asking the question.	• Graduate students and faculty could benefit from having their questions referred to a subject specialist. • Subject specialists could gain information regarding collection and instructional needs by having questions referred to them.
Markgren, Ascher, Crow, & Lougee-Heimer (2004)	UNIV – LB	QUAN	• Found 64 percent of e-mail questions sent when in-person reference desk was staffed. • In one library desk and telephone questions were declining while e-mail questions increased. • Many in-depth research questions were submitted by nonaffiliated users.	• Shows a need to provide multiple access points and equal levels of service to users who prefer different methods of communication.
				(Continued)

Table 8.1. Summary of Research on E-mail Reference Questions and Implications for Practice *(Continued)*

Author	Setting	Methodology	Major Findings	Implications for Library Services
Sullivan (2004)	PL – LB	QUAN	• Half of questions were research questions vs. ready reference. • The proportion of student questions were small, but took the longest to answer compared to all of the other categories.	• Should public librarians limit the amount of time spent on answering research questions? • What information or level of participation should be required by the user when asking research questions?
Fennewald (2006)	UNIV – LB	QUAN	• Categories used to classify questions at physical reference desk can be applied to questions answered online.	• The ability to use the same standard categories for in-person and online questions allows for standardization in reporting and analysis of data to improve library services.
Mon & Janes (2007)	PL – ONL	MIX	• Users most often cited helpfulness and usefulness of answer in their thank-you response. • Librarian responses that used more words and were not standard FAQ responses received more thank-you e-mails from users.	• An analysis of e-mail thank-you messages by users can indicate what factors users value in an e-mail reference service.
Shachaf, Meho, & Hara (2007)	UNIV – LB	QUAL	• Different user needs and perceptions of the library and librarians in questions from three different countries. • The librarian responses from the three different countries varied based on their professional culture.	• The need to consider many different cultural variables when designing global collaborative virtual reference services.

(Continued)

Table 8.1. Summary of Research on E-mail Reference Questions and Implications for Practice *(Continued)*

Author	Setting	Methodology	Major Findings	Implications for Library Services
Shachaf & Snyder (2007)	UNIV – ONL	QUAN	• African American students sent more messages than Caucasian students. • Significant differences in the type of requests between the two groups. • The writing styles of the two groups were found to be similar.	• Examining the differences and similarities of user groups will help librarians address the needs of diverse groups, in order to help them to be academically successful.
Jones, Kayongo, & Scofield (2009)	UNIV – LB	QUAL	• Coding of the content of e-mails and chat transcripts can be used to create a searchable Frequently Asked Questions (FAQ) service.	• A searchable FAQ of questions derived from questions submitted by users can be an important point-of-need tool for future users.
Westbrook (2009)	PL – ONL	QUAL	• 1,184 sent to the Internet Public Library that were considered "out of scope" by librarians because they asked to find a fact or opinion, or asked for multiple pieces of information. • Users needed requested information in order to understand or learn, and often wanted to contact a person directly or indirectly in order to gain clarity.	• This type of analysis can help librarians develop reference service training and policies from the perspective of the users.

• Analyze "out of scope" e-mail reference questions to better educate users of use guidelines, and to possibly create new services (Carter & Janes, 2000; Westbrook, 2009).
• Analyze the e-mail responses of users, to the librarian's answer of an e-mail reference question, to see if it indicates their need was met (Carter & Janes, 2000; Mon & Janes, 2007).
• Decide how to respond to the needs of unaffiliated users, especially those that send in-depth research questions that require more time to answer (Markgren et al., 2004; Moeller, 2003).

- Acknowledge and respond to the possible different needs of users by culture and race (Shachaf et al., 2007; Shachaf & Snyder, 2007).
- Monitor and perhaps limit the amount of time spent by librarians on e-mail questions (Powell & Bradigan, 2001; Sullivan, 2004).
- Determine the usefulness of e-mail reference to provide answers to in-depth research questions (Sullivan, 2004; Schwartz, 2003).

Classifying e-mail reference questions in categories, and determining who is asking questions and when they are asking can yield valuable information. However, studies that analyze these e-mail questions to better understand the information need from the user's perspective are potentially far more valuable (Duff & Johnson, 2001; Jones et al., 2009; Schwartz, 2003; Shachaf et al., 2007). Determining themes and patterns in e-mail reference service delivery provides opportunities for a better understanding of this mode of reference including appropriate level of instruction, clearer communication, and more effective responsiveness to user needs to ensure that librarians provide the best level of service for the future. Although librarians are delivering new modes of VR, e-mail has now become a traditional service that appears to be firmly established and continues to be vibrant.

References

Abels, E. G. (1996). The e-mail reference interview. *RQ, 35*(3), 345–358. Retrieved June 17, 2011, from http://www.rusq.org/.

Abels, E. G., & Liebscher, P. (1994). A new challenge for intermediary-client communication: The electronic network. *Reference Librarian, 41/42*, 185–196. Retrieved June 17, 2011, from http://www.tandf.co.uk/journals/titles/02763877.asp.

Bushallow-Wilbur, L., & DeVinney, G. (1996). Electronic mail reference service: A study. *RQ, 35*(3), 359–372. Retrieved June 17, 2011, from http://www.rusq.org.

Carter, D. S., & Janes, J. (2000). Unobtrusive data analysis of digital reference questions and service at the Internet public library: An exploratory study. *Library Trends, 49*(2), 251–266. Retrieved June 17, 2011, from http://www.press.jhu.edu/journals/library_trends/index.html.

Croft, R., & Eichenlaub, N. (2006). E-mail reference in a distributed learning environment: Best practices, user satisfaction, and the reference services continuum. *Journal of Library Administration, 45*(1/2), 117–147.

Duff, W. M., & Johnson, C. A. (2001). A virtual expression of need: An analysis of e-mail reference questions. *American Archivist, 64*(1), 43–60.

Fennewald, J. (2006). Same questions, different venue: An analysis of in-person and online questions. *Reference Librarian, 46*(95/96), 21–35.

Gilbert, L. M., Mengxiong, L., Matoush, T., & Whitlatch, J. B. (2006). Assessing digital reference and online instructional services in an integrated public/university library. *Reference Librarian, 46*(95/96), 149–172.

Grogan, D. (1992). *Practical reference work* (2nd ed.). London: Library Association Publishing.

Hahn, K. (1998). Qualitative investigation of an e-mail mediated help service. *Internet Research: Electronic Networking Applications and Policy, 8*(2), 123–135.

Howard, E. H., & Jankowski, T. A. (1986). Reference services via electronic mail. *Bulletin of the Medical Library Association, 74*(1), 41–44.

Jahoda, G., & Braunagel, J. S. (1980). *The librarian and reference queries: A systematic approach.* New York: Academic Press.

Janes, J. (2003). *Introduction to reference work in the digital age.* New York: Neal-Schuman.

Janes, J., Hill, C., & Rolfe, A. (2001). Ask-an-expert services analysis. *Journal of the American Society for Information Science & Technology, 52*(13), 1106–1121.

Jones, S., Kayongo, J., & Scofield, J. (2009). Ask us anytime: Creating a searchable FAQ using email and chat reference transcripts. *Internet Reference Services Quarterly, 14*(3), 67–81. doi:10.1080/10875300903256555.

Lederer, N. (2001). E-mail reference: Who, when where, and what is asked. *Reference Librarian, 35*(74), 55–73.

Lee, L. S. (2008). Reference services for students studying by distance: A comparative study of the attitudes distance students have towards phone, email and chat reference services. *New Zealand Library & Information Management Journal, 51*(1), 6–21.

Markgren, S., Ascher, M. T., Crow, S. J., & Lougee-Heimer, H. (2004). Asked and answered—online: How two medical libraries are using OCLC's QuestionPoint to answer reference questions. *Medical Reference Services Quarterly, 23*(1), 13–28.

Moeller, S. E. (2003). Ask-a-librarian: An analysis of an e-mail reference service at a large academic library. *Internet Reference Services Quarterly, 8*(3), 47–61.

Mon, L., & Janes, J. W. (2007). The thank you study. *Reference & User Services Quarterly, 46*(4), 53–59.

Nilsen, K., & Ross, C. S. (2006). Evaluating virtual reference from the users' perspective. *Reference Librarian, 46*(95/96), 53–79.

Portree, M., Evans, R. S., Adams, T. M., & Doherty, J. J. (2008). Overcoming transactional distance: Instructional intent in an e-mail reference service. *Reference & User Services Quarterly, 48*(2), 142–152.

Powell, C. A., & Bradigan, P. S. (2001). E-mail reference services: Characteristics and effects on overall reference services at an academic health sciences library. *Reference & User Services Quarterly, 41*(2), 170–178.

Ross, C. S., Nilsen, K., & Radford, M. L. (2009). *Conducting the reference interview* (2nd ed.). New York: Neal-Schuman.

Schilling-Eccles, K., & Harzbecker, J. J. (1998). The use of electronic mail at the reference desk: Impact of a computer-mediated communication technology on librarian-client interactions. *Medical Reference Services Quarterly, 17*(4), 17–27.

Schwartz, J. (2003). Toward a typology of e-mail reference questions. *Internet Reference Services Quarterly, 8*(3), 1–15. doi:10.1300/J136v08n03_01.

Shachaf, P., & Horowitz, S. (2006). Are virtual reference services color blind? *Library & Information Science Research, 28*(4), 501–520. doi:10.1016/j.lisr.2006.08.009.

Shachaf, P., Meho, L. I., & Hara, N. (2007). Cross-cultural analysis of e-mail reference. *Journal of Academic Librarianship, 33*(2), 243–253. doi:10.1016/jacalib.2006.08.010.

Shachaf, P., & Snyder, M. (2007). The relationship between cultural diversity and user needs in virtual reference services. *Journal of Academic Librarianship, 33*(3), 361–367.

Stacy-Bates, K. (2003). E-mail reference responses from academic ARL libraries. *Reference & User Services Quarterly, 43*(1), 59–70.

Stoffel, B., & Tucker, T. (2004). E-mail and chat reference: Assessing patron satisfaction. *Reference Services Review, 32*(2), 120–140. doi:10.1108/00907320410537649.

Sullivan, D. (2004). Characteristics of e-mail reference services in selected public libraries, Victoria, Australia. *Reference Librarian, 41*(85), 51–80.

Vandecreek, L. M. (2006). E-mail reference evaluation: Using the results of a satisfaction survey. *Reference Librarian, 45*(93), 99–108.

Westbrook, L. (2009). Unanswerable questions at the IPL: User expectations of e-mail reference. *Journal of Documentation, 65*(3), 367–395.

PART III

REFERENCE IN ACTION—
INNOVATIVE INITIATIVES
FORGING THE FUTURE

Implementing Intriguing Initiatives and Extending Outreach

## CHAPTER 9

Rolling Out Roving Reference in an Academic Library

Sara Davidson

Overview

This case study examines a roving reference model at the University of California, Merced Library, which employs undergraduate library student assistants. Library staff initiated the service with student employees in fall 2009 in response to conflicting data regarding the reference needs of library users. Based on the data collected, the majority of questions took less than five minutes to answer and questions related to printing and finding known items were asked most often. One of the greatest challenges has been how to effectively market the service in order to raise the number and complexity of questions. In the accompanying literature review, it is apparent that library staff members tend to be comfortable with traditional reference models while roving reference calls for flexibility and new ways in which to engage with users. Though there are many possibilities for roving reference models, libraries with wireless capabilities and non-quiet study areas may be most interested in initiating a roving reference service.

Introduction

Libraries are characterized by rich resources and services. At academic libraries, resources include collections of books, journals, and databases targeted at curricular needs, while services regularly consist of research instruction classes and one-on-one assistance, the latter often provided at a reference desk. While the University of California, Merced Library has a robust and relevant collection and shares effective search strategies with users through classes and in-person consultations, it does not offer a traditional reference desk. When the library opened in fall 2005, the leadership deliberately chose not to staff a reference desk with librarians even though this service has long been considered a staple of academic libraries. The library service points are staffed primarily with undergraduate student assistants and occasionally with permanent career staff. Librarians provide reference assistance through other means such as 24/7 chat, scheduled research consultations, e-mail, and drop-in meetings. Our reference model relies heavily on electronic forms of contact and also on our student assistants who connect with and refer students, faculty, and staff to librarians for more in-depth research assistance. There have been moments when we have wondered if we were doing the right thing, especially as information needs increase due to significant student population growth each year. Though our inaugural class consisted of approximately 800 students, in its sixth year our campus enrolled almost 4,200 students. This rate of student growth far exceeds the growth in numbers of permanent library staff. During this time of change, the library staff implemented a roving reference service with selected library student assistants trained to answer reference questions as a method to both gauge and meet reference needs.

Literature Review

Why Roving Reference?
Roving reference involves moving beyond the reference desk to the library's floor to ask users if they need assistance. It is not a new concept, with numerous libraries, both public and academic, having implemented variations on the roving reference theme for years. The reasons for initiating a roving reference service emerge out of librarians' strong customer-service values and their understanding of users. As strong customer-service advocates, librarians wish to meet users at their point of need. Roving reference is viewed as a proactive service in which library staff "take the transaction to the patron" (Burek Pierce, 2006, p. 39) since users may be unaware of service points or may be unlikely to approach staff at a reference desk. This service can foster a friendly, approachable atmosphere in which users receive assistance in a nonthreatening manner; it can be extremely helpful for users who experience library anxiety, a phrase first coined by Constance Mellon (1986, p. 163). Users experiencing library anxiety are often characterized by a "reluctance to ask librarians for help" (Carlile, 2007, p. 136). In addition, some users may not even be aware of the extent of their information needs and available resources. Many students entering academic libraries are often inexperienced and underprepared and can be easily overwhelmed by resources (Smith & Pietraszewski, 2004, p. 249). Roving reference can be effective in reaching timid and/or inexperienced users.

Influence of Technology and Electronic Information
While efforts to improve customer service and meet user needs are influential in initiating roving reference, libraries have specifically implemented this service due to the growth of electronic resources and the increase in available technology such as wireless routers and mobile computing devices. Courtois and Liriano (2000) found that roving reference started in the late 1980s when Online Public Access Catalog (OPAC) terminals and CD-ROM stations were installed and librarians anticipated that users would need assistance in using these tools and resources (p. 289). Many of these stations were installed in reference areas, though some were located at the ends of stacks in close proximity to book collections. Bregman and Mento (1992) affirmed this observation by referring to the "explosion of electronic resources" (p. 634) as the impetus to begin a roving service

at the O'Neill Library at Boston College in fall 1989. Their goal was to assist users in "differentiating between the various electronic information systems and learning the skills of searching each one" (p. 634). Similarly, during Kramer's (1996) roving reference pilot activity at the Frank E. Gannett Memorial Library at Utica College, she targeted the OPAC and CD-ROM areas as places where users would likely require assistance.

Following the years of OPAC terminals and CD-ROM stations, more libraries obtained the infrastructure to provide widespread wireless computing. The increased availability of wireless capabilities with its possibilities to "boost public service" (Huwe, 2003, p. 35) encouraged libraries to explore roving reference models, especially those reaching further than the reference section of the library (Courtois & Liriano, 2000, p. 289) since library staff could by that time roam with the resources which were previously available only at a desktop computer or a CD-ROM station. Librarians at West Campus Library, part of Texas A&M University Libraries, required a wireless network before implementing a roving reference pilot designed to explore reference needs that may have gone unasked in the upper floor of their library building. In addition, they wanted to experiment with new technology (Smith & Pietraszewski, 2004, p. 251). When librarians started the service, they used a tablet PC with a wireless network interface card (p. 251) and were able to use software to record transactions (p. 253). The Westerville (Ohio) Public Library initially equipped their rovers with a wireless headset and tablet PC, then looked to upgrade to devices which would bring together "search, phone, and text-message functions" (Burek Pierce, 2006, p. 39). Forsyth (2009) examined the use of Vocera voice badges in a number of public library systems. These devices run on a wireless network (p. 74) and have been used for both internal staff communication and roving reference services. Staff in both the Seattle Public Library (pp. 78–79) and Orange County Library System (OCLS) in Florida used the badges while roving (pp. 80–81).

Models and Staffing Challenges

The technology hurdles have diminished as wireless networks have increased and as mobile technologies proliferate. Some of the bigger challenges have involved determining a workable model. Variances in the models of roving reference have included differences in the length of shifts, what portion of the shift includes roving, and if staff perform any other activities while roving. Libraries have had to decide if roving reference will be considered a separate activity from a regular reference desk shift (Lorenzen, 1997, pp. 53–54). King County Library System (KCLS) in Washington initially tried having library staff cover the information desk and rove during a one-hour shift but decided that this did not work well (Pitney & Slote, 2007, p. 56). In addition to staffing considerations, Lorenzen (1997, p. 54) and Forsyth (2009, p. 74) wrote that a roving reference service would likely influence changes to physical space, including the reference desk area, either before or after implementation. KCLS made infrastructure changes to support roving reference, including a redesign of the reference desk (Pitney & Slote, 2007, p. 60).

Other changes could occur at the reference desk beyond physical changes. Bregman and Mento (1992) called out roving reference as a method to minimize librarian stress since answering questions where the electronic resources were located allowed library staff to offer "immediate assistance and instruction" (p. 635), and rovers served as an additional resource to which reference desk staff could make referrals (p. 636). Since a roving reference service usually requires more staffing, successful implementation may involve decreasing other activities in which library staff have been involved. For this reason implementing a roving reference service requires a careful evaluation of available resources and priorities. Pitney and Slote (2007) wrote that roving reference meant more face time with users and that workloads had to be reexamined to ensure they were manageable (p. 55). Susan Studebaker, of Columbus Metropolitan Library (CML), made a similar observation, remarking that the transition to roving reference meant more staff were needed in the stacks and, therefore, CML decided to eliminate "behind-the-scenes work that had less impact on the public" (as cited in Burek Pierce, 2006, p. 39). Fritch and Mandernack (2001) confirmed this observation, noting that implementing a roving reference service involves additional staff time. Their observation is based on offering roving services in addition to traditional reference desk services (p. 302).

Though libraries have strong advocates of roving reference, implementation examples highlight that some staff may not embrace the roving reference model. Don Barlow of Westerville Public Library revealed that while the majority of staff enjoyed providing roving reference, others were unable to abandon traditional library service and therefore left (Burek Pierce, 2006, p. 39). Not all librarians at West Campus Library at Texas A&M wanted to participate in a roving reference pilot. For example, the act of walking and carrying a tablet PC was not appealing to some (Smith & Pietraszewski, 2004, p. 254). Courtois and Liriano (2000) referred to "librarians who are unwilling to rove" (p. 289) as an ongoing challenge to roving reference services.

Types of Questions
Some staff may not embrace a roving reference model since it requires a proactive approach, which has the potential to be uncomfortable. In addition, the questions may not reach the bar of true reference questions. However, this has also been a chronic complaint at traditional reference desks. The top three categories of questions answered by roving reference staff at KCLS included ready reference, in-depth reference, and machine assistance. In addition, staff addressed security or behavior issues (Pitney & Slote, 2007, pp. 55–56). Kramer (1996) noted that she had many questions that would be considered appropriate for a professional. The most common questions she received involved helping students choose a new source, refine search strategies, and choose new subject headings (p. 74). However, her fourth most common question did involve assisting users with printing inquiries. The disparities in the types of questions referred to by Pitney and Slote (2007) versus those received by Kramer are most likely accounted for by the differences in library users and spaces where library staff roved. However, Kramer's questions still fell under the larger categories of ready reference, in-depth reference, and even machine assistance as reported at KCLS.

Training to Engage
The roving reference transaction is noticeably different from the reference desk transaction since the library staff member, rather than the user, is usually the conversation initiator. Even when library staff members are skilled at providing reference service at a reference desk, they will require additional training for this new role. Pitney and Slote (2007) explained this roving reference transaction as a "personal commitment by staff to

extend themselves to patrons throughout the library" (p. 59), which may be a new or unfamiliar skill to some and, therefore, an unanticipated challenge. Smith and Pietraszewski (2004) reflected on this issue: "the roving strategy [at West Campus Library, Texas A&M] underestimated the need to consider the interpersonal dynamics of the roving reference interaction" (p. 253). Pitney and Slote (2007) articulated that common sense works to a certain extent (p. 57), but additional training for this role is valuable. Additional training should include instruction in nonverbal communication and how to start conversations with open-ended questions (Burek Pierce, 2006, p. 39). The phrasing of questions can be important and should focus on assistance rather than possibly putting individuals on the defensive by insinuating that they need help (Lorenzen, 1997, p. 54). An example of a suitable question would be, "'Are you finding what you need?'" (Courtois & Liriano, 2000, p. 290). The challenge is to be approachable and proactive and yet, at the same time, aware of boundaries and appropriateness. Some of the loudest complaints regarding roving reference are related to privacy concerns. Reynolds (2005) wrote that these are most obvious in academic libraries and warned against watching computer monitors (p. 62). Courtois and Liriano (2000) offered good advice by instructing rovers to "[a]ddress the user before addressing their screen" (p. 290).

Varied Findings

In spite of these concerns and challenges, roving reference models do have benefits. At a time when reference desk numbers indicate that fewer individuals are visiting reference desks (Smith & Pietraszewski, 2004, p. 249), roving reference services provide opportunities to reach users at their point of need with individualized attention (Lorenzen, 1997, p. 55; Smith & Pietraszewski, 2004, p. 250). Library staff members have had different experiences with roving reference services. Kramer (1996) discovered that the students she helped through roving reference normally avoided the information desk and reference area (p. 71), so she was able to reach a broader user group. She found significant differences between the types of questions asked while roving versus those asked at the service points (p. 74) and, therefore, saw real value and service in her roving reference role. Smith and Pietraszewski (2004) reported on a six-week pilot with a fairly passive approach in which they recorded a total of six roving reference transactions. They concluded that students in the upper floors of the library were using the space for purposes other than in-depth research. At the same time, their assessment showed that those who received help were highly satisfied with the roving reference transaction (p. 253). The team was open to trying the service at another library location if funding could be obtained (p. 254). Many factors, such as space, approach, staff buy-in, training, marketing, user base, and initial goals, may influence the success of a roving reference service.

Identifying and Responding to Needs

The decision to begin a roving reference service at the University of California, Merced Library had its roots in conflicting information gathered from assessment findings. In spring 2009, library staff conducted surveys and focus groups with graduating students, both those who worked in the library as student assistants and those who did not. Findings from the survey data indicated that there was room for improvement in providing knowledgeable human assistance. In follow-up focus groups graduating library student assistants expressed a desire for librarians to be available at the front desk though this did not surface from other graduating students. Yet the data collected at the service desk did not support the conclusion that librarians were needed there. Very few questions were asked, and the majority of those asked required a short response time. Of course, some might argue that library users did not ask questions because they did not expect them to be answered by their peers or that answers were brief due to lack of knowledge by student assistants.

In light of this conflicting data, the decision was made to proceed with a roving reference service that would tap existing library student assistants to proactively offer library users reference assistance and, as needed, put those users in contact with librarians. The service would preserve the library's philosophy of providing librarians for on-demand reference rather than just-in-case reference at a desk. At the same time, it would put library users in touch with roving reference student assistants trained in assisting with reference questions. In providing the service, additional data on the type and number of questions being asked would be collected. This model varied in contrast to those roving reference models explored in the literature, since it relied completely on undergraduate student assistants for staffing this service. However, examples of using undergraduate students for reference purposes may become a more common practice, as indicated by a peer reference model at Kimbel Library at Coastal Carolina University in South Carolina, which employs upper-level undergraduates to provide "full reference service with minimal supervision" (Faix et al., 2010, p. 90).

Selecting and Training Student Assistants
The Roving Reference pilot employed library student assistants who already had experience in providing customer service at the library's main service points; for example, checking out books, answering directional questions, assisting users with Interlibrary Loan and printing questions, etc. These student assistants had a strong background in library operations, were interested in helping library users find and access information, and had excellent customer-service skills. In this new role, only students who willingly wanted to participate and who demonstrated strong skill sets for this type of work were employed. These students received additional training focused on informing them of the pilot's purpose and building skills in providing reference service. Library staff began by introducing students to the purpose of the program, their role in it, and work expectations during a roving reference shift. Library staff then addressed the topics of privacy, the reference interview, and various search strategies and tools that the student assistants could use to answer reference questions.

Providing Roving Reference
Student assistants who participated in the pilot continued to work shifts at the main service point in addition to one or two roving reference shifts each week. The project started with five roving reference student assistants who provided approximately 18 hours of service per week in two-hour shifts. For each shift they roved through the library a minimum of four times and made themselves available to answer questions and offer assistance. While roving they carried a small laptop and a walkie-talkie in case they needed to contact a librarian, staff supervisor, or other library student assistant. After

roving through the library, these student assistants were available at the consult desk, which is attached to the main service point. Library staff equipped the consult desk with a computer and a monitor that could easily be shifted to face the library user. Roving reference student assistants were encouraged to post to the library's blog and were required to submit an online debrief form at the end of each shift. On the form they recorded how many questions were asked (categorizing them by time spent on each question) and the types of questions asked. Further along in the pilot, a question was added to determine how many questions were answered while roving versus while at the consult desk area. Roving reference student assistants could also submit questions or comments via a form which librarians reviewed and responded to as needed. Red polo shirts, with an "i" (for "information") on the back, distinguished roving reference student assistants from their peer coworkers, who wore blue polo shirts. Rovers were scheduled for two-hour shifts Monday through Friday, with hours ranging from the early afternoon through the evening. Though the initial plan was to schedule all roving reference service hours late in the afternoon and into the evening when librarians were less likely to be available, it was necessary to work around student availability. Also, more students asked questions in the afternoons than in the evenings.

Examining the Data

After a semester of gathering data, it was determined that roving reference student assistants were not answering the number of questions expected, nor receiving as many reference-related questions as anticipated. After providing the service for 13 weeks, the student assistants had answered a total of 289 questions over 55 roving reference shifts for an average of 2.63 questions per hour. From the length of time it took to answer the questions, it is evident that most were not difficult or in-depth, reference-related questions. Instead, roving reference student assistants were primarily answering a number of basic questions that took no longer than five minutes per transaction. Our results were similar to those of Bregman and Mento (1992), who "found that about three-fourths of the rover interactions [at Boston College] lasted less than five minutes" (p. 635).

The following are fall 2009 results; total questions: $n = 289$:

- 52.2% <1 minute
- 32.5% 2–5 minutes
- 11.1% 6–15 minutes
- 3.8% 16–30 minutes
- 0.3% 30+ minutes

When calculating the types of questions that were asked most, data indicated that printing/printer-related questions were asked during 76.4 percent of the shifts ($n = 55$); finding a known item was asked during 47.3 percent of the shifts; and help locating specific materials was requested during 43.6 percent of the shifts. These data confirmed that the campus printing process was not intuitive or reliable. The data also indicated that roving reference student assistants handled questions about finding both online information and information in physical formats. Some of the questions answered by the roving reference student assistants included how to: (1) order resources through Interlibrary Loan services, (2) access resources remotely, (3) find peer-reviewed articles for psychology assignments, and (4) locate CDs on how to learn Spanish. These were the type of questions library staff members had hoped to see answered through this service. Overall, users were still asking more often about how to *print* a document than they were asking how to *find* a document; yet promise was seen in this model as roving reference student assistants were helping library users find and access information.

After a semester of data, some changes were implemented to the roving reference service, especially in the area of advertising and marketing. Even so, the results of the second (spring) semester were similar to those of the first (fall) semester, with the majority of questions taking less than five minutes to answer. In the second semester, the roving reference service averaged a lower percentage of questions per hour (1.61 questions per hour) than in the first semester. This finding includes a possible source of error as the calculations are based on the assumption that all shifts, 130 in total in spring 2010, ran a full 2 hours even though some shifts were shorter in length.

The following are spring 2010 results; total questions: $n = 417$:

- 55.2% <1 minute
- 31.9% 2–5 minutes
- 10.6% 6–15 minutes
- 2.2% 16–30 minutes
- 0.2% 30+ minutes

The top three types of questions remained the same, though printing questions dropped to second place. This may have been a result of students becoming increasingly familiar with printing procedures in the library by the spring semester.

Challenges and Changes

By examining the debrief form data and discussing the service with the roving reference student assistants after the fall 2009 semester, some challenges were discovered and some changes were made. One of the main challenges was highlighting and promoting the service. Though initially the service was marketed through table tents in the library, digital signage, screensavers on the consult-desk computer, and an advertisement in the student newspaper, it has taken time to make the service known and understandable. The roving reference student assistants have been regularly asked why they are wearing the red shirt. Though the term roving reference is used internally, most advertising has used the phrase "Ask Us" in an attempt to convey what the service is about and to address a concern that the average undergraduate library user may not understand what reference means. Though the "i" for information was selected as it was thought that it would be universally understandable, it does not necessarily convey the complete purpose of the service.

After brainstorming with the student assistants, other marketing strategies were incorporated. For example, free candy was available at the consult area when roving reference student assistants were on shift, and the treats were labeled with questions and statements to inform library users that students wearing the red shirts were available to answer questions. The candy also served as a conversation piece so *roving reference* student assistants could introduce individuals to the service. A bright-red "i" banner was placed by the consult-desk area to draw attention to the service, anticipating that having the "i" highly visible at the consult desk would inform library users of the service and prompt them to use it when they had questions in the stacks or at the consult desk. The student assistants also suggested incorporating their photographs on digital signage advertisements, so roving reference student photographs were combined with the "i" branding and the statement "Have a Question?" In addition, the librarians were more intentional about mentioning the availability of the roving reference service during library research instruction sessions. During summer orientations library staff advertised the service by using a red roving reference shirt as a show-and-tell object during face-to-face sessions with incoming freshmen. In addition, information about the roving reference service was incorporated into an iPod Touch Library Tour, which the majority of freshmen viewed in fall 2010.

The data revealed that most questions were asked at the consult desk rather than out on the floor and in the stacks. Over a sample of 77 shifts from the spring 2010 semester, it was discovered that during 31.2 percent of the shifts all transactions took place *while roving*, yet during 55.9 percent of the shifts all transactions happened at the *consult desk*. The remainder of the shifts (12.9 percent) included a mixture of answering questions on the floor or at the desk. This result could be tied to the challenges of assisting users proactively, while still respecting their privacy. Some roving reference student assistants have been more comfortable than others in approaching users who may need assistance. Though the most interest has been in going out into the physical space to assist users, the decision to have the roving reference student assistants spend time between roving rounds at the consult desk is largely dictated by the fact that the library's space of approximately 80,000 square feet spread across three floors can be covered in a relatively short period of time. Roving reference student assistants have also been asked to multitask while roving. For example, they make sure the printers are working, do head counts, etc. Sometimes the student assistants are viewed as police when they rove, especially on the fourth floor, which is designated as a quiet zone. Smith and Pietraszewski (2004) made a similar discovery after a six-week pilot of roving reference service in an academic library building, noting that "[t]he project team was not sure if the roving librarian was viewed by our student patrons as someone they could ask help from or if this wandering individual was serving as a monitor, policing the building" (p. 253). Though the roving reference student assistants' primary purpose is to assist library users with their questions, it can place them in an awkward position, since they do not want to ignore library policies and may feel compelled to intervene when they deem it necessary.

Conclusion
With only 1.91 questions per hour answered via roving reference (from fall 2009 through spring 2010), the benefits based on the hours invested may be questionable. Even so, the author is still pleased to see that these student assistants have helped library users and have also served as a resource for their peer student assistants who do not have more in-depth reference assistance training. Having this data has provided information indicating that staffing a reference desk with librarians would not be a good use of resources in the current environment. Roving reference student assistants have the knowledge to answer logistical questions in the library, as well as knowledge about information resources and search strategies, which makes them very flexible and valuable members of the staff.

Perhaps one of the greatest benefits of the service has been a closer working relationship with the roving reference student assistants who, as a group, feel more comfortable in referring questions to librarians than do some of the other student assistants who are not part of the pilot. Having information from the debrief form has alerted librarians to access issues, questions for follow-up, and the types of information most commonly needed by the library users. Shortly, these transactions will be entered in a new online database which will allow the librarians to gather and analyze additional information about each roving reference interaction. Overall, the roving reference service has provided users with another avenue through which they can obtain assistance, has made the· librarians increasingly aware of the types of questions users ask, and has equipped a group of student assistants with increased information-finding skills. Libraries reevaluating their reference services, providing a robust wireless network, and offering space beyond quiet study areas may wish to start their own roving reference pilot to meet and determine current information needs. The service will be continually monitored and evaluated to determine if additional changes are needed and if the service is valuable enough to continue long term. For now roving reference is still on a roll, being offered and actively promoted to our library users.

References

Bregman, A., & Mento, B. (1992). Reference roving at Boston College. *College & Research Libraries News* (10), 634–636.

Burek Pierce, J. (2006). Where reference librarians do rove. *American Libraries, 37*(2), 39.

Carlile, H. (2007). The implications of library anxiety for academic reference services: A review of the literature. *Australian Academic & Research Libraries, 38*(2), 129.

Courtois, M. P., & Liriano, M. (2000). Tips for roving reference: How to best serve library users. *College & Research Libraries News, 61*(4), 289–290, 315.

Faix, A. I., Bates, M. H., Hartman, L. A., Hughes, J. H., Schacher, C. N., Elliot, B. J., & Woods, A. D. (2010). Peer reference redefined: New uses for undergraduate students. *Reference Services Review, 38*(1), 90–107.

Forsyth, E. (2009). Fancy walkie talkies, Star Trek communicators or roving reference? *Australian Library Journal, 58*(1), 73–84.

Fritch, J. W., & Mandernack, S. B. (2001). The emerging reference paradigm: A vision of reference services in a complex information environment. *Library Trends, 50*(2), 286–305.

Huwe, T. K. (2003). Casting a wider net with roving reference. *Computers in Libraries, 23*(3), 34–36.

Kramer, E. H. (1996). Why roving reference: A case study in a small academic library. *Reference Services Review, 24*(3), 67–80.

Lorenzen, M. (1997). Management by wandering around: Reference rovering and quality reference serviced. *The Reference Librarian, 28*(59), 51–57.

Mellon, C. A. (1986). Library anxiety: A grounded theory and its development. *College and Research Libraries, 47*(2), 160–165.

Pitney, B., & Slote, N. (2007). Going mobile: The KCLS roving reference model. *Public Libraries, 46*(1), 54–68.

Reynolds, M. (2005). Operation rover. *Library Journal, 130*(7), 62.

Smith, M. M., & Pietraszewski, B. A. (2004). Enabling the roving reference librarian: Wireless access with tablet PCs. *Reference Services Review, 32*(3), 249–255.

CHAPTER 10

Business Community Outreach: Exploration of a New Service Role in an Academic Environment

Patrick Griffis and Sidney Lowe

Overview

Literature describing libraries that support community economic development indicates that the majority of business community outreach initiatives are developed by public libraries. Academic libraries should also expand their roles by reaching out to business-people in their surrounding communities to build key partnerships and to illustrate the value of a research university by marketing their services and resources. Recently, the Dean of Libraries at the University of Nevada, Las Vegas (UNLV) made it a priority to build upon relationships with local business groups by making presentations at meetings and luncheons. The libraries' Business Librarian became involved by creating resources for business research, providing reference consultations, conducting workshops, and working with community agencies on business plans and start-ups. This chapter discusses many benefits and challenges of business community outreach for academic libraries, describes common business information needs, and offers best practices for business reference and referrals. This new collaborative service role can potentially increase an academic library's value to its community.

Background

The role for libraries in supporting economic development in their communities has been well documented over the past few decades. It was inevitable that a collective work would emerge documenting business community outreach initiatives and best practices. Such a book was published by Bleiweis (1997). The majority of initiatives documented were from public libraries, with very few coming from academic libraries (Bleiweis, 1997). A decade later, a survey of business community outreach initiatives and best practices building upon the work of Bleiweis' book was published in a report by Sharpe and Stierman (2007) of Western Illinois University Libraries that reveals that the majority of business community initiatives documented are still being developed by public libraries with relatively little representation from academic libraries (Sharpe & Stierman, 2007). This finding is not surprising, considering the focus of public libraries on community outreach, but for some academic libraries it is becoming more important to reach out to their surrounding communities to connect with people and to market library services and resources.

A special issue of the *Journal of Business & Finance Librarianship* focusing on business librarianship and entrepreneurship includes many case studies detailing entrepreneurship outreach initiatives from academic libraries. In the introductory article MacDonald (2010) outlines entrepreneurial outreach initiatives in the issue, stating that they "describe three very different approaches libraries have taken to align themselves with a key mission of the university—economic development" (p. 159). This chapter elaborates on the previous work in describing the exploration of a new role in business community outreach as a whole, which includes, but is not limited to, entrepreneurship outreach.

The University of Nevada, Las Vegas (UNLV) has played a vital role in the local community for more than 50 years. It offers a variety of civic and cultural opportunities and events for its students, faculty, and staff, and also for the Southern Nevada community (http://communityrelations.unlv.edu/). UNLV's on-campus libraries comprise a main library and three branch libraries. Lied Library is the 300,000 square-foot main campus library at UNLV. It opened in January 2001, and replaced an outdated building which was no longer big enough for the university community's increasing population of students and faculty. It is an attractive, spacious, and comfortable learning space, providing information resources and services in person or by web access.

Research assistance is provided by a 25-person reference service pool largely comprised of librarians, paraprofessionals, and student interns. The skills and experiences of these individuals vary widely, but training is ongoing. Subject liaison librarians are trained in the basic resources of subject areas under other liaisons, but referrals are typically made to subject experts in cases of in-depth research questions. For example, business reference queries are often referred to the Business Librarian, who also provides basic training in the area of his subject expertise for other liaisons. The Business Librarian is the first point of contact for business-related research, but also among the library faculty is a Hospitality Librarian who specializes in tourism and hospitality resources.

Outreach to the Business Community

In addition to responding to business reference questions, in the past year, Lied Library has been motivated to reach out to the business community of Southern Nevada to initiate and participate in business events and activities, and to develop key community partnerships. The recent decline in the housing industry and in overall employment in Las Vegas has resulted in an increase in the number of local residents who are seeking to start their own business ventures. Local community agencies are focusing their efforts more on business start-ups, as small businesses tend to have a significant impact on employment. Small business development and exporting of goods and services from Las Vegas and Nevada have been identified as the solutions toward economic recovery. The Las Vegas-Clark County Library District provides resources and services for job seekers and maintains limited business resources, but does not have staff specialists focusing on business, or services tailored specifically for the business community. The public libraries focus on contributing to economic development through their Southern Nevada Non-Profit Information Center and Patent and Trademarks Collection. As such, members of the business community with needs beyond the resources and staff expertise of the public libraries in Southern Nevada are commonly referred to the UNLV Libraries for assistance.

In 2008, the University administration and other higher education system administrators began communicating with local community members about the value of a research university. Their message emphasized economic diversification and development as a key benefit to the business community. UNLV's Dean of Libraries advanced the message further by demonstrating the value of a research library to professionals in the community through meetings and presentations. With the support and collaborative efforts of the UNLV Libraries' Advisory Board, the Dean made it a priority to build upon relationships with local business groups. She was invited to speak at CEO group luncheons, Rotary Club and Chamber of Commerce meetings, and at an Executive Conference to discuss how the libraries can assist professionals with business and other areas of research (Iannuzzi, 2009). The Business Librarian became involved and created business resource handouts and research guides, and provided individual reference consultations for business community members. He also increased outreach efforts with community agencies supporting business start-ups, such as the Nevada Small Business Development Center, which offers courses for launching new businesses to local community members. He gave presentations on business research for developing business plans and provided training on the library resources to assist with research.

Common Information Needs and Requests

The most common request is for information that is required to develop a business plan that will be used to obtain financing for a new business venture or an expansion of a current business venture (new product, service, or new geographic location to provide existing product or service). Library users need information about the industry their venture will operate within, as well as information about the market for their product or service, to demonstrate the viability of their business venture to financiers. Consequently, they need industry reports and market research reports. They also need information on competitors and often request lists of similar companies to their venture in a specific geographic area. Business library users tend to need detailed financial information on potential competitors.

Their needs also include consumer research data to identify the demographics of the consumers they will be targeting for their product or service, as well as the most effective ways to market their product or service to them. They also request a list of potential financiers or funding sources for their business venture. As such, they need lists of granting agencies and foundations, as well as business loan banks and venture capitalists. Less often, business community library users need literature on current business trends for professional development activities such as developing business training sessions for employees and producing company newsletters. They need articles in a topical area from business presses, such as journals and magazines, as well as newspapers. Also, these library users need to conduct research to make informed investment decisions and to track their personal investments (stocks, bonds, etc.). Sometimes library users need career-related resources such as career guidebooks, résumé-writing manuals, and websites for job searching.

Scenario-Based Outreach Presentations

Another service offered for business library users is custom-designed workshops. Much of the time, research consultations occur at the point of need, but group sessions tailored to specific business needs are routinely scheduled by the Business Librarian. One approach that has been used in meetings with the business community is scenario-based outreach presentations, which work well and can be described as a kind of storytelling technique to engage participants. These scenarios illustrate library services and resources by using realistic examples of research assistance so that people become interested in how the librarian might be useful to them, and also enlightened about the availability of resources to meet their needs. A sample scenario could be one in which a reference librarian is assisting an entrepreneur who wants to open a comic book and gaming store, but has limited funds. To attract investors or lenders the entrepreneur needs a business plan that includes demographics and other statistics about the potential market, and he or she is wondering whether Las Vegas or Reno, Nevada, would be the best start-up location for this new business. How will he or she convince a bank that there are enough customers out there to generate enough income to pay off a loan? This type of scenario used during a presentation to the business community enables librarians to promote increased awareness and understanding of library services and available resources. Since there are some access restrictions for community users, it is important for librarians to emphasize what *can* be offered, and to focus less on what cannot be provided.

Benefits of Outreach

For academic libraries, promoting library resources and services to community business library users, as well as the level of reference services delivered to them, is very different from that of public libraries. At Lied Library, we believe that a balance must be achieved. We want to make positive connections and to provide assistance, but the daily reality is that some policy-based restrictions exist for community users that can be construed as negative if not communicated in a positive light. These limits are in place because the primary constituents are our students and faculty. However, the librarians are working to achieve that balance by providing optimal assistance utilizing those guidelines for library use while building collaborative relationships within the Las Vegas business community.

One of the benefits of outreach to the business community is that participating in business-based meetings or workshops and providing research assistance (such as help with business plans) promotes the value of the academic library in a community and increases awareness of its services and resources. UNLV Libraries have documented business outreach initiatives in their newsletters to community members, and many of the community agencies that have partnered in these efforts have also documented the initiatives in their newsletters. The reverse also happens; librarians become aware of community services that can be helpful to their users and other staff, and it increases their reference knowledge base. This reciprocal benefit is evidenced at the UNLV Libraries through its Business Community Resources Guide, which includes a list of local community agencies and resources that can support business start-up and growth. Another advantage to making connections and building relationships with business partners is that it can lead to exciting and unexpected opportunities for external fundraising. The contacts made through business outreach activities of the UNLV Dean of Libraries and the Business Librarian have significantly expanded the potential donors maintained by the Libraries' External Relations Department.

Another benefit arising from business outreach activities is that collaborative activities and research assistance with people from one agency or company often connect the library to other organizations within the community, and new relationships are formed. Such a relationship was shaped with Nevada Industry Excellence (NIE), a company designed to improve efficiency in business operations. NIE invited the Business Librarian to participate in an exporting workshop for local manufacturers called ExporTech. A similar relationship was developed with the Nevada Small Business Development Center. The Business Librarian was invited to participate in a business plan workshop for local entrepreneurs called NxLevel. In addition, the Dean of Libraries was asked to join and is now an active member of the Las Vegas Rotary Club. At one of their meetings, she promoted library services by saying,

> I am here to tell you about this valuable resource in your own backyard.... The UNLV Libraries provide onsite access to hundreds of databases, millions of electronic articles from more than 20,000 journals, newspapers, and other sources of information. This is content we license for our students and faculty—it is at the heart of teaching and research—we may have 10,000 students a day walking through our doors—but we also have over 3 million searches a year in our databases. (Iannuzzi, 2009, n.p.)

This type of direct participation widens the community's understanding of the library and the university's role and mission.

Outreach Challenges

Such benefits garnered by outreach do not just happen without being accompanied by a few challenges. In many ways, public libraries are able to assist community users with their research without regard to their status because they serve the general public, and every library user is entitled to the same level of assistance. In academic library settings, since community users have some limitations to their access privileges, creativity and diplomacy are often required by librarians to enhance the effectiveness of the research process for the business community user. One particular challenge faced at UNLV Libraries is that because academic libraries purchase subscriptions to licensed databases intended primarily for users affiliated with educational institutions, there are restrictions on commercial use. Library policies allow nonaffiliated community users access to proprietary research databases with specific restrictions. They must come into the library to use the designated guest computers located behind the reference desk (no remote access), and log in as a guest researcher. These computers have no Internet access, except to government-based websites. Printing and e-mailing are occasional obstacles, but it is also our policy to accommodate library users whenever possible, so they are frequently assisted with courtesy printing or e-mailing files by staff from the nearby reference desk.

Another particular challenge faced at UNLV Libraries is that clients who work with businesses are often accustomed to having research done *for* them, and do not necessarily recognize the difference between professional research services and assistance by an academic library professional. Explaining to a business community user what can and cannot be accomplished or provided is sometimes difficult, especially when the research help meets their needs but also "opens the door" for the possibility of services that exceed the scope of the librarian's time or expectations. Often, business community members expect the Business Librarian to prepare marketing lists and business plans instead of assisting them in preparing such products themselves. Research assistance scenarios that exceed the scope of the librarian's time or expectations are those business queries requiring "expert advice," which is a common challenge for legal or medical-based queries. The librarians can end up on the proverbial slippery slope if reference help is interpreted (rightly or wrongly) as advice to the library user. To avoid misunderstandings or potential legal liability, it is best to offer information while avoiding analysis and to refer library users to experts who are qualified to provide analysis.

In addition, there are challenges in providing services within the time frames of busy professionals when they contact the library for help requiring immediacy, as staff assistance is often limited for assistance to members of the business community. The UNLV Business Librarian serves as the primary contact for assisting them, but cannot always be available when needed because of competing job responsibilities. Also adding to the insufficiency of staff availability, academic libraries face challenges in the adequacy of library resources for meeting community users' research needs, necessitating referrals to other agencies or services. Library users may want high-quality marketing resources, and available databases sometimes fall short of their expectations. The stakes of business research can be extremely high. For businesspeople, the bottom line is about money, making business deals and decisions, creating accurate financial reports, writing a successful business plan, submitting excellent grant proposals, and so on.

There are some other common concerns that can accompany reference transactions with users from the business community. As noted above, they can expect more than can be given, and information from libraries is considered to be "free," even when the library user knows a report or data may be coming from a very expensive database. Non-business librarians and staff are often not familiar or interested in the subject matter, and business questions can be complex and confusing. If the Business Librarian is unavailable, staff can offer incomplete or even incorrect information if they do not use a thorough reference interview to find out what the user needs. Business jargon such as "profitability ratio" or "earnings per share" can cause seasoned reference veterans to temporarily freeze if their training or context for this type of terminology is lacking.

Best Practices for Business Reference and Referrals

The best starting place for determining the right approach to business reference and referrals is usually a good reference interview to determine true needs. One technique is to assign a category or area for what the library user is describing; resources are arranged by business-related categories such as finance, marketing, local resources, etc. Appropriate questions to ask the users include the following: Are they building a business plan? Making an investment decision? Looking at a new market, product, or company? Once the need is established it is possible to match it with the appropriate resources that are grouped and listed on a readily available bibliography or subject guide. If it is appropriate to refer a library user to another agency or person, here are a few suggestions:

- Develop a list, website, or handout of community organizations that support and provide information or courses on business start-ups and expansion.

- Develop a network of community organizations that support and provide information or courses on business start-ups and expansion on social media professional sites such as LinkedIn.
- Include local community services organizations in a resources guide for the surrounding business communities.
- Refer library users to experts who can provide guidance with business plans, business financing, or professional investment advice.
- As lists and guides are developed, become familiar with them, share them with other staff, and have them ready for distribution.

For reference service staff members who need baseline knowledge to point people with business-related questions in the right direction, the following checklist should help:

- For company directory information either keep a couple of basic, current directories (local, state, and national) nearby, bookmark them, or know how to look them up quickly.
- Extensive and authoritative e-resources can be located through the Business Reference and Services Section (BRASS) of American Library Association's (ALA) Reference and User Service Association's (RUSA) website, available at http://www.ala.org/ala/mgrps/divs/rusa/sections/brass/index.cfm. There are several LibGuides related to business topics that can be found at http://brass.libguides.com/index.php.
- Extensive and authoritative e-resources can be located through the Business and Finance Division of Special Library Association's (SLA) website, available at http://units.sla.org/division/dbf/index.html. A wiki related to business resources can be found at http://wiki.sla.org/display/SLADBF/Home.
- When using a search engine such as Google to look for business or company information, searches can be refined by a site domain, such as dot-gov (.gov) for federal and state government-based websites.

Other bits of knowledge for the business reference toolbox include industry and market research reports, investment information, funding sources from banks, venture capital, nonprofit funding sources such as foundations and grants, and resources for job searching and career information. References for learning how to find such information include the BRASS LibGuides.

Maintaining communication and collegial relationships with community businesspeople will perpetuate goodwill and build new connections. Keep library information packets and website URLs readily available, and include community library users in mailing lists for sending updates, newsletters, fundraising materials, and other communiqués. Ask them to share their library experiences with other library stakeholders and with their business peers. Libraries should track interactions to provide an account of outreach activities to administrators, publicize initiatives, include personal accounts of library users, and consistently emphasize the library's impact on the business community.

Conclusion

This new role in providing library services to support the local business community through proactive outreach efforts is a win-win collaboration that builds connections with professionals in the community to forge a significant integration of the academic library into their professional lives. This role supports UNLV's efforts to spread awareness of the value of a research university within the community, which Oakleaf (2010) advocates that all academic libraries undertake in the Association of College and Research Libraries (ACRL) Values Report. The challenges of this new role are not insurmountable and are worth overcoming to enable the libraries to interact with the local community in innovative ways. These types of interactions can raise the profile of the library to stakeholders and community members and can also change perceptions about libraries as a whole, and increase their value to the neighboring businesses and individuals. In addition, this new service role has the potential for a domino effect by influencing other libraries to broaden their range of services because it encourages people to utilize libraries. Library staff, especially those who provide frontline reference services, may also begin to see the benefits of business community outreach efforts.

Oakleaf (2010) states that "library services and resources support institutional engagement in service to their communities by providing community members . . . locally, nationally, and globally" (p. 139) with information that is of high quality, is valid, and meets their needs. For UNLV Libraries, this new service initiative represents the start of a new collaborative adventure in supporting the community engagement efforts of its university.

References

Bleiweis, M. (1997). *Helping business: The library's role in community economic development: A how-to-do-it manual.* New York: Neal-Schuman.

Iannuzzi, P. (2009, August). *Quality business information in an era of infoglut: UNLV Libraries' support of the Las Vegas business community.* Presentation at a meeting of the Las Vegas Rotary Club, Las Vegas, NV.

MacDonald, K. (2010). Entrepreneurship outreach: A new role for the academic business librarian. *Journal of Business & Finance Librarianship, 15*(3&4), 158–160.

Oakleaf, M. (2010). *Value of academic libraries: A comprehensive research review and report.* Chicago: Association of College and Research Libraries.

Sharpe, K. B., & Stierman, J. K. (2007). *Libraries and community economic development: A survey of best practices.* Retrieved June 9, 2011, from http://www.alliancelibrarysystem.com/rural/documents/bestpractices.pdf.

## CHAPTER 11

Embedded Librarians:
The Community Reference Project

Colbe Galston, Katherine Johnson,
Elizabeth Kelsen Huber, and Amy Long

Overview

Douglas County Libraries began an initiative called Community Reference in order to help the library prove its value to the community in a new way. Community Reference is a way to "focus on helping librarians more effectively identify and articulate both their value and the contributions of the institution" to the community (Durrance & Fisher, 2003, p. 25). In 2009, Douglas County Libraries asked the authors to create some structure around the concept. They created a process, defined new terms, built a data collection tool using Wordpress, and proposed the first Community Reference Project. In 2010, Douglas County Libraries began using this new process. This chapter provides a report of progress and discusses the process that was developed for the Library District.

Introduction/History

Libraries are constantly evolving and changing to adapt to the needs and desires of their users, especially during times of economic crisis when libraries are in danger of having service cuts or of being closed entirely. At Douglas County Libraries, positive changes have occurred inside our buildings, from obtaining cutting-edge technology and implementing self-service systems to redesigning our spaces. While these changes have been vital, they have failed to address the library's presence in the community, or in some cases, the lack thereof. Were the libraries truly demonstrating our value to our communities beyond the physical space, materials, or virtual space?

This question was one of many posed by James LaRue, Library Director for Douglas County Libraries in Colorado. Over the past several years, LaRue explored and came to define the value of libraries in the community using the term *Community Reference*. The concept is born from the underlying power of libraries to be transformational and to build communities. Overlaying that foundation is the intrinsic value of libraries to our communities, and specifically, the role of librarians in our communities. Working closely with the administrative team at Douglas County Libraries, LaRue explored ways in which to demonstrate those values to the community. From those discussions the idea emerged of librarians interacting with the community and demonstrating their skills beyond the physical space of the library.

Douglas County Libraries believe that the community has relevant questions that need answering, and those questions are not coming into the library as traditional reference questions, but are being discussed at community meetings. These questions could range from choosing a historically appropriate name for a new park to developing strategies to increase economic development in a downtown area. In addition, communities in our county may be facing similar issues or asking the same questions, yet are completely unaware that another Douglas County city is grappling with the same issue. LaRue often experienced this firsthand as he attended various meetings throughout the county and started to hear the same topics and themes mentioned repeatedly.

These issues and questions are important to our communities, which are looking for ways to solve them. Librarians are passionate about reference and research and are best suited to provide the necessary assistance to research the issues and answer the questions at little or no cost to the community. Consequently, via the Community Reference model, the librarians are perfectly positioned to provide information and solutions that add value to the community and demonstrate the value of Douglas County Libraries in the community.

Approximately two years ago, Community Reference became a district initiative. The district encouraged professional librarians to connect with key community groups and become involved in the activities of those groups and paid them for their time associated with those groups. As with all new ideas, some staff and branches embraced the concept and sought out groups to work with while others were unsure of their role. At this time there was very little structure and definition to the initiative. Staff members were simply encouraged to become engaged in the community. The result was that everyone (staff, supervisors, and associate directors) had a slightly different interpretation of Community Reference. There was very little consistency in what people were doing or thought they should be doing. Thus, while our work had been valuable, it did not have the impact that it should. Consequently the district realized how important it was to provide some structure around this concept. The needed structure included developing a process, guidelines, scope, definitions, and a data collection tool.

The three key components of Community Reference that Douglas County Libraries adopted in 2009 are Embedded Librarians, the Community Reference Project Blog, and the first Community Reference Project. In addition, continued evaluation of these processes is required.

Embedded Librarians

Historically used in special and academic libraries, the concept of the librarian leaving the physical library and serving their users where they are found—classrooms, project teams, academic departments, or virtual space—has been dubbed "embedding." This concept finds that having librarians integrate with the groups they serve helps them "contribute important information to the customer group in a timely fashion, even anticipating unrealized and unexpressed needs" (Shumaker & Tyler, 2007, p. 2). The embedded librarian functions as the information expert for his or her group, providing accurate and timely research, and also maintains the internal knowledge of the group, capturing and organizing the output.

Douglas County Libraries identified this model as an ideal way for librarians to begin connecting with patrons in a new environment, demonstrating our considerable skills, and discovering more about the community. This experiment with embedded librarians began in 2006 when LaRue was invited to attend the meetings of the Parker Downtown Development Council, an informal group of property owners, businesspeople, and town staff who were trying to increase economic development in downtown Parker, Colorado. Soon the Parker Library Manager and librarians began attending meetings on a regular basis and serving as the secretaries for the group—taking minutes, maintaining group e-mail communications, and performing special research, both at the behest of the group and when the librarians thought it would inform the conversation. When the group was asked to describe the value of the library's service over several years, they mentioned the importance of the expert research the librarians provided, the communication that was facilitated, and also the credibility that a partner like the library brought to a fledgling organization.

Douglas County Libraries decided this was an initiative they wanted to expand to become an expectation for all professional staff in the district, so they gathered the authors of this paper to help make this happen. It was quickly determined that there needed to be a way for librarians to evaluate their embedded experience—to be sure the experience was more than sitting in another meeting, that it had value for both the library and the community group. Librarians could work with any group in the community, but after about three months of active participation, the librarian should determine that: (1) the group adds value to the community; (2) the library is essential to helping the group achieve its goals; and (3) participating in the group helps the library be more visible and valuable to the community. These evaluative questions give the librarians a way to measure their impact and ensure that the library is getting the best possible value for the time and effort.

Embedded assignments vary from branch to branch, depending on the needs of the community and the groups and types of partnerships available. Patty Van Eysden, a business librarian at Phillip S. Miller Library, is an early example of embedded librarianship, serving as a mentor for businesses engaged in continuing education with the Castle Rock Economic Gardening group. She ran demographic research for the group to determine which area businesses to invite to participate in their business boot camp and supports the businesses through this multi-week training. She also created a presentation, along with the Economic Gardening marketing expert, which highlighted the library's resources for entrepreneurs and small businesses.

Parker librarian Amy Morgan is embedded with the Women's Crisis and Family Outreach Center. She supports both the center and the individuals it serves by bringing the library to the families who gather there. The librarian maintains a satellite collection for the center, conducts computer classes, offers résumé training, and provides a popular children's storytime. The families fill out feedback forms when they finish their time at the center, and they consistently identify the library services as the bright spot during a difficult time.

In another example, when Castle Pines Library opened in 2009, the professional staff immediately began embedding themselves in the community. They started making contacts with local groups. Librarian Kyra Hahn began attending city council meetings, metro district meetings, and a few meetings in the neighboring community of Castle Pines Village and is now the Business Librarian for Castle Pines Library. Librarian Beth Dalton began making contacts with the schools in the area as the school liaison and began partnering with them on various outreach services inside the local classrooms in addition to contacting local businesses to discover if they wanted to offer any specials for library patrons during the library's grand opening. Amy Long, the Department Head, started attending Chamber of Commerce and Economic Development Council meetings and now sits on the Economic Development Council board and acts as the secretary for the Chamber of Commerce board. Sharon Lauchner, Manager of Lone Tree Library and Castle Pines Library, attends Castle Pines Business After Hours, Chamber of Commerce events, local events and festivities, and also schedules various one-on-one meetings with local leaders. Community Reference has been an integral part of the Castle Pines Library since it opened, and the professional staff are excited by the possibilities and participate fully as they attend meetings, document highlights, and share information across the district via the Community Reference Project Blog.

School Liaisons

Before Community Reference became a district initiative, Douglas County Libraries started another outreach program called school liaison similar in scope to Community Reference. School liaisons are librarians who build relationships with local elementary, middle, and high schools. This partnership between the library and the schools includes library use instruction in the classroom, helping teachers by providing research and resources around special projects or curriculum, booktalks for students, facilitating library tours, and volunteering at literacy events. This approach builds a connection with both the schools and the students, and many kids come into the public library to see their own personal librarian. The schools assist the library by promoting library events, encouraging students to use the public library, and including the library in their events as well. It has been a partnership that benefits two organizations with similar missions, and the librarians who serve as school liaisons are in essence embedded with the schools they support. School liaisons have been encouraged to participate and share information they have learned from their contacts with the schools. Since the Community Reference Project began, we have looked to the embedded librarian experience that school liaisons have developed as a model for how to embed librarians into community groups.

The process of embedding librarians in local organizations is the cornerstone of Community Reference. This new service model allows the library to demonstrate its value to strategically targeted groups, helping us to become deeply knowledgeable about the issues facing the community at large. While the procedure continues to evolve, the district has never questioned the value of these relationships for both the librarians and the community.

Strategically Targeting Organizations for Embedding

There are three strategies to targeting organizations for embedding. The first strategy involves the managers and department heads working together to look at key organizations in the community and deciding where to embed librarians. They look for groups and organizations that will create mutually beneficial partnerships. The librarians bring skills to help a group, which, in turn, may help support the library by mentioning to other community organizations or leaders the types of collaborations and projects that have been successful. This strategy works toward changing perceptions of what a librarian can do for their group and what the library can do for the community. The partnership also demonstrates the library's value in the community as a catalyst for community achievement and an active participant in creating what the community will become.

The second strategy to targeting organizations happens organically. As librarians attend meetings in the community, they will naturally hear of additional meetings. New groups will form, the contacts from one group will lead librarians to new groups, and simply being part of various community groups will bring additional embedded librarian opportunities to the librarian's attention.

The third strategy to targeting organizations is by request, when an organization approaches the librarians and asks that a representative be sent to their meeting. By this continued involvement in community groups and valuable contribution of library services outside the walls of the library, the aim is to cultivate a reputation that will establish the library as a necessary and essential part of any community group. By so doing, the hope is that any new group formed in the community will approach the library for a representative. There is no traditional marketing plan at this time for Community Reference, but it is possible something in the future will be developed if word of mouth does not generate the attention necessary to make the service successful.

Part of targeting strategic organizations is a process of refinement. Librarians may attend many different groups at first to determine if they are appropriate for a partnership with the library. In order to determine if the library and the community group can form a mutually beneficial partnership, we developed three questions: (1) Is the group adding value to the community? (2) Is the library essential to helping the organization achieve their goals? (3) Will participating in the group help the library be more visible and valuable to the community?

If the answer to all three questions is yes, then the group is one in which the library should seek to participate. If the answer to any of the three questions is no, then the librarian and supervisor should prudently consider how to proceed. The librarian's time is valuable and the key to successfully engaging the community in this way is to choose the organizations and meetings that are best worth the investment of time required.

Expectations

It is important to manage both the group's expectations as well as the librarian's personal expectations. Through early embedded librarian experiences the needs of the group were sometimes overwhelming for the librarian, leading to conflict between the work of the community group and the required tasks within the library. Therefore, it is important to clarify the librarian's role in the group early in the embedded experience. It also may be necessary to determine how long the librarian will participate in the group. At times, the commitment may be indefinite. At others, it is possible that the librarian will only commit to the group through the completion of a specific project or time period. The librarian will need to work out these details with his or her supervisor shortly after determining the value of participating in the group.

Once the librarian has clearly defined expectations for the community group, he or she can begin work as an embedded librarian, which involves balancing group needs and the librarian's other responsibilities. This task can be challenging at times, especially when it comes to scheduling and staffing. However, on an individual level, balance, or relative balance, can be achieved by constant communication between the librarian and his or her supervisor. The supervisor should monitor which meetings are being attended, what project work is being done, and how much time librarians are spending both inside and outside the library. In some cases, supervisors may reassign other responsibilities for the short term or permanently to provide time for project work. If that is not an option, there may be opportunities to work at home on certain tasks or even to reevaluate the original project or expectations with the group. The supervisor's role is to provide enriching opportunities for his or her staff, balance the staffing needs of the library, and communicate how the role of librarians is changing and continues to evolve.

Douglas County Library staff members hired under the original job description have had to adapt and change their focus as Community Reference has been added to their job expectations. The revised job descriptions for librarians include requirements for community involvement for professional staff. As the district refines the position in the future, the value of community involvement will influence decisions and district direction for the Douglas County Libraries leadership team.

Staffing

Balancing staffing at service points with community assignments poses challenges for each library, and there are several models currently being used at Douglas County Libraries. Due to technological advances and more user-friendly interfaces, some tasks formerly undertaken by librarians may be given to paraprofessionals, freeing the librarian to perform tasks that do require a professional. Building easy-to-use interfaces and providing education and training for end users also will free librarians from routine questions and permit them to focus on more complex research problems (Keiser, 2010).

The Highlands Ranch Library has three service points that require staffing for up to 12 hours daily. Considering the number of service points and service hours, it is challenging to keep the desks staffed with professional librarians. Historically, the staffing model has called for each desk to have at least one, and in some cases, two librarians, most often at the reference desk. However, this model is changing quickly as library staff and administrators recognize the value of professional staff in the community. Currently, it is not uncommon for desks to be staffed solely with paraprofessionals. This model has caused concern about a drop in service level for both professional and paraprofessional staff. Our paraprofessional staff can answer the majority of questions received at either desk. This level of expertise has been achieved via training and collaboration between paraprofessional and professional staff as they assist users. Another challenge at Highlands Ranch Library is part-time librarians. Of eight librarians on staff, only three are considered full-time. Part-time librarians are not able to be as deeply involved in community groups as their full-time counterparts. Overcoming the time constraints of a part-time employee requires consistent communication among the librarians, the supervisor, and the branch scheduler for public services staff. It also requires a bit of negotiating with the schedule and flexibility when a community group meeting conflicts with duties inside the library or days off. The key points are communication, training, and flexibility.

Another type of staffing is demonstrated at one of the smaller branches, Castle Pines Library. Castle Pines Library is a 2,300-square-foot building with no reference section. It relies on the larger branches to supplement its newer and mostly popular collection. There are four paraprofessionals and three professional librarians on staff including the on-site supervisor. Most of the questions that the staff members receive at a branch like this may be answered by the paraprofessionals. Originally, the professional staff members were scheduled for about half of their budgeted hours, and the other half was designated as "flex time," so they may schedule meetings, attend community meetings, or cover open shifts. This structure provides for keeping a professional in the building 90 percent of the time, while ensuring flexibility to fully participate as embedded librarians in the community. However, this resulted in a fractured team that did not function as well together since they did not have as much face time. Castle Pines has now moved to a model that schedules all professionals in the building but adjusts the scheduled shifts as needed for meetings in the community and within the library.

At Parker Library, the librarians have developed flexibility around their more traditional scheduling. This practice allows them to cover for one another when it is necessary to work the desk and send someone to attend a community meeting at the same time. They communicate often about who is attending which meetings and are very aware of the balance between community participation and covering the desk. In this model, it is rare that the reference desk is not staffed with a professional librarian.

In addition to flexibility and communication, it is essential to have a supervisor who is on board with the new direction and supportive of this initiative. It is also vital to have the support of the scheduler to ensure that the library has the appropriate staffing to meet public service needs while adapting the schedule to allow librarians to attend meetings. With the flexibility of staff, supervisors, and librarians, the library can begin to add value to the community by actively participating in community groups, enhancing the community perception of the library.

Community Reference Project Blog

The Community Reference Project Blog (see Figure 11.1) was created to help the district unify Community Reference efforts. It is a central tool to organize and share information that is being gathered by embedded librarians and school liaisons across the district. The blog, Figure 11.1, was created in WordPress (http://wordpress.com/), which was chosen because the format is conducive to promoting dialogue and collaboration among librarians. It is a virtual meeting ground for librarians because time is valuable and face-to-face meetings can take a lot of coordination. According to Gordon and Stephens (2006) internal weblogs are a great way to share knowledge and experience. They are a powerful tool for communication and help reduce paper clutter and e-mail.

The Community Reference blog is currently set to "private," meaning only Douglas County librarians or key administrative staff can access the blog. This allows librarians access to the information and the discussion of community meeting highlights without opening the content to public scrutiny, preventing any potential political ramifications of posting information from community meetings in a public blog. It is possible that the blog will be opened up to the public at a future date. By allowing local leaders and officials of Douglas County to access the blog, valuable information about the county they serve is provided. That would turn this data collection tool into a product of librarian research and knowledge, which in itself can add value to the community.

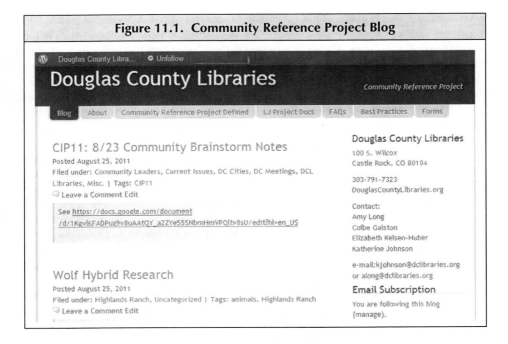

Figure 11.1. Community Reference Project Blog

The blog contains information on all aspects of Community Reference. This includes a flowchart, which shows the process Douglas County Libraries uses to identify Community Reference Projects, propose projects, and evaluate them upon completion. The flowchart is paired with a glossary for defining key aspects of Community Reference. The blog also includes the Community Reference Project proposal form and evaluative tools that may be used by managers and directors when evaluating project proposals. Last, it includes evaluation forms to be used by staff and community groups upon completion of a Community Reference Project.

The content librarians are expected to post on the blog includes narratives on current issues in the county, biographies of community leaders, and brief minutes from various community group meetings, such as city council, economic development committees, cultural and community associations, and metro districts. While it is possible to find this information online, having a librarian attend gives the library an opportunity to make contact with each organization and leader. Embedded librarians throughout the district post this information in one place, which makes it easier to see the big picture. In addition, the embedded librarian is able to filter out information and focus on the areas the library might need to know or be able to help with. While it is possible to identify large themes without a tool like the blog, the Community Reference Project Blog exists to help all librarians in the district focus on hyper-local issues that the library can assist with. The economy, funding, and growth are general concerns that affect many Colorado communities, but this blog exists to help us discover what issues Douglas County specifically faces.

The blog is monitored continually by two staff members who approve new posts and look for themes that appear in the community. All embedded librarians are encouraged to be active participants in the blog, posting information and looking for themes as well. Staff may sign up to receive e-mail updates as items are posted to the blog, allowing them to stay current without having to check the blog itself. The blog is searchable through tags and predesignated categories created according to geographic location, community groups, and government entities. The categories feature allows staff to access posts that have been tagged with that particular category.

By collecting this information and analyzing it, librarians should be able to find common themes, issues, or problems throughout the county, which they may propose as Community Reference Projects. Once a Community Reference Project is approved, a team representing a cross-section of librarians throughout the district will be created to collaborate, conduct research, hold interviews, and perform analysis. The goal for the project is to offer a solution to a community-wide problem while also demonstrating how valuable the public library is to our communities.

Community Reference Project

By definition, the Community Reference Project is a project proposed by Douglas County Libraries professional staff that will answer needs, problems, or questions that may apply to more than one community group, possibly across the entire district. The project may involve original data collection such as interviews or surveys, but may also include gathering existing data. These data will be gathered, understood, and compiled into a final product that does not simply list resources, but draws conclusions and makes recommendations. This final product may then be presented to groups throughout Douglas County, as well as to District Round Table or the Board of Directors. The final product could also be submitted for publication to journals or other relevant sources. The projects will be subject to review from many angles within the library and the community. Projects are the direct result of embedded librarian work and data collected via the Community Reference Project Blog. Without these essential pieces the district would be unable to identify broad yet hyper-local themes in Douglas County.

In June 2010, the administrative team for Douglas County Libraries, called District Round Table, branch managers and the Community Relations Manager, met to review and approve the first Community Reference Project for Douglas County Libraries. This proposal was written by the authors of this paper and proposed in 2010. Our group set forth the goal to complete a Community Reference Project in 2010 to provide staff with a participatory experience model, to understand the concept of Community Reference Projects. The first Community Reference Project is on higher education in Douglas County.

The theme of higher education came to our attention very organically during a discussion of common issues in Douglas County. During the discussion, Amy Long mentioned a conversation she had with two Castle Pines City Council members hoping to bring higher education to their city, including an idea of partnering with the public library to do so. Amy also heard from a neighboring city council meeting that they were discussing a possible partnership with a local community college to come in and provide refresher training for their medical community. Katherine Johnson was aware of a former employee who had written a report for another Douglas County city on the economic benefits of higher education institutions for the local community. The Associate Director of Public Services, David Farnan, shared with the group that he had conversations with at least two other cities who were working on various projects to bring higher education to their cities. This conversation demonstrated to the team the value of sharing information from community groups with other professionals throughout the district in order to identify a common area of interest throughout Douglas County. The Community Reference Project Blog is an attempt to virtually duplicate this organic process.

The Higher Education Community Reference Project team first met in August 2010. Administrators assigned a librarian from each branch, and two Associate Directors oversaw the project and assisted with community contacts, direction, and scope. The project team consisted of Amy Long from Castle Pines North in an advisory capacity, Adult Services Librarian Suzanne LaRue from Castle Rock Library, Business Librarian Lynn Sigman from Lone Tree Library, Business Librarian Mary Knott from Highlands Ranch Library, and Adult Services Librarian Jeanie Straub from Parker Library. David Farnan, Associate Director of Public Services, and Rochelle Logan, Associate Director of Research and Collections, were the project owners. The project also included Jamie Halgren, a student at the University of Denver who completed her practicum with the library.

The project team began by developing the scope and goals for the project: to examine, clarify, report on, and discuss the economic benefit of higher education in the community, higher education needs, the perspective of local higher education institutions on the county; and the various forms higher education may take, including a public library partnership, satellite locations for existing institutions, technology lab for distance learners, or a full campus installation. The group met about half a dozen times between October 2010 and February 2011. Each member of the group conducted interviews. The group started with a literature review on the subject while simultaneously interviewing about 21 people, including a combination of community members and contacts at Colorado higher education institutions. Jamie Halgren created an online survey that was e-mailed to more than 140 additional community and education contacts. All of this information was gathered together to write a report for community leaders and educational institutions to inform them about the topic. The end report was given to the community and educational institutions in Colorado, but is available on our website as a downloadable file. It has had a very positive reaction and has showed staff what a Community Reference Project can do! The final report can be found and read at this website: http://douglascountylibraries.org/files/HigherEdinDouglasCo.pdf.

Evaluation

One of the most important aspects of the Community Reference Project process is evaluation. It is important to evaluate any new process to establish best practices and to adjust to successes and failures. Evaluative tools throughout the process help staff and project teams stay on track and achieve the goals of Community Reference. There are three key evaluative tools in the process. The first, discussed previously, occurs when targeting a community group. The librarian is asked to evaluate that group to ensure that time is well spent by asking questions about value of the collaboration to the group and to the library.

The Community Reference Project Blog is the second evaluative tool. By reviewing the entries, tags, and categories, librarians can discern what type of content is most important to post from their community meetings. They can compare the effectiveness of their targeted community groups to those of other librarians. Most important, the information gathered on the blog should help librarians identify additional Community Reference questions similar in scope to the Higher Education Project. After the project is proposed and completed, the final evaluative tools are used. When a project is complete the final product will be presented to District Round Table, the Community Relations Manager, and branch managers to determine the success of the project and its readiness for presentation to the community. Once approved, the project may be presented to the community along with a survey evaluating the project's relevance and usefulness.

Next Steps and Conclusion

The Community Reference concept is in full swing with librarians embedded in various community groups across the district. The first Community Reference Project is complete and the Community Reference Project Blog is up and running. The expectation is that as staff read the blog posts and post pertinent information to the blog they will see a theme emerge for a potential Community Reference Project for 2011. The blog may become accessible to core members of the community outside of the library near the end of 2011 as a virtual catalog of the community. The viability of that possibility will be determined by library administrators, with input from those who have worked on developing the formal process for Community Reference in this district. The district management team will also evaluate all aspects of the Community Reference tools to look at challenges and successes, and to advise on refinements to any aspect of the process.

The Community Reference concept embraced by the library community will be a valuable practice for libraries and librarians to provide in the upcoming years. As Tyckoson (2007) states, "Amid all the hype and the changes, the important factor to remember is that we serve our community's needs. Helping and guiding and interacting with users... will do as much to keep the library relevant and vital as any new technology or program" (Tyckoson, 2007, p. 113). Community Reference will elevate the status of librarians and libraries while adding value to communities. It will hopefully "reinforce the library's role as a positive community force, breaking down the more traditional view of the library as an institution, and opening it up as a true public space" (Muzzerall, McLeod, Pacheco, & Sharkey, 2005, p. 266). One important goal is that, in time, the community will feel that a meeting should not start until the librarian is present. Creating this reputation and successful partnership with local community groups is the first and most crucial step in the Community Reference process. The same could hold true in any setting, whether academic or special libraries. The librarian should have a seat at the table with key administrators and policymakers to provide information and resources that will inform their decisions and help to create a strong and viable community.

References

Durrance, J. C., & Fisher, K. E. (2003). Determining how libraries and librarians help. *Library Trends, 51*(4), 541–571.

Gordon, R., & Stephens, M. (2006). How and why to try a blog for staff communication. *Computers in Libraries, 26*(2), 50–51.

Keiser, B. A. (2010). Libraries of the future-today! *Searcher, 18*(8), 18–54.

Muzzerall, D., McLeod, P. L., Pacheco, S., & Sharkey, K. (2005). Community development librarians: Starting out. *Feliciter, 51*(6), 265–267.

Shumaker, D., & Tyler, L. A. (2007). *Proceedings from Special Libraries Association annual conference: Embedded library services: An initial inquiry into practices for their development, management, and delivery.* Retrieved November 18, 2010, from http://www.sla.org/pdfs/sla2007/Shumaker EmbeddedLibSvcs.pdf.

Tyckoson, D. A. (2007). That thing you do. *Reference & User Services Quarterly, 42*(2), 111–113.

## CHAPTER 12

Virtual Reference: Variations on a Theme in Academic Libraries

Beth Avery, Elizabeth Brodak, Julie Fronmueller, Nancy Huling, Paul M. Mascareñas, Erin McCaffrey, Sylvia Owens, and Karen Sobel

Overview

Chat, text, and vendor reference services are presented through the lenses of librarian experience; level of usage/popularity; patron satisfaction; and the differences in collaboration models. The pros and cons of a single institution versus a cooperative are addressed. It is the contention of the authors that the factors of staffing, service, and patron base necessitate a level of collaboration not found in traditional reference. The differing experiences with chat/instant messaging (IM) including LibraryH3lp and Meebo; text/short message service (SMS) including Mosio and InfoQuest; and vendor-based virtual reference services (VRS) such as Tutor.com, InstaService, and QuestionPoint are discussed. Partial results of user and librarian surveys conducted to assess librarian and college student use of a cooperative VRS in fall 2009 and spring 2010 are presented.

Introduction

Remember the old question "What came first—the chicken or the egg?" When discussing the evolution of virtual reference (VR) it seems that there is a similar question that can be phrased: "What came first—the Internet or electronic publishing?" Speaking as information providers, the Internet and electronic publishing are both integral parts of providing reference service in a virtual world.

The robust interconnected world of Internet reference came into existence in 1992 when the U.S. Department of Education created AskERIC, one of the first formal online reference programs. AskERIC took the reference desk into cyberspace and significantly changed the process. Virtual question-and-answer services emerged and by the end of the decade, sites were logging impressive statistics. The reference interview had started to go digital. Internet usage increased and patrons began to expect information to be delivered quickly at any time or on any day (Stahl & Kresh, 2001).

A truly virtual library experience, though, depended on the electronic accessibility of information. Beginning in 2000, electronic content moved from simple indexing and abstracting or aggregator services to information being produced and available only electronically. The physical boundaries of the library started disappearing in the same way distance education was blurring campus boundaries and allowing the library to reach outside traditional reference service models (Bower & Mee, 2010).

This chapter explores the differences among the various technology-driven reference services available. Chat, text, and vendor services are evaluated through the lenses of the following questions: How does the product work? How is it staffed? What is the level of usage/popularity? What are the differences in collaboration between multiple institutions, citing the pros and cons of a single institution versus a cooperative? The following section provides a description of various VR formats, and a comparison of how they are operating in a variety of academic settings. In addition, promotion and marketing initiatives are discussed for each.

Chat/IM Reference Services[1]

LibraryH3lp at the Auraria Library, Denver, Colorado

The Auraria Library in downtown Denver serves a student population of approximately 48,000 in programs from the associate's degree to the doctorate. Three institutions of higher education share the Library—University of Colorado at Denver, Metropolitan State College of Denver, and the Community College of Denver. Auraria Library serves both a high ratio of nontraditional students and a large number of distance education students. LibraryH3lp (http://libraryh3lp.com/) serves both groups well. LibraryH3lp is used to staff Aurania's in-house chat reference service called "AskAuraria." Currently, all questions go into a single queue. One librarian at a time is assigned to staff AskAuraria from 8 a.m. to 6 p.m. However, all librarians are encouraged to "hover" on AskAuraria, picking up chats when the volume of questions coming in is high. LibraryH3lp's robustness has proven valuable while handling high volumes of online traffic.

The ability to embed widgets throughout the Library's webpages, class guides, databases, and more makes it easy for off-campus students to get help from a librarian. Nontraditional students who may not have experienced IM for social purposes report feeling comfortable with LibraryH3lp's simple interface. LibraryH3lp used at Auraria was created by a librarian (Pam Sessoms of UNC-Chapel Hill) and her programmer husband (Eric Sessoms of Nub Games), specifically for libraries. It offers great versatility in terms of features and setup, yet both novice library patrons and librarians find it easy to pick up. Librarians typically operate LibraryH3lp using Pidgin (http://www.pidgin.im/), a free chat client, or other Jabber-based (http://jabber.org/) open source-chat clients. Patrons can ask questions using widgets embedded in websites, text messages, and popular IM software such as Google Talk and AIM. LibraryH3lp functions well on most mobile devices. The administration module allows librarians to read transcripts, gather statistics, design queues for special types of questions, and more. And, believe it or not, LibraryH3lp bears a reasonable price tag (based on enrollment or related patron statistics).

Auraria has used LibraryH3lp since July 2008. Students immediately caught on, despite little formal advertisement. Usage went steadily upward for the first year of AskAuraria's existence. Since that time, it has maintained a fairly consistent up-and-down pattern following the academic year (more questions at exam time, fewer over the summer, and so on). On an average mid-semester day, AskAuraria receives about 30 questions.

The Auraria Library has not formally advertised the chat reference service. However, most library instructors demonstrate AskAuraria during instruction sessions, and encourage their students to try it later. Many other students simply give the chat boxes a try, since they are scattered throughout the Library's pages, databases, and class guides.

Meebo at the University of North Texas (UNT)

The University of North Texas (UNT) has more than 36,000 students enrolled in bachelor's, master's, and doctoral programs, and more than 2,000 faculty. Sixteen percent of the students live on campus. Most classes have an online component and more than 15 percent of the students are enrolled in online programs only.

Meebo Messenger (http://www.meebo.com/), used by UNT Libraries, allows access to all the major IM networks (AIM, Yahoo!, Windows Live Messenger, Google Talk, ICQ, and Jabber) in a single buddy list, right from a browser. One can sign into multiple Meebo accounts at once and the software allows for the transfer of files and saving of the conversation history. It is free and open source. However, as with many other free online tools, advertising appears at the bottom of the Meebo page. UNT is using Meebo for its stand-alone chat reference service. It is staffed Monday through Friday 8:00 a.m. to 6:00 p.m., though individual librarians may hover at any time.

The University of North Texas Libraries launched the Meebo reference service at UNT in September 2009 as an additional virtual reference point. The statistics vary widely depending on the point in the semester and how many hours it is staffed. There was a high of 104 questions in October and a high in the spring semester of 91 questions in April. As expected, January and May were the lowest months with around 10 questions each.

The publicity for the UNT Meebo has been primarily the placement of the widget prominently on the AskUs page. This page describes all of the reference services available. The reference services are pointed out in all instruction classes. Flyers for all services are distributed at all the reference points in the four libraries. While the usage is constant, it is low compared to other reference services offered.

AskAcademic at Austin Community College, Texas (ACC)

Austin Community College (ACC) libraries serve more than 40,000 students in associate's and certificate programs, of which approximately 15,000 are distance learners, and 3,000 faculty and staff. The college has recently become a member of the AskAcademic (http://askacademic.org/) collaborative. It was the second out-of-state college to join this collaborative, which had been the academic portion of AskColorado, a statewide virtual reference service (VRS), and split into a separate service after a pilot project in 2008 added academic institutions in Texas. AskAcademic works well for ACC because it serves as the primary "after-hours" chat reference service. AskAcademic provides an additional access point to reference services for students district wide. Library Services Dean Julie Todaro is committed to providing seamless access to reference services to constituents across eight full-service campuses, eight counties, nine regional centers, and a variety of business and community locations. In supporting the overall mission of the college, which is ultimately about supporting student success and retaining students who graduate and join the workforce or who transfer to a four-year institution, AskAcademic is another important tool to use to support academic achievement.

As one of the newest members of the AskAcademic collaborative, Austin Community College has been using the product since April 19, 2010, when the college launched the service. From April through July, there were 89 chat sessions originating from ACC students. Librarians answered eight chats. Usage has increased and shows a pattern of starting slowly with the number of questions increasing as the semester progresses. In spring and summer semesters 2011, there were 175 chat sessions originating from ACC students. Librarians answered 107 chats for the cooperative. The rest were answered by other librarians in the cooperative.

Austin Community College Library Services' Public Relations team designed posters and bookmarks and distributed hundreds to campus libraries and posted in student areas. AskAcademic was announced on the faculty electronic discussion list and to the head of the college's Distance Learning Department. The Extension/Distance Learning Librarian created a link to AskAcademic on the Library Services Tab in Blackboard, so every distance learning student and any Austin Community College students can access it from Blackboard. During New Faculty Orientation, Library Services Dean and PR Librarian present all library services to new part-time and full-time faculty. The AskAcademic bookmark image was placed on the library's homepage for a week before the end of the spring semester and at the beginning of the summer session and periodically throughout the semester (e.g., midterm, finals, etc.). The Library Services webmaster created a blog entry about AskAcademic, added AskAcademic to the ACC Library's Help Page, and created an additional AskAcademic information webpage. AskAcademic table tents are placed in library study carrels, group study rooms, and quiet study areas. Librarians announce the service to students during information literacy and library presentations. Many of these PR efforts are launched each semester. Austin Community College students are using the service and usage has increased each month since April 2010.

QuestionPoint at the University of Washington (UW)

The University of Washington (UW) is a three-campus system with multiple libraries, 43,000 students enrolled in bachelor's, master's and doctoral programs, and 50,000 staff. The UW Libraries has used Online Computer Library Center's (OCLC) QuestionPoint (http://questionpoint.org/) since its inception in 2002. QuestionPoint is a complete question management system that integrates e-mail, chat, an instant messaging widget (QWidget), and text messaging. Questions received in person, by phone, or via personal e-mail can be added to the system. Subscribers have the option of participating in the 24/7 chat cooperative, staffed by member libraries and OCLC-employed backup librarians. The system provides a knowledge base and tools that support seamless follow-up, referrals, and reports.

For more than ten years, a homegrown e-mail system was used to forward information and reference questions to the appropriate unit or individual. Tracking whether or not a question was answered was impossible and relied on the recipient to confirm that a response was received. There was also no way to determine overall use of the service or traffic patterns. A "one-stop" service was important for UW users and librarians, so that questions coming through e-mail, chat, and text could be seamlessly moved to the appropriate expert and easily tracked.

More than 100 UW units, branches, and subject librarians have accounts on QuestionPoint, which allows them to scan for questions at any time. The Information Technology Division checks the list often to determine frequent problems users have interacting with the website. They are then able to implement solutions. In addition to the main UW account, subaccounts exist for the campuses at Bothell and Tacoma, and for Special Collections, the Health Sciences Library, and the Law Library. They receive questions directly and librarians can refer questions between accounts.

UW was a beta site for QuestionPoint e-mail in 2002. From 2002 to 2005, UW collaborated with Cornell University in offering a chat service using the 24/7ref.org software. For those three years, QuestionPoint was used for e-mail and 24/7ref.org for chat. When OCLC acquired 24/7ref.org in 2005 and integrated it into QuestionPoint, UW parted ways with Cornell, implemented chat, and joined the 24/7 cooperative. Use has grown steadily since 2002, but inquiries tripled when the move was made to the 24/7 service. Users no longer had to remember when the service was staffed, and the service witnessed increases in both e-mail and chat statistics. Another spike occurred when the "QWidget," QuestionPoint's simplified, IM-chat product (questions still go into the library's question queue) was added. The service is staffed with two and sometimes three people from 9:00 a.m. to 5:00 p.m. Monday through Friday.

After subscribing to QuestionPoint, one of the major achievements was placing a persistent link to the service on all of our webpages. Previously, each unit had a "contact us" link that went to a unit e-mail account. Many of the branch libraries are minimally staffed, which meant that users sometimes had to wait several days for a response to questions such as "How do I access this journal article online?" By centralizing the management of questions, a team of librarians is able to respond in a timely manner seven days a week to e-mail and texts, and follow up quickly on chats, and to refer in-depth subject questions to the subject librarian.

The University of Washington Libraries has relied on the front-and-center placement of our AskUs link on all of its webpages. Each time the links to the QWidget or AskUs link in our databases are installed, an increase in usage is seen. Another major marketing effort is through instruction and orientation programs, where subject librarians promote the service. Several years ago, library buildings were papered with table tents advertising the service. Some students took advantage of this information, making contact from the upper floors of the buildings, but it is not clear that it resulted in service growth. Our text service, added in early 2010, has been minimally used. Its availability is highlighted through the library webpage, in class instruction, and at service desks, but it is clear it is necessary to mount a campaign to let students know of its existence.

Tutor.com at Regis University, Colorado
Regis University is a residential college with more than 1,400 traditional-age students enrolled in bachelor's- and master's-level programs. Regis is one of 17 Association of Jesuit Colleges and University (AJCU) libraries participating in the service. Librarians from multiple institutions can be signed in to staff a shift for the service, as well as to staff queues for their home institutions. The service is 24/7 with Tutor.com's Librarians

by Request (http://www.tutor.com/) staffing the overnight hours as well as providing backup staffing.

Tutor.com—Ask A Librarian software is collaborative VR software licensed from Tutor.com. Tutor.com is currently focusing on their Ask A Librarian Express service, in addition to their online tutoring services, and has no plans to upgrade or further develop the Ask A Librarian software. Tutor.com's Ask A Librarian software works for the AJCU Virtual Reference Project because of the collaborative nature of the service.

The Association of Jesuit Colleges and Universities Virtual Reference Project started in 2004, and Regis joined in 2005. There was a big jump overall in questions asked per year from 2005–2006 to 2006–2007. Usage has been steady the past few years. In 2009–2010 there were about 11,700 questions asked in total across the service. For the 2009/2010 academic year, Regis' statistics are up about 100 questions asked over the previous year.

Each participating institution in the Association of Jesuit Colleges and Universities Virtual Reference Project is responsible for their branding and marketing. At Regis, the service is branded "Ask Us!," while others have branded theirs Ask a Librarian, Ask Live, Get Help, Live Help, and Chat with a Librarian. Regis launched its service with posters, postcards, bookmarks, and an e-mail blast. A new marketing campaign will launch for fall 2010 with bookmarks, posters, and an e-mail blast to distance learning students. Regis has seen usage slowly increase over the years. At Regis, there is a large distance learning population; however, the service is not linked in the university's course management system so students that could potentially utilize the service the most are not always aware it exists. Those patrons that do use the service rate it highly. In 2009–2010, 94.84 percent of users who filled out the satisfaction survey indicated they would recommend the service to a friend.

SMS- or Text Message–Based Services[2]

My Info Quest: Adams State College, Colorado

Adams State College (ASC) has approximately 2,500 on-campus students, more than 10,000 students in the Extended Studies program, and 123 faculty. My Info Quest (http://www.myinfoquest.info/) is used by ASC and is a collaborative text-messaging reference service that enables users to send questions via short message service (SMS) text messages on their mobile phones. The cost and feasibility of having a dedicated cell phone to provide text reference was a concern for many libraries. As a result, the My Info Quest pilot was attractive to many libraries that could not afford a dedicated cell phone for reference. The My Info Quest pilot project is powered by the SMS reference software and systems generously donated by Altarama (http://www.altarama.com/). A shared Gmail.com account is used as the platform for answering questions. Users receive answers on their mobile phones in a matter of minutes. The pilot project is currently free for participating libraries with the agreement to staff at least two hours per week. Currently more than 60 libraries are participating in the project. As of this writing, My Info Quest is open 80 hours per week, with an eventual goal of 24/7 service. Service hours will expand as additional libraries join.

Librarians at ASC have been staffing My Info Quest text messaging service since the pilot project began in July 2009. In the first full month of launching My Info Quest there were 282 questions asked and answered. By the end of 2009, the text messaging service fielded an average of 500–800 questions per month. In June 2010 the collaborative answered more than 850 questions and in February, My Info Quest broke 1,000 questions. My Info Quest continues to average 800 questions per month. The service is advertised more at the beginning of semesters and at midterm and final exam periods. There has been increased usage during those time periods, but there may be little or no causality. Increased usage could be attributed to increased demand for library services in general.

To participate in the pilot phase of My Info Quest, ASC Nielsen Library agreed to promote the service by placing the logo and portal for the text messaging service on its homepage. Since making the service available not only to the nationwide collaborative but to the local community of users, use statistics by patrons in the local area code have risen from approximately five text messages to an average of 20–25 text message questions per month.

Mosio at Colorado State University–Pueblo

Colorado State University at Pueblo (CSU-P) has more than 5,000 students enrolled in bachelor's- and master's-level programs and almost 500 faculty. The University Library at CSU-P uses the Mosio Text a Librarian Service (http://www.textalibrarian.com/). Students may text questions to the library using a number and keyword. Questions are received on a micro board, which is a secure dedicated website for each subscribing library, where questions and answers are archived. Librarians must log in to the micro board using a username and password in order to see the patron's question. Patrons are assigned a number and their anonymity is protected. However, the micro board does keep track of how many questions that a particular patron's phone has sent. This is useful for tracking follow-up questions. Librarians are able to create templates with answers to frequently asked questions and set up an auto response for when the library is closed or the service is unavailable.

The CSU-P Library started using Mosio just over a year ago, at the beginning of the 2009–2010 school year. In August 2009, 34 questions were received, which was the busiest month so far. In June 2010, when classes were not in session for the majority of the month and the campus population had decreased significantly, there were only two questions. Usage seems to follow the ebb and flow of the semester and the changes in campus population. Text a Librarian is busier at the beginning of semesters, especially the fall semester, when new students arrive on campus, and during peak testing and homework periods. With only one year of data to analyze, it would be difficult to predict how the service will grow.

This service has been promoted in many ways at CSU-P. All librarians involved in instruction have highlighted the service in their instruction sessions; flyers have been distributed; table tents were set up in the dining hall at the beginning of the fall semester; the service is featured prominently on the library webpage; promotional items with the keyword and number were handed out at student orientations and events, and the service was featured on the library's blog. It is difficult to tell if increased usage in certain months is due to increased demand for assistance from a librarian, or to an increase in advertising. The library has attempted to advertise the service more at the beginning of semesters and at midterm and final exam periods. There has been increased usage during those time periods, but there may be little or no causality. Increased usage could be attributed to increased demand for library services in general.

Cooperative versus Stand-Alone Service

The following section reveals whether each service is operating as a cooperative or as a stand-alone. It discusses how each VRS works, whether it is serving multiple institutions or a single institution, and describes the pros and cons from each institution's perspective.

LibraryH3lp

The Auraria Library participates in AskAcademic, a 24/7 cooperative chat reference service currently covering Colorado and Texas. Auraria's Web Librarian designed a widget that directs students to AskAuraria when an Auraria librarian is signed on. When no one is signed on to AskAuraria, the widget displays a link to AskAcademic. Students seem to use the two services fairly seamlessly. The 24/7 coverage makes this combination quite worthwhile. Librarians have not discovered any significant downsides.

Meebo

The University of North Texas (UNT) Libraries staff the Meebo IM service as a stand-alone service. The pluses are that students get the answers to peculiar questions about the UNT website or resources from the UNT librarians. In addition, since it is easy to create the Meebo widget, each subject librarian can put a chat widget on their subject guides and students can ask questions when they are available. The downside is the staffing is limited. The widgets on the subject pages are only staffed when the subject librarian signs in and there is no consistency in hours staffed between subjects. The widget on the general reference page is staffed fewer hours than the library is open. So while it is more convenient to IM from a webpage rather than phone, and many students prefer IM to talking to a person, it does not expand the hours of reference coverage any.

AskAcademic

AskAcademic is a cooperative that is customer-service driven. In addition, Austin Community College (ACC) District is a single institution with multiple campuses and sites. For accreditation purposes, it's important that the institution is in compliance with distant learning associations' guidelines for serving distance learners. ACC has the services that are required, but AskAcademic gives the college another opportunity to provide seamless access to references services and to meet more students' and faculty's information needs—anywhere, anytime. AskAcademic has a "collaborative communication infrastructure."

There are multiple ways to remain in contact with other members (e.g., Intranet, blog, wiki, Delicious bookmarks, forums, electronic discussion lists, e-mail, telephone conferences, face-to-face meetings, chat). Because of its cooperative nature, AskAcademic is dynamic and open to change because its members direct change, not one person. A cooperative offers the collective expertise of its members. AskAcademic provides access to answers to difficult or challenging reference questions. It provides professional development opportunities for its members. It also helps staff increase online reference skills and offers members opportunities to work with colleagues outside of one's own institution.

AskAcademic is a great value for the money and time invested since the cooperative has a sliding scale based on each institution's budget and resources.

However, as well as advantages, some disadvantages have been found. Austin Community College librarians who staff AskAcademic have not had much opportunity to pick up very many chats during their shifts Friday evenings, and Saturday and Sunday afternoons. Austin Community College also uses stand-alone virtual chat reference software that all librarians (full-time and adjunct) answer during their shifts on the reference desk when all eight campus libraries are open. This software must be loaded and licensed for eight reference desktop computers, which presents a set of challenges not found with AskAcademic. Working in a VR chat environment has inherent challenges, such as the lack of verbal and nonverbal cues. InstantService software does not allow librarians to see another agent's chat transcript in progress. InstantService software also does not provide SMS capability.

QuestionPoint

The University of Washington Libraries is in several cooperatives, all through QuestionPoint. UW participates in the AskWA academic library cooperative (http://ask.wa.gov/), answering questions for other academic libraries in the state. It is also part of the QuestionPoint 24/7 service and staffs the cooperative for 12–15 hours each week (in addition to the libraries' local coverage). The system is designed to allow us to monitor one or multiple groups. Many staff members, for example, turn on only the local queue. Others monitor both the local and the state academic queue, and there is a small group of librarians that staff all of the queues. The Health Sciences Library has its own QWidget and librarians are able to transfer live chats to them during the hours they monitor. In the Washington State cooperative and through the global QuestionPoint account, questions can also be transferred via e-mail to other QuestionPoint member libraries in the state and beyond.

The advantages to cooperatives far outweigh any disadvantages. Students have access to a librarian 24 hours a day, 7 days a week, all year. The librarian can help with getting started on a topic or—one of the most common questions—how to log in to licensed resources from home. There is no need for users to remember service hours, since chat is always available. Because QuestionPoint maintains one list of questions, one can quickly check to see if a user who came through e-mail immediately logged on to chat for an answer. If the question was sufficiently answered in chat, there is no need for follow-up. We often peruse our list of questions by 7:00 a.m. and can follow up on chats that came in overnight. Users have been impressed with this service. Each QuestionPoint library completes a policy page, to which there is a link within the chat interface. This helps the librarians in the cooperative to rapidly track down local library and campus information. Another appreciated feature is that questions can be referred to experts throughout the world, from whom some substantial responses have been received that impress our faculty and graduate students. The disadvantage is that occasionally the assistance from the cooperative is less than ideal. This can happen for a multitude of reasons, from trying to juggle too many users to failing to read the question to not checking the policy page. However, poor service is rare and the system makes it easy to submit quality reports and to follow up with users.

Tutor.com

Regis is in a cooperative through the Association of Jesuit Colleges and Universities (AJCU). The project works well because participating institutions share similar missions and resources; that is why Regis originally joined the AJCU project rather than a statewide collaborative. The 24/7 service is the biggest pro and is a huge selling point when marketing the service to students and faculty. Each participating institution has a project page with links to catalogs, databases, remote-access information, library hours, etc., to assist librarians in answering questions from patrons at their institution. However, it can be challenging because users do not always realize that the librarian they are chatting with is not a librarian at their home institution.

Each participating institution has a VR coordinator and the coordinators work hard at communication. The coordinator group uses a wiki and a Google group for regular communication, in addition to meeting face-to-face on an annual basis. The face-to-face meeting has allowed for strong relationship building among the coordinators, making regular communication more effective. Of the current participating institutions, 14 of the libraries are using another chat service to answer local questions during some hours. These include LibraryH3lp, Meebo, Pidgin, and Gmail chat.

My Info Quest

There is definitely going to be positive alongside negative aspects with any collaborative project, especially one like My Info Quest, which includes more than 60 libraries spanning across the United States and Canada. Obviously, the first considerations are training, staffing, and communication. Training was provided from the beginning of the My Info Quest project. Each library was responsible for attending training sessions held online and monthly advisory meetings. Keeping up with policy implementations is each participating library's responsibility. Each library is also responsible for making sure its assigned shift is staffed.

An advantage of this size of cooperative is the knowledge base in which to serve patrons. Serving the patron base of multiple institutions is a challenge. As a collaborative text message reference service, it works. My Info Quest is multiple institutions serving a patron base of potentially thousands. As a concerted effort, each library agrees to provide the best reference service, just as they would in their own institution. Eventually, My Info Quest text messaging service will cost each institution to participate. The advantage of multiple institutions helping to buffer the software price is that it will help bring down the cost for each individual institution of a manageable cost-effective resource for patrons.

On the possibly negative side, since this is a grassroots effort, members must assume responsibility for running the organization, taking an active part in committee work, and making sure their staff is properly trained. As with all group efforts, it seems some organizations participate more than others, and this is not necessarily based on size of the organization.

Mosio

Text a Librarian, as used at CSU-P, is a stand-alone service. One of the factors driving the decision to adopt the service was the displacement of the Library, librarians, and library services while the library building was undergoing renovation. The library building is the tallest building on campus and centrally located. It is usually easily accessible and obvious to the students. The Library's current location is in the basement of the Union Center, and has to be accessed through a corridor containing the entrances to the Student Activities office, the Office of International Programs, a café, the Diversity Office, and Student Support Services. The main print collection is in storage, and items must be requested via the library catalog and retrieved by student workers. The University Archive and Special Collections is in yet another building, in a makeshift space in what used to be science classrooms. Librarians' offices are scattered over five buildings across the campus. The Library staff felt they needed to make themselves and their services as accessible as possible during this difficult time.

The most important advantage of the stand-alone service is being able to help students with local questions about Library and campus services. Text a Librarian service is seen as an extension of the reference desk and another way to serve students. Many questions received are of a local nature (related to campus locations and services, or to specific databases), and librarians feel that they are the best people to answer those questions. Since the answers to Text a Librarian questions are short due to the constraints of the technology, follow-up with students can be accomplished via-email, phone, or in person, if necessary. Often, they can be referred to another campus department or entity, such as tutoring, financial aid, advising, etc. What can probably be seen as a con of the Text a Librarian service is the fact that the service is only staffed when the library is open. The service does send an automated reply to students if the library is closed and the patron must wait to receive a reply until a librarian is back on duty. However, very few questions have been received when the library was closed, so that may indicate that a 24/7 service is not optimal for campus.

Staffing Issues
Each institution has different staffing models, including shared approaches, staffing at the physical reference desk, or staffing from home. The following section describes these configurations.

LibraryH3lp
The vast majority of staffing is performed by librarians from their offices. Originally, Auraria intended for some coverage to be provided from the reference desk. However, the demand for in-person reference service was too high for librarians to reasonably do both at once. Shifts can, however, easily be covered from any location. LibraryH3lp provides a "web chat" module that allows librarians to easily staff by signing in online. Librarians who prefer to staff using a Jabber client such as Pidgin can download Pidgin software online. AskAuraria's application manager offers to install this on librarians' personal laptops. The few librarians who do staff from home enjoy it. The author of this section likes staffing while working on documents in her living room. She can also take her laptop into the kitchen, turn the alert sounds up, and monitor AskAuraria while baking.

Meebo
UNT uses librarians and College of Information graduate students to staff the service, which is available for the core hours the library is open. Most of the time, it is staffed

from the offices. However, when the library is closed for weather and on holidays it is possible for librarians to staff from home. In low-library-use times, such as semester breaks, it can be staffed from the reference desk rather than the offices.

AskAcademic

In February 2010, Austin Community College adjunct faculty librarians were encouraged to volunteer to staff AskAcademic. The AskAcademic cooperative has varying requirements for the number of hours an institution staffs the service based primarily on the size of the institution. Five adjunct librarians staff AskAcademic in 2-hour shifts from the reference desk at their respective campuses for a total of 10 hours per week. Two librarians staff two hours each on Fridays, another staffs the service for a couple of hours on Saturday afternoons, and another staffs AskAcademic on Sunday afternoons. A fifth librarian alternates Saturday and Sunday staffing. Adjunct librarians' reference desk hours often change per semester; however, this core group of librarians has maintained the same staffing schedule with relatively few changes. They seek coverage from other librarians in the cooperative or from each other as needed.

QuestionPoint

The University of Washington has a team of librarians who are assigned a day each to monitor the question list. On their assigned day, they answer and assign questions and follow up on chats. For chat, a self-scheduling process is used through a shared calendar. A call goes out each morning to the chat staff electronic discussion list to fill vacancies in the schedule. The librarians can monitor chat from home or office. VR is monitored at a public desk only when there is no one available. The availability of the service was critical a few years ago, when a snowstorm closed the campus for three days at the end of the fall quarter. All of the chat hours were covered with librarians at home who responded to hundreds of questions about how to return books and whether or not overdue fees would be assessed when users were unable to journey to campus.

Tutor.com

There are staffing tiers for the Association of Jesuit Colleges and Universities project— eight, six, or four hours per week—based on the institution's full-time enrollment. Regis is responsible for staffing eight hours per week. Regis has a large distance learning population which puts Regis in the first tier for staffing the service. It has sometimes been a challenge to staff eight hours per week because Regis has fewer librarians than some of the other larger institutions in the project. Regis librarians staff the service from their offices or from home. The service is not staffed from the reference desk because the desk is single staffed. The Ask A Librarian provider software is not compatible with Macs and that has caused some frustration for librarians wishing to staff from home. Staffing has been on a volunteer basis, with librarians from the Reference, Distance Services, and Electronic Services Departments all participating.

My Info Quest

Two reference librarians staff My Info Quest. Nielsen Library at Adams State College agreed to staff the service two hours per week. Librarians staff from their desk while the option to staff from home or while on the road is not out of the question, as long as Internet connectivity is available.

Mosio

At Colorado State University–Pueblo, staffing for the service is shared among all of the librarians. The library faculty already used an on-call system to ensure that the reference desk is covered at all times. Librarians take turns being on call one weekday every other week. It was decided that the on-call librarian would be the primary person to staff the Text a Librarian service, with the librarian at the reference desk being the secondary person. This accomplishes two things: the service is constantly staffed by at least one person, and the librarian at the reference desk is free to assist patrons at the desk without ignoring the Text a Librarian patrons.

Conclusion

Part of the evaluation of the original pilot project with University of North Texas and AskAcademic was a survey to see how the librarians felt about answering questions for other academic libraries and how the users perceived the service they received. When adding an out-of-state library to what was a one-state cooperative, there were some questions about how well VR librarians would be able to answer questions for the patrons of libraries they had never even seen and if the patrons would think they were receiving inferior service because "their" librarians were not answering their questions.

Fifty-nine percent of the 38 librarians who answered the survey said they frequently or mostly answered questions from users not at their institution. Eighty-two percent of the librarians were comfortable or very comfortable answering questions from users not at their institution. Eighteen percent were somewhat uncomfortable, and none indicated that they were very uncomfortable.

Of the 165 students answering the question, equal numbers said they did or did not know they were speaking to a librarian who was not at their institution. An additional 20 percent said they did not know. However, more than 60 percent of the total respondents did not answer this question. It could not be determined whether they did not answer the question because they did not understand the question, or if it did not matter to them. Almost 70 percent strongly agreed that the information they received from the interaction was helpful. More than 80 percent said it was helpful or possibly helpful to be able to contact a librarian electronically, while only 17 percent said it was not helpful or did not matter.

The perception that only local librarians can best answer questions from their local users is fairly common. However, the authors involved in a cooperative think that the additional hours they are able to provide and the additional expertise gained are very important and far outweigh any disadvantages.

The academic library of today is challenged to provide support for students and faculty not only on campus, but also around the world. On-campus learners and distance learners alike demand access to content and services outside the boundaries of the physical library, and libraries have risen to the challenge by developing a suite of reference services. As library users spend more of their time in virtual space it is important that libraries be accessible to them there. The standard model of face-to-face now must be complemented by telephone, e-mail, chat/IM, and text, and because it is possible, the expectation is 24/7 service. The variations on the themes of service configurations, staffing models, and marketing strategies provided here are offered as examples of how a common goal of providing choice and convenient VR can play out successfully in different academic environments.

Notes
1. The following authors discuss chat/IM services as used in their institutions: (1) Karen Sobel of Auraria Library, Colorado (Auraria); LibraryH3lp; (2) Beth Fuseler Avery of University of North Texas (UNT); Meebo; (3) Sylvia Owens of Austin Community College, Texas (ACC); AskAcademic (powered by InstaService); (4) Nancy Huling of the University of Washington (UW); QuestionPoint; and (5) Erin McCaffrey of Regis University, Colorado (Regis); Tutor.com.
2. The following authors discuss SMS or text message–based services as used in their institutions: (1) Paul M. Mascareñas of Adams State College, Colorado (ASC); My Info Quest (powered by Altarama software); and b) Julie Fronmueller, Colorado State University–Pueblo (CSU-P).

References
Bower, S. L., & Mee, S. A. (2010). Virtual delivery of electronic resources and services to off-campus users: A multifaceted approach. *Journal of Library Administration, 50*(5–6), 468–483.
Stahl, J., & Kresh, D. M. (2001). Online, virtual, e-mail, digital, real time: The next generation of reference services. *Art Documentation, 20*(1), 26–30.

Additional Readings
Connaway, L. S., & Radford, M. L. (2010). Virtual reference service quality: Critical components for adults and the Net-generation. *Libri, 60*(2), 165–180.
DeHart, D. L., & Viles, A. (2007). Virtual reference service in southeastern academic libraries: A study of availability. *The Southeastern Librarian, 55*, 36–40.
Lipow, A. G. (2003). *The virtual reference librarian's handbook.* New York: Neal-Schuman.
Meert, D. L., & Given, L. M. (2009). Measuring quality in chat reference consortia: A comparative analysis of responses to users' queries. *College & Research Libraries, 70*(1), 71–84.
Peters, T. A. (2002). E-reference: How consortia add value. *The Journal of Academic Librarianship, 28*(4), 248–250.
Rourke, L., & Pascal, L. (2010). Learning from chatting: How our virtual reference questions are giving us answers. *Evidence Based Library & Information Practice, 5*(2), 63–67.

## CHAPTER 13

Managing Mayhem: Wrestling with Academic Library Reference and Outreach Challenges

Kari A. Kozak and Leo P. Clougherty

Overview

Bringing academic libraries into the spotlight has always been difficult, but even more so during this challenging time. Over the past year at the University of Iowa, four branch libraries were merged into other existing locations, material was moved into off-site storage, and the Sciences Library was created while offices in buildings that no longer have libraries were retained. A variety of outreach strategies to the community and general public—as well as those associated with the university—have been offered to help users understand that the Library as a place still exists and has valuable resources, and to increase exposure and raise awareness of its resources. These efforts included creating a website with links to the various subjects that used to be independent libraries, hosting exhibits, and giving presentations. Events, exhibits, and posters for different events (including Earth Day, Pi Day, Mole Day, fiftieth anniversary of the laser's invention, and more) have showcased the collections and given different subject areas time in the spotlight. These projects have provided opportunities to reduce the confusion that may have been created by the closures and increase use and awareness of library resources. The changes taking place at the University of Iowa's Sciences Library highlight ways that it has evolved to ensure that users continue to look to and access its resources. This chapter explores challenges and describes the lessons learned from experiencing these changes.

Introduction

Merging libraries and rejuvenating marketing strategies is becoming more common in academic libraries. Many institutions have had to face closures or mergers over the years, which can be contributed, at least in part, to budget constraints and trends of falling statistics for in-house use of materials, circulation, and photocopying. The Academic Research Libraries from 2001–2002 (Martell, 2005) report that decreases in usage statistics can be seen at a wide variety of locations. Statistics from many individual institutions also show this decline, including the California State University Libraries, the University of Washington, the University of Idaho at Moscow, Augusta State University, and the University of Maryland (Carlson, 2001; Hiller, 2004; Martell, 2005).

Mergers and closures can be seen at a wide variety of academic library locations. For example, the University of Wisconsin-Madison merged three health science libraries into one (Hitchcock, Sager, & Schneider, 2005). The University of Pittsburgh has closed one of the four libraries in the Health Sciences Library System (Czechowski, Barger, Fort, & Maxeiner, 2010). At the Ohio State University, in 1993, six separate departmental libraries were merged into the Science and Engineering Library (Opperman & Jamison, 2008). Louisiana State University has closed its chemistry library (Armstrong, 2005). This did not affect only academic libraries. The Engineering Societies Library, a department of the United Engineering Trustees, Inc., closed its doors in 1998 and had the collection dispersed between the Linda Hall Library in Kansas City and the New York Public Library (Cohen, 2000). Princeton University opened a new science library, Lewis Library, on September 11, 2008, which combined many of the University's science and technology spaces (Cliatt, 2008).

With these mergers and the decrease in print usage, gate counts at Ohio State University's Science and Engineering Library and Indiana University's Life Sciences Library had gone up (Opperman & Jamison, 2008; Winterman & Hill, 2010). This increase gives the Sciences Library hope that after the mayhem of the merging of the four branch libraries, a gate count increase can also be seen through invigorating reference, marketing, and outreach strategies.

Merging of the Branches
The traditional model of multiple library locations around campus was useful for many years. The collection was near the primary users; it kept the material out of the Main Library stacks so they were not outgrown; and it was easy for the library staff to learn and respond to the needs of the users who were on-site. With budget reductions hitting libraries nationwide, the University of Iowa Libraries needed to make plans for large cuts. Due to reduced usage and the electronic availability of so many science resources, the decision was made to close the Geosciences, Mathematics, Physics, and Psychology branch libraries and merge these collections into the current location of the Biological Sciences Library. In addition, the staff displaced by this merger would allow some flexibility in filling the duties of retired staff and some of the open positions with the least detriment to our users.

The closing and merger decisions caused pandemonium not only because it was a huge change for the campus, but also because it happened very quickly. The time between the decision to consider closing branch libraries and the first closure was only nine months. This time frame was so short because the budget savings needed to be realized before the next fiscal year, and the moves needed to be done between semesters when the user impact would be minimized. Due to the relatively short notice, the librarians and staff felt thrust into the project by everything happening so fast and furiously.

Before going ahead with this idea, the University Librarian first had to make sure that the remaining branch libraries and the facilities could handle the influx of materials, that the time frames for relocation would work within both the fiscal year and the breaks between classes, and that funding would be available from the university administration to pay for the moving companies and the purchase of any additional shelving required. Beyond these up-front questions, she also had to make sure that the campus administrators were convinced this was a necessary charge and that they would back the libraries mergers. This step was particularly important because of expected backlash from at least some of the faculty and students from the affected departments.

Understandably, some of the users were quite upset with the plans to close the branch libraries. It was convenient for them, as well as the libraries, to have the materials right at hand, especially in the laboratory-oriented sciences where it is more difficult to be away from the laboratory for long periods to do library research. Also, since each branch was located in their respective departmental buildings, most of the branches allowed the primary users (who were given keys) to have access 24/7. This access was very popular with faculty, because they could work on their own schedule and avoid the students who otherwise might keep them tied down with questions usually asked during office hours. One branch, Chemistry, had been moved out of its "parent building" for several years because of major construction, so the faculty were used to the idea of going some distance for materials and using electronic means, for the most part, to contact their subject liaison. The other departments' faculty and students put up some resistance to the plan.

Communicating the decision became a sensitive undertaking and required considerable political support. Once administrative support was in place, the University Librarian and the head of the involved branch library scheduled meetings with the heads of the affected university departments. In several departments, she also attended a faculty meeting to explain the necessity of the closure and respond to any questions. The users needed interaction through e-mail and telephone, and in person, with the library staff to get person-to-person reassurance that the library was still committed to providing the best service possible, and to see plans to soften the impact of changes created by the mergers.

In the end, the four science branch libraries listed earlier were closed, all but one of which the authors of this chapter staffed. A large percentage of each collection was sent to the off-site storage facility. The remainder of the Mathematical Sciences collection was moved entirely to the Main Library and shelved in its own separate section. At least part of the material from all of the other libraries was merged into what had been the Biological Sciences Library (BSL). Due to the need for additional space in the BSL stacks to house the merging collections, much of the BSL collection first had to be sent to storage. The remaining Psychology Library collection was sent to the Hardin Library for the Health Sciences with only the reference collections and the reserve materials to BSL. The entire collections from the Geoscience Library and the Physics Library had to be either stored or merged into BSL.

Closing libraries is not an easy thing, especially when merging more than one simultaneously. Before the actual moving process began, numerous decisions needed to be made and many library staff meetings were held involving all of the affected library departments and branches. Most decisions involved interaction between staff from two or more libraries regarding the amount of material that could be added, and therefore, how much material needed to be sent to storage. Some of these decisions were more complicated and involved a wide variety of library staff from technology to cataloging to access services. The most important decisions were in which order the moves would take place and setting reasonable timetables for preparation and the logistics for actual library moves.

The manager of each branch being closed needed to decide what to send to storage versus to the library where the collection was moving and confirm with the receiving library's staff how much material they could hold. The receiving library's staff also had to decide the materials' arrangement and whether it would be kept separate or integrated. For the branches being closed, faculty involvement was vital both for gauging needs and for being interested in the end result.

The moves were staggered because of logistics. The Mathematical Sciences and Psychology Libraries were moved in January 2010, while the Geoscience and Physics Libraries were moved in May–June 2010. Staff from each branch was located at both ends to supervise the movers and to ensure that everything went to its proper place. Because some of the shelving was reassembled for use at the storage facility, most moves were done in stages with some items being placed in storage, and then some moved to merge into another library while more shelving was relocated.

Actually moving the libraries seemed almost anticlimactic after all the planning. What had previously seemed like a logistical nightmare went fairly smoothly. In the end, four libraries were emptied of 259,799 volumes plus all of the furniture, files, and shelving. Fifty-five thousand maps and their cases were transferred to the Main Library. Up to 78 percent of some collections were sent to the remote storage facility (about 182,000 volumes) and the rest was combined into other collections. Four staff members were reassigned to different positions around the library system. When all was finished, between each of the sciences buildings, 17,750 square feet of space and 193 seats were lost in total, as well as seating in Main and Hardin Library for the Health Sciences (HLHS) to accommodate the influx in materials.

The final piece of the moving puzzle was selecting a new name for the merged science collections. The staff consulted with users and came up with the name "Sciences Library." To finalize the name change, the University Librarian had to get campus approval and work with the campus offices to have maps and signs changed.

Outreach and Marketing Challenges

Communication became essential in order to reach the faculty, staff, and students in the University departments affected by the mergers. Signs (similar to Figure 13.1) were designed to guide users who were looking for the library in its old location to the new Sciences Library. The signs proved to be an effective way to communicate the changes to those who did not receive the related e-mails, attend faculty meetings, or visit the libraries in the months leading up to the closing.

Since the branch libraries were in the same building as the science departments, many of the faculty and students developed the idea that the library was part of the department, just like the rock lab or glass shop. But after the mergers, the feeling that the library staff is part of the departments has been lost. The librarians no longer have daily faculty and graduate student contact, or see people at the reference desk, or have any more "water cooler" chats unless a conscious effort is made to look for people. Librarians, and the faculty, staff, and students, have lost the serendipity of browsing all of the collection and having reference talks at the desk where the topics ebb and flow as they will. Also, conversations one participates in while in the hallways going to coffee or lunch have been lost, which are chance encounters that are unplanned, but often very enlightening.

Figure 13.1. Moving Sign at Physics Library

The Physics Library has moved

To the
Sciences Library

Which includes Books, Journals, Reference, & Reserve for:
. Biological Sciences
. Geosciences
. Physics & Astronomy

Also, Reference & Reserve for:
. Chemistry
. Psychology

Located At:
120 Iowa Avenue
Iowa City, IA 52242
(The former Biological Sciences Library)

Contact Information
(319) 335-3083
lib-sciences@uiowa.edu
www.lib.uiowa.edu/sciences

All of the mayhem just discussed created challenges that must be faced. The branch libraries were used to a "captive" audience who always came in for help. The traditional model was easy and convenient for the users and for librarians. With this no longer the case, it is necessary to make it easier or quicker for users to visit the library or consult librarians than it is to use only Google or talk to their friends at other universities. As the authors see it, the only way to avoid being caged and isolated is to break out. In other words, it is necessary to make an effort to reach out where users were previously coming to the library. Communicating with users has become a huge priority. The librarians now do more blogging than ever, and even blogged the move itself (see http://blog.lib .uiowa.edu/science/2010/05/).

Going to the Users
With the mergers and the loss of the public spaces in each of the departments, the Sciences Library began to look at different ways to reach its users. The idea of embedded librarianship began to take on more importance. The librarians now attempt to have offices in each of the science buildings in order to maintain a physical presence with the departments. The Science Education and Outreach Librarian, who is also the physics liaison, maintains an office in the building housing the Physics Department. The Psychology and Education Librarian supports two offices: one in the building with the Psychology Department and one with the Education Department. The Head of the Sciences Library now has an office in the Sciences Library as well as one in the Chemistry Building. These offices allow librarians to interact closely with the university departments. Many of the faculty and staff do not venture out to the Sciences Library with any regularity, so having offices in the buildings with these departments allow us more chances for interaction. Walking through the hallways, it is possible to share friendly conversation, and learn about new and ongoing projects, events, or research studies that are going on in the departments. This presence also provides a physical reminder for the faculty and staff that librarians are available to help if they have any questions or problems. The serendipity of these meetings enables staff to learn about different library opportunities ranging from chances to speak in a classroom to upcoming seminars to attend, to learning about current research by faculty and staff.

With the changes, what has been added also becomes important. Librarians are required to become more positive about possibilities and have become more "sales ori- ented." That is, they are trying to explain and communicate the library's worth more clearly. The Sciences Library now has added 14 additional computers and another printer to attract students. The new library also hosts open houses with free food and drinks, in addition to making free coffee available every morning and all day during finals week.

Reaching the users also includes a focus on user education and providing instruction whenever possible. Instruction is provided to a wide variety of users in many different science and math fields and to everyone from incoming freshmen to faculty. For the underclassman, instruction is delivered in a variety of venues. An example is teaching in undergraduate classes such as Organic Chemistry Lab. The first assignment for the Organic Chemistry Lab is a chemistry literature assignment where the students visit the Sciences Library and learn how to use the resources to find chemical data and other relevant information. A one-credit course titled "Library Research in Context: Science and Technology" is open to all students. In the past, this class has been taught in person with speakers from the different parts of the library discussing available databases and resources. Next semester, this class will be taught asynchronously online. To assist graduate students, librarians provide overviews of library services and resources in most of the orientation classes that take place within the first weeks of classes or even the week before classes start. In these sessions, instruction focuses on where to find materials in the library, how to navigate library websites, and demonstrations of pertinent databases. With the faculty and staff, individual demonstrations of services and databases are found to be the most useful and can be personalized to focus on only what these users want to learn. These sessions are often brief, and librarians typically teach them on very short notice, due to the busy schedules of many faculty and staff and the need for focused learning to help with their current projects. Broad overviews of all the library services and resources are not usually necessary or appreciated.

In addition, attending faculty meetings provides an opportunity to inform faculty and staff about changes in the libraries and that individual demonstrations are available for everyone. Departmental seminars also provide a platform for learning about research being conducted as well as an informal setting for informing faculty and staff about services and resources offered by the library.

In addition to the faculty, staff, and students in the departments directly served by the Sciences Library, many other departments and groups are potential users of the library. One of these groups is Women in Science and Engineering (WISE). The librarians created a specific guide just for these students, who were given tours of the Sciences Library including demonstrations and instruction on using the library webpage, specialized databases, and citation management software. WISE is also part of a program called Living-Learning Communities. These communities live together in the dorms and the students are linked by common interest and degrees. They often have special programming and classes to enhance student success. The librarians are involved in several of these programs to provide students with an overview of library services and resources as well as personalize the library so the students are aware of an individual librarian that they can go to for help.

Showcasing the Library

In addition to going to the users, the library needs to continue to advertise the library as well as to market the changes that have taken place with the mergers. Advertising the library can be a challenge and requires a variety of strategies. The University of Iowa Sciences Library utilizes many approaches including highlighting collections, planning exhibits and events, maintaining a blog, as well as presenting to and working with groups outside the university. Highlighting collections provides the users with opportunities to see what resources are available for them. One way to do this is to create eye-catching exhibits which offer users a glimpse of the collections when visiting the library. Creating these exhibits and events requires making posters along with planning for artifacts and books for display as well as coordinating with the public relations coordinator. Many of the exhibits and events at the Sciences Library focus on different holidays or anniversaries.

One event was for the International Year of Astronomy in 2009. The University of Iowa Libraries provided a talk titled "Hour of Astronomy" (see Figure 13.2). This presentation featured rare books from Galileo and Tycho Brahe, star charts and celestial atlases, and the papers and diaries from James Van Allen. In addition to the university community, the Cedar Amateur Astronomers, a local club open to anyone with an interest in astronomy, were invited to attend. Another outside activity was a presentation on weather and climate books at the Iowa Book Festival. This festival is open to the public and features presentations about books on a variety of subjects and sessions with authors.

Figure 13.2. Hour of Astronomy

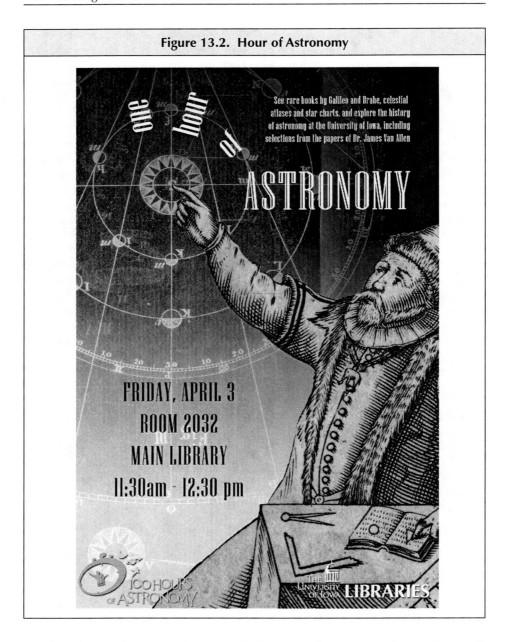

The Sciences Library now features a display case in the entrance. This may be an old idea but it receives attention and good comments while allowing the library to showcase the different collections. The first display was of interesting items from the branches which were brought together to form the Sciences Library. These included microscopes, old teaching kits for geometry, interesting geodes, and a mushroom viewfinder. Some of the items on display are unique parts of the prints collection that new users may have never seen before.

The display case exhibits now focus on different anniversaries, birthdays, or days of celebrations and allow the library to highlight a wide variety of collections as well as to provide different groups on campus opportunities to showcase artifacts. Some of the events commemorated are well-known, including Earth Day or Halloween, while others are not as renowned, such as Mole Day or Pi Day. The goal is to have as much variety in the exhibits as possible and to highlight each collection (e.g., astronomy, biology, chemistry, geosciences, and physics) at least once a year. For the more general exhibits, the library tries to have books from each collection showing the real diversity of the library.

The library celebrates Earth Day every April 22 (see Figure 13.3). This involves creating posters and trivia about conservation, earth history, and recycling to display around the library. Books about the Earth, rocks, soil, and endangered animals are showcased. The library also hands out chocolate balls with wrappers that make them look like little globes.

Science of Halloween provides opportunities for books from a wide variety of collections to be displayed (see Figure 13.4). This includes books on bodies and bones, candy, paranormal, potions, witchcraft, and vampires. For the most recent of these, the

Figure 13.3. Earth Day Poster

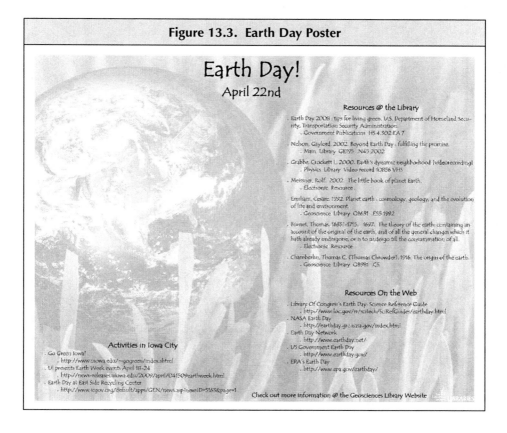

Figure 13.4. Science of Halloween

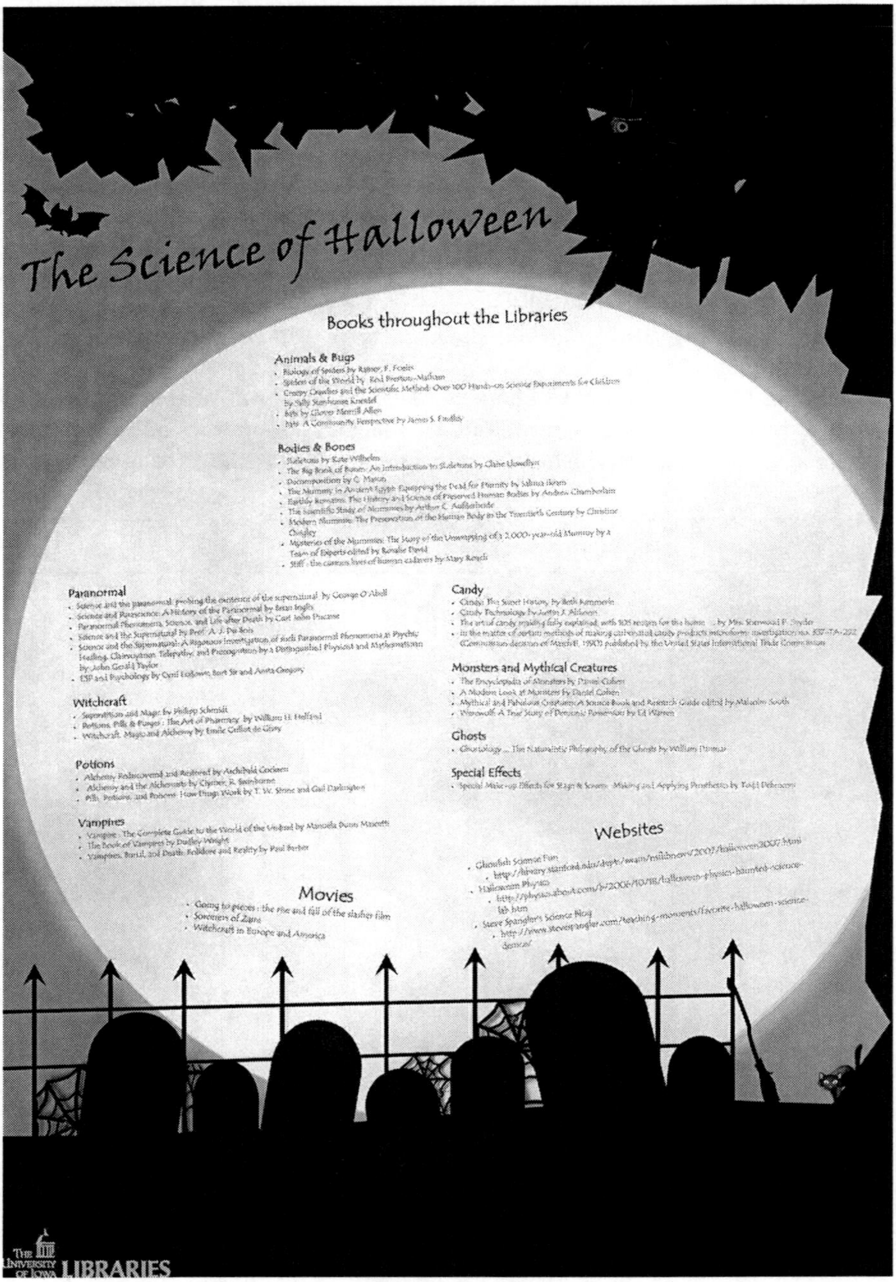

The Science of Halloween

Books throughout the Libraries

Animals & Bugs

Bodies & Bones

Paranormal

Witchcraft

Potions

Vampires

Movies

Candy

Monsters and Mythical Creatures

Ghosts

Special Effects

Websites

THE UNIVERSITY OF IOWA LIBRARIES

library borrowed a bat skeleton and a mounted bat specimen from the University of Iowa's Museum of Natural History. The Geoscience Department Repository loaned the library several artifacts as well, including a fossil tooth, a Smilodon skull, and two snake heads. Spider webs and paper bats were used to decorate the whole library in the Halloween theme. This exhibit was one of the favorites for both the library staff and the students.

Some of the lesser known events include Pi Day and Mole Day. Pi Day is March 14; for this celebration of the mathematical term pi (equivalent to 3.14) the library displays books and artifacts related to using mathematics. Trivia questions are placed throughout the area asking users to define, for instance, what the "formal" definition of pi is, or who the first scientist to use pi was. This year the library also gave away pie to the students, staff, and faculty in honor of Pi Day.

Mole Day celebrates the mole, a unit of measurement in chemistry. To calculate a mole into molecules, Avogadro's number (6.02×1023) is used, which is why the celebration takes place at 6:02 in the morning or at night on October 23 (10/23). For this exhibit, the library borrowed mounted moles from the University of Iowa's Museum of Natural History and created moles from fabric, each of which was decorated as a different element or compound. For example, some of the moles were decorated as gold, iron, TNT, and arsenic. The library included in the exhibit a special collections copy of the first journal article by Avogadro written in 1811, as well as the English translation. In the display case, jars were filled to visually demonstrate a mole of sugar, salt, water, and chocolate. In addition, the Mole Day exhibit featured trivia disseminated around the library.

The Main Library has a large area for exhibits, which the Sciences Library staff has used. In 2009 was the fiftieth anniversary of laser innovation. An exhibit area was created featuring many parts of the laser and displaying a timeline and history of its development, illustrations of how the laser works, highlights of current research on campus using the laser, and the laser's many uses, including medical, industrial, and entertainment applications. Laser pieces were borrowed from the Physics and Astronomy Department. The posters were designed by the Iowa Memorial Union's Marketing and Design Department (see Figures 13.5 and 13.6). The exhibit featured working lasers, which were set up on a switch so they could be turned on for one minute at a time. A DVD player was also continuously playing a scene from *Ocean's 12* called the Laser Dance. This demonstrated both how the laser ran the DVD and how lasers can be used in the security industry. Opening night of the *50 Years of Laser Innovation* exhibit featured demonstrations of different uses of the laser by a Physics instructor and graduate students. Preparing the "Current Research on Campus" section provided an excellent opportunity to talk with faculty about their research.

Marketing the New Sciences Library

In addition to the exhibits and events, the library had to change marketing strategies with the mergers of the four libraries into one and the scattering of several collections to different locations around campus. The marketing of the library mergers took on three different strategies: bookmarks (see Figure 13.7, p. 208), LibGuides, and website redesign. The bookmarks are also an old idea, but the Sciences Library decided to create these handouts for service points, events, and classes. They provide information on available collections, hours, location, and contact information and offer a brief

Figure 13.5. Laser Exhibit Poster A

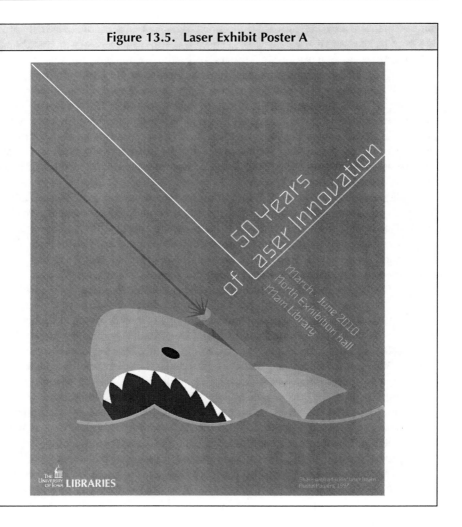

description of what parts of different collections are located at the Sciences Library. This information has been difficult to explain given that the library houses only the reference and reserve collection for chemistry and psychology and the rest of those collections are located in the Hardin Library for the Health Sciences.

With the mergers, the Sciences Library needed to develop a new web presence. Each of the individual libraries had their own webpage so the information from these pages was converted into resource guides. At the University of Iowa Libraries, resource pages were designed for each of the subject areas. The library used LibGuides to create these pages. All these subject guides are linked from the Sciences Library new homepage so that all the information can be gathered together in one place (see Figure 13.8, p. 209). A news blog and a mobile interface were also added to the new Sciences Library webpage for a more updated look.

Figure 13.6. Laser Exhibit Poster B

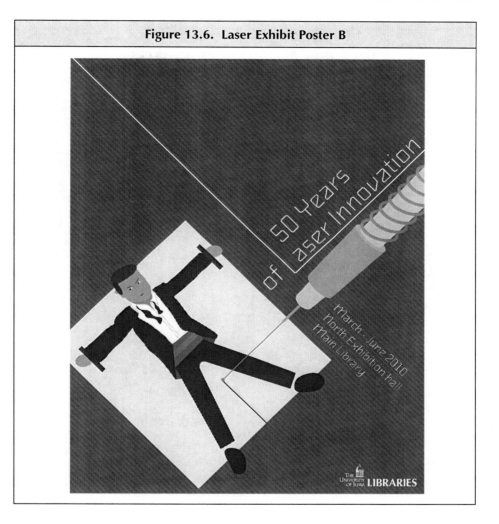

Future Projects

The Sciences Library is continuing to experiment with different forms of outreach to strengthen ties with the science departments, with several projects underway. One is to implement Meebo Chat for just the Sciences Library. The Main Library and several other branches already have these in place. Another project is obtaining plasma televisions for each of the three floors of the Library. These televisions will allow for continuous slide shows of events, exhibits, and key resources. They can also be connected to a computer which can then be used as large screens during presentations. A quick response (QR) code scavenger hunt is a venture to attract the students to the library. This hunt will have the students use their smartphones to get clues from the QR codes created by the library that will send them on a voyage to explore all parts of the library.

Figure 13.7. Sciences Library Bookmark

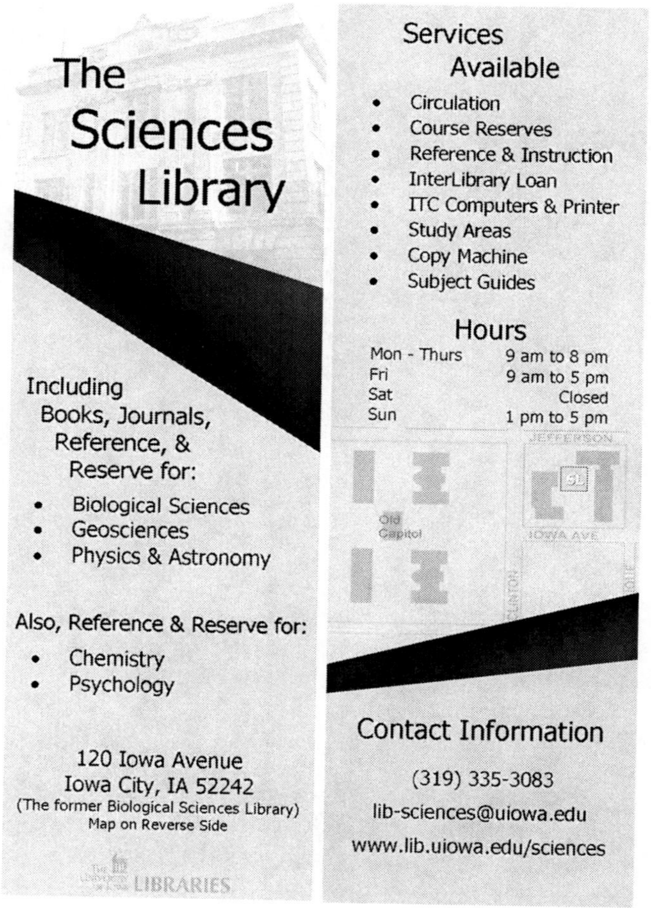
The Sciences Library
Including Books, Journals, Reference, & Reserve for:
• Biological Sciences
• Geosciences
• Physics & Astronomy
Also, Reference & Reserve for:
• Chemistry
• Psychology
120 Iowa Avenue
Iowa City, IA 52242
(The former Biological Sciences Library)
Map on Reverse Side
LIBRARIES
Services Available
• Circulation
• Course Reserves
• Reference & Instruction
• InterLibrary Loan
• ITC Computers & Printer
• Study Areas
• Copy Machine
• Subject Guides
Hours
Mon - Thurs 9 am to 8 pm
Fri 9 am to 5 pm
Sat Closed
Sun 1 pm to 5 pm
JEFFERSON
SL
Old Capitol
IOWA AVE
CLINTON
Contact Information
(319) 335-3083
lib-sciences@uiowa.edu
www.lib.uiowa.edu/sciences

Conclusion

The mayhem created by the drastic changes with merging or storing so much of the collections and closing several service points has forced the library staff to change reference and outreach strategies. These changes are ongoing and will continue to involve a wide variety of projects. This chapter describes some of the new ways the library is reaching out to users—trying to make them aware of what the librarians can do and what resources are available to them. There is some evidence of success. Gate count has risen almost 25 percent since our outreach efforts were started, and webpage hits are rising. As Martell (2005) said, "Libraries are no longer bounded; they are boundless. Our users need our assistance as never before. Our challenge is to discover the roles we must develop in order to be of greatest benefit to them and to society" (p. 451). The librarians

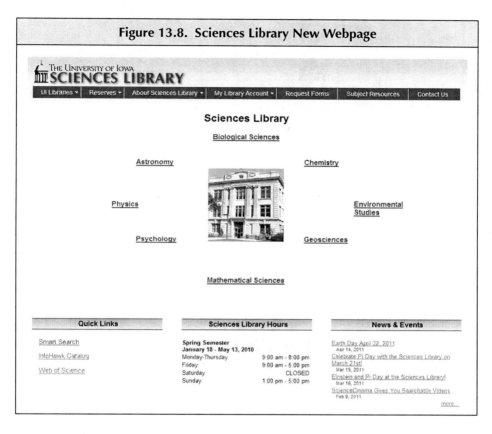

Figure 13.8. Sciences Library New Webpage

at the University of Iowa are continually striving to put together a package of new services, outreach, teaching, and marketing that works. The goal is to keep ourselves in the lives of our users and get them "in the door," whether physically or virtually.

References

Armstrong, W. W. (2005). The closing of the LSU chemistry library. *Issues in Science and Technology Librarianship, 44*(5). Retrieved from http://www.istl.org/05-fall/article5.html.

Carlson, S. (2001). The deserted library. *Chronicle of Higher Education, 48*(12), A35–A38.

Cliatt, Cass. (2008, September 3). Lewis Library fact sheet. Message posted to http://www.princeton.edu/main/news.

Cohen, A. (2000). ESL: Engineering societies library: End of a special library. *Science & Technology Libraries, 19*(1), 3–20.

Czechowski, L., Barger, R., Fort, M., & Maxeiner, G. (2010). Letting go: Closing a branch library of the health sciences library system, University of Pittsburgh. *Library Resources & Technical Services, 54*(3), 153–163.

Hiller, S. (2004). Measure by measure: Assessing the viability of the physical library. *The Bottom Line, 17*(4), 126–131.

Hitchcock, M., Sager, R., & Schneider, J. (2005). And then there was one: Moving and merging three health science library collections. *Issues in Science and Technology Librarianship, 44*(5), 1.

Martell, C. R. (2005). The ubiquitous user: A reexamination of Carlson's deserted library. *portal: Libraries and the Academy, 5*(4), 441–453.

Opperman, B. V., & Jamison, M. (2008). New roles for an academic library: Current measurements. *New Library World, 109*(11/12), 559–573.

Winterman, B., & Hill, J. (2010). Continued viability: A review of the life sciences library at Indiana University in a time of institutional change and proposed branch library downsizing. *Science & Technology Libraries, 29*(3), 200–215.

SECTION III.2

Collaborative Solutions and Successes

CHAPTER 14

Cooperative SMS: The My Info Quest Journey

Beth Avery, Karen Docherty, and Shaye White

Overview

The history and evolution of the My Info Quest collaborative text or short message service (SMS) reference initiative is presented in this chapter. An academic and public librarian discuss the implementation of My Info Quest in their libraries, including the pragmatics of the service, advertising, queries received, and improvements in user service. The authors then discuss the challenges that libraries face when providing a SMS reference service like My Info Quest.

Introduction

Texting has quickly become a popular and effective way of communicating. Walking down the streets, sitting in meetings, and just about everywhere, people are using their handheld devices to text. Those text or short message service (SMS) messages sent from computers, cell phones, and other handheld devices may only be a maximum of 140 to 160 characters, but more and more information is being conveyed that way and, of course, longer messages can be split into several messages.

According to a September 2010 Pew Internet & American Life Project study, "Cell phones have moved beyond fashionable accessory and into the realm of life necessity—just as many adults have a cell phone as have a computer" (Lenhart, 2010, p. 4). Cell phone users range from 57 percent of those 65 years old or older to 90 percent of those in the 18–29 age group, with the average user sending and receiving 10 texts a day. This average is up from an average of five just eight months previously, and there are no gender differences in who is texting. Interestingly, those who are heavy texters are also heavy voice-calling users.

One of the responses to a Yahoo! Answers (http://answers.yahoo.com/) question illustrates why texting has become so popular with youth: "I do it because its [sic] easier to keep private than a phone call. I'm a college student, and i [sic] have 7 people sharing my dorm, so its [sic] hard to keep a call private. Texting is easier, quicker, more private, and to the point. Plus, I can't make calls in class, but I can text. And I have an unlimited plan, so I might as well use them [sic]" (Greg, 2009, p. 1).

In an effort to reach users where they are, many libraries and commercial services have developed reference services based on texting. The collaborative/cooperative model emerged as libraries realized that a cooperative offers the opportunity to staff more hours than an individual library can and to share the expertise of the member libraries. The software is easily used in a cooperative setting. While there are several text-messaging reference cooperatives, My Info Quest was one of the earliest multistate collaboratives. Other library collaboratives are Ask A Librarian (Florida), QandANJ (New Jersey), KnowItNow24x7 (Ohio), and Washington County (OR) Cooperative Library Services. Many libraries have implemented a text reference service. Most text reference services used in libraries use an interface which allows the question sent from a cell phone to be answered using a computer. Popular SMS software used in libraries include Mosio/Text a Librarian, Altarama, and LibraryH3lp. There are several commercial SMS reference services available including ChaCha (free; http://www.chacha.com/), KGB Answers (99 cents per answer; http://www.kgbanswers.com/), and Google SMS Search (free; http://www.google.com/mobile/sms/search/).

A special double issue of *The Reference Librarian* (January 2011) is devoted to the mobile revolution in reference. An overview of SMS reference includes a description of the major library vendors (Brannon, 2011). An article on the launch of the Cornell University Text a Librarian service discusses the beta testing, staffing, and training issues, as well as gives an analysis of the types of questions received (Cole & Krkoska, 2011). An evaluation of the first five years of the Southeastern Louisiana University (SLU) service showed that while there are some obstacles to SMS reference there are important reasons to offer this reference mode (Stahr, 2011). For some students SMS was the entry to more interaction with the librarians. The users are pleased with the service, and approximately 10 percent of the messages received at SLU were thank-yous (Stahr, 2011, p. 18).

My Info Quest

The Alliance Library System (ALS) of East Peoria, Illinois, had a tradition of cooperative virtual reference services (VRS) (http://alliancelibrarysystem.com/). These services began with a Library Services and Technology Act (LSTA) pilot project used to develop *Ready for Reference*, a VRS for eight academic libraries. This project merged with the North Suburban Library System's public library service to form My Web Librarian, which in turn expanded and merged with the Ask?AwayIllinois VRS. With this background of providing cooperative reference services and the increased use of cell phones rather than voice to transmit data, it was natural to expand reference services to the ever-increasing number of texters.

In late 2008 Lori Bell, Director of Innovation for the Alliance System, sent out a call for libraries to join a pilot project to form a collaborative SMS reference service that would include all types of libraries anywhere in the world. As a result, My Info Quest was formed and held its first organizational meeting online in March 2009. This pilot project, which had its soft launch in July of that year, started with approximately 50 libraries, and by 2010 had more than 70 libraries and individuals. Participants used Altarama software (http://www.altarama.com/), which sent the users' SMS messages to a shared Gmail account that librarians used to answer questions. PeopleWhere software was used for scheduling. The original aim was to add enough libraries to be open 24/7. As of August 2010 the service had 74 libraries and had grown from being staffed less than 70 hours to 83 hours per week.

Pilot project member libraries were asked to attend the training, to staff the service two hours per week, to place a link to the service on their website, to publicize the service to their users, and to join the committees that were being formed. A Google group was formed to enhance communication among the members. My Info Quest became a collaborative guided by an advisory committee made up of representatives who meet monthly to address issues and set policies. Other groups were formed and are responsible for setting standards and guidelines, providing online training, and developing marketing materials.

The service is easy for users to access by texting the My Info Quest phone number or by pointing the camera in their cell phone at the quick response (QR) code that many member libraries have placed on their websites. The service strives to answer all questions in less than 10 minutes. Following the policies of most of the libraries involved, there is a disclaimer that the service does not provide medical, tax, or legal advice. Librarians are supposed to limit their responses to no more than two SMS text messages long, or a total of 320 characters. As the service has evolved, some librarians have found that they actually have reference interviews with people, and this does take more than 320 characters. However, with the advent of unlimited texting for many cell phone plans, this is not the issue it was at the beginning of the service when many people paid per message. From July 2009 through September 2010, 8,862 questions were answered. The highest month in use so far was February 2010, when about three questions were answered per hour of coverage.

Marketing

Early in the pilot project a marketing/public relations group was formed. First, the group developed talking points that could be used to explain the service to potential member libraries and potential users. The talking points for libraries addressed such issues as what the service was, how it would operate, the monetary and labor costs involved, and how the service would be governed. The talking points for users included a basic overview of the service, including letting them know that they may not be texting with a librarian from their home library, how to ask a question, what kinds of questions could be answered, costs, how soon they could expect an answer, and privacy issues since texting is not a secure form of communication. Next a tagline was created to convey this was a reference service. Of the 18 possible taglines submitted by patrons, a survey of My Info Quest participants narrowed it to the top four most popular. From these the committee selected "txt 4 answers."

Because libraries of many sizes were included in the project and many of them did not have a publicity department, the committee created customizable publicity pieces including bookmarks, postcards, press releases, and public service announcements. These were created in Microsoft Word so that libraries without access to more sophisticated tools could easily modify the pieces. The bookmarks have the My Info Quest logo, the tagline, the website URL, and the phone number in the largest letters on the front. Figure 14.1 shows the front of the bookmark.

The back of the bookmark was designed to be easily customized. It had three lines of text: You can text your questions anytime. Messages will be answered {INSERT CURRENT DAY AND HOUR INFORMATION HERE} central time. A service brought to you by: {INSERT YOUR LIBRARY INFORMATION HERE}. There is also enough white space for the library to include its logo. Figure 14.2 shows the back of the bookmark. All of the pieces were intended to make sure the users knew it was a service brought to them by their local library.

Since academic libraries would most likely have to publicize the service every semester, a checklist with various ideas to choose from was developed to make the marketing a little different each semester. After it was developed it was apparent that many of the items on the list would be useful for any type of library to use to publicize the service.

The complete marketing efforts are discussed in a recent article by Avery, Docherty, and Lindbloom (2011). As the project evolves, the committee is compiling the best of the publicity being done by member libraries and continuing to develop additional publicity pieces for all member libraries to use.

Evaluation

Evaluation in the early stages has been through collecting basic statistics of use by number of questions and area code distribution of the questions. Beginning in late fall 2010, a user service perception survey is being distributed and evaluated by Lili Luo at the San Jose State University, School of Library and Information Science. The survey link was first distributed as a signature line to the responses. The full evaluation will identify: the types of information needs that can be fulfilled by SMS reference services; the issues and potential obstacles that need to be addressed before implementing SMS

Figure 14.1. My Info Quest Bookmark, Front

Figure 14.2. My Info Quest Bookmark, Back

You can text your questions anytime. Messages will be answered
Monday-Friday from 8:00 a.m to 9:00 p.m. Central time.

A service brought to you by: {INSERT LIBRARY INFORMATION HERE}

reference services; the important features to consider when choosing a vendor; and the costs and benefits of offering these services.

The Libraries and Staffing

The service is staffed by librarians from 28 academic libraries of various types, from community colleges to research universities; 23 public libraries ranging from a two-person library to countywide systems; two special libraries; two middle schools; one multi-type library system; five graduate library assistants; and three librarian volunteers. It is staffed for 68 hours per week, and during times of high use, it is double staffed.

The Paradise Valley Community College and Rio Salado College Experience

Two of the ten Maricopa County Community Colleges District (MCCCD), Rio Salado College (RSC) and Paradise Valley Community College (PVCC), chose to participate in the My Info Quest pilot project. MCCCD is located in Maricopa County in central Arizona. It includes the entire Phoenix metro area, with a population of nearly four million. The District has more than 250,000 students taking credit and non-credit courses. Locally, RSC and PVCC named the SMS service Ask! Txt 4 Answers to better parallel the name of the District's existing 24/7 live chat service, Ask a Librarian. For the purposes of this article, the SMS service is referred to by the collaborative's name, My Info Quest.

As with most libraries, the main reason RSC and PVCC decided to try texting is because many of the current students and perhaps equally important, the future students, are texting, and doing so in impressive numbers. This pilot project was an easy way to experiment with SMS to find out if it would be a viable way to provide reference service.

Reasons for Joining My Info Quest

The pilot project seemed like a perfect opportunity because of the minimal effort on the part of the staff and the costs involved, while allowing experimentation with texting technology. It also provided a venue to partner with colleagues around the United States and Canada, to learn from each other, and to see if a collaborative staffing model would work in an SMS environment like it works so well in chat cooperatives. My Info Quest participants receive many hours of service coverage for their users and in return contributed only a couple of hours each week to the project. Other than staff time, there were no additional costs to participate.

Usage

Usage statistics are kept for both the overall number of My Info Quest SMS transactions as well as for each participating institution. One transaction is defined as a series of message exchanges between a librarian and a user that focus on one question. While use of the service has been light for the two colleges, it has started to see growth. Between September 2009 and June 2010 the entire My Info Quest service had more than 7,900 transactions from all participating libraries. During this same time frame, Rio Salado College and Paradise Valley Community College had only 52 transactions. By comparison, live chat service was more active for these two colleges, with 1,806 live chat sessions between September 2009 and June 2010.

Although a formal survey of students has not yet been conducted, there are several possible explanations for the reason that texting usage is so low. Perhaps students see texting as social, and therefore do not select it as a service option. Another possibility is that when students are online, they elect to use chat or instant messaging (IM), since links are available at the point of need. In addition, when students are away from a computer and would want to use the service, perhaps they are not aware of how to access it. Another strong possibility is that, because of its relatively recent implementation when compared to traditional library services, students simply do not know about the SMS service. Radford and Connaway (2005–2008), in their study of live chat reference, conducted online surveys and interviews with nonusers of VRS and found that the single most important reason that people did not use chat was that they were not aware that it existed.

The Ask a Librarian chat service, now flourishing, started slowly as well. The MCCCD chat service began in 2001 with a pilot project which offered the service on a limited basis. Today, all ten colleges in the District participate in the service with backup services for 24/7 coverage provided by QuestionPoint contract librarians (hired by QuestionPoint) and cooperative librarians (academic librarians from other colleges and universities who are members of the QuestionPoint global cooperative). It took time to develop support from librarians and to promote the chat service to faculty, staff, and students. Usage took off once buy-in with colleagues was achieved and regular and persistent marketing was in place. The same promotional effort must also be put forth with the SMS service.

Marketing

Marketing is an important component of any library service. Sometimes minimal marketing is enough to spread the word, but other times targeted, thoughtful, and continuous marketing is necessary. Marketing efforts of Rio Salado College and Paradise Valley Community College have included: well-placed and visible buttons on the main library pages which lead to secondary pages that provide the service phone number and library service code (library service codes are three-letter codes used by the My Info Quest participants to differentiate among libraries; project members use service codes to be able to identify a texter's library affiliation and to aid in gathering statistics); articles in the *Arizona Republic* newspaper (Staudacher, 2009, November 14) and on the AZFamily (http://www.AZFamily.com/) website (Staudacher, 2009, November 20); a presence in the RioLounge, Rio Salado College's social networking space, and on the Rio Salado "Current Students" page; and word-of-mouth promotion in library use instruction classes. While these efforts represent a nice start in promoting the SMS service, the low usage indicates this area needs greater attention.

Questions from the Local Area Code

Due to the way the My Info Quest service was implemented on the collaborative level, users are asked, but not required, to enter their library's three-letter service code when submitting questions. Since service codes tend to be inconsistently used, Rio Salado College and Paradise Valley Community College instead tracked usage by the area codes for the metropolitan area. This method is also imprecise since users may be texting from a device with one of the local area codes, but may be actually living elsewhere (attending college out-of-state, recently relocated, etc.), but area codes still provide more complete data than does use of service codes.

Here is a sampling of the kinds of questions asked by users texting from the local area codes and answered by My Info Quest librarians:

QUESTION: How do i go about getting a transcript and who dp i [*sic*] call

ANSWER: Hello. Do you mean an academic transcript? Which institution are you inquiring about? This is a national service. I'd be happy to look it up once I know where to look. ThxTxt4Ans

QUESTION: Rio salada [*sic*]

ANSWER: Hello. You can fax, phone, online [*sic*] or in person request a copy. http://www.riosalado.edu/selfserve/Pages/transcripts.aspx Fax to (480) 377-4741 or my.maricopa.edu TksTxt4Ans

QUESTION: What is the difference between "affect" & "effect"? RSC

ANSWER: The answer to this is too long for a txt. Please see this web site http://bit.ly/deYCPs

QUESTION: Is "The God Delusion" a book worth reading?

ANSWER: "worth reading" is a matter of opinion. the [*sic*] book is well reviewed & author Richard Dawkins is a successful speaker and scientist in England. does [*sic*] that help?

QUESTION: Writing a definition paper on a single word. What are some examples of words with many definitions in differant catgories [*sic*]?

ANSWER: Words with many meanings include JACK, PLAY, CAN, FOOT, DRAW, JAM, HEAD, CHEER, CHECK, LIE, and SPELL. There are many others. Thx 4 askN My Info Quest!

QUESTION: where can I find info on bowhead whales?

ANSWER: The National Marine Fisheries Service has a good webpage about bowhead whales. http://bit.ly/9jK1IY

QUESTION: How many stomachs does a cow have?

ANSWER: Cows have a four-chambered stomach, according to www.crazyforcows.com

QUESTION: Who was known as the Son King?

ANSWER: Louis XIV (5 September 1638–1 September 1715), known as the Sun King (French: le Roi Soleil), was King of France and of Navarre.

These questions illustrate the typical range of questions texted by Rio Salado College students during the My Info Quest pilot. Many were ready-reference questions and easily answered by supplying a brief response and URL. Surprisingly, few questions required local library knowledge and few were complex enough that they would have benefited from library instruction, as is usually the case with the MCCCD Ask a Librarian chat service.

The Pioneer Library System Experience

The Pioneer Library System (PLS) serves the area just south of the Oklahoma City Metro including Cleveland, McClain, and Pottawatomie counties. This service area is very large with both rural and urban areas and several institutions of higher education. More than 240,000 people live in the area and represent a diverse population that is very mobile. Currently, PLS consists of nine hometown libraries and eight information stations to serve approximately 170,000 registered card holders. The system continues to grow, with a new branch set to open in 2011; it will boast several outreach locations, and many new services.

The PLS's Virtual Library, begun in 2008, is a stand-alone branch that patrons can access 24/7. Three staff members manage all of the web-based access to information and resources. Services are offered through websites, Facebook, research databases, and the Overdrive collection of audiobooks (http://pioneer.lib.overdrive.com), e-books, and videos. In 2010, a Virtual Library card type was established, and is available for patrons to utilize all the online resources without stepping into a library building.

Reasons for Joining My Info Quest

When the opportunity to join the My Info Quest SMS reference service was presented to the Virtual Library in July 2010, it was immediately seen as a chance to try something new and to expand the library's services. Previously, PLS only offered reference service through an e-mail contact form and there were no plans to offer chat or text reference in the near future. Since the pilot project did not cost any money and the time commitment was minimal, it seemed like the perfect opportunity and had great potential.

Staffing

All three of the PLS Virtual Library staff members are trained to answer questions during the library's assigned My Info Quest SMS reference shift. Usually, two staff members are on at a time so one person is not overwhelmed with questions. Since the staff members' desks are located close together, discussion about the questions, including where to find information or how to approach a difficult question, is easily accomplished if needed. Questions can be "claimed" so double answers are not sent to users. When answering questions, the expectation has been set for standards that apply to other forms of reference (i.e., that answers will come from reliable sources and that librarians will avoid opinionated responses). Each question is treated seriously and priority is only given based on the order in which questions are received. The Virtual Library staff members have the attitude that no question is too awkward or difficult to find an answer. With only three staff members, it is easy to hold one another accountable and work together for an answer.

The response time of ten minutes that has been set by the My Info Quest group is always a goal, but a correct or appropriate answer is the most important goal, so staff may take more time to find an answer. When more information is needed from the user, the staff does not hesitate to ask clarifying questions.

Usage

After only a few months, PLS noticed that users were responding well to the SMS reference service. The primary telephone area code for the service area, 405, had some of the highest usage rates, according to the monthly My Info Quest statistics reports. The 405 area code accounted for 12.5 percent of all questions asked between June 2009 and December 2010. Each month during that time, the 405 area code made up between 7 percent and

29 percent of questions. In terms of number of questions, February 2010 was the heaviest used month with 239 texts (23 percent of total My Info Quest texts). Compared with other participating libraries, PLS had the highest usage rate. The second highest usage rate was 9.7 percent for the 309 area code. It was surprising how much usage the small promotion campaign was creating and that approximately 47 percent of total 405 area code users accessed the service more than once.

Marketing

PLS chose to perform a small promotional campaign to introduce My Info Quest SMS reference service to the public. The promotion consisted of posters, flyers, and an online banner created in-house.

Each of the nine physical library branches received one or two large posters to hang up in the library and approximately 100 small flyers (see Figure 14.3) to place at the information desk beside flyers for upcoming programs. To promote My Info Quest SMS

Figure 14.3. My Info Quest Flyer

reference online, an article was placed on the front page of the main website and a banner (see Figure 14.4), which rotates along with other banners, was placed at the top of all the website pages. The article was on the front page for a few months, and was then moved to another section of the website, where it has remained. The banner has been revised to include a quick response (QR) code (see Figure 14.5), but it remains in rotation at the top of all the website pages.

This small promotional campaign was successful in introducing the SMS reference service, and people began using the service shortly after the information was displayed. Since the promotion worked so well and patrons continue to use the service, PLS has not increased publicity.

Questions from the 405 Local Area Code

After looking at the questions asked and answered by My Info Quest, PLS was able to determine how patrons use the SMS reference service. The questions fall into five categories:

1. Ready reference
2. Local library services and resources
3. Specific research
4. Opinions
5. About My Info Quest

The questions asked through texting are very similar to the types of questions asked in person or over the phone at the library branches.

A few examples of questions sent in by users from the 405 area code are provided here. These are a representative mix of the types of questions asked. Requests are made for information about buying items, popular music, foreign language translations, and even medical information. All questions are treated seriously and answered by My Info Quest staff.

Figure 14.4. My Info Quest Banner 1

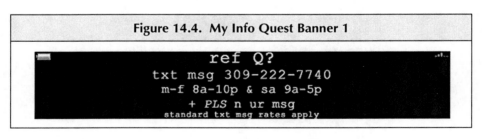

Figure 14.5. My Info Quest Banner 2

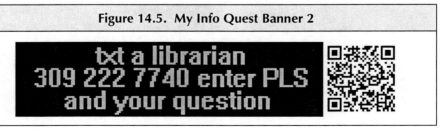

QUESTION: Should I buy the new evo phone from sprint?
ANSWER: Personally, I would look on blogs and in mags for reviews and compare with what I want the smartphone to do. My current carrier's contract provisions might also B a Factor. [*sic*]

QUESTION: What is the chorus to "your not the only one" by The Throwaways?
ANSWER: Just look at what you've started/ Just look at what you've done/ Just look at what you've started/ You're not the only one

QUESTION: How do you say "blue" in samoan?
ANSWER: Looking @ diff sources - depends on what u want to say. lanumoana = sky colored, moana = sea blue, uliuli = blue black or dark color. Does this help?

QUESTION: How can marijuana harm the human body How can exstacy hurt a person How can heroin harm the body How can cocain harm a persons body How can mushrooms harm a persons bady [*sic*]
ANSWER: All of these drugs adversely affect the brain, heart, lungs, and mental health. For more info visit www.nlm.nih.gov/medlineplus/.

QUESTION: How do i make peanut butter balls [*sic*]
ANSWER: Ingredients: ½ lb. butter, softened (2 sticks) 1 can flaked coconut 4 cups powdered sugar (1 lb) 1 cup nuts, chopped 1 tsp. vanilla food grade paraffin wax ½ cup peanut butter ½ lb. graham cracker crumbs 1 large pkg. semi-sweet chocolate bits. Instructions: Stir together butter, peanut butter, coconut and powdered sugar. Let stand for a few minutes. Shape mixture into balls. Melt a 1-inch square of paraffin wax with the chocolate bits in saucepan. Dip ball into mixture and place on parchment paper. Cooks Note: Use Baker's Dipping Chocolate or substitute your own tempered chocolate in place of the paraffin, if desired. Refrigerate until serving. (from cooks.com)

QUESTION: How many teeth does the average hippo have?
ANSWER: wikiped: average hippo age 5–10 had 100 teeth while the youngest had 40 and the biggest had 100.

QUESTION: What is the tallest building ever made?
ANSWER: the Burj Khalifa in Dubai, United Arab Emirates is the tallest building in the world at 2,717 feet. A structure is defined as a building if at least 50% of its height is made up of floors containing habitable floor area. if not, they are defined as towers

QUESTION: How many days does it take to walk to mexico from baton rouge while carrying a dead body? [*sic*]
ANSWER: It's roughly 625 miles by road from Baton Rouge to Matamoros; see http://bit.ly/985WSz

Reflections
Looking back at the past year of My Info Quest text reference service, the PLS Virtual Library staff has seen positive and negative aspects of offering the service. Among the positives is the fact that several patrons are return users. This is very satisfying, as it means they found the service useful and want to use it again. The PLS service area

includes several rural areas that do not have Internet, so cell phones are a primary means of communication and the text reference service reaches those patrons. Finally, My Info Quest has allowed patrons to have questions answered outside the hours of operation, which fits into the Virtual Library's goal of providing access 24/7.

On the negative side, PLS has found that some patrons text several questions in a row, chat with the librarian, or ask inappropriate questions, which takes away from the intended use of the service. Since My Info Quest is staffed by libraries across the United States and Canada and questions can come from anywhere, this can lead to mistakes or the inability to answer questions. It is difficult to answer questions about another library's services or resources when a website is the only available information. Not being face-to-face with the patron adds a layer of difficulty as well. Finally, some questions are too intensive to answer in a text and shortening answers is always a challenge, as answers must make sense and yet be 160 characters.

Overall, joining My Info Quest has been a great experience for the Pioneer Library System. The text reference service has allowed the library to serve the information needs of patrons beyond what can be provided by the library staff. The PLS staff has enjoyed the ability to help patrons and learn some interesting pieces of trivia along the way. The partnership with more than 60 libraries across the United States and Canada has been a welcome opportunity to form connections that would not otherwise exist.

Challenges of SMS Reference
After staffing the My Info Quest service for nearly a year, librarians from Paradise Valley Community College and Rio Salado College identified several challenges, discussed in the following section.

Providing SMS Reference Seems More Difficult Than Synchronous Chat
Without the ease and convenience of a live chat conversation, it is difficult to do a reference interview. Without knowing whether or not the user has an unlimited texting plan, there was concern about texting a clarifying question and costing the user money. Efforts were made to make educated guesses about the user's real need and to tailor the response into a maximum of two text messages, but to seek clarification when necessary.

Provide the Answer, Not Just the URL
While there are a growing number of library users that have smartphones with web access, many do not yet have this capability. Therefore, it is important to try to answer the question as best as possible *and* provide a shortened URL for more information. A URL by itself, even if pointing to the perfect answer, will not help the patron without web access.

Character Limitations and an Instructional Mission
How do you provide a complete answer in less than 320 characters? Text messaging works great for short-and-sweet questions, but the ability to provide instruction is sorely lacking. It is possible to suggest a database name, send a shortened URL to access it, and recommend a few search terms, but any sort of explanation will likely not fit into so few characters. This reality is at odds with the instructional mission of academic

libraries, but SMS reference can at least steer students in the right direction and perhaps initiate a relationship between the student and the library.

Mix of Library Types
The collaborative nature of the project presents the challenge of serving patrons from other library types. At the Rio Salado and Paradise Valley Community Colleges librarians are frequently helping students do research for papers, format citations, select databases, and evaluate sources, so they were less familiar with the wide range of questions that public library colleagues receive on a regular basis.

Software (Gmail) Limitations
Unlike with chat, there is no audible notification when a new question has arrived, which means that staff members must constantly monitor the Gmail interface for new message arrivals. Librarians cannot see when other librarians are logged in; at best librarians can see that somebody is logged in and what the IP address is at that location. In addition, with the Gmail interface, there are no automated usage reports. Lili Luo from San Jose State University oversees a manual process for gathering and evaluating activity. As mentioned previously, users are asked to enter service codes that identify their libraries when submitting their questions. However, they frequently leave off the codes, so it is difficult to have accurate data for individual libraries.

Scheduling Concerns
Not surprisingly, in this grassroots, collaborative effort where there is no centralized authority, there can be challenges to scheduling. One frequent concern is that monitors do not show up for scheduled shifts. The group has developed strategies for minimizing missed shifts, but even so, some hurdles persist. An early problem that seems to have been resolved was librarian monitors being present when they were not scheduled. This practice created confusion about who was supposed to be answering questions and was probably due to the newness of the service and an eagerness by librarians to try it. Another scheduling consideration is creating a schedule that works for both users (ample service hours) and librarians (shifts that fit into a library's schedule).

Answer Quality and Consistency
As with any collaborative reference service, issues of answer quality and consistency arise. To address these issues, policies and procedures were established and a best practices team was formed. Librarians also frequently use the project list to discuss complicated questions and to share ideas for how to best answer sticky questions.

Conclusion
While a few challenges have been presented in forming this collaborative reference service, it is important to recognize what a tremendous experience this has been for project participants (see Table 14.1). The librarians involved are a group of dedicated, generous, and innovative professionals who have spent many hours—some on their personal time—to get the project off the ground. Of course, the library users are the beneficiaries of this effort. Because of the collaboration, library users have access via texting for most hours of the day to librarians that provide quality answers to all questions.

Table 14.1. Comparison of Services					
Presenter/ Institution	**Platform**	**Stand-Alone/ Collaborative (Name)**	**Start Date, Growth, & Usage**	**Publicity**	**Staffing**
Karen Sobel, Auraria Library (CO)	LibraryH3lp	Stand-alone	July 2008; good start & growing; average 30 questions a day	Nothing formal, part of instruction, embedded on pages	Office, home
Beth Avery, University of North Texas (TX)	Meebo	Stand-alone	September 2009; variable by staffing, time; & semester; high 104/month, low 10/month	Widget on reference services webpage, part of instruction, link on most library webpages	Office, home, reference desk
Sylvia Owens, Austin Community College (TX)	InstaService	Multistate Collaborative (AskAcademic)	April–July 2010; 22 ACC student sessions/month	Posters & bookmarks, link on all webpages	Reference desk
Nancy Huling, University of Washington (WA)	QuestionPoint (QP)	National Collaborative (QP 24x7 & AskWA)	Beta site 2002–2005; grown steadily; tripled usage	Persistent link on all library webpages, QWidget or AskUs link in databases, part of instruction	Office, home
Erin McCaffrey, Regis University (CO)	Tutor.com	Collaborative (Association of Jesuit Colleges & Universities)	2004; consistent growth; average 1,000 per month	Branded with posters, bookmarks, & e-mail	Office, home
Paul Mascareñas, Adams State College (CO)	Altarama	National Collaborative (My Info Quest)	July 2009 pilot; growing; up from 2 to 25 per month	Logo & portal on library homepage	Office, home
Julie Fronmueller, Colorado State University– Pueblo (CO)	Mosio	Stand-alone	August 2009; growing; high 34/month, low 2/month	Flyers, table tents, part of instruction	Office, reference desk

The project has been determined to be a success by most of the participating libraries. As the pilot project sponsored by the Alliance Library System is drawing to a close, the Advisory Committee evaluated various SMS reference software packages in the summer of 2010. As of January 1, 2011, the My Info Quest project is funded totally by the participating library/systems from the United States and Canada. While several libraries decided to leave the cooperative when it became a service with a modest fee, many libraries continue. As of July 2011, 11 academic libraries, 13 public libraries, 2 regional library systems, and 6 librarian volunteers provide 77 hours of service. My Info Quest is expanding and continues to add members and hours of service.

My Info Quest allows participating libraries to offer an innovative service to their users and brings librarians out from behind the "reference desk." Participating libraries can meet users at their point of need, lower costs by sharing responsibilities for staffing and developing materials, and offer extended hours. Still, the biggest benefits of being involved in cutting-edge cooperative projects like this are the opportunity to work with a fantastic network of colleagues and being able to develop new and expanded services for users. By taking advantage of cooperative pilot projects using new technologies, librarians are able to showcase themselves as the techno-savvy, up-to-date professionals they are.

References

Avery, B. F., Docherty, K. J., & Lindbloom, M. C. (2011). Collaborative marketing for virtual reference: The My Info Quest experience. *The Reference Librarian, 52*(1/2), 36–46.

Brannon, S. (2011). SMS reference. *The Reference Librarian, 52*(1/2), 152–158.

Cole, V., & Krkoska, B. B. (2011). Launching a text a librarian service: Cornell's preliminary experiences. *The Reference Librarian, 52*(1/2), 3–8.

Greg. (2009). Why do people love to text? Retrieved July 2, 2011, from http://answers.yahoo.com/question/index?qid=20090816172123AAU8uqI.

Lenhardt, A. (2010). Cell phones and American adults. Pew Internet and American Life Project. Retrieved July 2, 2011, from http://www.pewinternet.org/Reports/2010/Cell-Phones-and-American-Adults/Part-1-Adults-and-cell-phones-Ownership-and-use/Cell-ownership-in-the-United-States-remains-steady-since-2009.aspx.

Radford, M. L., & Connaway, L. S. (2005–2008). Seeking synchronicity: Evaluating virtual reference services from user, non-user, and librarian perspectives. Retrieved July 2, 2011, from http://www.oclc.org/research/activities/synchronicity/default.htm.

Stahr, B. (2011). Text message reference services: Five years later. *The Reference Librarian, 52*(1/2), 9–19.

Staudacher, D. (2009, November 14). Have a question? Text a librarian. *Arizona Republic*, p. D10.

Staudacher, D. (2009, November 20). Your questions answered by Rio Salado librarian. Retrieved March 21, 2011, from http://www.azfamily.com/home/related/Your-questions-answered-by-Rio-Salado-Librarian-70656537.html.

Additional Readings

Jensen, B. (2010). SMS text reference comes of age: The My Info Quest collaborative. *The Reference Librarian, 51*(4), 264–275.

Luo, L., & Bell, L. (2010). Text 4 Answers: A collaborative service model. *Reference Service Review, 38*(2), 274–283.

Pearce, A. (2010). Text message reference at NYU Libraries. *The Reference Librarian, 51*(4), 256–263.

Pearce, A., Collard, S., & Whatley, K. (2010). SMS reference: Myths, markers, and modalities. *Reference Service Review, 38*(2), 250–263.

Pope, K, Peters, T., & Bell, L. (2009). InfoQuest: Using text messaging to answer reference questions. *Library Hi Tech News, 26*(8), 12–13.

Stahr, B. (2009). SMS library reference service options. *Library Hi Tech News, 26*(3–4), 3–15.

Wortham, J. (2010). Cellphones now used more for data than for calls. *The New York Times*. Retrieved July 2, 2011, from http://www.nytimes.com/2010/05/14/technology/personaltech/14talk.html.

## CHAPTER 15

Collaborative Virtual Reference Really Does Work, but It Takes a Tribe

Kris Johnson, Patrick Farrell, Kristen Laughlin, Paul M. Mascareñas, and Amy Sieving

Overview

Several well-written guides exist for launching and maintaining virtual reference services (VRS) (Kern, 2009; RUSA, 2010), including ones that are cooperative in nature (RUSA, 2007): libraries joining forces to answer queries for one another in an effort to provide longer and more consistent service hours. What those guides lack are advice related to the practical realities concerning buy-in and human nature. These intangibles factor into the success of any enterprise, and aspects of cooperative reference services that are not easily quantifiable in general return-on-investment analyses. This article focuses on those intangibles, using a model outlined in Seth Godin's (2008) popular book *Tribes: We Need You to Lead Us* to describe the ongoing successes and challenges faced at AskColorado, one of the first and longest-running statewide cooperative VRS in the United States. Librarians from AskColorado describe in their own words "the tribe" and how being part of the tribe benefits them personally, as well as the health and success of the tribe overall.

Introduction

Offering continuous service since September 2003, AskColorado (http://www.askcolorado .org/) is one of the oldest statewide VRS in the country, and during this time per capita usage of the queues has at times equaled that of states four and five times larger than its own. The service has always had a tribal genesis. It was started as a grassroots effort by librarians in the state, from all types of libraries, and today continues to be member supported and governed. The organization has faced several challenges over the years, and has made many changes. During this time, other state- or province-wide cooperative VRS have been formed, later to be dissolved, often with little fanfare, publicity, or documentation, including AskMontana (http://askmontana.org/), AskAway (British Columbia; http://askaway.org/), MassAnswers (Massachusetts), InfoAnyTime (Connecticut), and KANAnswer (Kansas). Discontinuation of nine VRS services, including three consortial (cooperative) services, was profiled by Radford and Kern (2006.) What has AskColorado done differently that has allowed it to survive and prosper? What formula can be taken from AskColorado and applied by other libraries in other states to ensure viability of future VRS cooperatives? The answer is not simple, but lies in basic principles—principles centered on community and belief in a common goal, principles outlined in Godin's 2008 book *Tribes*. While AskColorado did not purposely set forth to follow Godin's *Tribes* philosophy from the beginning, similarities were noticed after *Tribes* was published and the AskColorado coordinator made a concerted effort to draw parallels to the book in outreach to the membership in the form of presentations and gifts of the book to members of the steering committee. A search of the library literature finds that while *Tribes* is briefly mentioned by two library practitioners (Stephens, 2011, p. 211; Zamora, 2009, p. 3), besides AskColorado, no other library consortium has systematically applied Godin's work to its organization.

Key themes from Godin centered on *connection, shared interest, leadership*, and a *desire for change* are central to the success of any human-based organization. At its core, VRS cooperatives are human- (not technology-) based organizations. If only one piece of advice could be offered to others seeking to start a cooperative VRS, or to improve an existing cooperative, it would be this: do not look at the venture as one centered on technology, and instead focus on the human aspects. Do not analyze the service like a database subscription, focusing on metrics and coverage comparisons alone. This approach would be like analyzing the success of a reference desk service using usage hash mark statistics and tracking whether the librarians showed up on time for their shifts. Per-question metrics applied to VR in particular, have always been, at best, misleading (Eakin & Pomerantz, 2009). What is the real cost of not having a service to field questions at the point/time of need? What if the question is never asked of the library because the assumption is made that the library obviously is not the place to ask? What is the cost of bad service, or no service? Those intangibles are what will be discussed in this chapter. Let us start then with key points from Godin combined with a history of AskColorado paired with examples that tie into his themes.

Tribes: Key Points and Examples

1. "A tribe is a group of people connected to one another, connected to a leader, and connected to an idea" (Godin, 2008, p. 1).
   - Idea: The only way to create a truly successful 24/7 reference service in the twenty-first century is to collaborate. (Collaborative VR really does work!)
   - Group: AskColorado member libraries and librarians
   - Leader(s): Committees; individual, exemplary librarians; coordinator/project manager

As previously mentioned, AskColorado was started by libraries throughout the state. Early on, libraries in Colorado picked up on the importance of offering service to patrons electronically, in real time, and without "hours" (i.e., 24/7). They also knew the only way to do this was to collaborate. No libraries in the state were wealthy enough to offer a 24/7 service alone, and all knew that in the twenty-first century, to remain relevant in the eyes of the public, the service must always be available, because people today may work around the clock and do not want to think about hours.

It is also important to know some background about Colorado and its people. Knowing this background information helps to be able to better contextualize the information so as to apply or compare it to other situations. Home to the Continental

Divide, Colorado presents many geographic barriers. At 103,730 square miles, Colorado is the eighth largest state in the United States area-wise. Separated into two main halves by the Rocky Mountains, traveling through the state can be time-consuming, and in the winter often difficult or dangerous. In contrast to this, though, in terms of population, Colorado ranked #22 in 2009 with a total population of about 5 million (5,024,748) (U.S. Census Bureau, 2010). These statistics help give the state its unique flavor in terms of the challenges, as well as benefits, for library resource sharing and other collaboration. Colorado communities have a long history of local control, autonomy, and self-sufficiency, in part because of the geographic distances and, in part, because of that decidedly Western mentality unique to the homesteaders and ranchers. Colorado's library community draws from these extremes, with a preference for local control combined with a history of collaboration. The key thing about this is that in Colorado, libraries share with their communities the practice of collaboration, and geography and population play a key role.

Librarians in the state began discussing VR informally, but seriously, around 2001. The Colorado Resource Sharing Board (RSB; now defunct) charged the Colorado State Library with formally investigating the level of interest in VR in Colorado. This action resulted in two statewide library discussion forums in the spring of 2002 and a groundswell of interest in the topic. Based on the level of interest generated, on April 3, 2002, the RSB authorized the creation of a Virtual Reference Collaboration Committee. This committee (comprised of librarians around the state from multiple library types) was charged with continuing to examine the issues related to collaborating on VR on a statewide basis, to investigate different models of VR, and to make recommendations to RSB about which model should be adopted in Colorado and how to proceed with organizing and funding the effort. A symposium was hosted in summer 2002 with the goal of educating Colorado librarians about collaborative VR (see http://www.webjunction .org/cvrd-2002). The resulting efforts led to recommendations from the Committee, which in turn led to the RSB recommending that the Colorado State Library apply for Library Service and Technology Act (LSTA) grant monies to launch the service. It did, and LSTA monies continue to subsidize the organization today.

2. "Tribes need leadership. Sometimes one person leads, sometimes more" (Godin, 2008, p. 2).
   AskColorado's leaders consist of the following:
   - Committees and subcommittees:
     – Steering Committee
     – Quality Assurance Subcommittee
     – Policies and Procedures Subcommittee
     – Software Selection Subcommittee
   - Individual, exemplary librarians
   - Coordinator/project manager

Because the Colorado State Library has been subsidizing AskColorado by directing LSTA funds into the service from its inception in 2003 to date, the impression among some has been that LSTA funding dictates what the service can do and can be; thus the service is run by the State Library. However, from the very beginning, the service has not subsisted on LSTA funding alone, because the Committee decided that in order to work toward sustainability, Colorado libraries should be asked to contribute financially based on a sliding scale. This method of joint funding continues today, and is what makes Colorado's collaborative VRS unique from many other statewide services. Currently, about one-third of the operating budgeting comes from Colorado libraries, and two-thirds from LSTA grant funds. Colorado libraries also contribute significantly what are called "in-kind" contributions in the form of staffing the service. The in-kind contributions, when calculated hourly, actually represent the largest portion of a participating library's contribution.

In addition, while the Institute for Museum and Library Services (IMLS) has specific restrictions on how the LSTA monies can be *spent*, these are totally unrelated to AskColorado governance. In reality, all decisions for AskColorado are made by one of three committees comprised of librarians from member libraries: Steering, Policies and Procedures, and Quality Assurance. A fourth committee, the Software Selection Subcommittee, convenes every other year, and makes recommendations to the Steering Committee regarding software selection. Thus decision making is centralized with the tribe, which then guides the direction of the organization.

The AskColorado service is member based. In 2009–2010, the cooperative consisted of 74 member libraries and around 200 librarians. Members set the policies; members select the software; members govern. The organization is analogous to a food co-op, or public radio. It is member and grant supported and run. As such, the members of the co-op make the major decisions that affect the organization, led by the expertise and guidance of a project manager who believes "if it isn't broken, make it better, and if it is, do something to change it." The organization is always mindful of the baseline philosophy that combining human and financial resources is the only way to create a truly successful 24/7 reference service in the twenty-first century.

3. "A group needs only two things to be a tribe: a shared interest and a way to communicate" (Godin, 2008, pp. 1–2).
   - Shared Interest. The official objectives established by the organization are as follows:
     – AskColorado Objective: Colorado libraries are *collaborating* to provide a 24/7 online chat reference service that efficiently and effectively meets the information and learning needs of Colorado residents.
     – AskAcademic Objective: Academic libraries are *collaborating* to provide a 24/7 online chat reference service that efficiently and effectively meets the information and learning needs of their students, faculty, and staff.

In the early stages of forming the organization, objectives were written. Those objectives remain today. The objective for AskAcademic was written in 2010, due to a change at the academic queue of the organization, which will be discussed in more detail later in this chapter.

4. "People want connection and growth and something new. They want change" (Godin, 2008, p. 2).
   - Librarians in the AskColorado organization connect significantly with these aspects of the tribal ethos.

- Connection and Growth: Geographic isolation; professional isolation
- New: Skills, patrons, ideas
- Change: Every year our service has made changes

As mentioned previously, and to be elaborated on in the "In Their Own Words" portion of this chapter, AskColorado meets the needs of Colorado libraries and librarians partly due to the challenge presented by the state's geography, and partly due to the innovative nature of VR that engenders new skills and enthusiasm for reference service. Here, however, the focus on point #4 will center on *change*.

Led by the expertise, philosophical views, and guidance of a project manager, the organization has undergone many changes over the years. Some major changes the organization was willing to make include:

- selecting a new chat software from a non-library vendor;
- bringing into the fold two Texas academic libraries (The University of North Texas and Austin Community College);
- rebranding and securing the domain name AskAcademic;
- starting an after-hours librarian service (from scratch);
- discontinuing a Spanish queue; and
- highlighting exemplary transcripts in order to improve customer service.

All changes were decided upon by the membership. Here is a full list of all the changes the cooperative has made since inception in 2003:

2004:
- Offered companion "Live Homework Help" service
- Separated academic queue out of general queue (initially, the academic queue was combined with a general, public queue)

2005:
- Discontinued "Live Homework Help" project

2006:
- Started "Live Help Queue" for state government

2008:
- Rebranded: New logo, tagline, website
- Closed "Live Help Queue"
- Added an academic library from Texas to academic queue

2009:
- Selected new software vendor (non-library vendor)

2010:
- Implemented new software from InstantService (now Oracle Live Help on Demand)
- Expanded and branded the academic queue: two Texas academic libraries
- Launched AskAcademic.org domain (http://www.askacademic.org/)
- Discontinued Spanish service
- Created staff Intranet using Drupal
- Started the ASK After-Hours service to staff evenings, nights, and weekends

Rationale for these changes could comprise a chapter in itself, but one significant change worth highlighting in detail was the evolution of the academic queue of AskColorado into a separate and distinct brand: AskAcademic (now considered a partner queue). AskColorado always had a College Research queue as part of a suite of four queues offered to patrons (K–12, General, Spanish, and College Research), but when approached by a university library outside the state of Colorado interested in joining, made the decision to branch out with distinct identity more inclusive to partnering academic institutions spanning multiple states. In December 2008 the queue began answering questions for students from the University of North Texas, and in February 2010 launched a distinct website (http://www.askacademic.org/) with a new logo for AskAcademic. As of 2011, AskAcademic is comprised of 13 academic libraries from Colorado and Texas.

5. "Some tribes are stuck. They embrace the status quo and drown out any tribe member who dares to question authority and the accepted order" (Godin, 2008, p. 5).
   - AskColorado strives to avoid becoming stuck by encouraging change and library/librarian input via our committee governance.
   - Coordinators' philosophical view is that ongoing change is positive and encouraged.

As just mentioned, the cooperative has striven to encourage and embrace change, and cooperative input into creating that change. The goal has been to encourage members from participating libraries to speak up when they are not happy. Culturally, this goal has not always been an easy thing for some libraries to achieve. In fact, the organization has been presented, at times, with dissatisfaction from select libraries that resulted in a lack of communication, and with those libraries later leaving the cooperative. Ironically, after the fact one library mentioned to the coordinator that their library would be happy to send feedback regarding why they decided to leave the cooperative. In this instance, the feedback was appreciated, but it was communicated back to the library in question that in order for the cooperative to function effectively, feedback needed to be presented in advance of leaving, not retrospectively.

So, one key to the longevity of the AskColorado Cooperative has been ongoing, honest feedback from member libraries. Sometimes that feedback has been uncomfortable, but the resulting changes that ensued due to it have served to benefit and strengthen the cooperative overall.

To illustrate some of the key themes from Godin (*connection, shared interest, leadership, desire for change*), several librarians from member libraries will now describe, in their own words, their thoughts on the organization, how they have personally benefited from participating, and the tribal ethos underlying the benefits received.

In Their Own Words

Patrick Farrell—Public Librarian, Jefferson County Library, Colorado

I work at Jefferson County Public Library (JeffCo) (http://jeffcolibrary.org/), a large county library system serving more than 500,000 residents through 10 library locations, an online library, and a variety of outreach services, and have staffed AskColorado/AskAcademic (ASK) since fall 2007. Recently, JeffCo changed our method of staffing ASK, moving from a decentralized system spread between the branches, to a centralized staffing model based in one department. I serve as the in-house trainer and contact person for the ASK staffers in that department.

JeffCo Library gets a great deal of value from its participation in ASK. Our librarians have the opportunity to network and learn from other librarians. In addition, because many of our local patrons are primarily remote users, the service provided to participating libraries is an important step toward meeting our patrons where they are.

In addition to staffing the service, I am a co-chair of the Quality Assurance (QA) Subcommittee. Our committee is charged with overseeing the quality of the service using evaluation procedures and feedback to help maintain high standards of reference service. Our committee reviews transcripts each month to identify trends and issues, to recognize librarians providing exemplary service, and to troubleshoot potential issues. Members of our group are also responsible for planning the annual ASK Workshop, and identifying other training opportunities throughout the year. Recently, we have been seeking out new opportunities to facilitate communication between members of the cooperative. The committee has attempted to engage more through forums and electronic discussion lists. Members also make themselves available to other staffers during their scheduled shifts to answer questions or generate discussion. The annual workshop is treated as an opportunity to expand conversations among staff rather than simply presenting content. People have generally responded positively to this opportunity to meet other members in person, share tips and tricks, and ask questions. Attendees at the most recent workshop found these discussions and the information shared to be one of the most valuable aspects of the workshop and requested that there be more time for discussion and an opportunity to compile what was generated for use by other members at our next workshop. In my experience, the opportunity to make meaningful professional connections has been a major benefit of participating in ASK, and being able to talk shop with librarians with different backgrounds or different levels of experience is always educational.

ASK functions as a tribe by creating conditions for all staff to be leaders, not only by having the opportunities to influence policy and training initiatives, but also by creating the conditions for collaboration and information sharing between members. Communication channels such as electronic discussion lists and forums via our staff intranet allow members to ask questions and share expertise. Members serving on committees are responsible for creating an environment in which communication is quick, frequent, and low risk.

There is no single platform that makes tighter communication possible. A tribe like ours needs to continually look for the best tools and identify new opportunities to let its members communicate. Communication is especially important in the case of ASK since its members are spread out geographically and many will never meet face-to-face. A great deal of the work of the QA Subcommittee is dedicated to making staff feel supported and valuable and therefore invested in the service. If communication is disjointed, unilateral, or merely punitive in nature, the relationship between members might change for the worse.

My participation in ASK has made me a better librarian. Discussing VR issues with other librarians never ceases to give me new ideas about how to approach questions or solve problems. A great deal of my work is done from my desk. I do not regularly staff a reference desk so I have learned most of my reference skills by participating in this community. Much of my other work is done with other people in other buildings, so an environment in which most communication is virtual is the norm for me. In addition, because much of my work involves online resources, staffing ASK is actually ideal for developing a knowledge base about online searching and information sources. While the work does not necessarily require a specific set of technological skills, it does help to be fearless about trying new things and sharing those experiences. I have found that I can develop these skills more quickly in a collaborative environment.

Ultimately the collaborative and its members are focused on some common goals. In addition to the broad goal of maintaining a high-quality statewide VRS, many of the discussions I have both with colleagues at my own library and with other ASK members revolve around the roles we play in building information literacy among our patrons. ASK sees a large amount of K–12 traffic, and while many of these users are skilled at negotiating the web or communicating virtually, they may not be as far along in terms of their ability to analyze and evaluate information online. VR providers are in a unique position to help students improve their research skills at the point of need.

Paul M. Mascareñas: Academic Librarian, Adams State College, Alamosa, Colorado

Participating in AskColorado/AskAcademic (ASK) gives the librarians at Adams State College Nielsen Library (ASCNL) access to a knowledge base outside of our library for our community of users. Many libraries, such as ASCNL (http://www.adams.edu/library/) located in the south central part of Colorado, are separated from numerous other library systems on the Front Range and Western Slope. Being a member of the ASK collaborative reduces distance and connects librarians, students, and community members from all over the state of Colorado, as well as the faculty, staff, and students from the participating libraries in Texas.

An example of the VR collaborative experience that bridges libraries and librarians is participating in committees. The Quality Assurance (QA) Subcommittee requires reading of monthly transcripts for exemplary service and provides oversight for potential difficult interactions. This practice allows members of QA to ensure excellent VR service. Not only does the virtual medium lend itself to reference questions and answers, but also training can take place on a virtual platform to guarantee every librarian is adequately equipped to staff AskColorado/AskAcademic. Furthermore, a VRS in a collaborative model challenges traditional reference desk librarians to open up their skill set to a wider audience and use an additional set of communication tools.

VR does require technical competencies. In saying that, some skills utilized at the reference desk are transferrable to VR. Librarians are familiar with using databases and library catalogs, and Internet searching. Being able to navigate the more traditional research targets and using a web/chat interface to communicate with a student could be cause for alarm. However, the advances and ease of current chat software make the seemingly difficult reference interview manageable, enjoyable, and effective. Software and supportive technology allows librarians to carry on a conversation or reference interview while sending appropriate resources to their student or patron. In addition, our current software (Oracle Live Help on Demand) also allows for librarians to communicate with each other via instant messaging (IM) directly in the software while simultaneously staffing the service. This feature has proven useful when a student asks a difficult question and assistance from the collaborative is needed.

Being a part of a collaborative VRS gives the librarian an opportunity to instruct and, more important, learn. Providing reference service to patrons from around the state of Colorado, as well as academic patrons from Texas, gives the librarian a chance to experience other library systems and resources. Teaching styles and techniques may vary when a librarian assists a young student in finding information about Egypt or a question arises from a community college student needing to know how to get into his or her library databases. VR also provides the user with anonymity to ask "embarrassing" questions. Sometimes this is the only outlet for a potential personal question to be asked.

VR in a collaborative system gives libraries across the state the opportunity to make an impact and difference in the daily lives of their communities. ASK brings the resources of each library and knowledge base under one umbrella, which means our local community also has access to a myriad of brain power.

This collaborative service or "tribe" of librarians has definite "shared interest." Not only do reference teams provide excellent research assistance at reference desks, by phone, through e-mail, and roaming but also, given the means by which to provide this type of service virtually, librarians can expand their reach to other patrons around the state. Student and community expectations of instantaneous information are satisfied with virtual reference. In addition, with a cooperative virtual reference, it helps to buffer the cost of providing patrons with 24/7 service. Libraries are always asking to do more with less and ASK is doing great things by pooling resources.

Additional benefits to participating in a collaborative reference service include reference agility. It is important that libraries and librarians remain true to their original intent, and that is to provide excellent resources for their communities. Defining "community" with the advent of the Internet and the web has broadened the demographic we serve and the way in which we serve patrons' needs. Many library mission statements support this venture, specifically citing the creation of not only physical but virtual spaces to promote information literacy. Ultimately, librarians are still responsible for finding, evaluating, and retrieving credible information for their users. VR allows reference librarians to expand their scope and reach the greatest number of users. According to Godin (2008), "The Internet allows some organizations to embrace long distance involvement. This is the new leverage" (p. 116). VR provides the leverage for librarians to remain relevant in the ever-evolving world of our users.

Amy Sieving: Public Librarian, Wilkinson Public Library, Telluride, Colorado

The title of this chapter, "Collaborative Virtual Reference Really Does Work, but It Takes a Tribe," is an accurate summary of the VR situation. AskColorado/AskAcademic (ASK) is successful only because there are so many great people involved. I do not believe that a team of librarians paid to staff ASK full-time would provide the same high level of service that the participating collaborative librarians currently offer. Providing VR is intense work, and it is difficult to do well for more than a few hours each week. Since ASK has a large team of dedicated librarians, we can handle that with intensity and provide excellent customer service.

According to Godin (2008, p. 1), "A tribe is a group of people connected to one another, connected to a leader, and connected to an idea." The ASK tribe works so it incorporates all of these criteria. The librarians who staff ASK are connected to one another through means such as the e-mail mailing list and the staff intranet. The librarians are connected to leaders, through the coordinator and the members of the committees. Finally, all ASK tribe members are connected to the idea of providing patrons with outstanding VR.

Wilkinson Public Library (http://www.telluridelibrary.org/) is located in a rural, isolated area of the state. The nearest college is 65 miles away, and as such, the librarians here do not get many "real" reference questions. We certainly keep busy showing patrons how to print documents and how to use the Internet, but we do not get much practice using reference skills and conducting a proper reference interview. ASK gives me and two other librarians at Wilkinson Public Library the opportunity to use all of the reference skills that we learned in library school. ASK helps us keep those skills current even when we do not get regular in-depth questions from face-to-face patrons.

This geographic isolation touches on another reason that being part of ASK is beneficial for me and for other rural librarians: It helps us to become part of the Colorado library community. Telluride is pretty much in the middle of nowhere, and it is tough for us to make it all the way up to Denver for conferences. Even meetings in Grand Junction usually require an overnight stay, but still we are not as connected to the rest of the state as we would like to be. I assume that many rural libraries feel a similar disconnection from the metro areas. Staffing ASK helps to connect me to Colorado librarians on a more frequent basis. Even simple things like covering a shift for another staffer help me feel like part of the group, and it is nice to be able to recognize names when attending conferences. Furthermore, ASK offers access to many professionals who are willing and able to help with reference queries. I do not know anything about legal matters, but just knowing that we have contacts at the Colorado Supreme Court Library through ASK serves as a reference security blanket. ASK has exposed me to this whole group of people who are also excited about providing reference, and their enthusiasm is contagious. ASK staffers share great tips and tricks and contribute to the AskColorado online bookmarking site (http://www.delicious.com/askcolorado).

I staff ASK during an early morning shift, so during the school year there is heavy traffic from classes visiting the site. Frequently we will be bombarded with 15 or 20 kids all at the same time. Although the questions are usually fairly basic, like "Where did Pizarro go in his explorations?" or "What kind of foods did Mayans eat?" it really takes some focus to be able to help these students get answers quickly. Another fun challenge is taking on two or three questions at the same time. There is enough lag time while patrons look at the information sent to them and then reply that staffers can usually do that. This really helps to hone search skills and forces staffers to search efficiently. It is also challenging to find websites that can be used by students as references for assignments, sites more substantial than user-created online encyclopedias such as Wikipedia (http://www.wikipedia.org/). This also helps keep library databases in mind. It is easy to forget about our useful library databases on a day-to-day basis, but this type of practice helps to keep reference skills sharp.

Rural library patrons may experience frustration that their libraries are only open limited hours and that they do not have access to librarians outside of these hours. ASK provides all Colorado library patrons (and even those who do not have library cards— hopefully those people are encouraged to use their physical libraries as well) with an opportunity to ask questions and get help with any question at any time. Colorado libraries provide a wide array of online resources, but many patrons are unaware that these resources exist. Since many people conduct research in an online environment, VR is crucial to providing 24/7, at-home access to our patrons. If a patron is researching a topic at home on the couch and runs into a problem, calling a library or actually walking into a library is a bit of a hassle. Fortunately, clicking the "Ask-a-Librarian" button and chatting online with a friendly librarian is definitely not a hassle. VR is crucial for libraries to stay relevant in an environment where everyone is online all the time.

As part of the preparation for this chapter, I was reading some online reviews of the book *Tribes: We Need You to Lead Us* (Godin, 2008), and one person was disappointed that although the book was inspirational in terms of making one want to become a leader, it did not really outline the steps involved in becoming a leader. That made me think that the great thing about ASK and other similar tribes is that they provide a place for people like me. I am definitely not a leader (maybe as my career progresses I will hopefully grow into that), but ASK provides a place for me to easily contribute an hour each week doing something that I enjoy to help make the ASK tribe sustainable, and I really appreciate that.

Kristen Laughlin: ASK After-Hours Librarian

AskColorado/AskAcademic (ASK) allows every participating librarian to contribute something helpful and meaningful that makes the cooperative better as a whole. There are many micro-leadership opportunities within AskColorado; librarians can take the lead based on their unique skills and experience. Some are great at working with children, some have an excellent grasp of business resources, some are tech savvy. No single librarian is an expert in all areas, but if we allow everyone to have a voice and contribute when they have something to share, then we all learn and become better at VR.

One example of an ASK librarian taking the lead is Tracy Treece, with her contribution to the way we handle math questions. We work with many students who have questions about math homework, and it can be a challenge to help them without actually tutoring them. Tracy started using videos from a variety of math help and online video-sharing sites to help students better understand their math homework. When she shared this idea with the other librarians, we loved it, and started using it as well. Often a demonstration of solving a problem in real time is more helpful to a student than a written explanation. Because Tracy took the lead on trying a new approach and then shared it with the cooperative at large, the librarians and their patrons all benefited.

This kind of informal sharing of techniques and ideas is possible for two reasons. The first is that we are the opposite of a hierarchical, traditionally structured workplace. Our organization encourages leadership and innovation by all participants. The second reason is that we have multiple, accessible channels of communication within the organization that allow us to spread our ideas quickly to all of our members. Our staff intranet and electronic discussion list are central to our success, and are especially important to the after-hours librarians, because we have no "home library" where we share staffing duties with coworkers. These tools empower us to communicate among ourselves, and solve problems in an informal, participatory manner. Without these tools, we would be far less effective.

This ability to communicate across the cooperative allows us to learn from one another on a regular basis, which is of tremendous importance because of the variety of questions we receive. After-hours librarians staff both the public and academic queues, and because we often staff late in the evening, we get a particularly mixed bag of questions. We may get in-depth research questions from college students, business-related questions, and questions from younger patrons that range from homework topics, to pop culture, to how to make your own hairspray. We have to be nimble and flexible in order to work across the various disciplines, and we count on our fellow librarians to share resources and tips so that we can serve all of our patrons well.

One concern many librarians have about working within a VR consortium environment is the potential lack of access to a patron's electronic resources. We serve many patrons at many different libraries, and we do not have accounts at all of these libraries, so we cannot necessarily access information from a specific library's databases. However, as long as we can see which databases the library uses, we can help the patron form a search strategy. Our familiarity with databases in general and our ability to teach search skills are all we need. We can recommend databases that would be appropriate for a given topic, and keywords that will give good results. This way, patrons get instruction in searching, which will help them in the future, as well as with the current research question. If patrons have questions we cannot answer, such as technical issues, we can refer them to their home libraries. Often they just need to know where to start. This practice is another example of how working together and sharing ideas and questions as a group is helpful to all of the ASK libraries. If one librarian has a question about resources or procedures at a specific library, she can ask the group and solicit advice and feedback that everyone can see, or she can ask a representative of the library in question, and share the response with the group. We have all learned tips and tricks about using our various member libraries' websites from one another, via our staff intranet and our e-mail mailing lists.

ASK, and virtual reference in general, are important because we need to meet our patrons where they are. Not everyone will come to the library. Even if patrons do visit the library, they often come in for fiction or movies. When they are doing research, they go to Google first. If they have a research question while they are online at home, sitting on their couch with their laptop at 10 o'clock at night, we have to meet them there, and assist them there. It is especially important to have the after-hours service, so that patrons can get help at any time. We have to show that we are relevant and indispensable. The web is a messy place; it's a disorganized resource with huge variations in quality of information, and we can help them find good information that they don't even know is there—but we cannot do that if we stay behind the reference desk and only work nine to five.

It is not possible for the staff of a single library to be there 24 hours a day for their patrons. By working together as a cooperative organization, we help one another serve all of our patrons better. We are there for them whenever they need us, and we are better librarians because we learn from one another on a continual basis.

I believe that working for ASK helped me get my previous job at an all-online university, and my current job as a community college librarian with an emphasis on serving distance students. Working as an ASK After-Hours Librarian prepared me to assist students with all types of research, in large part because of how much I learned from my fellow librarians. As an after-hours librarian, I get a great mix of questions, including both academic and business questions, which translates into familiarity with resources that help all of my students. Helping distance students is second nature to me now, because I am used to using chat and e-mail as tools to provide resources and bibliographic instruction.

Godin (2008) tells us that leaders motivate, connect, and leverage the members of their tribe in order to make the tribe successful. The most important element of this in a statewide VRS cooperative is connection. The fact that we can communicate with one another, and that we have opportunities to see one another at workshops and events throughout the year, allows us to motivate one another. When one librarian posts a great new idea or tip on the intranet or via a mailing list, we feel good about learning something new, and we feel motivated to contribute ourselves. Godin also says that leaders trust members of the tribe to do what they do best, rather than micromanaging. Allowing the competent and capable librarians who participate in ASK to pose questions to one another and solve problems as a group is what makes us work so well. It is an organic and sometimes messy way to approach a problem, but we do arrive at great answers, and it gives us all an opportunity to learn along the way.

One of the main lessons of *Tribes* (Godin, 2008) is that organizations that destroy the status quo, by delivering something awesome to their customers, will win. We do this at ASK, because we provide a real, live person to help you, day or night. That person is a skilled VR librarian, who has learned from fellow librarians. We have the tools to help our patrons because we are allowed to lead, we are motivated, and we are connected.

Conclusion

As mentioned in their own words, these are just a few of the positive intangibles inherent with a collaborative VRS for the librarians that participate in AskColorado/AskAcademic:

- Networking and learning from other librarians
- Opportunities for leadership and professional growth
- Occasions to make meaningful professional connections outside of one's home library
- Meeting our patrons where they are: online
- Patrons receiving excellent service that is seamless with their use of their physical, home libraries

One librarian participating in a workshop in Colorado commented that for her, ASK acted as her only professional organization focusing on reference services. None of the state and regional professional associations provided a reference subgroup, or any programming or training related to reference services. Without the ASK organization, she had no access to continuing education, hands-on practice with real and difficult reference questions, and camaraderie with a network of other librarians interested in reference and with the expertise to share. Thus, the value to her library from participating in the ASK collaborative went beyond mere usage statistics from residents of their county, and included professional development benefits impossible to calculate in monetary terms, with a return on investment to the library in the form of a librarian much more apt to provide excellent reference service to the library's constituents.

It truly does take a *tribe* for collaborative VR to work. It is that network of people— not technology—that makes the VR cooperative successful. The people work well together to provide a successful product or service because they believe in the common goal of providing excellent service to all library patrons, and it is that ethos that forms the foundation of the common goal needed in order to sustain the tribe.

References

Eakin, L., & Pomerantz, J. (2009). Virtual reference, real money: Modeling costs in virtual reference services. *portal: Libraries and the Academy, 9*(1), 133–164.

Godin, S. (2008). *Tribes: We need you to lead us.* New York: Portfolio.

Kern, M. K. (2009). *Virtual reference best practices: Tailoring services to your library.* Chicago: American Library Association.

Radford, M. L., & Kern, M. K. (2006). A multiple-case study investigation of the discontinuation of nine chat reference services. *Library & Information Science Research, 28*(4), 521–547.

RUSA. (2007). Guidelines for cooperative reference services. *Reference and User Services Quarterly, 47*(1), 97–100.

RUSA. (2010). Guidelines for implementing and maintaining virtual reference services. *Reference and User Services Quarterly, 50*(1), 92–96.

Stephens, M. (2011). What's next? Tracking tech trends. In D. Zabel (Ed.), *Reference reborn: Breathing new life into public services librarianship* (pp. 203–214). Santa Barbara, CA: Libraries Unlimited.

U.S. Census Bureau. (2010). *Colorado Quick Facts.* Retrieved June 9, 2011, from http://quickfacts.census.gov/qfd/states/08000.html.

Zamora, G. (2009, July/August). Help SLA build our alignment tribe. *Information Outlook, 13*(5), 3.

## CHAPTER 16

Collaborate to Succeed: Implementing New Reference Services with SPLAT

Amy Vecchione and Memo Cordova

Overview

Libraries face shrinking budgets and increased user demands, yet library users expect librarians to provide the latest reference and information services. New applications are created daily and library staff may find it difficult to keep up with these innovative technological tools and developments in social media. Idaho has come up with a new way to stay ahead of the game. SPLAT (Special Projects Library Action Team) offers a collaborative model to meet these challenges and enhance library reference services. This model engages a diverse group of library staff chosen from different libraries, skills, and geographic regions. As a team, this group works with a statewide focus to experiment with new trends and share what they learn with the entire library community. The model follows the mantra to make many mistakes quickly when learning new technologies and trends, and to compile best practices so that others do not have to do so. An anonymous, web-based survey was sent to anyone who has interacted or worked with SPLAT members in the past and its focus was on perceptions of the impact SPLAT has had on their library work (see Figure 16.1 for the complete survey). Preliminary results indicate that this model has been successful in its implementation. This chapter presents a collaborative model that can be used in any region to help many libraries come up to speed simultaneously.

Introduction: Futuring in Libraries

Many libraries do not have the time to think about future needs as they are so busy thinking about the needs of users now. The need for libraries to innovate in order to remain relevant is not a new one. Futuring is defined as the imagining and exploring of future and present needs, and is a type of predictive action that will help make decisions about library services. This imperative is well described in an article by Staley and Malenfant (2010) which explains that futuring will increase relevance for libraries: "For academic librarians seeking to demonstrate the value of their libraries to their parent institutions, it is important to understand not only the current climate but also what will be valued in the future so that they can begin to take appropriate action now" (p. 173). Futuring should be an activity in the strategic planning process of libraries. Groups like SPLAT can facilitate this process by vetting tools, services, and new ideas on a regular basis. As budgets are being cut, administrators and library staff members are facing

---

Figure 16.1. Assessment of the Special Projects Library Action Team

For the past four years, the Special Projects Library Action Team (SPLAT) has aimed to "act in the 'crow's nest' capacity, searching for innovation, proposing and leading experiments and pilot projects, and discovering new opportunities." As a result SPLAT has been involved in several projects, its members attended numerous conferences, and their ideas written on the SPLAT blog (http://splat.lili.org/).

The purpose of this survey is twofold: to learn of your experiences with SPLAT, and to determine if SPLAT is on track to fulfilling its mission. Please complete this survey if you have had any experience(s) with SPLAT.

The entire procedure will take about five minutes and can be completed anywhere there is Internet access. There will be no costs to you as a result of taking part in this study, other than the time spent to participate. This survey is anonymous and voluntary. You are free to exit the survey at any time.

If you have questions or concerns about participation in this study, you should first talk with the principal investigators:

Amy Vecchione   Memo Cordova
Assistant Professor/Librarian   Assistant Professor/Librarian
Boise State University   Boise State University
1910 University Drive   1910 University Drive
Boise, Idaho 83725   Boise, Idaho 83725
(208) 426-1625   (208) 426-1270
amyvecchione@boisestate.edu   memocordova@boisestate.edu

If for some reason you do not wish to do this, you may contact the Institutional Review Board, which is concerned with the protection of volunteers in research projects:

Institutional Review Board
Office of Research Compliance
Boise State University
(208) 426-5401

1. **What type of library are you affiliated with?**
   - ❑ Special   ❑ Public
   - ❑ School   ❑ Other: _____
   - ❑ Academic   _____

2. **Please indicate your skill level using these tools or conducting the following tasks:**

   using new media, like tumblr   **uploading a video to YouTube**
   - ❑ Expert   ❑ Expert
   - ❑ Proficient   ❑ Proficient
   - ❑ Novice   ❑ Novice
   - ❑ Not Applicable   ❑ Not Applicable

   setting up & using rss feeds   **sharing links, like Delicious**
   - ❑ Expert   ❑ Expert
   - ❑ Proficient   ❑ Proficient
   - ❑ Novice   ❑ Novice
   - ❑ Not Applicable   ❑ Not Applicable

   downloading mp3s   **sharing photos online**
   - ❑ Expert   ❑ Expert
   - ❑ Proficient   ❑ Proficient
   - ❑ Novice   ❑ Novice
   - ❑ Not Applicable   ❑ Not Applicable

(Continued)

Figure 16.1. Assessment of the Special Projects Library Action Team *(Cont'd.)*

2. **Please indicate your skill level using these tools or conducting the following tasks:** *(Continued)*

streaming online media, like Pandora or Last.fm
- ❏ Expert
- ❏ Proficient
- ❏ Novice
- ❏ Not Applicable

copying and pasting
- ❏ Expert
- ❏ Proficient
- ❏ Novice
- ❏ Not Applicable

accessing e-audiobooks
- ❏ Expert
- ❏ Proficient
- ❏ Novice
- ❏ Not Applicable

gaming
- ❏ Expert
- ❏ Proficient
- ❏ Novice
- ❏ Not Applicable

tweeting
- ❏ Expert
- ❏ Proficient
- ❏ Novice
- ❏ Not Applicable

blogging
- ❏ Expert
- ❏ Proficient
- ❏ Novice
- ❏ Not Applicable

accessing databases
- ❏ Expert
- ❏ Proficient
- ❏ Novice
- ❏ Not Applicable

creating accounts on the web
- ❏ Expert
- ❏ Proficient
- ❏ Novice
- ❏ Not Applicable

accessing e-books
- ❏ Expert
- ❏ Proficient
- ❏ Novice
- ❏ Not Applicable

using a social network
- ❏ Expert
- ❏ Proficient
- ❏ Novice
- ❏ Not Applicable

editing and using wikis
- ❏ Expert
- ❏ Proficient
- ❏ Novice
- ❏ Not Applicable

setting up a blog
- ❏ Expert
- ❏ Proficient
- ❏ Novice
- ❏ Not Applicable

3. **In which of the following ways have you interacted with SPLAT? Choose all that apply.**
- ❏ I talked to someone on a couch at a conference.
- ❏ I have read about SPLAT on LIbIdaho, The Scoop, the ICFL website, etc.
- ❏ I attended a presentation at a conference.
- ❏ I participated in training in my library by a SPLAT member.
- ❏ I read the blog.
- ❏ I participated in SPLAT 101.
- ❏ I have heard about SPLAT from colleagues.
- ❏ Something else? Please write it in: _____

_____

_____

_____

(Continued)

Figure 16.1. Assessment of the Special Projects Library Action Team *(Cont'd.)*

4. What are your impressions of SPLAT? Please choose your answer for each concept on the matrix scale.

SPLAT members have helped me learn new tools and technologies
❏ Strongly Agree
❏ Agree
❏ Neither Agree nor Disagree
❏ Disagree
❏ Strongly Disagree

Services or policies have changed at my library because of SPLAT
❏ Strongly Agree
❏ Agree
❏ Neither Agree nor Disagree
❏ Disagree
❏ Strongly Disagree

I have integrated some tools I've learned from SPLAT into our library services
❏ Strongly Agree
❏ Agree
❏ Neither Agree nor Disagree
❏ Disagree
❏ Strongly Disagree

SPLAT helps me stay current
❏ Strongly Agree
❏ Agree
❏ Neither Agree nor Disagree
❏ Disagree
❏ Strongly Disagree

SPLAT has helped me understand better new social media or tools
❏ Strongly Agree
❏ Agree
❏ Neither Agree nor Disagree
❏ Disagree
❏ Strongly Disagree

5. What specific new ideas, technologies, or tools have you learned from SPLAT? Please provide examples.

_____
_____
_____

6. Have you shared anything you learned from SPLAT with others?
❏ Yes   ❏ No

7. What are your impressions of SPLAT overall?

_____
_____
_____

8. How can SPLAT become more effective at meetings its mission? What suggestions do you have for SPLAT? Please be as specific as possible.

_____
_____
_____

9. Do you have any other comments not addressed in the questions above? Please indicate those comments here.

_____
_____
_____

difficult decisions. Trying to determine potential growth for libraries is imperative because administrators and library staff members may cut those services, or collections, that they think are unnecessary in upcoming years, although they may not have had the opportunity to participate in or be informed by futuring. Despite this, librarians rarely participate in futuring themselves. Since each region, city, community, or user group is different, who is better at predicting the future needs of those groups than the librarians that serve them? Futuring is no longer simply necessary to predict the trends and their effects on libraries, but change is happening so quickly that it is also necessary in order to reach out to current or potential user groups.

Furthermore, little modeling has been done to help libraries conceptualize what futuring would look like. SPLAT is among the first statewide collaborative futuring groups for libraries, and can serve as one potential model: the grassroots team of innovation representatives. Rubleske, Kaarst-Brown, and Strobel (2010) found that "While we know that libraries (like most service providers) typically innovate through the adoption of technological and organizational innovations, few attempts have been made to conceptualize this process" (para. 1). They also claim that libraries have not fully developed their instruments nor fully studied models for innovation in asserting that "there is a conspicuous lack of conceptual frameworks for understanding thoroughly the 'front end' of service innovation" (para. 11).

Futuring is also crucial because of the risks libraries potentially face in this current economic crisis. Focusing solely on current users' needs means that libraries risk becoming obsolete if they do not adapt to new technologies. The Association of Research Libraries (ARL), and Stratus, Inc., recently published a guide that points out this danger as well, stating that "The temptation to 'wait and see' is appealing but exposes libraries to the risks of irrelevance and replacement" (Association of Research Libraries, 2010, p. 7). The guide looks at scenarios for academic libraries in 2030, which were carefully assessed on their potential impact and likelihood of occurrence by experts, library panels, focus groups, and the author participants. The authors of this document espouse that few libraries participate in scenario imagining, or futuring, stating that "Scenario planning is a tool that a few research libraries have used, but is largely new to the library community" (Association of Research Libraries, 2010, p. 7). Conducting a localized set of scenarios specific to a library or regional user group, however, would be quite beneficial. Using the documents from the Idaho Library Futures Conference, and some of the more current scenarios from various reports, any library, or group of library staff, can commence a fruitful discussion about library planning for the future.

By encouraging this collaborative model, new ideas, not yet brought forth, may come to light, which in turn would serve all libraries. A SPLAT-like team from any region can develop their own scenarios to investigate based on community needs and can then initiate a conversation from that imagined future much like the Idaho Library Futures Conference.

SPLAT members use the *Horizon Report* as a back channel for futuring purposes. This report addresses core fundamental changes in information technologies and education. Though geared toward universities and colleges, it is applicable to any institution that is vested in providing education. The *Horizon Report* consists of many great scenarios to discuss with such a group (Johnson, Smith, Willis, Levine, & Haywood, 2011). This document suggests the emerging technologies that will impact higher education, which will in turn impact us. Also included is information about the likelihood of the scenario coming to fruition, as well as the years until the technology reaches widespread adoption. The report focuses on new technologies and how they may be incorporated into educational settings, but libraries will have to respond to these technologies also as they increase in adoption. For example, the 2011 report highlights technologies that will become mainstream quite soon—"that is, within the next 12 months—are mobile computing and open content" (Johnson et al., 2011, p. 5)—including mobile technologies and e-books. Both of these trends have significant impacts for libraries. Any library would find it beneficial to discuss scenarios based on the potential futures outlined in this report.

The SPLAT Team

The SPLAT Idea
The SPLAT initiative was developed over the course of three days. Participants engaged in futuring discussions and thus developed a lengthy list of challenges, trends, and scenarios that libraries currently experience, or are likely to encounter in the next few decades. Participants also identified driving forces that would influence the way libraries meet the challenges of the future, including the following:

- Generational shifts in communities and library customers
- Population growth and increased diversity, but limits to revenue/taxes
- Changing technology challenges and opportunities
- Education and literacy needs increasing
- Information ubiquity, transparency, and challenges to privacy, freedom, and intellectual property
- Loss of place, roots, and stability (Idaho Commission for Libraries, 2006, p. 2)

This steering committee proposed four statewide strategies, based on seven regional meetings where the above issues were discussed, to direct libraries toward a preferred future of relevance and community engagement:

1. Develop ways to reach digital natives.
2. Innovate by creating a Special Projects Library Action Team (SPLAT) to act in the "crow's nest" capacity, searching for innovation, proposing and leading experiments and pilot projects, and discovering new opportunities. This initiative will begin with a statewide team, but could later be extended to regions or localities.
3. Establish an Idaho libraries brand or identity. Seek professional assistance to establish a dynamic brand identity for Idaho libraries as a whole.
4. Produce scenarios. Create a scenario development effort, involving a team of people who work year-round to produce several alternative plausible scenarios for the future of libraries, and update and communicate these scenarios periodically. (Idaho Commission for Libraries, 2006, p. 6)

Following the recommendations of the steering committee, a design team was formed to implement the SPLAT initiative. In spring 2006, the team solicited applications to libraries across the state for individuals who demonstrate forward thinking. By fall 2006, the team had selected a dozen individuals to form SPLAT. Members are innovation representatives. They engage in a futuring process by which each member will seek out, experiment, and learn how best to implement tools to current reference practices and services to a variety of libraries. Each member tries to see what trends are on the horizon, and what users are demanding, as a way of trying to predict which services and technologies will create a positive impact on the user experience. This meta-thinking concept presupposes a set of thinking models SPLAT members take to heart:

- Leaders everywhere: SPLAT members encourage all library staff to experiment, and apply what they learn to better their own reference or public service challenges.
- Passion for libraries: SPLAT members are passionate about libraries, their place in the community, and the people they serve.
- Flexibility: Ideas and implementation: SPLAT members encourage awareness and use of emergent social media tools and services, and apply practices to reference models, outreach, collection, and community development.
- Experimentation: Trial and error: SPLAT members seek out, learn, and experiment with gadgetry, online tools, and social media (SM) models—a process that can result in successful practices that enhance reference service models, or can admittedly fail. Both outcomes inform understanding of what constitutes a good tool or reference service practice.

SPLAT members participate in quarterly futuring meetings and share ideas on the SPLAT blog (http://splat.lili.org/). Each member brings ideas, predictions, tools, and suggestions to discuss and shares viable ways libraries can integrate or enhance reference services based on the current trends. Once the ideas are vetted, SPLAT members share their favorite endeavors with the larger library community. Successful efforts include SPLAT 101, an online course for library staff to learn about web technologies and social networks; conference presentations on emergent trends, SM, and social software; the aforementioned SPLAT blog devoted to current tools and trends; and peer-to-peer discussion and education. These endeavors serve to demystify evolving tools and to exploit web-rich technologies. SPLAT's ongoing efforts result in enhanced reference services, policy changes, and in an understanding of experimentation. Overall, this initiative increases the number of positive user experiences at libraries.

How SPLAT Fosters Innovation

Several authors indicate that the primary model of innovation consists of a top-down administration level approach (Rubleske et al., 2010; Katsirikou & Sefertzi, 2000). The top-down approach is systematic in its conceptualization, but nonlinear. As Katsirikou and Sefertzi (2000) explain, innovation is a systematic process that does not take place in a linear fashion "but rather a system of interactions, of comings and goings between different functions and different players whose experience, knowledge and know-how are mutually reinforcing and cumulative" (p. 706). This system is more effective in informing the adoption of a new idea or tool. Our observations are that innovation can arise from a bottom-up approach by those who are leaders on the front lines.

The SPLAT meetings are largely social interactions. During these meetings, or prior to them, team members experience the mindful interactions described by Rubleske and colleagues (2010). These mindful interactions draw a strong comparison to the system of interactions described by Katsirikou and Sefertzi (2000). Mindful interactions are defined as "the perceptual (*feeling*) and cognitive (*thinking*) awareness of some 'discriminatory detail' (e.g., an object's potential usefulness)" (Rubleske et al., 2010, para. 19; italics in original). These interactions are similar to inspirations, realizations, or great ideas. Though their study indicates that these mindful interactions come from administrators and subsequently lead libraries to adopting innovation, the SPLAT model takes a bottom-up approach where the team of innovation representatives is always looking for these new service possibilities. Rubleske and colleagues have a very helpful model, however, if one is to consider that individuals who come from a collaborative team may experience mindful interactions.

Rubleske and colleagues describe that these interactions first come from an experience outside of the library with vendors, colleagues, individuals from other outside organizations, and as personal consumer. SPLAT meetings often include guests from related fields, or individuals who are inspiring experts on a certain topic. As forward-thinking experimenters, SPLAT members are consumers of new tools and technologies. Each member becomes the resident expert on a certain new topic, such as e-books, geolocation, or text message reference. By including background information about the user groups served, and the knowledge of what can be done within the library, team members are able to conceive and implement new services.

In addition, the authors have observed both in meetings and found to be reported in the library literature that not all innovation adoption comes from such a systematic process. Some of the elements to SPLAT's success have been the result of the casual, unsystematic approach that SPLAT takes, and this serendipity is perhaps what arises out of the mindful interactions. Katsirikou and Sefertzi's (2000) model differs by identifying that "innovation is composed of the systematic retrieve of changes and systematic analysis of the opportunities which these changes could contribute to economic and social improvement" (p. 705). SPLAT looks for new ideas and its members become inspired. This idea resonates much more with the model proposed by Rubleske and colleagues (2010), who posit that innovation in libraries is due to an administrator who is always thinking about how these interactions may result in "*new service possibilities for customers*" (Rubleske et al., 2010, para. 19; italics in original). In the SPLAT model, the frontline staff members are always thinking about new service possibilities for their users. This team shares, implements, and adopts new services in a nonsystematic manner.

Current Framework of SPLAT

SPLAT members vet ideas and projects on an ongoing basis, both individually and as group-think, and these are showcased or disseminated at the local level as well as in regional and state conferences. This grassroots level of interaction and dissemination of online tools and awareness produce improved service experiences at libraries on all levels, and can prepare library staff to better serve individuals who come to the reference desk with questions about FourSquare (http://www.foursquare.com/), their Android phone, or WorldCat (http://www.worldcat.org/) apps; library staff have an amplified awareness, or have developed a working knowledge of these developments thanks to SPLAT.

SPLAT 101

SPLAT 101 is an educational initiative consisting of online learning modules that came about in a meeting as a solution to help bridge the digital divide among library staff. The goal was to educate reference staff on the newer tools in libraries so that if a patron were to approach the desk with a question about any technology, such as wikis, the staff could say that they are aware of wikis, that they are familiar with them, and that they could help. This brought about a larger discussion within SPLAT about the concept of a unified reference service, and our team felt this was a positive step toward that ideal. Many participants in the online course SPLAT 101 engaged in several different modules where they learned how to use the technology in their library, and subsequently adopted the tool, such as using a wiki, to serve as their internal website. SPLAT 101 was further refined by Idaho Commission for Libraries (ICfL), who formalized the tools offered by the original online modules in the SPLAT blog into a permanently available, independent of SPLAT's blog, online course that is freely available to anyone (http://libraries.idaho.gov/splat101).

Reference tools make up the bulk of SPLAT discussions, due in part to the larger make-up of the group who serve as reference staff in some capacity. Unsurprisingly, one of the first initiatives SPLAT members instituted to their respective libraries was the implementation of chat and short message service (SMS) reference services. Members experimented with tools like Meebo (http://www.meebo.com/) and Google Voice (http://www.google.com/voice) initially, and further evaluation encouraged libraries to implement a combination of chat and SMS tools such as LibraryH3lp (http://library h3lp.com/), and Google Chat (http://www.google.com/talk/) or other services which best suited a specific library setting or need.

Another area of experimentation has been in collection management, particularly social online collection networks like Shelfari (http://www.shelfari.com/) and LibraryThing (http://www.librarything.com/). The author showcased LibraryThing as part of a staff presentation to his library, which resulted in its use as a viable collection development tool for Boise State University's Albertsons Library. This site has enhanced the selection and order of printed materials, and replaced the inefficient use of routed journals and trade magazines for collection awareness of newly published materials. Another example of innovative experimentation is the use of LibGuides (http://www.springshare .com/libguides/). A SPLAT member saw the potential of LibGuides as a viable tool for management of subject-related materials for his library. He experimented personally with it before making his case to his library's administration for its adoption. After further study, LibGuides became the main library subject management tool for Albertsons Library. Awareness and experimentation of potentially beneficial online products and SM sites like LibraryThing and LibGuides serve to improve and challenge traditional library services.

SPLAT members have encouraged the use of free or low-cost social software tools such as Zoho (http://www.zoho.com/) and Google Docs (http://docs.google.com/), as these can be used to enhance library computing services as alternatives to costly proprietary office programs, and require no hardware or software installation. In addition, tools such as Google Sites (http://sites.google.com/) and Wetpaint (http://wikisineducation .wetpaint.com/) are wiki tools used as effective platforms for conference planning and project management, and can function as intranets.

SPLAT members routinely use and experiment with videoconferencing tools like Skype (http://www.skype.com/) and Google Video (http://video.google.com/) to collaborate and visually communicate within specific library groups, SPLAT members, or the larger library community. Last, the continued rise of social networks like Facebook (http://www.facebook.com/), YouTube (http://www.youtube.com/), Flickr (http://www.flickr.com/), and Twitter (http://www.twitter.com/), provide SPLAT members ample experimentation to utilize these networks as outreach venues. Most served libraries now boast an online social presence thanks to the awareness brought on by SPLAT member presentations at conferences, via peer-to-peer conversations with library leaders, and via updates to the SPLAT blog.

The SPLAT blog is a key component in these efforts, not only as an awareness tool for potentially beneficial technological innovations for libraries, but also as an authoritative theater where SPLAT members personally experiment, use, and vet innovative tools and practices. As each SPLAT member is committed to post regularly to the blog, a guaranteed stream of fresh ideas, musings, and sometimes radical notions emerge regularly. These endeavors add value to current library services, and can sometimes challenge the sometimes staid thinking of libraries as being mainly concerned with just books.

Assessment of SPLAT

Members' Reactions

Most of the evidence for SPLAT's success has been anecdotal. Individuals report that they are now using wikis as the intranet in their library, or that their teens love their new blog at their school library. One of the most touted successes of SPLAT has to do with Teacher Librarian Glynda Pflieger's work at the Melba School District, a small-town district with a population of 439 people located in Southwest Idaho. Pflieger took SPLAT 101 and as a result was able to change policies throughout the Melba School District so students and teachers alike can use more new technologies. Prior to Pflieger's interactions with SPLAT, many social media sites, such as Gmail, MySpace, Facebook, YouTube, and Google Docs, were banned from use, and therefore blocked, at her school library. Their new policy "includes email, streaming video, and social networking among the acceptable uses of Internet" (Persichini, 2010, p. 3). Pflieger is now the School Library Consultant at the ICfL, and will help to encourage this kind of change throughout the state.

Ann Joslin has stated "two most visible successes of SPLAT are the informal technology mentoring members provided at the ILA [Idaho Library Association] conferences and the SPLAT 101 courses on Web 2.0 tools" (personal communication, January 22, 2010). Based on the survey data that the ICfL collected after the completion of SPLAT 101, 72.1 percent of the participants expressed that they learned something new and enjoyed taking the course. Participants of SPLAT 101 also mentioned how they were implementing the new tools at their library. "We're all doing SPLAT 101 at our library. We're thinking about an internal blog and an internal Wiki where we can put out [a] procedures manual and keep it up to date. Thanks for all the info!" (Dewey, 2008, para. 56). There were also many comments posted anonymously on the SPLAT 101 site. SPLAT 101 participants had felt intimidated by the new technology in the past, but now found it so easy to learn, with one anonymous participant writing "Amazingly I created my own blog. I'm not a big fan of computers in general but slowly but surely I am getting the hang of some things" (Anonymous, 2008, para. 57).

Survey Assessment

Survey Design

Until last year, most of the assessment of SPLAT has been in the form of personal and electronic feedback, or casual reports. The SPLAT user group is geographically and technologically diverse. Many library staff members have come forward with stories about how SPLAT has changed and impacted their work life, but this is not a very formal analysis. The first step was to design the survey instrument that was sent to any library staff members in the region served (see Figure 16.1 for survey, pp. 242–244). The recruitment plan consisted of crafted messages to be sent via e-mail, Twitter, and Facebook. One e-mail message was sent to those who partook in SPLAT 101, and another e-mail message was sent to the LIBIDAHO e-mail list.

The respondents are primarily library staff members within the region who have taken SPLAT 101 or interacted with SPLAT in some way. The questions were designed around the activities SPLAT has undertaken in lieu of the mission of SPLAT. This should provide information where our gaps are in regards to accomplishing its mission. The authors also hope to learn about the experiences that individuals have had with SPLAT. The survey questions inquired about certain technologies that they have learned to use from SPLAT or that they use on a regular basis. Also critical to the SPLAT assessment is where the most valuable experiences took place. One survey item is a multiple-checkbox question allowing respondents to indicate where they interacted with SPLAT (i.e., conferences, e-mail, SPLAT 101, library visit, etc.). Respondents also were asked to complete open-answer questions to explain more fully the detail of their experience. This analysis should help determine where to focus SPLAT efforts, or where the most impact has been. The survey also asks respondents to specify if they have shared what they have learned from SPLAT to see how viral the impact has been. Overall, the authors hypothesize this survey will also show SPLAT members where to focus efforts and where there is a lack or disconnect between our activities and mission.

Survey Results

SPLAT 101 was the most formalized aspect of SPLAT, and therefore we have analyzed the survey results of the 240 respondents who completed the course (see Figure 16.2). Of the 240 participants, 120 completed all of the modules of SPLAT 101 and took the post survey. More than 80 percent of these 120 respondents reported that they learned something new. Most of the tools shared with the library community are conveyed through posts made to the LIBIDAHO electronic mailing list, the SPLAT blog (http://splat.lili.org/), SPLAT 101, and through SPLAT's casual mentorship at conferences, which takes place, literally, on couches in the hallways of statewide and regional conferences (Vecchione & Cordova, 2011).

For this assessment, the authors wanted to determine which SPLAT efforts were highly rated in order to focus and strengthen the program. In addition, these data will

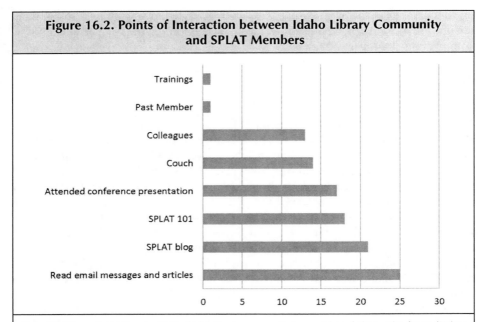

Figure 16.2. Points of Interaction between Idaho Library Community and SPLAT Members

Note: SPLAT members interact with the Idaho library community in a number of places. This figure displays the number of respondents who indicated where they had interacted with SPLAT. This would mean that more individuals interact with SPLAT via the Idaho library electronic mailing list and other publications more so than the SPLAT blog.

be correlated with respondents' comments to determine which activities produce the most positive outcome to the most people. Based on the data analyzed to date, it seems that most people learn about SPLAT ideas through the electronic mailing lists and written articles. These data could shape the methods and activities that SPLAT conducts.

Some of the more significant preliminary findings indicate a large change in libraries as a result of SPLAT. The authors intend to use this survey to learn more about what SPLAT is doing well, and about how SPLAT can improve. It is planned that the same web-based, anonymous survey will be used repeatedly over time to see how SPLAT has improved, and also will be used to inform and improve assessment techniques. Of the questions asked, these three indicators seemed to tell the most interesting story: Based on their interactions with SPLAT initiatives: (1) did policies at your library change, (2) did you learn something you implemented at your library, and (3) have you learned something that you have shared with someone else? Not only did an overwhelming majority of individuals learn something new from SPLAT, but they also integrated those tools into their library. This could possibly be due to the vetting process that SPLAT undergoes with each new innovation that allows library staff members to more easily understand and subsequently implement these new technologies.

Though originally it was expected that the number of individuals whose policies had changed would be quite small, we asked this question and found that a significant portion indicated that within their library a policy had changed (see Figure 16.3). Of

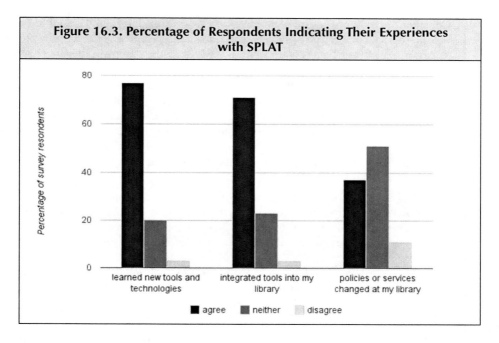

Figure 16.3. Percentage of Respondents Indicating Their Experiences with SPLAT

the 37 respondents, 37 percent agreed that policies had changed at their library as a result of SPLAT, and 51 percent said that they neither agreed nor disagreed. This group, the one that indicated neither, is hypothetically having a lot of discussions that are going to potentially lead to a change. Since a great deal of library policies are about what cannot happen (not using Facebook, not using mobile technology), this means that a change in those policies results in more users experiencing an increase in the relevancy of their libraries. Ultimately when this change takes place and "Rules and outdated policies fall away in favor of breaking down barriers to service and collections" (Stephens, 2011, p. 7), the library users experience greater access to information.

Creating Your Own SPLAT

Any group of individuals who work in libraries can create their own team of innovation representatives, and the concept is quite scalable. Some libraries have created their own teams within their library that are charged to seek out applicable innovation. A library, or group of librarians, can create a team of innovation representatives in any region. This model could be applied countywide, for a branch only, or for a specific region or area. For those who are considering starting their own SPLAT-like team in their region, here are some issues to consider:

- Identify the location or region that makes the most sense, and identify those boundaries. A countywide network could work well in some places just as some libraries have a team that just resides within their branches alone. Creating a statewide group can be feasible with the proper tools, such as web-conferencing software, and other collaborative utilities.

- Consider the individuals you would want on your team. They would need to be willing to experiment and consider many different perspectives. According to Katsirikou and Sefertzi's (2000) analysis, "Innovation requires a diverse rich-information and interactive environment where people with different perspectives work together towards a common objective, with accurate up-to-date information and the proper tools" (p. 706). SPLAT members have found this to be true. When recruiting members, you will want diversity of career, position, and type of library. Meetings should be held in an unfamiliar and interesting location that will inspire the group. This space also needs to have the proper tools, including wireless Internet to support all kinds of devices. All members should be prepared to share their experiences, initiatives, new ideas, and adopted tools.

- Gathering information about the future of libraries is an important key, as local groups will need to explain in certain terms why a tool or innovation is a good idea. Hard facts, data, and a thorough evaluation are recommended. Documents like the Vision 2020 report (Idaho Commission for Libraries, 2006) have helped to garner support from administrators. SPLAT members relied heavily on the book *The Fifth Discipline Fieldbook: Strategies and Tools for Building a Learning Organization* (Senge, 1994) during the nascent stages of SPLAT. To achieve buy-in, library staff members used the activities described in this book to help with the difficult conversations about issues that come up as technology evolves.

- This need to establish buy-in is not an uncommon feature of change. As mentioned earlier, not all library staff members are willing to make the changes to adapt to new user needs and potential changes in library roles: "Any change in a library brings with it both opportunity and outcry—often both, and from both patrons and staff" (Griffey, 2010, p. 21). Those initiating change will need to make careful plans and decisions about which tools to implement, when and with what preparation.

Some examples of these issues include adopting a new practice like SMS reference, or allowing students to access Facebook in the school library because some believe that these are not library tools. SPLAT members continually hold discussions in their local community and at conferences to assist in change and technological adoption. It is important to keep in mind that a new idea can be hindered if it has not been fully fleshed out. Having a group to share and vet ideas with is key for that success. Once the idea has been vetted and the group fully understands the potential uses in libraries, then the group should share this idea in some kind of initiative. Teams like SPLAT apply new initiatives, some of which fail while others succeed, but find that evaluating these initiatives too early can impede their success. Abram (2007) indicates that this is true among many groups of second-stage early adopters: "New initiatives are exciting. Don't let your strategies fail by evaluating them too early" (p. 160), and SPLAT has found this to be true. Trying to push new technology without a purpose or library use can be difficult. As Michael Stephens (2011) points out, "The response to ongoing change should be constant and purposeful—based on thoughtful planning and grounded in the mission of libraries" (p. 3), and therefore any suggestions made to one's own library need to be couched in the mission and strategic plan of that library.

However, the reader should not assume every idea or tool vetted by SPLAT has received wide support, or even realization. As SPLAT members have varied backgrounds and experiences, so do the ideas they bring forth, which might make their implementation dependent on the type of library or population they serve. Add to this the scope, budget, staff buy-in, and technical proficiency of libraries, and it is sometimes difficult to bring an idea to fruition. That is why a steady exploration of innovation and tool utilization is a key component of SPLAT's mission, as some projects will prove more effective in an academic library setting, say, rather than a school one. Indeed, Griffey (2010) states that "technology, more than most aspects in libraries, is a huge moving target" (p. 93). But developing an awareness of the shifts and turns of the social media environment allows SPLAT members to identify opportunities that can benefit libraries accordingly.

When initiating change, the SPLAT members are patient, benevolent, and ultimately casual, rather than being pushy and insistent. Being patient and casual allows late adopters to initiate contact when they feel most comfortable. SPLAT members have found this to be the best way to implement new tools.

Conclusion

Libraries adopt numerous ideas and technologies, but the methodology for the means of adoption is not well understood. In this article we discuss two primary models: an administration-led model, and a grassroots approach. Our experiences as SPLAT members and our research indicate that the grassroots SPLAT model can be easily implemented and constructed, and has great potential to benefit library staff, services, and the larger community. The concept of futuring is a necessary ingredient for library staff to effectively meet the needs of current users, and to determine new ways to reach out to new users. A team of innovation representatives can be created in any region by starting on the grassroots level. Members of the team can develop ideas and vet tools in a non-systematic way by proposing ways to adopt the innovations, and support these with experiences and data. As innovative representatives, team members are leaders who share their expertise in a collaborative, benevolent manner intended to improve reference services in libraries.

References

Abram, S. (2007). *Out front with Stephen Abram: A guide for information leaders*. Chicago, IL: American Library Association.

Anonymous. (2008, May 6). SPLAT 101: Blogs. [Web log comment]. Retrieved June 29, 2011, from http://splat.lili.org/splat101/blogs.

Association of Research Libraries, & Stratus, Inc. (2010). *The ARL 2030 scenarios: A user's guide for research libraries*. Washington, DC: Association of Research Libraries.

Dewey, J. (2008, May 6). SPLAT 101: Blogs. [Web log comment]. Retrieved June 29, 2011, from http://splat.lili.org/splat101/blogs.

Griffey, J. (2010). *Mobile technology and libraries*. New York: Neal-Schuman.

Idaho Commission for Libraries. (2006). *A vision for libraries in 2020*. Retrieved June 17, 2011, from http://libraries.idaho.gov/files/2020vision-document.pdf.

Johnson, L., Smith, R., Willis, H., Levine, A., & Haywood, K. (2011). *The 2011 horizon report*. Austin, TX: The New Media Consortium.

Katsirikou, A., & Sefertzi, E. (2000). Innovation in the everyday life of libraries. *Technovation, 20,* 705–709.

Persichini, G. (2010, January). *Libraries linking Idaho. Steering committee meeting.* Retrieved June 17, 2011, from http://libraries.idaho.gov/files/20100107MinGper.pdf.

Rubleske, J., Kaarst-Brown, M., & Strobel, T. (2010, October 22–27). How do public library administrators generate and evaluate ideas for new services? A proposed model based on evidence from Cuyahoga County Public Library. *ASIST 2010.* Retrieved June 17, 2011, from http://www.asis.org/asist2010/proceedings/proceedings/ASIST_AM10/submissions/35_Final_Submission.pdf.

Schrecker, D. (2010, May 6). Listening to students. [Web blog post]. Retrieved June 17, 2011, from http://librarycloud.blogspot.com/2010/02/wired-campus-chronicle-of-higher.html.

Senge, P. M. (1994). *The fifth discipline fieldbook: Strategies and tools for building a learning organization.* New York: Currency, Doubleday.

Staley, D. J., & Malenfant, K. J. (2010). Futures thinking for academic librarians: Higher education in 2025. *Information Services and Use, 30,* 57–90.

Stephens, M. (2011, February). *The hyperlinked library.* Retrieved June 17, 2011, from http://tametheweb.com/2011/02/21/hyperlinkedlibrary2011/.

Vecchione, A., & Cordova, M. (2011). [Assessment of the Special Projects Library Action Team]. Unpublished raw data.

Assessing Reference and Tracking User Behavior

Using Libstats Statistical Tracking Software to Assess Library Services for Strategic Planning

Emily K. Chan and Lorrie A. Knight

Overview

In today's numbers-driven environment, organizations need to quantify performance and impact for planning and administrative purposes. Strategic planning connects current positions to future directions. Data collection and analysis is one vital piece that informs the process. The University of the Pacific Library is successfully using an open-source management system to track all library employee-mediated interactions. This software has been especially illuminating for the librarians who offer reference services. The following information is collected from every reference interaction: duration of exchange, method of asking, time/date stamping, patron type, question type, and the question and answer provided. The amassed data help to measure use patterns to inform the delivery of reference services.

Implementation of a reference statistics system provides opportunities for strategic and individualized training and development, adjusting staffing levels to meet user needs and patterns, and measuring the effect of librarians' instructional sessions on reference traffic. Moreover, since all Library service points are incorporated into this management system, peer-to-peer information sharing can be facilitated, aggregated, and managed.

Collected data can be analyzed and tailored to different audiences. Data points are both quantitative and qualitative. Quantitative data can be organized and manipulated through spreadsheet applications to generate reports. Qualitative data can be aggregated to demonstrate the range and diversity of the questions fielded by the librarians or searched as an information archive. Data can be mined to demonstrate the Library's effectiveness and contributions to the university's educational mission. Reference-tracking software is a powerful tool to manage service points, provide data to administrators, and support strategic service evaluation and planning.

Introduction

In today's numbers-driven environment, organizations need to quantify performance and impact for planning and administrative purposes. Strategic planning can be defined as "deciding and refining organizational objectives and working consistently and persistently to translate those objectives into actions and outcomes. It requires insight and foresight to interpret past events and present trends to determine future directions" (Corrall, 2009, p. 5047). At University of the Pacific, planning is an important and ongoing activity. Data collection and analysis is one vital piece that informs the process.

University of the Pacific Library is successfully using an open-source, web-based management system to track library employee-mediated interactions. The use of the software has greatly expanded the library's abilities to assess services by providing detailed quantitative and qualitative data in a highly customizable format. This opportunity prompted the authors to explore the potential strategic implications for use of the information. They wanted to know if the statistics could provide "insight" by documenting connections among various library programs, best practices in staffing and training, collection development needs, and the overall relevance of the library to the mission of the university. Similarly, the statistics could offer "foresight" by suggesting future directions for the library.

University of the Pacific, located in Stockton, California, is a private institution of approximately 4,800 students. The university offers a wide array of programs, including undergraduate- and graduate-level courses in liberal arts, business, education, international studies, and health sciences. There are two library facilities, the Main Library and the Health Sciences Branch. The libraries are serviced by seven professional librarians who have faculty rank.

The Pacific library followed the typical pattern of statistic-keeping common to most academic libraries. Libraries have long histories of collecting data, including circulation counts, gate counts, books shelved, interlibrary loan, reference encounters, and instruction sessions. Traditionally, the recorded data have been used for reports to national and state organizations, on-campus administrative entities, external stakeholders, such as donors or friends' groups, and internal operational reviews. This use of data can be seen as a form of summative assessment, as the information is tabulated and recorded, but given little weight in planning or analysis. Kendon Stubbs (1986) observed that library statistics "can at least be used as the drunkard uses the lamp post—for support if not illumination" (p. 19). One possible explanation for this gap is that the traditional statistics were simply numeric and did not offer useful qualitative insights.

In recent years, the librarians at Pacific adopted new methods for statistic tracking. Instruction statistics, formerly collected on a paper form and tabulated by student assistants, moved to an online spreadsheet, accessible via a common folder. The spreadsheet greatly expedited recording, tabulating, and reporting on efforts and gains made in the area of instruction. Reference statistics were recorded via a paper form, which was kept on a clipboard at the reference desk. In 2007, the iconic reference statistics hash marks on paper were abandoned in favor of an open-source system called Libstats, available at http://code.google.com/p/libstats/. The web-based form greatly expanded the amount and categories of data collected about patron interactions. No longer just a tool for recording, as in the past, the new form allowed the numerical data to be supplemented with qualitative information, sorted in numerous ways, and adapted for alignment with the library's goals.

Literature Review

A brief review of the literature guided the analysis of the emerging trends in the collection and use of library statistics. Although several articles (Carlson, 2001; Martell, 2005) report the decline in the numbers of basic transactions, many others argue that simple counting systems do not adequately reflect the changing reference landscape (Gerlich & Berard, 2010). While the prevalence of online databases with full content may have made patrons' physical visits to the library less frequent, those who do come to the library may need more in-depth assistance and require more time with the librarians. Librarians are also providing reference services in a wider variety of methods, such as instant messaging (IM), which may not be indicated in the current recording structures. The persistent problem of ambiguity and inconsistency in how the statistics are recorded and reported may also contribute to these issues (Applegate, 2008). Smith (2006) provides a thorough discussion of the traditional purposes for tracking reference statistics and many of the inherent problems and limitations. He also points out that many librarians perceive the need for statistics to be externally driven and not especially relevant to their work.

Concerned that the traditional methods of reference tracking present a false picture of the relevance of the service, librarians are seeking new systems to record data that incorporate descriptive and qualitative information. Hoivik (2006) emphasizes that the majority of library statistics consist of counting tangible objects and encounters. Through the act of counting the number of study rooms, carrels, books, and materials, libraries imply that the compilation of resources is important. Likewise, libraries approach their services along the same vein and count the number of users who use the facility. Reporting to national organizations or agencies has driven the statistics that are collected. One of the most important organizations, the Association of Research Libraries (ARL), requests the following information from their member libraries: counts of collection additions and deletions in all formats, personnel expenditures, and number of contacts between library employees and the public (ARL, 2010). The simple counting of books, users, and interactions has provided a means for libraries to compare their work with other libraries, but has done little to shed light on how to alter library services to meet users' needs. Poll (2003) refers to these types of statistics as input and output data. Input data includes the annual expenditures toward employee wages, increases to the collection, square footage of the physical building, and how that space may be utilized (through multi-use or study spaces). Output data is driven by the movement of library materials from off the shelves within and out of the library building. Other important data points include interlibrary loan requests fulfilled, number of students and classes attending library use instruction sessions, and number of reference transactions.

Libraries are more than their collections, however. The currently reported input and output data do little to signify the value that a library adds to the academic enterprise nor do they capture the impact of the services and resources of the library. In a rapidly changing, increasingly online environment, libraries no longer have a monopoly on physical or electronic resources. A recent Online Computer Library Center (OCLC) report (2010) notes that 83 percent of college students initiated their research by using a search engine. Furthermore, 50 percent of them rated information obtained through the search engines to be just as trustworthy as information obtained through the library. To adjust to this new landscape, libraries need to focus upon and obtain better quantitative and qualitative data that demonstrate the worth of libraries and librarians and their collective expertise and experience in providing reference services.

A more thorough collection process is reported by Dennison (1999), who describes a library that also records levels of difficulty, in addition to simple numbers. He applied a statistical test to determine the highs and lows of reference desk activity. This approach to data analysis illustrates ways in which robust tracking can provide both operational and evaluative information. Smith (2006) describes the development of an in-house online tool to enhance reference tracking.

Following a thorough review of current practice, a web-based form was created, tested, and deployed at Pacific. The new system has been successful in addressing staffing issues, providing rudimentary quality assessment, and even illuminating the value of the data collection process as a whole. An Australian library was an early adopter of Libstats, the open-source tool selected at Pacific, as reported by Jordan (2008), who offers recommendations for implementation and reports that the use of the system has been very successful.

Changing trends in reference service have also prompted the development of new processes for data gathering. At Indiana University-Purdue, librarians found their manual tracking of statistics to be labor-intensive and of limited administrative use (Garrison, 2010). The true work of the librarians was trivialized by the brief reports. This finding provided the impetus to create an online form that could be used at every point of contact. By allowing librarians to fully document the complexity of their user interactions, the importance of having subject specialists providing in-depth research consultations could be substantiated (Garrison, 2010). In a similar vein, Feldman (2009) describes the development of a specialized form in response to a change to a reference referral system. By providing many options for data entry, the new form highlights the in-depth level of research assistance offered by the librarians, suggests opportunities for library instruction, and addresses the distinctions in levels of reference service.

Pacific's Former Methods for Collecting Statistics

The Main Library has four service points: Circulation, the Information Commons (IC) Student Help Desk, the Media Studio Help Desk, and the Reference Desk. The Health Sciences Branch (HSB) has one central service point. All of the service points at the Main Library serve unique purposes. For example: items that circulate can only be checked out at the Circulation Desk, advanced technological assistance is offered by IC student assistants, complex audiovisual assistance is provided by student workers in the Media Studio, and information assistance from librarians is only available at the Reference Desk.

Prior to 2007, when Libstats was first adopted, Pacific's Circulation Department collected the following statistics: gate counts, counts of library users at certain times of the day in specific parts of the library, circulation and use of materials within and checked out of the library, and the number of instances in which individuals made requests to use study rooms after they were all reserved. Data on individual transactions with users were not collected.

Beginning in 2006, student assistants at the Information Commons (IC) Student Help Desk documented their interactions across three categories: log-in/wireless, media, and software. Interactions were logged in an Excel spreadsheet on a shared drive, which indicated the date and time period for each interaction. Results were compiled and reported to the administration on a yearly basis at the conclusion of the fiscal year. Recently, similar data have begun to be collected by staff at the Media Studio service point to address the need for advanced audiovisual assistance.

Pacific, like many academic institutions across the United States, dedicates a significant amount of employee time, training, and resources toward the provision of traditional and virtual reference services. Prior to adoption of Libstats in 2007, this investment of librarian hours was tabulated using paper tally forms, where the librarian would apply a hash mark for each contact made during a given time frame (see Table 17.1). In this form, transactions were tracked for every hour and assigned to one of three categories: Reference Questions, Computer Support, and Directional Information. One could only indicate the number of transactions per category per time period. Aspects, such as the complexity of the question, how the question was being posed (e.g., walk-up, IM, e-mail, or phone), and the duration of interaction, could not be captured using these traditional

Table 17.1. Pacific's Historical "Hash Mark" Form Used Prior to 2007				
Month:		**Week:**		**Year:**
Day of the Week:		**Reference Questions**	**Computer Support**	**Directional Information**
	900–1000			
	1000–1100			
	1100–1200			
	1200–100			
	100–200			
	200–300			
	300–400			
	400–500			
	500–600			
	600–700			
	700–800			
	800–900			

methods for collecting data. At the end of an academic session or year, a student would compile the number of hash marks on the paper sheets by adding the number of hash marks there were for every hour in each column. This primitive and unreliable data collection method was the extent of reporting for this important service. The lack of detail for a reference transaction resulted in uni-dimensional reporting.

Furthermore, the onerous task of translating the physical forms to usable statistics ensured that statistics and the insight on user behavior trends could only be viewed in a historical context. Librarians were unable to critically examine how well reference services were being utilized in a timely fashion with the intent to optimize staffing levels and leverage librarian energies most appropriately.

A Modern Solution: Using a Web-Based, Online System

Using a web-based, online system for the collection of employee-mediated interactions was proposed to automate the tabulation process. A number of benefits that could be realized:

- Centralized, online collection of employee-mediated interactions
- Standardized data points
- Customizable fields to account for unique service locations
- Searchable archive of questions and answers
- On-the-fly reporting function
- Statistics that demonstrate the value of librarians and library employees

Libstats (http://code.google.com/p/libstats/) is an open-source software program that allows libraries to collect information from employee-mediated interactions. This free program requires PHP, which "is a widely-used general-purpose scripting language that is especially suited for Web development and can be embedded into HTML" (http://www.php.net/), and PHP-Extension and Application Repository (PEAR)::DB (http://code.google.com/p/libstats/). Libstats not only allows a library to customize and collect data on all employee-mediated interactions, it also provides the ability to create reports on the fly. Basic data collection fields include location, patron type, question type, time spent, and question format. Data that are also collected includes initials (of the respondent), date with backdate function, question, and answer. The latter two fields—question and answer—allow for extensive writing about an interaction.

Pacific's reference team incorporated this system in spring 2007 to automate the collection of reference statistics (see Figure 17.1). Libstats provides both quantitative and qualitative information. Quantitative information can be obtained from the following general fixed fields: location, patron type, question type, time spent, and question format. It is important to note that all of the responses may be customized to accommodate a library's needs and answer specific strategic planning questions.

Libstats has numerous fields in which data can be entered, including those discussed in the following sections.

Location Field

This field denotes where the question was handled by the library employee. The selections can be customized to include all of the library's service points. Pacific had six selections,

Figure 17.1. Pacific's Libstats Page

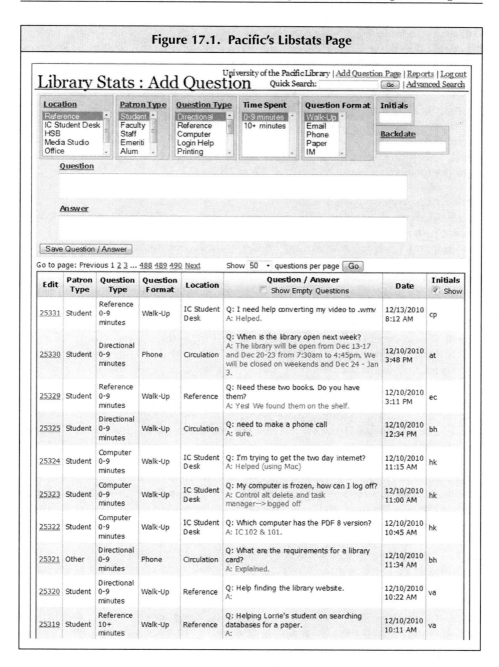

incorporating its four service points in the Main Library, the central service point in the Health Sciences Branch (HSB), and adding a field for questions that take place in librarians' offices.

Patron Type Field
This field offers the ability to designate the user's demographic group, allowing attention to be paid to the constituencies the library serves. Pacific chose Student, Faculty, Staff, Emeriti, Alum, and Other as its selections.

Question Type Field
The types of questions posed by the user are captured in this field, which offers insight on what question types are being tackled by each service point. Pacific chose Directional, Reference, Computer, Log-in Help, Printing, and Wireless to delineate the level of expertise required to assist the user.

Time Spent Field
This field allows one to designate the length of the interaction to assist in informing staffing patterns. At the beginning, Pacific chose 0–9 minutes and 10+ minutes for its fixed response fields to streamline the process of data reporting.

Question Format Field
This field specifies how the individual contacted the service point. As librarians devote more time and energy to creating alternative methods for contacting the reference desk, it will be important to assess the use and value of such services. Pacific selected Walk-up, E-mail, Phone, Paper (i.e., U.S. Postal Service), and IM as the responses for this field.

Qualitative information is available through the Question and Answer fields. Library employees may input the specific question that the user posed, as well as enter the response that was given. In essence, recording transactions facilitates the building of a knowledge bank, a record of the value of the service in context. An embedded search box and advanced search feature in the program allow one to find and filter transactions based on keywords (see Figure 17.2). Thus, one can search the archive to obtain answers that may be of use for one's current interaction.

Taking into account all of the data points available through Libstats, library employees and reference librarians can now document the context for all user interactions. Instead of recording a reference transaction through a simple hash mark on a piece of paper, a librarian may access the secure submission form and select the corresponding fields to contextualize each transaction. Furthermore, every question can be saved, creating a massive database of the work and expertise leveraged at the Reference Desk.

It should be noted that the Libstats program retains the selections for the previous transaction, thus expediting the recording process, should many of the same types of questions be fielded successively. Furthermore, every question logged into the system is automatically time- and date-stamped. Backdating or altering the date and time to record transactions after the fact is simple and available through an editing feature available on all transactions.

Libstats provides on-the-fly reporting and a data-dump feature for more complex transactional queries. The built-in Reports feature offers the following options: Data Dump, Questions by Date, Questions by Patron Type, Questions by Question Format, Questions by Time of Day, and Questions by Weekday (see Figure 17.3).

Figure 17.2. Using the Search Feature in Libstats*

Library Stats : Search Results

University of the Pacific Library | Add Question Page | Reports | Log out
Quick Search: [Go] | Advanced Search

Go to page: Previous 1 Next   Show 50 ▾ questions per page [Go]

Edit	Patron Type	Question Type	Question Format	Location	READ Scale	Question / Answer Show Empty Questions	Date	Initials ☑ Show
23458	Faculty	Reference 0-9 minutes	Email	University Library Reference		Q: Crissy, I have discovered a book titled "Hydrology and Water Resources of **Africa**" by Mamdouh Shahin, published in 2003 by Kluwer Academic. I believe it is held in the library; could you check to see if this is true? If so, I can come by to check it out. A: This was an email mistakenly sent to a librarian at the law school. She forwarded it to me and I sent an email back to the professor telling him we have this book electronically and showing him how he can retrieve it.	10/14/2010 9:18 AM	va
19602	Student	Reference 10+ minutes	Walk-Up	University Library Reference		Q: Help with social and educational reforms in post-apartheid South **Africa**... A: Helped.	4/15/2010 7:29 PM	ec
16201	Student	Reference 0-9 minutes	Walk-Up	University Library Reference		Q: Number of immigrants from **Africa** to the United States. A: U.S. Statistical Abstract	11/19/2009 10:56 AM	ch
16200	Student	Reference 10+ minutes	Walk-Up	University Library Reference		Q: Scholarly articles on waste management in **Africa**--non-technical. A: Academic Search Complete	11/19/2009 10:56 AM	ch
12098	Student	Reference 10+ minutes	Walk-Up	University Library Reference		Q: I'm looking for information on clinical trials done in South **Africa** prior to the 1990's. Can you help? A: We searched all flavors of EBSCO, PubMed, Google, IPA, and a couple others, all to find a handful of articles that touch on the history of clinical trials in **Africa**.	5/04/2009 2:36 PM	r3p
11386	Student	Reference 10+ minutes	Walk-Up	University Library Office		Q: Need to know about the historical aspects of reproductive health clinical trials in South **Africa**. A: Helped her. CINAHL, ScienceDirect, Wiley, SCOPUS, PubMed/MEDLINE. Went over RefWorks and how to use them in concert for researching.	4/08/2009 1:55 PM	ec
11094	Student	Reference 10+ minutes	Walk-Up	University Library Reference		Q: student needs books/articles about smallpox in 19thc **Africa** A: JSTOR, HNYT	3/26/2009 1:13 PM	lk
1483	Other	Reference 10+ minutes	Walk-Up	University Library Reference		Q: How can I find articles on Morocco's recent election on the 8th of September? A: Searched open web with patron. Not so much (surprisingly) on the BBC news webpage, but struck gold with the Guardian U.K. – had relevant	9/16/2007 2:30 PM	MM

*Searching for the term Africa

Report types include the following:

1. Data Dump

    The Data Dump report allows one to download all of the collected data during a user-specified date range (see Table 17.2). One can limit based on library (if

Figure 17.3. Available On-the-Fly Reports through Libstats

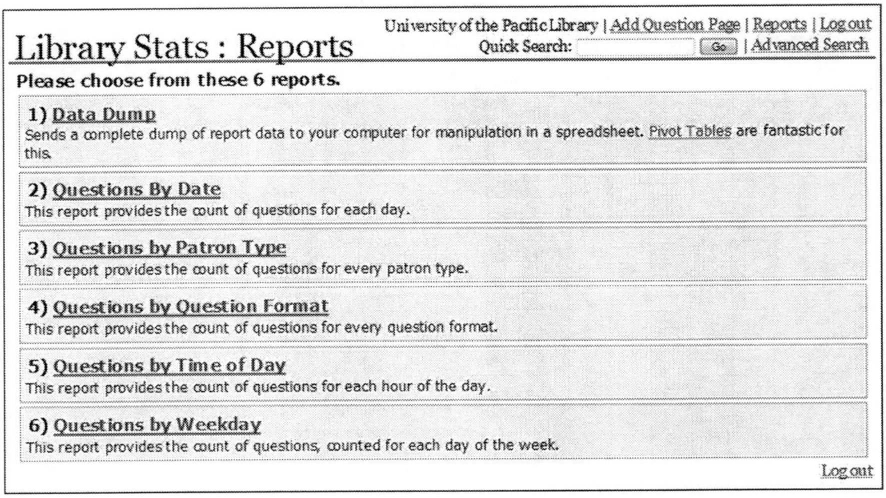

Library Stats : Reports

University of the Pacific Library | Add Question Page | Reports | Log out
Quick Search: [____] [Go] | Advanced Search

Please choose from these 6 reports.

1) Data Dump
Sends a complete dump of report data to your computer for manipulation in a spreadsheet. Pivot Tables are fantastic for this.

2) Questions By Date
This report provides the count of questions for each day.

3) Questions by Patron Type
This report provides the count of questions for every patron type.

4) Questions by Question Format
This report provides the count of questions for every question format.

5) Questions by Time of Day
This report provides the count of questions for each hour of the day.

6) Questions by Weekday
This report provides the count of questions, counted for each day of the week.

Log out

multiple library collections have been created) and location. The information is downloaded as a comma separated value (.csv) file. Thus, it is not advisable to utilize commas in the Question and Answer fields, as this will parse out portions of the text (Breitbach, 2009). Transforming the data into a manageable form will take more time and greater effort.

Once the data are exported into a spreadsheet software program, the data can be manipulated in a variety of ways. Sorting, filtering, and charting functions can be utilized to create information sets based on criteria that are unavailable through the built-in reporting options, such as Time Spent and Question Type.

2. Questions by Date
The Questions by Date report (see Figure 17.4) plots out the number of transactions per day for a given time period. Days of the week are identified, as well.

3. Questions by Patron Type
The Questions by Patron Type report enumerates the types and percentages of populations that are being served at library service points for a specified date range. In Figure 17.5, total questions received at the Reference Desk and the relative percentages of the groups that visited the Reference Desk are identified.

4. Questions by Question Format
The Questions by Question Format report offers a way to track how library users are making contact with library employees. At the Reference Desk, especially given the emphasis and dedication of resources to the addition of new services, such as instant messaging, it is important to track their utilization by library

Table 17.2. Example of Data-Dump Feature with Minimal Formatting

ID	Question	Answer	Patron Type	Question Type	Time Spent	Format	Half-Hour	Date	Day	Initials
25019	Student needs help with a sociology paper	Found some articles and theories.	Student	Reference	10+ min	Walk-up	9:30 AM	12/1/2010	Wed	lk
25021	Need info and images about American Sign Language	We have some!	Student	Reference	10+ min	Walk-up	10:30 AM	12/1/2010	Wed	lk
25022	Do you have a heavy duty stapler?	At Circ	Student	Directional	0–9 min	Walk-up	10:30 AM	12/1/2010	Wed	lk
25028	Need help with powerpoint. Is there anyone there who can assist me?	If you come to our multimedia studio, one of our student assistants should be able to work with you.	Student	Directional	0–9 min	Phone	12:30 PM	12/1/2010	Wed	Va
25033	FACEWORK AS USED BY SOCIOLOGISTS	Did not want to go online; insisted on print, so checked opac and we had four print titles— three of them in HM!!!	Student	Reference	0–9 min	Walk-up	2:00 PM	12/1/2010	Wed	Ch
25035	SPSS on laptops?	Yes.	Student	Reference	0–9 min	IM	2:30 PM	12/1/2010	Wed	Ch

Note: Two data fields—Added Stamp and Question Time—have been removed from this example in the interest of clarity and brevity. These data points duplicate the information provided by the Question Half-Hour and Date fields.

Figure 17.4. Questions by Date Report

Library Stats : Finished Report

University of the Pacific Library | Add Question Page | Reports | Log out
Quick Search: [   ] [Go] | Advanced Search

University Library | Reference
Questions By Date from 20101201 through 20110101

Date	Weekday	Question Count	Percentage
12-10-2010	Friday	7	5.8%
12-09-2010	Thursday	6	5%
12-08-2010	Wednesday	6	5%
12-07-2010	Tuesday	8	6.6%
12-06-2010	Monday	13	10.7%
12-05-2010	Sunday	8	6.6%
12-03-2010	Friday	31	25.6%
12-02-2010	Thursday	13	10.7%
12-01-2010	Wednesday	29	24%
Totals	**9**	**121**	**100%**

Import Data to Excel

Log out

Figure 17.5. Questions by Patron Type Report

Library Stats : Finished Report

University of the Pacific Library | Add Question Page | Reports | Log out
Quick Search: [   ] [Go] | Advanced Search

University Library > location: Reference
Questions by Patron Type from 20101201 through 20110101 - Full Report

Patron Type	Question Count	Percentage
Alum	2	1.7%
Emeriti	2	1.7%
Faculty	1	0.8%
Other	10	8.3%
Student	106	87.6%
Totals	**121**	**100.1%**

Import Data to Excel

Log out

patrons. Use may be tracked on a weekly, monthly, annual, and multiyear basis. In Figure 17.6, the methods by which Pacific Library users contacted the Reference Desk during December 2010 are provided.

5. Questions by Time of Day
   The Questions by Time of Day report offers an hour by hour view of transactions at a particular location for a specified date range. This report can indicate which hours have the highest and lowest volume of traffic. Maximizing the open hours of the Reference Desk (i.e., extending and contracting reference hours) could be entertained only after obtaining this type of data. Figure 17.7 shows the allocation

Figure 17.6. Questions by Question Format Report

Library Stats : Finished Report
University of the Pacific Library | Add Question Page | Reports | Log out
Quick Search: [Go] | Advanced Search

University Library | Reference
Questions by Question Format from 20101201 through 20110101

Question Format	Question Count	Percentage
IM	28	23.1%
Phone	14	11.6%
Walk-Up	79	65.3%
Totals	121	100%

Import Data to Excel

Log out

Figure 17.7. Questions by Time of Day Report

Library Stats : Finished Report
University of the Pacific Library | Add Question Page | Reports | Log out
Quick Search: [Go] | Advanced Search

University Library | Reference
Questions by Time of Day from 20101201 through 20110101

Hour Begin TO End	Question Count	Percentage
08-PM TO 9	3	2.5%
07-PM TO 8	9	7.4%
06-PM TO 7	2	1.7%
05-PM TO 6	10	8.3%
04-PM TO 5	11	9.1%
03-PM TO 4	19	15.7%
02-PM TO 3	8	6.6%
01-PM TO 2	12	9.9%
12-PM TO 1	14	11.6%
11-AM TO 12	13	10.7%
10-AM TO 11	10	8.3%
09-AM TO 10	10	8.3%
Totals	121	100.1%

Import Data to Excel

Log out

of questions by hour received at the Reference Desk in December 2010. More than 20 percent of the questions were received from 2:00 to 4:00 p.m.

6. Questions by Weekday

The Questions by Weekday report indicates the number of questions received at a location for a specified date range, broken down by the day of the week. This report may be helpful in identifying the days of the week with highest and lowest volume to adjust staffing levels accordingly. Pacific Library eliminated Saturday reference hours after obtaining sufficient historical and convincing data that

Figure 17.8. Questions by Weekday Report

University of the Pacific Library | Add Question Page | Reports | Log out

Library Stats : Finished Report
Quick Search: _____ [Go] | Advanced Search

University Library | Reference
Questions by Weekday from 20101201 through 20110101

Weekday	Question Count	Percentage
Sunday	8	6.6%
Monday	13	10.7%
Tuesday	8	6.6%
Wednesday	35	28.9%
Thursday	19	15.7%
Friday	38	31.4%
Totals	**121**	**99.9%**

Import Data to Excel

Log out

there was little need for this specialized service on Saturdays. Figure 17.8 (above) indicates that Wednesdays and Fridays were the busiest weekdays in December 2010.

Value of Qualitative and Quantitative Data Retrieved from Libstats

The reporting features of Libstats may be utilized in a myriad of ways. On-the-fly reporting allows one to quickly determine historical trends and obtain information that can inform staffing concerns. Built-in reports and reports created from the data dump provide quantitative data and contextualize interactions in a much more comprehensive and meaningful way.

Individuals may utilize the quantitative data to identify high- and low-volume times and days for individual service points. Certainly, staffing and service offerings may adjust to optimize both time and skill set needed. Knowing who uses the library is important, as programming and outreach efforts can attend to those who are not using the library. Understanding how user populations are contacting the Reference Desk is critical; methods of communication are changing. For example, in the 2007 fiscal year IM service was added to Pacific's traditional methods of contact. To assess its value and contribution to the reference statistics, one can map out the increasing gains on an annual basis.

The data-dump feature allows for multilayer reporting. For example, one can identify the percentage of students who posed reference questions via the IM format. Furthermore, one can identify how many of those reference questions were between 0 and 9 minutes and how many were 10 or more minutes. This segmentation allows one to truly identify how demographic groups are utilizing library services.

The qualitative data available via Libstats has been evaluated and found to be highly beneficial, as well. Libstats offers inherent training and development opportunities. Individuals who are new to the job or to a service point may be instructed to review past transactions to learn of the various situations that are encountered at that location. In essence, one can become familiarized with all of the transactions at a particular location. Questions and answers are provided, creating a knowledge repository of reference transactions, policies, and procedures. Furthermore, as an ongoing assessment tool, the answers may be monitored, with the goals of instruction, quality control, and professional growth. Library staff who provide an incorrect answer or response may be informed of a better solution. This repository can promote knowledge sharing and gains in expertise.

Libstats helps to create an accessible and flexible knowledge bank of experiences. The ability to cite the diversity of questions answered helps to promote the expertise and skill set of the librarians. Further mining of the qualitative data can indicate systemic issues—for example, repeated questions on a specific topic may indicate a lack of signage, collection development gaps, or the opportunity to extend instruction via the library's website or other modes.

It is important to note that Libstats is limited by the human element. Library employees may forget to input statistics, especially during busy times when they have answered a number of queries in a consecutive fashion. Fortunately, Libstats has a back-date function that allows for data entry during less busy times. Furthermore, individual interpretations on the classification of questions (e.g., is this question directional or reference?) will always be debated.

Libstats is not a panacea for the collection of all necessary library statistics. Any library will continue to count the use and circulation of its physical and electronic materials, as well as use of its physical spaces. Libstats, however, can contextualize and more thoroughly detail human service interactions and can qualitatively indicate the complexity of reference work. In this climate of assessment and accountability, quantitative report functions can strengthen a case to amend staffing and service hours or to justify additional hires. The usefulness of Libstats' applications as archive and knowledge bank for training, development, and assessment ensure its worthy place in the library repertoire.

Librarians who hope to use this product to collect data about reference interactions should expect to have several conversations about the level of detail and the types of information that should be captured for each transaction. While technical personnel can easily install and maintain the product, the librarians are responsible for the more difficult process of identifying the information collected and the degree of granularity. Maintenance is minimal once the installation and customization decisions have been made.

Future Directions

During the past three years of Libstats' implementation and use, the Pacific Library has not established a quantitative scale to indicate the level of expertise needed to answer the question, like the Warner Model (Warner, 2001). Previously, the Time Spent category was used as a method by which to segregate minor from major transactions. This data element was the only quantitative element that could begin to connote complexity.

Recently, Libstats added a new data field to their offerings. This field allows for the addition of the Reference Effort Assessment Data (READ) Scale to the normal collection of data points. Pacific Library included that new field for the spring 2011 semester with the hope of better elucidating the value and impact that librarians have on the academic mission of the university. In spring 2011, Pacific Library began to utilize the READ

Scale. The READ Scale attempts to assist in the determination of the "skills, knowledge, techniques and tools utilized by the librarian during a reference transaction" (Gerlich & Berard, 2007, p. 7) using a 6-point scale. Items on the scale correlate to how much time is spent on the transaction, the multitude of resources consulted, and the types of activities completed in order to fulfill the request. The goal of adopting the READ Scale is to better identify the skills needed to successfully answer reference questions for staffing and training purposes. While this creates some inconsistencies with past and current data, the enrichment of information captured is a worthwhile trade-off. Analysis of the data is in its preliminary stages.

Another future direction is to fully document instructional impact both in the classroom and at the reference desk. Libstats may provide documentation as to the synergy between reference and instruction. One student learning outcome of Pacific Library instruction sessions is to recognize the various ways to seek help from reference librarians. Librarians at Pacific intend to use Libstats reports to assess the achievement of this outcome. Libstats can also identify instructional opportunities. At the Reference Desk, librarians often encounter assignments that suggest an instructional session would be of value to students. By indicating these interactions in the online form, the subject liaison can follow up accordingly. The use of Libstats can support the Library's goal of continuously improving information competency in students through excellent service.

Conclusion

Following its implementation in 2007, the librarians at University of the Pacific have found using Libstats to be meaningful. It is expected that further refinement will enhance its usefulness. While this example centered on an academic library application, the benefits of this open-source system can be realized by any type of library. The customizable fields in the form can be adapted to any organization intent on learning more about the work that is done on a daily basis. The changing information environment has also challenged the traditional "reference desk" and prompted the exploration of new service models. As mobile devices play an increasing role in reference service, Libstats can be modified to capture that data.

Tracking and using statistics effectively can inform strategic decision making, guide the development of new programs, and assess the overall success of the library in serving its educational mission. Strategic planning involves an analysis of past and current positions with an eye toward future directions. Libstats can document patron services and highlight areas for transformation. Strategic planning requires "cultivat[ing] multiple information streams so that the plan reflects accurate, relevant, and up-to-date information" (Wayne, 2011, p. 13). Coupled with other organizational documentation, information from Libstats can serve as one vital stream of input in the strategic planning process, while offering evidence of librarians' critical role in the academic enterprise.

References

Applegate, R. (2008). Whose decline? Which academic libraries are "deserted" in terms of reference transactions? *Reference & User Services Quarterly*, 48(2), 176–189.

Association of Research Libraries. (2010, September 28). *ARL statistics worksheet*. Retrieved June 9, 2011, from http://www.arl.org/bm~doc/10arlstatistics.pdf.

Breitbach, W. (2009). Libstats. *The Charleston Advisor, 11*(1), 44–45.

Carlson, S. (2001, November 16). The deserted library: As students work online, reading rooms empty—leading some campuses to add Starbucks. *Chronicle of Higher Education,* A35–38.

Corrall, S. (2009). Strategic planning in academic libraries. In M. J. Bates & M. N. Maack (Eds.), *Encyclopedia of library and information sciences* (3rd ed.) (pp. 5047–5058). New York: Taylor & Francis. doi:10.1081/E-ELIS3-120008654.

Dennison, R. F. (1999). Usage-based staffing of the reference desk: A statistical approach. *Reference & Users Quarterly, 39*(2), 158–165.

Feldman, L. M. (2009). Information desk referrals: Implementing an office statistics database. *College and Research Libraries, 70*(2), 133–140.

Garrison, J. S. (2010). Making reference service count: Collecting and using reference service statistics to make a difference. *The Reference Librarian, 51*(3), 202–211.

Gerlich, B. K., & Berard, G. L. (2007). Introducing the READ Scale: Qualitative statistics for academic reference services. *Georgia Library Quarterly, 43*(4), 7–13.

Gerlich, B. K., & Berard, G. L. (2010). Testing the viability of the READ Scale (Reference Effort Assessment Data): Qualitative statistics for academic reference services. *College & Research Libraries, 71*(2), 116–137.

Hoivik, T. (2006). Comparing libraries: From official statistics to effective strategies. In T. K. Flaten (Ed.), *Management, marketing and promotion of library services based on statistics, analyses and evaluation* (pp. 43–64). München, Germany: Saur.

Jordan, E. (2008). An open source online tool for collecting and reporting on statistics in an academic library. *Performance Measurement and Metrics, 9*(1), 18–25.

Martell, C. (2005). The ubiquitous user: A reexamination of Carlson's deserted library. *portal: Libraries and the Academy, 5*(4), 441–453.

OCLC. (2010). *Perceptions of libraries 2010: Context and community.* Retrieved June 17, 2011, from http://www.oclc.org/reports/2010perceptions/2010perceptions_all.pdf.

Poll, R. (2003). Measuring impact and outcome of libraries. *Performance Measurement and Metrics, 4*(1), 5–12.

Smith, M. M. (2006). A tool for all places: A web-based reference statistics system. *Reference Services Review, 34*(2), 298–315.

Stubbs, K. L. (1986). "On the ARL library index." In *Access and Services: Shaping the Future.* Minutes of the Meeting of the Association of Research Libraries (106th, Cincinnati, Ohio, May 16–17, 1985) (pp. 18–20). Washington, DC: Association of Research Libraries.

Warner, D. G. (2001). A new classification for reference statistics. *Reference & User Services Quarterly, 41*(1), 51–55.

Wayne, R. (2011). The academic library strategic planning puzzle: Putting the pieces together. *C&RL News, 72*(1), 12–15.

## CHAPTER 18

Analyzing the Past to Invest in the Future: Usage Statistics for Research Guides from Multiple Data Sources

Carrie Forbes and Christopher C. Brown

Overview

After adopting Springshare's LibGuides product at the end of 2009, the reference librarians at the University of Denver's Penrose Library began an assessment project to determine usage patterns of the library's research guides created by LibGuides. LibGuides usage data and Google Analytics trends were used to determine how students accessed and used the guides. Overall findings indicated that most users were interested in finding and using database links. Google Analytics searching data also showed that users were most often looking for course-specific guides. Furthermore, library instruction sessions increased the usage of these course-specific guides. Students accessing the research guides through a course management system spent the most amount of time viewing a guide. Changes made to the library's research guides based on usage data and recommendations for further studies on research guides usage are discussed.

Introduction

Springshare's LibGuides (http://www.springshare.com/libguides/) has received significant attention in the library community since the company first offered its software in spring 2007. Known for its "Web 2.0" functions, user-friendly interface, and customizable templates, LibGuides has transformed the way many libraries create, organize, and manage web-based research guides. After hosting research guides on a homegrown content management system for more than seven years, the reference librarians at the University of Denver's Penrose Library began using LibGuides at the end of 2009. Shortly thereafter an assessment initiative was begun to analyze how these guides are used by library patrons. Analyzing the use of LibGuides through the product's own statistical data as well as through Google Analytics (http://www.google.com/analytics/) has allowed the discovery of various usage patterns, such as the most frequently accessed guides and subsections of guides, the most frequently used links, whether users are on campus or off campus, and how students and faculty access and find the guides.

Analysis of these common patterns of user behavior has allowed improvements to be made to both the functionality and visibility of the research guides. Furthermore, analysis of user-entered searching data has helped reveal how users perceive the library. Given the amount of time and effort reference librarians have invested in research guide development, this kind of statistical analysis has given much-needed data on research guide usage patterns.

Literature Review

Research Guide Usage

Both Vileno (2007) and Smith (2007) provide thorough literature reviews of the history of research guides, from bibliographies to online pathfinders to LibGuides. Each identifies common concerns specific to online guides. Among these concerns are the amount of time librarians spend creating guides and the lack of usage data collected by librarians. For example, Vileno expresses concern about the sheer amount of time librarians spend authoring and editing guides, especially given that "few have reported using focus groups, surveys, or usability tests in order to discover their target audience's needs" (p. 448). In fact, Grimes and Morris (2000) found that fewer than half of the libraries they surveyed kept any kind of usage statistics on their research guides. The results suggest that academic librarians devote a great deal of time to the development and maintenance of research guides, but relatively little is done to monitor their use. Several authors have given various reasons for this lack of research guide usage data. Vileno (2007) noted that "it is assumed that clients will use a tool, simply because it is online" (p. 442) and because of this common assumption librarians do not test online resources, like research guides. Tchangalova and Feigley (2008) noted a striking indifference librarians have as to whether or not "users are even aware of the existence of subject guides" (para. 2). Staley (2007) also asserted that while there is a body of literature on subject guides which focuses on establishing guidelines, formats, and cost-cutting measures, very few of these studies' recommendations are backed by user-centered data.

Despite a lack of usage data, the main perception among librarians has been that research guides get little use from students. In fact, a large portion of the literature on research guides before the introduction of LibGuides questioned guide effectiveness overall, and sought to understand whether poor usage at some institutions was due to a lack of awareness about these resources. Tchangalova and Feigley (2008) found that users were not cognizant of subject guides, possibly due to "poor promotion and visibility" (para. 2). At San José State University, in California, a study revealed that students who learned about subject guides in library instruction sessions were the patrons most likely to use them (Staley, 2007). Other research has suggested that low usage is the result of online research guides that are modeled on pathfinder approaches and the print paradigm (Hemmig, 2005). Reeb and Gibbons (2004) questioned the usefulness of subject guides specifically, and advocated for the creation of course-specific guides for undergraduates as an alternative.

In recent years, a few authors have conducted usability studies or have administered surveys in an attempt to discover the usefulness of subject guides as research tools for students and faculty. In 2003, librarians from George Washington University in Washington, DC, conducted an online survey to determine the usefulness of their subject guides. They asked users, "Was this guide helpful?" and of the 210 respondents, 73 (34.8 percent) selected "very helpful," while 68 (32.4 percent), the second highest response, chose "not helpful." Patrons indicated frustration with encountering broken links and the exclusion of sites they perceived to be essential. The authors believed that a reason patrons responded negatively was that they did not understand the purpose of the guides. Like other librarians, they concluded that the terminology used to label these guides was too specialized (Courtois, Higgins, & Kapur, 2005). Tchangalova and Feigley (2008) found that "the majority of academic libraries do not offer an explanation as to the purposes of their guides" (para. 6). Similarly, Jackson and Pellack (2004) found that only 38 percent of guides had annotations to help users figure out what each link meant in context. Arnold, Csir, Sias, and Zhang (2004) conclude: "in order for online help to be effective, it must be fully integrated into the functioning of a library's Web site and available at a user's point of need" (p. 132).

More information about the context within which students use these guides is important for better practices in creating, maintaining, and evaluating them. Staley (2007) stated that research into subject guide use is still at an exploratory stage. There are still little, if any, statistically significant data indicating usage trends in different university communities. Morris and Del Bosque (2010) stressed that with the explosion of low-cost tools, more and more libraries are creating research guides, but that few studies have been conducted that evaluate how patrons use these new guides or whether the integration of Web 2.0 tools into research guides is effective.

LibGuides

LibGuides came on the scene in 2007 as a Web 2.0 solution that would make research guides useful again. Since then a number of academic libraries have implemented the service. In addition to confirming that LibGuides has made librarians' lives easier, researchers have found that teaching faculty appreciate the resources created and believe that they have improved student work (Horne, Adams, Cook, Heidig, & Miller, 2009).

Much of the research done concerning LibGuides as a research guide platform has focused on the integration of Web 2.0 technologies. Miner and Alexander (2010) discussed the use of LibGuides to effectively teach information literacy in political science and international affairs. The authors found that LibGuides provided a flexible and personalized experience for library research which reduced student apprehension and enabled faculty to guide students to a variety of sources and a multitude of perspectives. Little (2010) contends that LibGuides provides greater flexibility in web programming, thereby allowing even technologically inexperienced librarians to create guides. Little's analysis used the framework of Cognitive Load Theory, which provides guidelines for the design of instructional materials based on how users process information. Foster, Wilson, Allensworth, and Sands (2010) found, however, that simply promoting LibGuides-based research guides is not enough. It is the connection with a class, course, and subject librarian that ultimately makes research guides useful. Finally, Gonzalez and Westbrock (2010) created a set of best practices for working in LibGuides to help ensure that their librarians most effectively use the software.

Google Analytics

Because of the difficulty of conducting usability studies, many libraries are now turning to less intrusive methods to gather usage data. One such method is the use of third-party web analytics services. According to the Web Analytics Association, "Web analytics is the measurement, collection, analysis, and reporting of Internet data for the purposes of understanding and optimizing Web usage" (http://www.webanalyticsassociation .org/?page=aboutus).With web analytics, librarians do not need to worry about location-based problems inherent in paper-based surveys or about receiving inaccurate information. All the data are collected automatically with high accuracy. Examples of available web analytics tools include VisiStat (http://www.visistat.com/), StatCounter (http://statcounter.com/), and ClickTracks Pro (http://www.clicktracks.com/products/pro/index.php). By far the most sophisticated web analytics tool, though, is Google Analytics, which provides a hosted service for web analytics, through which collecting and analyzing web usage data can be done quickly (see http://www.webanalyticsassociation.org/?page=aboutus). It is a valuable tool for those who need to scrutinize their website's performance.

In particular, Google Analytics is now being used by a few libraries to monitor website traffic and the use of online resources. Most notably, Fang (2007) documented a case study performed at the University of Rutgers-Newark Law Library in New Jersey, in which Google Analytics was used to improve website usability. Turner (2010) discussed how library website managers can make better use of Google Analytics data by using goal-creation and goal-tracking processes. Betty (2009) used Google Analytics data to track usage of library tutorials and other digital learning objects. Finally, Fang and Crawford (2008) measured the usability of the online catalog by analyzing the transaction logs from the Online Public Access Catalog (OPAC) system and results from Google Analytics.

Given the benefits of both LibGuides and Google Analytics, it is surprising that there is relatively little literature on using Google Analytics to analyze LibGuide usage. To date, only a few research articles have been written on this topic. For example, Foster and colleagues (2010) used both LibGuides and Google Analytics to assess the impact of a marketing campaign on research guide usage. Rather than analyzing the LibGuides product itself, this chapter compares the usage data from LibGuides with Google Analytics to gain a better understanding of how students interact with information found on research guides at the University of Denver (DU) in Colorado.

Background

Founded in 1864, DU is a private institution, designated as a doctoral/research university with high research activity by the Carnegie Foundation classification (RU/H) (University of Denver, 2010). Strong in undergraduate, graduate, and professional programs, the university typically enrolls a fairly even distribution of students: in 2009 there were 5,343 undergraduate and 6,301 graduate students, and 793 full-time appointed faculty members (University of Denver, 2010). Undergraduate programs comprise more than 100 areas of study, ranging from traditional liberal arts to pre-professional concentrations. Though graduate programs at DU are also located across many of the traditional liberal arts disciplines, the vast majority of graduate students are clustered in the professional programs of the School of Engineering and Computer Science, the Daniels College of Business, the Sturm College of Law, the Graduate Tax Program, the Morgridge College of Education, the Graduate School of Professional Psychology, the Josef Korbel School of International Studies, and the Graduate School of Social Work. A large number of nontraditional students take programs through University College and the Women's College. Apart from the Sturm College of Law and the Lamont School of Music, which have their own libraries, the Penrose Library reference department serves this diverse community with seven full-time reference librarians, all subject specialists who work as liaisons to particular academic units, in addition to nine graduate student assistants and a paraprofessional.

The reference librarians at Penrose Library provide research and instruction services to the DU community through in-person consultations at the Research Center as well as through chat, text, phone, and e-mail services. The Research Center is a new model of reference service that began in the fall 2008 quarter. Graduate students answer quick questions (less than 15 minutes in length) at the Research Center desk and also make appointments for Research Center consultations with a reference librarian. The Research Center consultation area is situated directly behind the desk and is largely staffed by subject-specialist reference librarians. Students and faculty meet with the reference librarians for one-hour, one-on-one research consultations in this space, which has four workstations with comfortable task chairs and commercial-grade computers, each connected to two sets of widescreen monitors.

In addition to reference services at the Research Center, the reference librarians also provide general workshops and course-integrated instruction, as well as create supplemental educational materials like tutorials and research guides. After hosting research guides on a homegrown content management system for more than seven years, DU's Penrose Library began using LibGuides at the end of 2009. After a migration period, the new LibGuides platform became fully available to the DU community in early March 2010 with the launch of a new library website. The reference department uses LibGuides to manage various types of guides, including:

- subject guides,
- class guides,
- journal A-Z list (e-journal finder), and
- licensing pass-through pages.

The research guides are available to students, faculty, and staff through the library's homepage. Select subject and course guides are also embedded into DU's course management systems (i.e., Blackboard and eCollege).

Shortly after the implementation of the new LibGuides platform, the reference librarians began conducting a statistical analysis to understand user behavior patterns for these guides. An in-depth analysis was needed in order to determine which features of LibGuides to use and to discover how students accessed and used these guides. Analyzing use through LibGuides' own statistical data, as well as Google Analytics, various usage patterns have been discovered. These data have been used to make a number of changes to improve the visibility and usability of these guides.

LibGuides Usage Patterns

The LibGuides software tracks a wide variety of usage data to give librarians an overview of how their guides are being used. To view detailed LibGuides statistics, librarians need to log in to the system, select "My Admin" and "Usage Statistics," and then choose the type of report that they would like to view. Results can be viewed in the web browser or exported to Excel. Users with an administrator-level account can view statistics for any individual guide as well as system-wide statistics. Users with a general-level account can view statistics for guides for which they are creators/co-owners/editors. System-wide LibGuides statistics include a system summary, most-popular-guides list, homepage hits, and guide hits.

The general System Summary option gives librarians information on the total number of guides in the system, total number of pages, and total number of accounts as well as the complete number of homepage views and guide views (see Figure 18.1). Finally, the system summary also provides users with an analysis on the numbers of different content box types being used. Content boxes are the primary design element in LibGuides and they allow librarians to create different types of information. Common content box types allow users to create web links, RSS feeds, embedded audio and video, links to books in a library catalog, and more.

If users select Homepage Hits as an option under the general system reports, they will receive the number of homepage hits broken down by month (see Figure 18.2). The Guide Hits option provides data on the number of hits for each guide per month (see Figure 18.3). Usage reports for individual guides detail the number of hits for pages, widgets and APIs (application program interfaces), links, files, events, and books (see Figures 18.4 and 18.5).

Librarians should be aware that LibGuides only provides usage data for certain content boxes used in the system: Simple Web Links, Links and Lists, Books from the

Figure 18.1. General System Summary

Select Your Report: System Summary
Report Year: Not applicable to the selected report
Display Format: Standard: Best for viewing within your web browser
Run Report

System Summary *(generated 2011-09-26)*

# Guides	# Pages	# Content Boxes	# Accounts	Homepage Views (2011)	Guide Views (2011)
250	1526	3297	19	24160	71187

Content Box Types *(generated 2011-09-26)*

# Rich Text	# Simple Web Links	# Links & Lists	# Documents & Files	# RSS Feed	# Dates & Events
1409	46	1520	16	25	
# Embedded Media & Widgets	# Podcast Feed	# Interactive Poll	# Linked/Reused Box	# Del.ico.us Tag Cloud	# Books from the Catalog
36			88	5	108
# User Submitted Links	# Remote Script	# Google Web Search	# Feedback	# Google Book Search	# Google Scholar Search
21		6	6	2	6
# LibAnswers	# Links to Guides	# Partner Links & Search	# User Profile		
	1		2		

Figure 18.2. Homepage Hits by Month

Select Your Report: Homepage Hits
Report Year: 2010
Display Format: Standard: Best for viewing within your web browser
Run Report

Homepage Hits 2010 *(generated 2011-09-26)*

Homepage	Jan	Feb	Mar	Apr	May	Jun	Jul	Aug	Sep	Oct	Nov	Dec	Total
Homepage Hits	716	562	1023	1400	894	649	741	693	2825	5764	2534	847	18648

Figure 18.3. Guide Hits 2010

Select Your Report: Guide Hits
Report Year: 2010
Display Format: Standard: Best for viewing within your web browser

Run Report

Guide Hits 2010 *(generated 2011-01-01)*

Guide	Jan	Feb	Mar	Apr	May	Jun	Jul	Aug	Sep	Oct	Nov	Dec	Total
18th Century British Digital Collections	-	-	-	-	-	-	-	-	-	38	27	11	76
Academic Search Complete Database	-	-	-	-	-	12	9	5	4	-	-	-	30
ADM 1510 Foundations for Academic and Professional Development	109	106	57	66	8	2	11	14	13	48	6	-	440
ADMN 4849 Action Research for School Leaders	7	38	13	7	8	5	2	1	10	11	18	5	125
American Elections	5	-	6	15	2	3	-	8	4	35	19	12	109
American Government	-	4	13	6	1	-	-	-	13	29	4	3	73
American Youth Violence	-	-	9	9	-	1	5	2	2	10	12	6	56
An Italian Odyssey: 18th and 19th Century British Artists and Italy	4	22	1	7	19	6	-	5	5	4	6	3	82
ANTH 2020 Artifacts, Texts, and Meanings	-	-	-	23	26	2	-	-	3	7	3	2	66
Anthropology	-	2	8	1	8	1	-	3	2	30	35	17	107
APA Style Guide for Business	-	-	-	-	-	-	-	-	-	-	36	59	95
Archival Resources	-	33	143	104	48	52	44	24	76	49	29	30	632
Aristocrats 1660-1800	-	-	7	3	24	1	-	2	1	-	-	-	38
Art - eMAD Graduate Seminar	6	1	1	-	1	3	1	1	20	1	-	1	36
Art - Photography	9	14	4	5	14	2	6	1	120	21	2	4	202

Figure 18.4. "Marketing 2800 Research Guide" Page Hits 2010

"Marketing 2800 Research Guide" Page Hits 2010 *(generated 2011-01-01)*

Page	Jan	Feb	Mar	Apr	May	Jun	Jul	Aug	Sep	Oct	Nov	Dec	Total
Advertising	28	42	33	17	14	4	23	7	15	21	27	1	232
Articles	62	26	14	20	21	10	5	4	79	33	21	1	296
Citation Sources	15	14	6	10	1	1	-	2	74	62	21	1	207
Company Research	134	42	36	103	35	42	38	28	230	81	55	3	827
Course Tools	14	9	5	14	4	4	4	4	9	2	3	1	73
Google	4	2	3	2	1	1	2	3	9	4	6	1	38
Industry Analysis / Financial Benchmarks	-	-	-	-	-	-	35	9	36	20	11	2	113
Industry Overviews	131	39	23	114	42	33	25	13	183	70	48	5	726
Introduction	337	190	98	283	114	83	90	61	440	282	151	8	2137
Library Catalog	12	10	7	12	5	2	1	1	11	5	1	1	68
Market Research	171	139	40	178	54	32	38	13	169	136	104	2	1076
NAICS and SIC Codes	60	26	14	35	10	18	15	10	123	25	26	12	374
Patents	9	4	3	8	1	2	3	2	12	7	1	1	53
Product Research	80	48	19	40	15	16	10	6	64	39	13	1	351
SWOT / Market Share / Rankings	115	26	16	80	31	13	25	9	141	64	47	2	569
Totals	1172	617	317	916	348	261	314	172	1595	851	535	42	7140

Catalog, Documents and Files, and Dates and Events. The system has a high rate of accuracy for counting guide and page hits. It only counts the page hits from the public view and does not count the hits coming from administrative log-ins. For example, when librarians are logged in to the administrative module to create guides, previewing a new guide is not counted toward the number of guide hits.

After the implementation of LibGuides at the end of 2009, the reference librarians began keeping track of the usage statistics available through LibGuides. As the usage of the research guides continued to increase, the librarians decided to undertake a more robust

Figure 18.5. Research Guide Link Hits

Link	Jan	Feb	Mar	Apr	May	Jun	Jul	Aug	Sep	Oct	Nov	Dec	Total
Standard & Poor's NetAdvantage	2	-	3	-	-	1	2	-	1	1	1	-	11
Hoover's Online	72	9	12	49	11	26	12	5	51	13	14	-	274
ReferenceUSA	13	-	-	9	1	5	4	5	11	-	4	-	52
Business and Company Resource Center	18	4	1	18	6	8	4	6	19	9	12	-	105
Corporate Affiliations	16	1	1	2	1	2	1	3	6	-	3	-	36
Hoover's Online	1	-	-	3	1	3	3	14	48	21	13	-	107
ReferenceUSA	4	-	1	4	1	3	4	6	14	2	1	-	40
MarketResearch.com Academic	12	2	5	13	3	2	2	2	25	6	5	2	79
Mintel	33	4	6	21	2	2	5	1	56	22	9	1	162
MarketResearch.com Academic	29	41	5	35	15	7	11	2	27	38	10	-	220
Mintel	60	57	13	72	15	6	11	3	70	66	27	-	400
MRI Plus	36	14	3	60	8	3	2	-	12	28	-	-	166
Global Market Information Database	10	14	1	12	8	2	3	1	8	9	3	-	71
Snapshot Series	6	5	1	7	2	1	1	-	2	3	3	-	31
U.S. Patent and Trade Office - Patents	6	3	1	1	-	-	-	1	7	2	1	-	22

analysis of the usage data in LibGuides. Using data from January through December 2010, an analysis of all subject and course guides that had more than 200 hits was conducted, which amounted to 42 guides (see Figure 18.6). Guides used for the Journals A-Z list and Licensing Pass-Through Pages were not included in this part of the study.

The cutoff of 200 hits was chosen based on the amount of time LibGuides had been available to the DU community and the average number of hits for each guide. At the time of the study, there were 231 published and unpublished guides in the system. The reference librarians also compared the number of guide hits for each month to the library instruction schedule to determine if research guide usage increased with instruction. Finally, data on the number of link hits for each of the guides were categorized according to resource type to see which types of resources were being used most frequently. Based on the analysis of the data, the following trends were noted.

- A causal link between research guide usage and library instruction was found for course-related guides. Of the 42 guides analyzed, 14 were categorized as course-specific guides created specifically for a course or workshop. Comparing the number of guide hits for these guides against the library instruction schedule for the winter, spring, and fall 2010 quarters, it was noted that offering a library instruction workshop for a course increased guide usage by 25.2 percent during the month that the instruction was offered. Given the small number of guides in the sample and the fact that many of these guides were created specifically to accompany a library instruction workshop, the data are not all that significant. They do show, however, that students do use research guides more frequently after they are shown in an information literacy session. Rather than creating a general subject guide, librarians might better spend their time creating guides that they know will be used in a class.

- Thirty-one percent of guides in the study were related to business. Given that students in the Daniels College of Business make up 25 percent of all students (both graduate and undergraduate) at DU, this is also not a surprising statistic. Many of

Figure 18.6. Usage Statistics for LibGuides with 150 or More Hits	
Guide Name	Total Hits
Marketing 2800 Research Guide	3966
Marketing 4610—Marketing Strategy	2292
Security Analysis	781
Business Plan Research	748
Marketing 3950—Integrative Marketing Strategy	606
International Management and Marketing Resources	593
WRIT Classes—Interdisciplinary and Discipline-Based Resources	441
Archival Resources	424
Company Research	422
ADM 1510 Foundations for Academic and Professional Development	363
ENGL 2202—Renaissance Poetry & Prose	320
Research Funding & Grants for Graduate Students	309
Images	286
Creative Communities Workshop	277
Scholarly Communication and Open Access Resources	244
Ira M. and Peryle H. Beck Memorial Archives	238
RefWorks Tutorial	222
Economic and Statistical Sources	212
MALS 4020 Graduate Research and Writing	197
Ski/Snow Industry Resources	166
Country Studies	158
Industry Research	156
CUI 4058 Teacher as Researcher	152

the research guides for business courses are available through students' Blackboard courses, though, which may indicate that linkage in course management systems increases research guide usage. This finding is discussed in more detail later, in the Google Analytics portion of the chapter.

- Database resources were the most heavily used links on the guides. After analyzing the link hits in all 42 guides and then categorizing the links based on type (database link, book link, article link, or freely available web resource), database resources were found to have had the highest average number of hits compared with all other links. Database links do represent the majority (62 percent) of all links in the analyzed guides, but it was encouraging to note that students and faculty are accessing the databases through the research guides. This finding was also confirmed by the keyword search results from Google Analytics, which will be described in the next section of this chapter.

• Users expressed an interest in the library catalog by clicking on the pages, but did not conduct a search in the catalog itself. In addition to analyzing the link hits, the number of page hits for all analyzed guides was also reviewed. While all of the pages had different organizational structures, it was possible to categorize the pages by general type. A majority of the research guides in the data set had a page that gave users access to library catalogs, including Penrose Library's catalog. This access page was one of the five most heavily used types as measured by number of hits, indicating that users were going to the page. A further analysis of the link hits, however, showed that the number of times that users actually clicked through to the library catalog was quite low. Simply put, users were accessing the library catalog descriptive page in the research guides, but not following through with a search in the catalog itself. There are a number of plausible explanations for this occurrence. First, the library catalog page is often listed as the "Home" page for a guide, so the page hits may actually indicate only an interest in the guide and not an interest in the library catalog itself. Second, many of the guides in the analysis had a widget that searched the library catalog, rather than just a link to the catalog. Since LibGuides is not able to collect data on widgets, the actual number of users accessing the catalog from the research guides may be higher than indicated in the LibGuides statistics. Further investigation using Google Analytics and usability testing is needed to explain whether users access the library catalog from research guides.

Limitations to LibGuides Usage Data

While LibGuides usage data can provide an overall indicator of the popularity of certain guides, links, and pages, it does not give a holistic picture of how students and faculty use the library's research guides. Combining LibGuides usage data with data obtained from Google Analytics gives a more comprehensive picture of research guide usage.

Search Engine Indexing

Up to this point, this chapter has discussed using LibGuides' search statistics for analysis. In order to get a more complete picture of use, however, it is necessary to call upon outside sources as well. One possible source of statistics is from the search engines themselves. To discover to what extent the DU LibGuides site was being indexed by two major search engines, Google and Bing, intermittent "site-specific" searches of the search engines were done. That is, the authors searched site:libguides.du.edu for both Google and Bing several times per month to see how much content had been indexed. The results from both Google and Bing proved to be extremely erratic, as Figure 18.7 shows. The reason for this is obscure, with no known explanation on the DU side.

Since the search engines are not "talking" about how they perform their magic, and how often they do it, the authors are left to conjecture. About all that can be said is that

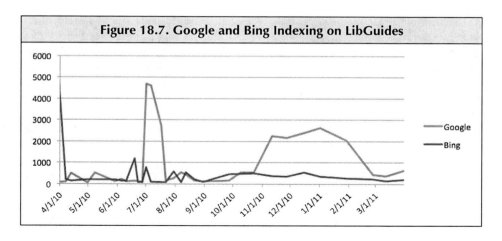

Figure 18.7. Google and Bing Indexing on LibGuides

for some periods of time the DU site was well-exposed, and at other times not well-exposed to search engines at all.

Google Analytics

In August 2006 Google Analytics became publicly available. To make use of this tool, web authors place a snippet of code into a webpage, or a template for dynamic web-pages, so that pages that are output can be picked up and tracked by Google Analytics.

Even though DU's LibGuides site was launched in October 2009, the Google Analytics code was not installed until February 2010, to coincide with the formal rollout of LibGuides to the academic community. Overall results show weekly ups and downs, with high points at the earlier part of the week, and low valleys on the weekends (see Figure 18.8).

Though it is useful to know the numbers of visits, the authors desired to know much more, including:

- How do users find our LibGuides?
- What interface do they use to access them?
- Who visits our LibGuides?
- What is the ratio of new/returning visitors?

- Is there visitor loyalty?
- What is the average length of visit?
- Do users click on LibGuides tags?

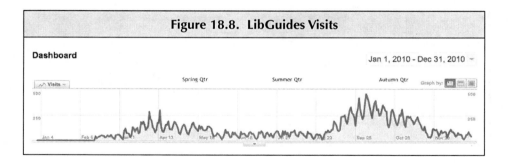

Figure 18.8. LibGuides Visits

According the Google Analytics, 7.41 percent of traffic came from "direct traffic," 84.88 percent was "referring sites," and 7.72 percent was sent by search engines. Direct traffic links are from within LibGuides themselves; the referring sites are links from sites such as the primary library website, which has a different Internet domain (http://library.du.edu/) from the LibGuides site. Users generally discover the research guides by accessing the internal content management system, thus accounting for the high percentage of referring traffic. DU uses two course management software systems, Blackboard (http://www.blackboard.com/) generally for the campus, and eCollege (http://ecollege.com/) for courses at University College, an alternative adult college of the university. Through Google Analytics it was discovered that users who entered the LibGuides through either of these course management systems spent about twice as much time studying the content as other visitors.

The authors were curious about Google Analytics' categorization of most-viewed pages. The number one slot was the "E-Journal Finder," the A–Z list of journals hosted on a LibGuide. Following that was the homepage itself, followed by a licensing pass-through page where, because of our license agreement with that publisher, users agree to legal terms, again hosted on a LibGuide. Right behind that was the LibGuide for "Cool Tools." This page, authored by the Science Librarian, linked to helpful widgets, downloads, and fun diversions the librarian thought that the users might enjoy. Together all the Marketing Guides were next in line.

LibGuides statistics could not distinguish between on-campus versus off-campus use, but Google Analytics could. On-campus access comprised 43 percent of use, whereas off-campus access was 57 percent. This affirmed what was already known: that remote library help has become a cultural expectation.

On the technology side, Google Analytics could tell which web browsers and operating systems were in use by the community (see Figure 18.9).

DU users access the website through a variety of browsers. Firefox (http://www .mozilla .com/) use is gaining on Internet Explorer's (http://windows.microsoft.com/en-US/

Figure 18.9. Visitor Browser and Operating Systems Combinations

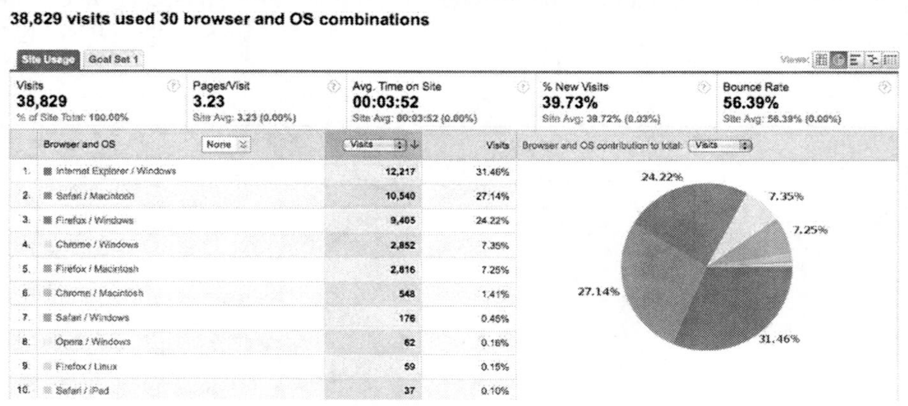

38,829 visits used 30 browser and OS combinations

internet-explorer/products/ie/home) dominance, but Macintosh Safari (http:// www.apple .com/safari/download/) use is also increasing. Google Chrome (http://www .google.com/ chrome/), first released in 2008, is gaining traction. Although only recently released, mobile devices show that at DU iPad is in the lead over iPhone, Android, and iPod devices.

Google Analytics generates some statistics that are more difficult to assign meaning to, such as new visitors (45.14 percent) and returning (54.86 percent) visitors. The visitor loyalty chart (see Figure 18.10) provides a more understandable view of visits and visitors, since it focuses on repeat visits.

Length of visit is most interesting. It has been assumed that users who visited a LibGuide for less than one minute are not really where they want to be, but that users who visited for more than a minute glean some value from the guide. With these assumptions it can be seen from Figure 18.11 that 27 percent of users were considered "actual users."

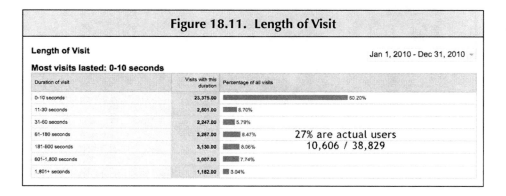

Figure 18.10. Visitor Loyalty

Visitor Loyalty

Jan 1, 2010 - Dec 31, 2010

Most visits repeated: 1 times

Count of visits from this visitor including current	Visits that were the visitor's nth visit	Percentage of all visits
1 times	15,426.00	39.73%
2 times	4,356.00	11.22%
3 times	2,610.00	6.72%
4 times	1,743.00	4.49%
5 times	1,302.00	3.35%
6 times	1,031.00	2.66%
7 times	845.00	2.18%
8 times	717.00	1.85%
9-14 times	2,701.00	6.96%
15-25 times	2,260.00	5.82%
26-50 times	1,981.00	5.05%
51-100 times	1,256.00	3.23%
101-200 times	822.00	2.12%
201+ times	1,799.00	4.63%

Figure 18.11. Length of Visit

Length of Visit

Jan 1, 2010 - Dec 31, 2010

Most visits lasted: 0-10 seconds

Duration of visit	Visits with this duration	Percentage of all visits
0-10 seconds	23,375.00	60.20%
11-30 seconds	2,601.00	6.70%
31-60 seconds	2,247.00	5.79%
61-180 seconds	3,287.00	8.47%
181-600 seconds	3,130.00	8.06%
601-1,800 seconds	3,007.00	7.74%
1,801+ seconds	1,182.00	3.04%

27% are actual users
10,606 / 38,829

DU's LibGuides implementation makes use of built-in tags. Although not the only way to access the various guides, the tags provide a relative indicator of LibGuide popularity. By far the most heavily used guide is for marketing (see Figure 18.12).

Perhaps one of the most interesting questions answerable by Google Analytics concerns keywords used to access LibGuides. At DU users can search within LibGuides or within a search engine such as Google or Bing to discover relevant guides. Figure 18.13 ranks, by popularity, keywords used to access the LibGuides.

Recommendations

LibGuides' native statistics together with those provided by Google Analytics provide complementary views of users' actions. While there are still many questions unanswered by the combination of these two analysis tools, it was possible to arrive at several recommendations after reviewing the data just presented.

It is necessary to conduct usability testing on the most used research guides. The results of this testing will provide more information on how students are actually using the guides. For example, LibGuides usage data, along with Google Analytics information, indicated that students are often using the research guides to access the databases. Further research needs to be done to find out how students search for the database links in these guides. The study results also indicated that students might be confused by the library catalog information in the research guides. Usability testing will help to discover why students may not be searching the library catalog and what can be done to improve access to this important resource. Usability testing is also needed to determine what terms or keywords would help students more easily find the article databases. Since

Figure 18.12. Most Frequently Used Guides

Content Performance					Views:
Pageviews **125,233** % of Site Total: 100.00%	Unique Pageviews **92,258** % of Site Total: 100.00%	Avg. Time on Page **00:01:44** Site Avg: 00:01:44 (0.00%)	Bounce Rate **56.39%** Site Avg: 56.39% (0.00%)	% Exit **31.01%** Site Avg: 31.01% (0.00%)	$ Index **$0.00** Site Avg: $0.00 (0.00%)

	Page None	Pageviews ↓	Unique Pageviews	Avg. Time on Page	Bounce Rate	% Exit	$ Index
1.	/	15,554	11,582	00:00:49	43.16%	38.49%	$0.00
2.	/EjournalFinder	14,491	10,270	00:04:27	71.56%	67.08%	$0.00
3.	/wos	4,673	3,730	00:05:06	79.63%	75.37%	$0.00
4.	/content.php?pid=137043&sid=	3,827	2,101	00:01:57	63.92%	50.74%	$0.00
5.	/admin.php	1,833	720	00:00:32	2.97%	2.13%	$0.00
6.	/marketing2800	1,597	1,326	00:00:38	9.38%	7.14%	$0.00
7.	/cool_tools	1,572	1,320	00:01:25	45.47%	42.81%	$0.00
8.	/index.php	1,379	899	00:00:44	18.92%	12.47%	$0.00
9.	/cat.php?cid=17757	1,178	791	00:00:35	83.45%	15.10%	$0.00
10.	/cat.php?cid=17722	1,122	771	00:00:26	25.71%	6.33%	$0.00
11.	/content.php?pid=73719&sid=550581	797	666	00:01:50	75.93%	27.10%	$0.00
12.	/login.php?pid=903	777	564	00:02:23	78.55%	71.17%	$0.00
13.	/cat.php?cid=17719	730	565	00:00:33	88.16%	38.49%	$0.00
14.	/medline-wok	717	499	00:04:01	62.82%	61.51%	$0.00
15.	/content.php?pid=73719&sid=551013	673	530	00:01:12	56.92%	15.30%	$0.00
16.	/immigrationpolicyhistory	666	491	00:01:01	15.79%	4.60%	$0.00
17.	/scifinder	644	505	00:04:34	76.56%	70.81%	$0.00

Figure 18.13. Most Frequently Used Keywords

Search sent 2,584 total visits via 1,722 keywords
Show: non-paid | total | paid

Site Usage	Goal Set 1				Views:
Visits	**Pages/Visit**	**Avg. Time on Site**	**% New Visits**	**Bounce Rate**	
2,584	**2.42**	**00:01:56**	**81.85%**	**60.53%**	
% of Site Total: 6.65%	Site Avg: 3.23 (-24.96%)	Site Avg: 00:03:52 (-50.09%)	Site Avg: 39.72% (106.09%)	Site Avg: 56.39% (7.33%)	

	Keyword	None	Visits ↓	Pages/Visit	Avg. Time on Site	% New Visits	Bounce Rate
1.	libguides.du.edu/art		97	1.97	00:01:56	1.03%	84.54%
2.	refworks		30	5.10	00:06:24	63.33%	63.33%
3.	book selection tools		28	2.00	00:00:58	96.43%	39.29%
4.	msls 4020		27	1.81	00:00:16	96.30%	74.07%
5.	libguides.du.edu		26	8.46	00:24:34	3.85%	15.38%
6.	penrose database		22	3.73	00:02:33	22.73%	54.55%
7.	naxos		21	2.05	00:00:22	47.62%	61.90%
8.	penrose library		20	2.25	00:00:33	90.00%	65.00%
9.	psycinfo		18	2.17	00:03:08	33.33%	72.22%
10.	research		16	4.81	00:26:46	6.25%	12.50%
11.	esther gil		14	2.29	00:00:41	100.00%	57.14%
12.	penrose		14	1.71	00:01:16	85.71%	78.57%
13.	university of denver refworks		13	1.46	00:00:22	61.54%	69.23%
14.	chicago manual of style du.edu		12	4.00	00:11:18	0.00%	41.67%
15.	educational testing and measurement		12	3.08	00:03:54	100.00%	33.33%
16.	restaurant industry code		12	1.67	00:02:38	100.00%	75.00%
17.	psycarticles		11	2.09	00:00:21	90.91%	27.27%
18.	restaurant sic code		11	1.18	00:00:06	100.00%	81.82%

database resources are of great interest to DU users, it is necessary to make sure the pages and tags in the guides use the terminology most familiar to students.

Since search results from Google Analytics indicate that students are primarily searching for the names of databases and classes, more LibGuides tags have been added based on these data. Any information gained from usability testing also can be used to generate more keywords for tagging purposes.

Because results showed that research guide usage increases with instruction, it is necessary to increase the promotion of research guides in DU classes. Google Analytics data indicated that many users were searching for the names of classes in the LibGuides search, so it would also be beneficial to increase the number of course-related guides. Finally, because Google Analytics data indicated that users coming from course management systems spent the longest amount of time using the guides, links to our research guides within Blackboard and eCollege will be added as appropriate.

Conclusion

Librarians spend a considerable amount of time creating and maintaining research guides, and often very little analysis is done to establish usage patterns. Through a relatively simple examination of the data provided by the LibGuides platform along with Google Analytics data, reference librarians can get a clearer picture of how their guides are used. Both LibGuides and Google Analytics data provide an unobtrusive means of data collection and at the same time allow librarians to discover trends that may need to be more fully evaluated through usability testing. Both statistical analysis tools will continue to be used in the hope that, over time, valuable longitudinal data can enable DU to make its research guides more useful and discoverable to students.

References

Arnold, J. M., Csir, F., Sias, J., & Zhang, J. (2004). Does anyone need help out there? Lessons from designing online help. *Internet Reference Services Quarterly, 9*(3/4), 115–134.

Betty, P. (2009). Assessing homegrown library collections: Using Google Analytics to track use of screencasts and flash-based learning objects. *Journal of Electronic Resources Librarianship, 21*(1), 75–92.

Courtois, M. P., Higgins, M. E., & Kapur, A. (2005). Was this guide helpful? Users' perceptions of subject guides. *Reference Services Review, 33*(2), 188–196.

Fang, W. (2007). Using Google Analytics for improving library website content and design: A case study. *Library Philosophy and Practice, 9*(3), 1–17.

Fang, W., & Crawford, M. E. (2008). Measuring law library catalog web site usability: A web analytic approach. *Journal of Web Librarianship, 2*(2&3), 287–306.

Foster, M., Wilson, H., Allensworth, N., & Sands, D. T. (2010). Marketing research guides: An online experiment with LibGuides. *Journal of Library Administration, 50*(5&6), 602–616.

Gonzalez, A. C., & Westbrock, T. (2010). Reaching out with LibGuides: Establishing a working set of best practices. *Journal of Library Administration, 50*(5), 638–656.

Grimes, M., & Morris, S. E. (2000). A comparison of academic libraries' webliographies. *Internet Reference Services Quarterly, 5*(4), 69–77.

Hemmig, W. (2005). Online pathfinders: Toward an experience-centered model. *Reference Services Review, 33*(1), 66–87.

Horne, A. K., Adams, S. M., Cook, M., Heidig, L., & Miller, C. (2009). Do the outcomes justify the buzz? An assessment of LibGuides at Cornell University and Princeton University. Association of Academic and Research Libraries, Seattle, WA. Retrieved June 9, 2011, from http://www.acrl.org/ala/mgrps/divs/acrl/events/national/seattle/papers/172.pdf.

Jackson, R., & Pellack, L. J. (2004). Internet subject guides in academic libraries: An analysis of contents, practices, and opinions. *Reference & User Services Quarterly, 43*(4), 319–327.

Little, J. J. (2010). Cognitive load theory and library research guides. *Internet Reference Services Quarterly, 15*(1), 53–63.

Miner, J., & Alexander, R. (2010). LibGuides in political science: A gateway to information literacy and improved student research. *Journal of Information Literacy, 4*(1), 40–54.

Morris, S. E., & Del Bosque, D. (2010). Forgotten resources: Subject guides in the era of web 2.0. *Technical Services Quarterly, 27*(2), 178–193.

Reeb, B., & Gibbons, S. (2004). Students, librarians, and subject guides: Improving a poor rate of return. *portal: Libraries and the Academy, 4*(1), 123–130.

Smith, C. H. (2007). Meta-assessment of online research guides usage. *The Reference Librarian, 47*(1), 79–93.

Staley, S. M. (2007). Academic subject guides: A case study of use at San José State University. *College & Research Libraries, 68*(2), 119–139.

Tchangalova, N., & Feigley, A. (2008). Subject guides: Putting a new spin on an old concept. *Electronic Journal of Academic & Special Librarianship, 9*(3), n.p.

Turner, S. J. (2010). Website statistics 2.0: Using Google Analytics to measure library website effectiveness. *Technical Services Quarterly, 27*(3), 261–278.

University of Denver. (2010). *Profiles 2009–2010.* Denver, CO: University of Denver.

Vileno, L. L. (2007). From paper to electronic, the evolution of pathfinders: A review of the literature. *Reference Services Review, 35*(3), 434–451.

CHAPTER 19

The Reference Ref:
How to Referee the Assessment Process
for Virtual Reference Services

Karen Biglin and Karen Docherty

Overview

This chapter reports research results from two studies at the Maricopa County (AZ) Community College District (MCCCD) which involved the evaluation of virtual reference (VR) transcripts, using customized rubrics. The first study was done at Scottsdale (AZ) Community College by the local VR librarian and was a pilot for the second one, which was a larger project by the ASK Coordinator that involved all ten MCCCD colleges. Recognizing that live chat reference presents a challenge to librarians who seek to provide high-quality information services, the authors were interested in developing methods to assess and improve VR. They realized that the chat transcript was an essential and unique tool in helping to evaluate VR transactions. The steps in the research process included identifying the components involved in VR transactions, specifying levels of service outcomes, creating a rubric, and then evaluating and scoring transcripts. The processes for both studies are explained in detail in this chapter.[1]

Introduction

Do librarians provide quality, accurate answers? Are they approachable? Do they give people a reason to use our services instead of Google? These questions, along with the expectation that librarians can show service standards and instructional goals are being met, make it clear that we need a process and a tool to help in assessment efforts. This chapter describes two assessment projects that developed and used rubrics based on RUSA (ALA/RUSA, 2010) and QuestionPoint (QuestionPoint 24/7 Reference Services, 2010) guidelines to evaluate a local and a District-wide Ask a Librarian virtual reference service (VRS).These assessment projects were conducted at Scottsdale Community College and Maricopa County Community College District (MCCCD).

Recent research provides theories as to the efficacy of virtual reference (VR). Gronemeyer and Deitering (2009) suggest that VR may be better suited to teaching students than face-to-face reference transactions. One possible reason for this is that VR shifts the control of the reference transaction away from the librarian, thereby making the power in the transaction more balanced between the librarian and the user. This shift in control may help students take responsibility for their own inquiry and learning. In a study of face-to-face reference versus VR, Moyo (2006) found that a significant amount of instruction takes place in both types of transactions; however, improving technology is an important enhancement in VR transactions. With these findings in mind, chat transcripts can be used to investigate the effectiveness of VRS. The authors of this article realized that being able to use chat transcripts as artifacts would be an objective way to evaluate VRS. As Smyth (2003) points out, a great benefit of chat transcripts is that they allow us to finally capture the elusive reference process. Objective assessment is valuable for VRS, as both the college and District strive to meet the requirements put forth by the regional accrediting body, the Higher Learning Commission (http://www.ncahlc.org/). With an awareness of the increasing importance of VRS, the authors sought to gather information from chat transcripts in order to analyze and improve the level of service and instruction.

To set the stage for understanding how the mechanics of the assessment process worked at the Maricopa Community Colleges, it is necessary to describe the District and its Ask a Librarian VRS. The District is located in Maricopa County in central Arizona. It includes the entire Phoenix metro area, with a population of nearly four million. There are ten Maricopa Community Colleges,[2] with more than 250,000 students taking credit and non-credit courses.

The Ask a Librarian VRS began in 2001 with a pilot project that offered the service on a limited basis. By 2006, the District hired a full-time VR Coordinator and contracted with a provider for 24/7 services. Today, all ten colleges in the District participate in the service, and staff it for 41 hours a week, 12 hours of which are double-staffed during the busiest times. Backup services for 24/7 coverage are provided by QuestionPoint (QP) contract librarians (hired by QP) and cooperative librarians (academic librarians from other colleges and universities who are members of the QuestionPoint global cooperative). Ask a Librarian is used mostly by students, who initiated a total of 7,852 chats in 2009–2010. The service currently only offers live chat, but will soon be offering a District-wide collaborative text reference service beginning in 2011.

Developing and Using a Rubric to Assess VR at Scottsdale Community College Library

At Scottsdale Community College, author Karen Biglin conducted an exploratory study to measure the contribution of VR service to student success. It was designed to answer the following questions:

- How well are students at Scottsdale Community College being served by the 24/7 Ask a Librarian service?
- Is there a way to measure the effectiveness of the service?
- Are there different levels of service, depending on service provider (in-house versus backup librarians)?
- Are the students getting high-quality, accurate answers?
- Do we give students a reason to use our services?
- How can seasoned librarians who are adept at the face-to-face reference interview improve their interpersonal skills in the relatively new medium of online reference?
- How can VRS contribute to student success?

It was decided to develop a rubric to address these questions. A rubric is a scoring tool used for assessment which has been widely and effectively used in higher education to evaluate student learning outcomes (Walvoord, 2004). Librarians use rubrics to evaluate student learning in information literacy programs and classes. Choinski, Mark, and

Murphey (2003) describe a study in which a conventional grading rubric was used as an objective tool for assessing learning outcomes in an Information Resources class. Results showed students scored lowest on the areas requiring higher-level thinking skills, such as the ability to distinguish between popular and scholarly publications. Research discussed by Knight (2006) used a rubric to assess information literacy skills among undergraduates in a first-year research and writing course. The study concluded that a rubric is a valuable assessment tool that provides a reliable and objective method for analysis and comparison. Oakleaf (2009) explains that one of the benefits of using rubrics is that they make instructor expectations clear.

The literature contains examples of methods used to evaluate VR services. Smyth (2003) identified three different models that could be used to classify the content of transcripts, while Avery and Ward (2010) studied chat transcripts in order to find ways to develop information competency skills through reference services. The unique aspect of the Scottsdale Community College study is that a rubric was specifically developed to measure the level of service offered by VR librarians, rather than to measure student learning. Without an existing model rubric to follow, the author created one based on the existing guidelines for VRS from RUSA's *Guidelines for Implementing and Maintaining Virtual Reference Services* (ALA/RUSA, 2010) and OCLC QP's *Best Practices for 24/7 Reference Cooperative Sessions* (QuestionPoint, 2010). The rubric was formatted in a table.

As can be seen in Table 19.1, the rubric included five categories: Greeting, Reference Interview, Quality of Answer, Interpersonal Skills, and Concluding the Session. Within each category, four levels of service were developed, with Level 4 being assigned to the top level and Level 1 being assigned to the lowest level. Within the Greeting category, for example, the four levels were as follows:

1. Level 4: A personal greeting is sent, self-identifying and indicating willingness to help. Library group or affiliation is identified, including a brief explanation about cooperative coverage (i.e., "Your library and my library are part of a nationwide cooperative...").
2. Level 3: A personal greeting is sent, but does not indicate willingness or identification.
3. Level 2: A personal greeting is sent, but is inadequate, abrupt, or incomplete.
4. Level 1: No personal greeting or affiliation is sent.

The author had prior experience in developing rubrics; therefore, creating a new one for this study was not a time-consuming process. The advantage of using a rubric was that it provided a relatively objective scoring tool to evaluate the VR skills of librarians. Stevens and Levi (2005) note that rubrics are useful in establishing performance anchors as well as providing detailed, formative feedback (p. 73). The disadvantage of the rubric was that it was not perfect, as creating a good rubric requires revision as part of an ongoing assessment process, and this was a first step. Later refinements to the rubric included adding a category for Instruction. Valuable results were discovered that were used to inform a larger process as described later in the section titled Ask a Librarian Assessment Project at MCCCD.

After having developed the rubric for all five categories, VR transcripts with students from Scottsdale Community College were collected over a six-week period for a total of

Table 19.1. Rubric Used to Evaluate Ask a Librarian Service at Scottsdale Community College	
Category	**Rubric**
1. Greeting	4. A personal greeting is sent, self-identifying and indicating willingness to help. Library group or affiliation is identified, including a brief explanation about cooperative coverage (i.e., "Your library and my library are part of a nationwide cooperative....").
	3. A personal greeting is sent, but does not indicate willingness or identification.
	2. A personal greeting is sent, but is inadequate, abrupt, or incomplete.
	1. No personal greeting or affiliation is sent.
2. Reference Interview	4. Reference interview is adequate to understand the question and the patron's information need. Patron's question is clarified before beginning the search.
	3. Reference interview is adequate, but does not clarify patron's question before beginning the search.
	2. Reference interview is somewhat adequate, but does not clarify patron's question, and fails to identify patron's information need.
	1. No reference interview.
3. Quality of Answer	4. Answer is complete and correct. One or more quality sources are used. Sources are at the appropriate level for the patron's research. In general, databases are preferable to Google or other general sources when assisting students with research projects. Adheres to all the QP Best Practices guidelines.
	3. Answer is incomplete, but mostly correct. Exactly one quality source is used. Adheres to most of the QP Best Practices guidelines.
	2. Answer is incomplete and mostly incorrect. All sources are dubious. Adheres to some of the QP Best Practices guidelines.
	1. Completely incorrect answer; no quality sources. Does not adhere to QP Best Practices guidelines.
4. Interpersonal Skills	4. Interpersonal skills create a welcoming atmosphere. Librarian chats frequently without long lags, and shows interest in the patron's question. Librarian uses positive phrasing; also uses scripts appropriately, as needed.
	3. Interpersonal skills create a mostly welcoming atmosphere, although there may be some lags, and/or not enough positive phrasing. Scripts are used appropriately, as needed.
	2. Interpersonal skills create a less than welcoming atmosphere. There are long lags and the librarian does not show adequate interest in the patron's question. Does not use much positive phrasing. Does not use scripts appropriately (too much or too little).
	1. Interpersonal skills are completely lacking and inadequate.
(Continued)	

Category	Rubric
Table 19.1. Rubric Used to Evaluate Ask a Librarian Service at Scottsdale Community College *(Continued)*	
5. Concluding the Session	4. The conclusion is complete: the librarian asks the patron if the question has been completely answered. If not, the session is coded for follow-up. Before coding, the patron's e-mail address and deadline is verified. If no more information is needed, patron is thanked for using the service and encouraged to return.
	3. The conclusion is mostly complete, but missing one of the follow-up components.
	2. The conclusion is not complete and is missing more than one of the follow-up components.
	1. Conclusion is inadequate, abrupt, or missing completely.

100 transcripts. Eighty-five of these were found to be usable after incomplete chats or disconnected sessions were eliminated. These 85 transcripts were printed out and scored using the rubric. The data were made anonymous by removing identifying names, e-mail addresses, etc. Only the information about the institutional affiliations of the librarians providing the service was kept (including the MCCCD librarians, QP's contract librarians, or QP's Academic Cooperative librarians). It was exciting to be doing the study, but reviewing and rating transcripts was a long and tedious process, taking three weeks to complete. The author's method was to read six or seven transcripts a day, rather than try to go through all of them at once. For this exploratory study, there was only one rater, but it is desirable to have two or more reviewers to achieve a higher degree of objectivity.

Although not all of the research questions were fully answered by the data analysis, preliminary results indicated that overall the scores were quite high, and some of the findings were useful for further study. The QP contract librarians were found to excel in the category of Greeting, with an average score of 4.0. As the point of first contact with students, a greeting is very important in setting the tone for the entire transaction. By studying how these librarians make effective use of greetings, often with welcoming scripts, it is possible to learn how to improve MCCCD's VRS.

The Reference Interview category had an overall score of 3.13, with the MCCCD librarians scoring 3.20. These are reasonably high scores, but there is still room to refine the VR reference interview. One possible strategy to improve this category is for librarians to clarify the question by asking open, neutral questions. The Quality of Answer overall category score was 3.06, with the MCCCD librarians scoring slightly higher at 3.20. This result may be because the MCCCD librarians are more familiar with the available resources.

Interpersonal Skills is the category in which the author from Scottsdale Community College was most interested. Radford and Connaway (2010) point out that it is important to remember that the VR user "is an individual human being on the other side of the computer screen, not a passive or unfeeling automaton" (p. 45). Most librarians did well in this category, with MCCCD librarians scoring the highest at 3.20. By reviewing the most positive interactions, the author gained insight into what makes a successful VR chat. Rapport-building strategies such as warmth, familiarity, patience, humor, and self-disclosure are important tools of the best VR librarians.

The category of Concluding the Session had surprising results, with the lowest overall score of 2.96. One possible reason for this score is that some sessions end abruptly because the student is in a hurry and disconnects. In this case, it is still important to close with an offer of further service if the student has any more questions. If the student has supplied an e-mail address, he or she will receive the ending messages, and more information can be provided for follow-up. The results of this exploratory research were shared with the internal MCCCD Ask a Librarian Committee, which led to further ongoing District-wide assessment and training processes.

Ask a Librarian Assessment Project at MCCCD
Witnessing the successful use of the rubric to evaluate chat transcripts at Scottsdale Community College, the MCCCD Ask a Librarian committee, composed of representatives from the ten colleges plus the VR coordinator, embarked on a District-wide assessment of their VRS. The Ask a Librarian committee, in a nutshell, wanted to know *really* how well they were doing, as service excellence outcomes can be especially difficult to measure. With a desire to go beyond informal transcript review and user surveys, the committee developed five goals for the assessment project:

1. To evaluate how the quality of the service provided by MCCCD librarians compared with the service provided by QP Academic Cooperative librarians and their contract librarians. MCCCD wanted to know if their patrons receive good service regardless of the librarian that serves them.
2. To determine if user survey results correlated with transcript evaluation results. In other words, do high transcript scores mean positive patron surveys? Do librarian perceptions of good service match those of patrons?
3. To identify areas where VR librarians need improvement to develop appropriate training.
4. To identify areas where VR librarians are doing well.
5. To develop local Ask a Librarian best practices that build on existing guidelines.

The assessment process began with the committee first identifying the goals for the project (just listed) and then building the rest of the process around them. The process, approved by the MCCCD Institutional Review Board (IRB), involved analyzing and coding every transcript from Maricopa users from a one-week period during spring semester 2009. The week was chosen because it represented a typical, mid-semester week that did not include any holidays. The process was initially designed to evaluate one week's worth of transcripts every semester so that quality and improvement could be continuously measured; however, after completing one cycle, the committee realized how labor-intensive the process was. With the consultation of the Institutional Research staff, the process was modified to score two weeks of transcripts from each spring semester. The results reported in this article reflect the first batch of transcript scoring, and are only the beginning of what is intended to be ongoing VRS assessment.

As with the Scottsdale Community College project, transcripts were gathered and stripped of all personal identifiers for both users and librarians. All transcript evaluation and scoring was done at the broad librarian level: Maricopa, QP contract, and cooperative. In an attempt to use a paperless process, transcripts were posted to individual members' folders on the committee's SharePoint site, rather than being printed and mailed.

The committee evaluated the transcripts using the rubric developed for use at Scottsdale Community College. Through an interrater reliability training process which will be discussed in the next section, the committee made several changes to the Scottsdale Community College rubric by changing the Quality of Answer category to Quality of Resources, and by adding Factual Information and Instruction categories, and an option for N/A (not applicable) to every category. The MCCCD rubric can be seen in Table 19.2.

Table 19.2. Rubric Used to Evaluate Ask a Librarian Service at the Maricopa Community Colleges	
Category	**Rubric**
1. Greeting	4. A personal greeting is sent and indicates willingness to help.
	3. A personal greeting is sent, but does not indicate willingness to help.
	2. A personal greeting is sent, but is inadequate, abrupt, or incomplete.
	1. No personal greeting is sent.
	N/A
2. Reference Interview	4. If necessary, patron's question is clarified at appropriate points during the transaction. Reference interview is adequate to understand the question and the patron's information need.
	3. Reference interview is adequate, but does not clarify patron's question at appropriate points during the transaction.
	2. Reference interview does not clarify patron's question and fails to identify patron's information need.
	1. No reference interview.
	N/A
3. Quality of Resources	4. One or more relevant resources are recommended. Resources are at the appropriate level for the patron's research. [In general, databases are preferable to Google or other general resources when assisting students with research projects.]
	3. Only one relevant resource is recommended when more are appropriate.
	2. All resources are dubious.
	1. No relevant resources are recommended.
	N/A
	(Continued)

Table 19.2. Rubric Used to Evaluate Ask a Librarian Service at the Maricopa Community Colleges *(Continued)*

Category	Rubric
4. Factual Information (e.g., directional information: phone numbers, hours, policies. This category does **not** include URLs or sources.)	4. Correct
	3. Mostly correct
	2. Mostly incorrect
	1. Incorrect
	N/A
5. Instruction Consider items such as how to: • Use search terms • Create search strategies • Select resources • Cite sources • Evaluate sources • Access resources (links)	4. Transaction includes detailed instruction.
	3. Transaction includes instruction.
	2. Transaction includes limited instruction.
	1. Transaction warranted instruction, but none provided.
	N/A
6. Interpersonal Skills	4. Interpersonal skills create a welcoming atmosphere. Librarian chats frequently without long lags and shows interest in the patron's question. Librarian uses positive phrasing; also uses scripts appropriately, as needed.
	3. Interpersonal skills create a mostly welcoming atmosphere, although there may be some lags, and/or not enough positive phrasing. Scripts are used appropriately, as needed.
	2. Interpersonal skills create a less than welcoming atmosphere. There are long lags and the librarian does not show adequate interest in the patron's question. Does not use much positive phrasing. Does not use scripts appropriately.
	1. Interpersonal skills are completely lacking and inadequate.
	N/A
7. Concluding the Session	4. The conclusion is complete: the librarian asks the patron if the question has been completely answered **or** if more help is needed. The librarian thanks the patron for using the service **and** invites the patron to use the service again.
	3. The conclusion is mostly complete, but missing one of the follow-up components.
	2. The conclusion is not complete and is missing more than one of the follow-up components.
	1. Conclusion is inadequate, abrupt, or missing completely.
	N/A

To minimize subjectivity in evaluating transcripts, two reviewers were assigned to score each transcript. If the average final scores from the two evaluators for a transcript differed by more than one point, a third reviewer was asked to review that transcript. Members were asked to access their batch of assigned transcripts from their SharePoint folders and to submit rubric scores electronically using an online rubric scorecard (survey).

The committee also collected exit survey data from users during the week that transcripts were collected to see if correlations existed between positive or negative survey responses and transcript scores. Twenty surveys were gathered, which is a small sample size, but reflects a typical response rate of 11.1 percent. Instead of using the standard QP survey questions, the committee selected a set of six questions, four of which were customized to address the rubric categories, and two of which were demographic questions.

Interrater Reliability: What and Why?

Conducting interrater reliability training is an essential part of the assessment process to help ensure replicable and reliable results. The Colorado State University's Writing@CSU Department defines interrater reliability as "...the extent to which two or more individuals (coders or raters) agree. Interrater reliability addresses the consistency of the implementation of a rating system" (http://writing.colostate/edu/guides/research/relval/com2a5.cfm). MCCCD's project had 11 members of the committee scoring transcripts; the interrater reliability training helped to ensure, to the extent possible, consistency in interpreting and applying the rubric. Not only did scorers want to make sure they were consistent with fellow members, they also wanted to make sure they were consistent among themselves—that is, to make sure that each committee member would apply rubric scores the same way from transcript to transcript.

There are a variety of ways to ensure interrater and intrarater reliability, such as the Attribute Gage R&R method used by The Ohio State University Libraries to reduce subjectivity in evaluating their e-mail reference transcripts. Their process was similar to the MCCCD process in that it sought to achieve repeatability (intrarater reliability) and reproducibility (interrater reliability) of results and involved reviewing coding (scoring) disparities and adding clarifying language to the definitions they used (Murphy, Moeller, Page, Cerqua, & Boarman, 2009).

Interrater reliability training was conducted at MCCCD prior to the start of the Ask a Librarian assessment process. First, three transcripts of short to medium length were made anonymous by stripping them of all personal identifiers at both the user and librarian level. Next, they were e-mailed to the committee along with a link to an online rubric scorecard. A deadline for scoring was set so that the Rio Salado College Office of Institutional Research (IR) could gather the results for group discussion. It is important to allow enough time to discuss the transcripts and rubric results and to plan an hour or two for discussion of one or two transcripts. It is possible, depending upon the number of evaluators and the level of comfort sharing opinions and ideas with one another, that only one transcript will be discussed in-depth in that amount of time.

The committee first looked at the scores to determine where the group agreed and disagreed. For categories in which there was substantial agreement, not much discussion was needed. For the categories with the greatest disagreement, there was quite a bit of discussion. Why did one person score a category a 4? Why did one person give the same category a 2? Why did fellow committee members interpret the rubric in different ways? As the committee went through the interrater reliability training process, it became obvious where changing words or adding definitions to the rubric would make it easier for all members to consistently interpret and apply it. Once interrater reliability testing had taken place and the rubric had been revised for maximum clarity by all reviewers, the actual scoring process began.

Interrater reliability training provides clarity to scorers about how to interpret the rubric categories and the scoring levels that comprise it. The detail just given is provided to encourage other libraries to use the rubric evaluation process. The discussion will enable each library to apply its own standards to the analysis process. One library may have far more stringent guidelines about what constitutes a high-quality reference interview than another library. Another library may decide that including in-depth instruction in a chat session is of critical importance for them, and they will be looking for evidence of it, such as explaining concepts and search strategies, in order to receive a high score. Yet another library may interpret the Instruction category more loosely.

Results

The Rio Salado College Office of Institutional Research compiled the transcript scores and correlations and presented them to the committee. MCCCD assessment results, as shown in Table 19.3, provide the overall average rubric scores for the three monitor groups.

The overall average rubric score was 3.233. However, the average rubric score varied by monitor group. The QP contract monitor group earned the highest average (3.35) of all three groups. The MCCCD monitor group earned a 3.26 average while the cooperative monitor group earned a 3.00 average.

Table 19.4 illustrates how the three librarian monitor groups fared in the seven rubric categories. The table indicates areas of strength: librarians earned the highest average (Average = 3.54) in the Factual Information category while Greeting (Average = 3.50) and Quality of Resources (Average = 3.47) were not far behind. These results show where improvements can be made: Instruction, the Reference Interview, and Concluding the Session.

Table 19.3. Average Rubric Score by Monitor Group	
Monitor Group	**Average Rubric Score**
Cooperative	3.00
MCCCD	3.26
QP Contract	3.35
Overall	**3.23**

Monitor Group	Greeting	Reference Interview	Quality of Resources	Factual Information	Instruction	Interpersonal Skills	Concluding the Session
Cooperative	3.16	2.86	3.33	3.45	2.42	3.06	2.74
MCCCD	3.29	3.22	3.46	3.67	2.79	3.35	3.01
QP Contract	3.91	3.09	3.58	3.43	2.61	3.30	3.25
Overall	**3.50**	**3.08**	**3.47**	**3.54**	**2.63**	**3.26**	**3.04**

Table 19.4. Average Score of Rubric Category by Monitor Group

A positive correlation appeared between the rubric score and student survey average, indicating that the two are related. However, the correlation was not significant. This could be due to the disparity between the low number of survey responses and the number of transcripts. Correlations also appeared between specific rubric categories and student survey questions. A positive correlation appeared between the Quality of Resources rubric category and the student survey statement "I received a better answer from Ask a Librarian than I would have found on my own." This correlation was significant when comparing Strongly Disagree responses to Strongly Agree responses, indicating that the Quality of Resources provided by the librarian did have an impact on the user's experience. The statement "I felt that the librarian was courteous and welcoming" was positively correlated to the Greeting and Interpersonal Skills categories. In both cases, the correlation was significant when comparing Strongly Disagree responses to Strongly Agree responses, indicating that a positive greeting and encouraging interpersonal skills positively affected the student's experience. Given the low numbers of both transcripts and survey responses, this will be an area of continued focus in future rounds of assessment.

Discussion

While the QP contract monitors received the highest overall score with a 3.35, the MCCCD librarians were close behind at 3.26. The contract librarians surpassed local librarians in use of a Greeting, Quality of Resources, and Concluding the Session. The success of the Greeting and Conclusion categories can likely be attributed to contract librarians being very consistent with their use of scripts. The surprise is the Quality of Resources category. Do the contract librarians recommend MCCCD library resources even more than MCCCD librarians do? The Scottsdale Community College results showed the MCCCD librarians scoring highest in this category, so perhaps this was an anomaly? Or perhaps further analysis of the transcripts needs to take place to understand this phenomenon. The next batch of MCCCD results may help to further understand what is happening.

Academic librarians who participate in the QuestionPoint cooperative received an overall score of 3.00. While the lowest of the three, this is still a solid score. The weakest areas for the cooperative librarians are Instruction, Concluding the Session, and the Reference Interview; however, the cooperative librarians scored well in the Quality of Resources, Factual Information, and Greeting categories.

The score for the Reference Interview category, defined as clarifying the patron's question at appropriate points during the transaction and being adequate to understand the question and the patron's information need, floats comfortably in the middle of the pack with a score of 3.08 across all librarian categories. According to a study done by Tucker-Raymond and Hyde (2006), "patrons expressed satisfaction 65 percent of the time when a reference interview was done but only 53 percent of the time when one was not done" (p. 16). Reference interviews serve not only to identify the real information need of the patron and increase the likelihood of an accurate answer, but can also demonstrate a librarian's interest, thereby building a connection with the patron.

Perhaps the relatively high overall score for the Quality of Resources category, 3.47, can be attributed to academic libraries subscribing to a core of the same electronic resources as MCCCD and having a general familiarity with student assignments, therefore making it easy for librarians to suggest resources. Quality resources are defined in the rubric as databases being preferable to Google or other general resources; in addition, higher scores were given when more than one resource was suggested, if appropriate for the question. Even when librarians may not have access to the same resources, they can usually identify other resources to suggest to a user. In some instances, students may have requested and received website recommendations during their chat, but transcript evaluators may have scored these transcripts lower, believing that resources offered through the library would have been preferable.

The Factual Information category, focusing on the accuracy of responses to policy-related and directional questions and not accuracy of resources recommended, received the highest overall score and the highest individual category scores for both the MCCCD librarians and the cooperative librarians. While other factors, such as interpersonal skills or use of a proper closing, may determine a user's perception of the effectiveness of a transaction, accuracy of factual information cannot be discounted.

The Instruction category, focusing on whether or not instruction was present, and at what level, was the highest for MCCCD of the three librarian groups, but the lowest scoring category overall. The rubric defines instruction as a transaction including detailed instruction with examples and/or how-to steps, instructing how to create search terms and strategies, select databases, search databases, cite sources, and/or evaluate sources. Given the instructional mission of MCCCD and its emphasis on teaching and learning, this area needs significant attention. Desai and Graves (2008) discuss the findings of three of their research studies about the important teaching role of reference librarians across mediums (instant messaging, chat, and face-to-face) and conclude that, "patrons wanted to be taught regardless of medium, and that librarians responded by providing instruction in all mediums" (p. 254). They note that "these patrons' consistently high desire for instruction reinforces the notion that the ideal teachable moment can be found in reference work" (p. 254). However, according to Radford (2008), chat users "get annoyed with elaborate instruction when it is forced rather than offered" (p. 112). Surely an instructional component, at least one that is offered to students, should be provided whenever appropriate. There can be real barriers to instruction in the chat environment, such as lack of time while juggling multiple users and software limitations that make instruction laborious and challenging. The advent of free and easy-to-use screen capture software as well as highlighting and voice-augmenting tools may make new ways of providing customized instruction easier in the future. While instruction is clearly taking place some of the time in MCCCD chat interactions, more effort needs to be placed on training librarians to integrate this mission-important and user-desired aspect into all sessions that warrant it.

The Interpersonal Skills category, defined in the rubric as creating a welcoming atmosphere, chatting frequently without long lags, showing interest in the patron's question, using positive phrasing, and using scripts appropriately, received relatively high scores across all librarian categories. This is very positive since the results of this study, while based on a small survey sample, suggest that encouraging Interpersonal Skills positively affected a student's experience. According to extensive research conducted by Radford, "users reported relational aspects as being crucial to success of the interaction more frequently than the librarians. Librarians, in contrast, were found to be more concerned with the quality of the information exchanged" (Radford & Connaway, 2008a). Radford and Connaway (2008b) have developed an extensive list of rapport builders designed to increase the positive relational aspects of a transaction. A few examples from the list include the use of greeting and closing rituals, deference (agreement to what is said, expressions of enthusiasm, offering thanks, asking others to be patient), and rapport building (familiarity, humor, repair/self correction, emoticons, ellipses, expressions of enthusiasm and encouragement) (see handout, p. 2, at http://www.oclc.org/research/activities/synchronicity/presentations.htm). These types of interpersonal skills were taken into consideration by reviewers when scoring the Interpersonal Skills category.

Librarians may believe that the Greeting and Concluding the Session categories are not as important as suggesting quality resources or providing instruction, but this may not be the case. The high scores across all three librarian groups for the Greeting category are good news because the results of this study suggest that as with the Interpersonal Skills category, a positive greeting positively affected the student's experience. Research done by Kwon and Gregory (2007) notes that "the strongest predictor of user satisfaction among all ten behaviors was 'Answered?' (for example, asking patrons if their questions have been completely answered)" (p. 145), so properly closing a session is very important. In addition, these authors noted that "the two follow-up questions ("asking if the question was answered" and "asking to come back for further assistance") were not significantly correlated with each other, and each behavior increased user satisfaction independently" (p. 146). Gers and Seward (1985), although referring to an in-person reference environment, contend that "[follow-up] may be the single most important behavior because it has the potential for allowing one to remedy lapses in other desirable behaviors" (p. 34). Thus, both the MCCCD librarians and the cooperative librarians would benefit their chat patrons by improving their consistency in always engaging in proper closing behavior. The general consensus among librarians who monitor VRS is that the use of too many scripts is off-putting to users. Perhaps the limited use of scripts at both opening (to greet and welcome the patron) and closing (to thank the patron for visiting and to invite him or her to return), is an ideal way to ensure consistent behaviors.

Conclusion: Adopting Continuous Assessment of VRS
The transcript results from this first wave of MCCCD VRS assessment address the goals that were laid out at the beginning of the project. The Maricopa community can feel

confident that cooperative and QP contract librarians are providing quality service to its students. Average rubric scores for all three librarian categories are above 3.0, showing that all librarians are providing good service overall.

The scores also illustrate, however, that there is room for improvement. Another goal of the project was to identify areas that need attention, which the evaluation process accomplished. It is clear from this first round of scoring that more instruction could be provided in sessions. In addition, attention must be given to the Reference Interview and Closing categories. Based on these results, the MCCCD VRS monitors have engaged in a Best Practices workshop to focus on these areas. Another round of transcript review will be conducted to measure the effectiveness of the workshop.

Yet another goal of the project was to identify areas of strength among VRS monitors, and this too was accomplished. Successful categories for all monitor groups were identified as Factual Information, Greeting, and Quality Resources; and, not far behind, Interpersonal Skills.

The next round of transcript evaluation will also be helpful to determine if there are any correlations between student survey responses and librarian transcript scores. The first round of scoring identified correlations, but most findings were not significant. This area is interesting, but needs further study. Finally, the results of this initial assessment effort allowed MCCCD librarians to develop a list of best practices for chat monitors to use as a guide for positive behaviors that should be employed in chat sessions.

This chapter has provided a framework for conducting a successful assessment process, starting with identifying project goals and getting the project approved by an institutional review board. Developing a measurement tool, such as a rubric, and providing interrater reliability training to ensure evaluators know how to use it are also important pieces of the process. Consulting with one's institutional research (IR) office is a great way to make sure the process used is valid. IR offices can also help with crunching numbers, identifying correlations, and presenting data. Once results are available, share them with library and institutional colleagues. Develop training around the results, and then assess again. Most important, use the results to improve library services.

Assessment of VRS is an ongoing process, and is being continuously refined at MCCCD. A process of continuous assessment and improvement is the key to student success in higher education. It is with the goal of constant improvement in mind that MCCCD developed a *process* for ongoing assessment of its VRS. The process involves an annual cycle of collecting and analyzing data, which is then used to formulate strategies for improving service. In this way, the Ask a Librarian service at MCCCD can be confident it is doing all it can in each VR encounter to help students achieve their educational goals.

Notes

1. Amigos Library Services funded a grant for the authors to present at the Conference. During this presentation, the authors had the opportunity to explain their research processes in-depth and to assist participants in hands-on development of rubrics.
2. Chandler Gilbert Community College, Estrella Mountain Community College, Gateway Community College, Glendale Community College, Mesa Community College, Paradise Valley

Community College, Phoenix College, Rio Salado College, Scottsdale Community College, and South Mountain Community College.

References

American Library Association. Reference and User Services Association. (2010). *Guidelines for implementing and maintaining virtual reference services.* Retrieved June 7, 2011, from http://ala.org/ala/mgrps/divs/rusa/resources/guidelines/virtual-reference-se.pdf.

Avery, S., & Ward, D. (2010). Reference is my classroom: Setting instructional goals for academic library reference services. *Internet Reference Services Quarterly, 15*(1), 35–51.

Choinski, E., Mark, A., & Murphey, M. (2003). Assessment with rubrics: Efficient and objective means of assessing student outcomes in an information resources class. *portal: Libraries & the Academy, 3*(4), 563–575.

Desai, C. M., & Graves, S. J. (2008). Cyberspace or face-to-face: The teachable moment and changing reference mediums. *Reference & User Services Quarterly, 47*(3), 242–254.

Gers, R., & Seward, L. J. (1985). Improving reference performance: Results of a statewide study. *Library Journal, 110*(18), 32–35.

Gronemeyer, K., & Deitering, A. (2009). I don't think it's harder, just that it's different: Librarians' attitudes about instruction in the virtual reference environment. *Reference Services Review, 37*(4), 421–434.

Knight, L. A. (2006). Using rubrics to assess information literacy. *Reference Services Review, 34*(1), 43–55.

Kwon, N., & Gregory, V. L. (2007). The effects of librarians' behavioral performance on user satisfaction in chat reference services. *Reference & User Services Quarterly, 47*(2), 137–148.

Moyo, L. M. (2006). Virtual reference services and instruction: An assessment. *The Reference Librarian, 46*(95), 213–230.

Murphy, S. A., Moeller, S. E., Page, J. R., Cerqua, J. R., & Boarman, M. (2009). Leveraging measurement system analysis (MSA) to improve library assessment: The attribute gage R&R. *College & Research Libraries, 70*(6), 568–577.

Oakleaf, M. (2009). Using rubrics to assess information literacy: An examination of methodology and interrater reliability. *Journal of the American Society for Information Science & Technology, 60*(5), 969–983.

QuestionPoint 24/7 Reference Services. (2010, May 17). *Best practices for 24/7 reference cooperative sessions.* Retrieved June 7, 2011, from http://wiki.questionpoint.org/247-Best-Practices.

Radford, M. L. (2008). From the editor: A personal choice: reference service excellence. *Reference & User Services Quarterly, 48*(2), 108–115.

Radford, M. L., & Connaway, L. S. (2008a). *Cordial connections: Evaluating virtual reference from user, non-user, and librarian perspectives using the Critical Incident Technique.* Paper presented at the Libraries in the Digital Age (LIDA) Conference, Dubrovnik and Mljet, Croatia, June 2–7. Retrieved June 15, 2011, from http://www.oclc.org/research/activities/synchronicity/resources/lida2008-radfordconnaway.pdf.

Radford, M. L., & Connaway, L. S. (2008b). *Getting better all the time: Improving communication & accuracy in virtual reference.* Handout presented at Reference Renaissance: Current and Future Trends Conference, Denver, CO, August 4–5. Retrieved from http://www.oclc.org/research/activities/synchronicity/resources/refren08-handout.pdf.

Radford, M. L., & Connaway, L. S. (2010). Getting better all the time: Improving communication and accuracy in virtual reference. In M. L. Radford & R. D. Lankes (Eds.), *Reference renaissance: Current and future trends* (pp. 39–54). New York: Neal-Schuman.

Smyth, J. (2003). Virtual reference transcript analysis. *Searcher, 11*(3), 26–30.

Stevens, D. D., & Levi, A. J. (2005). *Introduction to rubrics: An assessment tool to save grading time, convey effective feedback, and promote student learning.* Sterling, VA: Stylus.

Tucker-Raymond, C., & Hyde, L. (2006). Benchmarking librarian performance in chat reference. *The Reference Librarian, 46*(95/96), 5–19.

Walvoord, B. E. (2004). *Assessment clear and simple: A practical guide for institutions, departments, and general education.* San Francisco, CA: Jossey-Bass.

## CHAPTER 20

Leveraging OpenURL Click-Through Statistics to Study User Behavior

Justin Otto and Doris Munson

Overview

Eastern Washington University (EWU) uses WebBridge as their OpenURL link resolver. WebBridge statistics were analyzed to help answer questions about the use of free academic resources and how often a full text link is displayed. The use of open access journals linked to through WebBridge is increasing. They appear to be indexed by the library's databases, and they are being accepted as a valid form of scholarly communication at EWU. However, there are costs associated with providing WebBridge entree to open access journal articles and to free databases such as PubMed. PubMed users are more likely to click-through to interlibrary loan (ILL) than other WebBridge users. Surprisingly, WorldCat Local and RefWorks are major WebBridge origins. The likelihood that the user will get a link to a full-text article is 53 percent. Users do not get a full-text link or use ILL 36.7 percent of the time.

Introduction

An OpenURL link resolver is a tool that helps users obtain electronic content. It is used to bridge users from an origin, usually an indexing/abstracting database such as Web of Science or FirstSearch, to electronic periodical content like subscription-based electronic journals. SFX from Ex Libris, Article Linker from Serials Solutions, and WebBridge from Innovative Interfaces (http://www.iii.com/products/webbridge_lr.shtml) are three of the more commonly used OpenURL link resolvers. Eastern Washington University (EWU), a regional, comprehensive public university with approximately 10,000 students and 500 faculty members, has used WebBridge since 2004.

The act of clicking on a link to an article presented by a link resolver is often known as a *click-through*. Most OpenURL resolvers can log click-through events to varying degrees. The library at EWU has been capturing click-through data since 2007 with the intention of eventually examining the data for trends in user behavior and vendor indexing to make e-resources more responsive to the user community.

Many libraries are already logging data from their OpenURL resolvers, but since much of the existing work with click-through data has been in collection management, librarians may not think about how they can use the same data to gain insight into their users' behavior and how effective their services are in addressing their users' needs. The authors hope that this chapter's discussion of how users' interactions can be analyzed with free and open access academic materials can serve as an example of how librarians can do data-driven analysis with information that is already on hand.

As free electronic academic content like open access journals and PubMed (http://www.ncbi.nlm.nih.gov/pubmed/) have become more prevalent, WebBridge has been configured to work with them. The rapid proliferation of free electronic resources over the past few years makes their use an interesting case for study. EWU now has three years of OpenURL click-through usage data, and is using it to try to answer the following questions about free electronic academic resources in our library:

- Are open access journals getting used?
- What are the hidden costs of making open access journals available through Web-Bridge?
- Which of the subscription databases index open access journals?
- What is the likelihood that the user will get a link to a full-text article or will use the link to interlibrary loan?
- Is PubMed, a free indexing/abstracting database, actually free?

Recent Literature

There is a small but growing body of literature on the use of OpenURL resolver click-through data to study user behavior. Yi and Herlihy (2007) used click-through data from the SFX link resolver to specific targets, which they referred to as "SFX data by the number of sessions fulfilled" (p. 320), as one component of their study of the impact of an OpenURL resolver on the use of electronic scholarly resources at their institution. Trainor and Price (2010a,b) discussed using SFX click-through data to identify heavily used databases and journals as part of an effort to improve OpenURL resolver usability and performance. However, much of the literature on OpenURL and link resolvers to this point has not focused on user behavior itself, but rather employs user behavior to inform collection analysis decisions. Stengel (2004) used data on OpenURL click-throughs to interlibrary loan services to help identify journals for acquisition. Similarly, Stowers and Tucker (2009) looked at unsuccessful click-through requests for full-text articles to identify journals for future purchase. Gallagher, Bauer, and Dollar (2005) employed link resolver data in print journal cancellation decisions.

OpenURLs, Click-Throughs, and WebBridge: Start to Finish

Many libraries that provide electronic journals from multiple vendors have an OpenURL resolver. While many academic librarians use a resolver regularly, they may not know what it is doing behind the scenes to get the user to the article they want. The detailed mechanics of how OpenURLs and link resolvers work is outside of the scope of this chapter, but generally speaking, an OpenURL is an Internet address that includes metadata about the item in question. OpenURLs can be assigned to virtually any electronic item, but in academic libraries, OpenURLs are most commonly used in conjunction with electronic journal articles. The user starts by finding a citation in an *origin*. Origins are most often indexing/abstracting databases, but other article-locating systems, such as Google Scholar (http://scholar.google.com/) or bibliographic management software such as RefWorks or EndNote, can be configured as OpenURL origins as well. When the user clicks on the resolver link provided by the origin, metadata about the article are sent to the link resolver via an OpenURL. EWU has tried to make the OpenURL resolver link in the origin as obvious as possible, so it appears as a clickable yellow button labeled "Check for Full Text" (see Figure 20.1).

The link resolver compares the article metadata to data in its coverage database, which has information about the journals the library subscribes to. If the link resolver finds a match, a pop-up box in the web browser offers the user one or more links, or *offered links*, to the full text of the article (see Figure 20.2).

The act of clicking on an offered link in the pop-up box is known as a *click-through*. The link then connects the user to the *target*. The target is usually a webpage with a link to the full text of an article, not the full text itself (see Figure 20.3). The target can also be an interlibrary loan (ILL) request or other alternative link.

Figure 20.4 illustrates the patron's path, beginning with an indexing/abstracting database and finishing at the full text of an article.

Methodology

WebBridge Usage Statistics

The statistics available through WebBridge are limited, but can still be used to infer quite a bit about how EWU's electronic resources are being used. For a single click-through event, WebBridge logs (1) the origin, (2) what links were offered in the pop-up

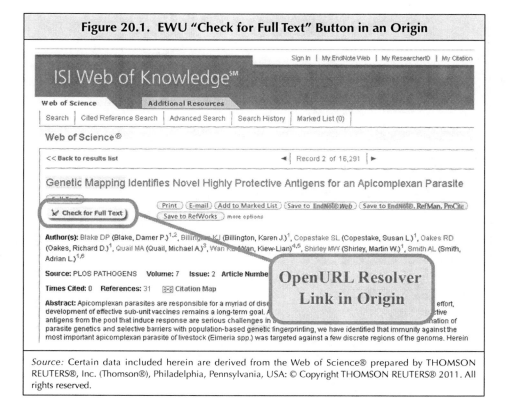

Figure 20.1. EWU "Check for Full Text" Button in an Origin

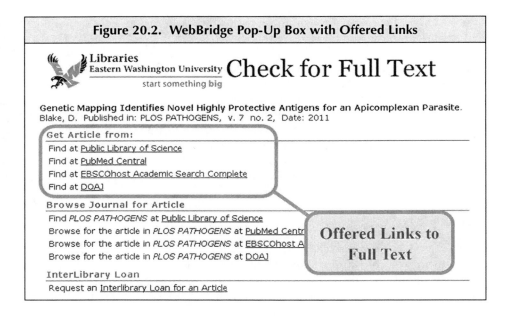

Figure 20.2. WebBridge Pop-Up Box with Offered Links

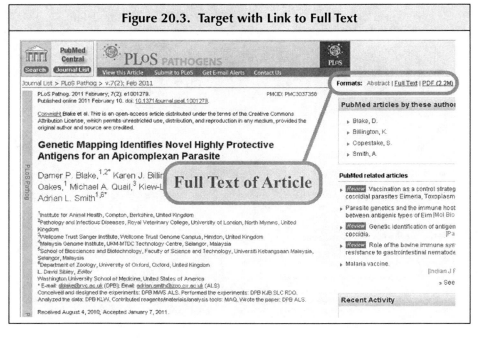

Figure 20.3. Target with Link to Full Text

box, and, (3) what target was clicked-through to (or if no links were clicked on). Unlike SFX, WebBridge does not collect journal-level data, so the actual journal that was clicked-through to is not known—only the target is known. WebBridge also does not

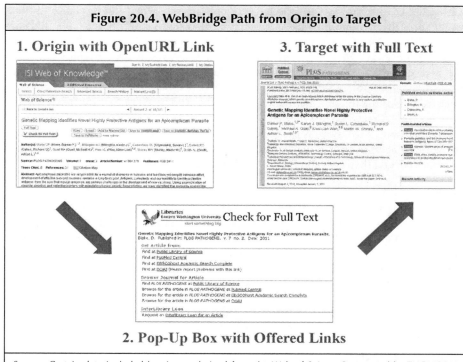

Figure 20.4. WebBridge Path from Origin to Target

1. Origin with OpenURL Link   3. Target with Full Text

2. Pop-Up Box with Offered Links

log any data about the user or his or her computer. Each click-through from start to finish is an individual, anonymous transaction.

Data Analysis

The data collected by WebBridge is logged using a series of numerical codes consisting of "1"s and "0"s. For instance, if a user clicks the EWU "Check for Full Text" OpenURL link in a database, but then does not click an offered link to the target, WebBridge logs the click-through to the target as a "0." If the offered link is clicked on, the click-through is logged as a "1." WebBridge can export data in comma-delimited format for use in a spreadsheet program such as Microsoft Excel. Once in a spreadsheet, click-through data can be sorted by column. WebBridge data were downloaded for the calendar years (not academic years) 2007, 2008, and 2009 and analyzed using Microsoft Office Excel 2007. The click-through data involving open access targets, PubMed, and ILL were extracted and analyzed. The open access data were sorted first by target, second by origin, and then third by whether or not the offered link had been clicked.

Total click-throughs were calculated annually for each open access target and origin. Some calculations required knowing the total number of full-text links to targets that were offered by WebBridge annually. In order to determine those totals, the authors subtracted the instances of a link that was offered only when there was no full text available—"Electronic Journals A-Z"—from the instances of a link that was always offered in every WebBridge transaction, interlibrary loan (see Figure 20.5).

As of the end of 2009, EWU offered 11 open access resources through WebBridge. The first four, the Directory of Open Access Journals (DOAJ), Highwire Press, Hindawi Publishing, and Public Library of Science were added before click-through data were collected beginning in 2007. Bentham Open Access and BioMed Central were added in 2008. In 2009, Freely Accessible Arts & Humanities Journals, Freely Accessible Social Science Journals, Medknow, Nature Open Access, and PubMed Central were included in the open access resource offerings. ProQuest usage data were also downloaded, summarized, and then compared to the WebBridge data.

Caveats to the Use of Click-Through Data

There are two caveats to keep in mind when analyzing click-through data with regard to open access journals. First, a click-through does not guarantee that the user got the article, only that the offered link was clicked on. If the article metadata do not exactly match between the origin and target, for example, the user could click on the offered link (and thus be counted as a click-through) but not get the article. In this sense, what our click-through data is really counting is the *intent* to get the article. Second, some database origins, such as ProQuest and PubMed, already provide their own direct links to open access titles. In such an instance, the user would bypass WebBridge and still access the article, thus not generating a click-through transaction for WebBridge to log.

Results and Analysis

Are Open Access Journals Being Used?

The data reveal that open access journals are being used, and that their use is increasing. Highwire Press and the Directory of Open Access Journals have received the most

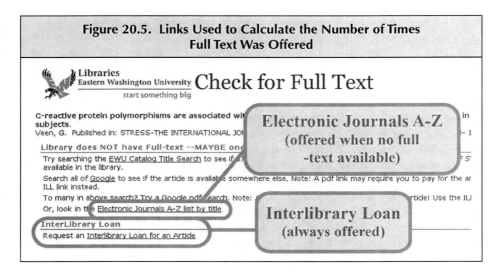

Figure 20.5. Links Used to Calculate the Number of Times Full Text Was Offered

click-throughs of the open access resources made available through WebBridge. PubMed Central, while only added in January 2009, quickly became the third most-used open access resource. The next two most frequently used resources are Freely Accessible Social Science Journals and BioMed Central, although their usage is much lower than that of the top three resources. The combined click-throughs for all other open access resources is less than the usage of BioMed Central (see Table 20.1).

While the numbers are not large in and of themselves, there is a definite increase in open access usage: 304 percent in 2008, and 73 percent in 2009. The use of open access is also increasing as a percentage of total WebBridge click-throughs (see Table 20.2). The open access journals we link to are being used, their use is increasing, and they are being accepted as a valid form of scholarly communication at EWU. One indication of this acceptance is that our sciences faculty requested that we include BioMed Central as a resource for them to link to.

Are the Databases Provided Enabling Open Access Journals to Be Found?

The volume of click-throughs to open access that begin with indexing and abstracting databases suggest that the open access journals our students are using do appear to be indexed by the databases provided. EBSCO was the most-often used WebBridge origin, followed by Web of Science and PubMed (see Table 20.3).

Table 20.1. Most Frequently Used Open Access Resources

Resource	2007	2008	2009
Highwire Press	107	588	678
Directory of Open Access Journals	180	514	604
PubMed Central	n/a	n/a	526
Freely Accessible Social Science Journals	n/a	n/a	107
BioMed Central	n/a	69	71
Other	5	8	55

Table 20.2. Increase in Open Access Usage

Use	2007	2008	2009
Total Click-Throughs to Journal Articles	13,790	22,012	31,092
Open Access	292	1179	2042
% Open Access	2.1%	5.4%	6.6%
% Increase in Open Access from Previous Year	n/a	304%	73%

Table 20.3. WebBridge Origins: Where Users Started from to Retrieve Open Access

Origin	2008	2009
EBSCO	304	521
Web of Science	262	408
PubMed	194	272
RefWorks	56	84
FirstSearch	54	77
WorldCat Local (from 9/1/09)	n/a	51
Other	82	103

As was mentioned earlier, some database origins already provide their own direct links to open access titles. The act of clicking a direct link is something WebBridge cannot count. For example, ProQuest offers EWU users direct links to the full text of articles from other vendors, because we get our coverage data from Serials Solutions, a ProQuest subsidiary. Any journals (including open access) that EWU has listed in Serials Solutions are offered as full-text links in ProQuest if ProQuest indexes the journal. ProQuest provides data on click-throughs from the direct links they offer, which we downloaded for 2007, 2008, and 2009 (see Table 20.4).

In 2007 and 2008, click-throughs to open access from ProQuest direct links far outnumbered those facilitated by WebBridge. But in 2009, WebBridge click-throughs slightly outnumbered those from ProQuest. This is likely due to the fact that in 2008, EWU switched from ProQuest to EBSCO as our primary database vendor, and EBSCO did not provide the direct linking that was available from the ProQuest/Serials Solutions arrangement. Hence, as more people used EBSCO, more people used WebBridge. When ProQuest and WebBridge click-throughs are combined for the 2007–2009 period, total click-throughs to open access articles increased by 41 percent from 2007–2008 and by 26 percent from 2008–2009 (see Table 20.4). Because the ProQuest direct linking

Table 20.4. WebBridge versus ProQuest Click-Throughs to Open Access Articles

WebBridge or ProQuest	2007	2008	2009
WebBridge	292	1179	2042
ProQuest	1992	2045	2010
WebBridge + ProQuest	2284	3224	4052
% Increase from Previous Year	n/a	41%	26%

click-throughs remained relatively constant over the three-year period, these percentage increases in usage are not as dramatic as those for WebBridge alone (see Table 20.2), but they still show a large increase in click-throughs to open access.

EWU's top two WebBridge origins for open access journal articles, EBSCO and Web of Science, are both paid subscriptions, as is ProQuest. When the WebBridge click-through data and ProQuest direct linking data are combined, we see that a large number of open access articles were accessed through these origins. This also indicates that users will use open access articles if they are available as WebBridge targets.

What Is the Likelihood That the User Will Get a Link to a Full-Text Article or Will Use the Link to ILL?

Calculations indicate that a full-text link is offered about 53 percent of the time. While analyzing open access click-through statistics, the question arose about how often the user gets the article through WebBridge using either a full-text link or ILL. However, in the age of Google instant gratification, even the option to get an article in a few days via ILL is considered a failed search by some. So the question of how often WebBridge offers a full-text link can also be thought of as, "How often does a user get what he or she would perceive as a successful result when using WebBridge?" It is impossible to answer this question exactly because a single WebBridge pop-up box can offer multiple links for the same article, each of which could be clicked on, generating multiple click-throughs. But it is possible to make an educated guess based on when certain links are offered.

Whenever a user clicks on the WebBridge icon in an origin (see Figure 20.1, p. 309), the resulting WebBridge results page always offers a link to ILL. On the other hand, the "Electronic A-Z list" link is only offered when WebBridge cannot offer a full-text link (see Figure 20.5, p. 312). The following formula was used to determine how often a full-text link was offered in 2009: (ILL link displays—Electronic A-Z list displays)/ILL link displays = percent full-text link displays. This formula allowed the authors to determine that a full-text link was displayed 53 percent of the time (see Table 20.5). Or, essentially, WebBridge did not provide an instantly successful result 47 percent of the time.

Table 20.5. How Often a Full-Text Link Was Offered in 2009	
Category	**Number of Times/Percentage**
ILL Article Links Offered	71,428
ILL Article Links Clicked On	7,133
Electronic Journal A-Z Links Offered	33,382
No Full Text Available	38,046
Full-Text Link Was Offered	53%
Full-Text Link Was Not Offered	47%
No Full Text or ILL Was Not Used	36.7%

If the number of times the ILL-offered link was clicked on is added to the number of times a full-text link was displayed, it can be deduced that users did not get a full-text link nor did they use ILL 36.7 percent of the time. In actuality, this figure may be a little lower because of the fall-back links WebBridge has been configured to offer when no full-text links are available (see Figure 20.5, p. 312). Fall-back links, like Google Scholar, are offered when no full-text resources are available. This analysis cannot tell if fall-back links find an item, only if they are clicked on.

A 53 percent immediate success rate is encouraging for us because EWU is not a PhD-granting institution, and does not have the extensive journal collections of a major research library. It is considered a success that the desired journal article is immediately provided more than half of the time, because it provides users with a successful search often enough that hopefully they will not lose faith in the library's ability to provide them with the materials they require. The fact that only 36.7 percent of users end their WebBridge transaction in what could be perceived as a failed search is also encouraging. Although the authors wish that more students were willing to use ILL to obtain their desired article, it is felt that EWU is doing a pretty good job of meeting faculty and students' needs with regard to journals if the majority of WebBridge transactions end favorably.

PubMed as a Free Origin

One cannot look at free resources without also considering free origins such as PubMed. One way to consider if a free origin is really free is by looking at whether its use generates other costs to the library, such as the cost of fulfilling ILL requests that start from that origin. According to our estimates, the "free" origin PubMed actually cost EWU $14,350.00 in 2009.

EWU began to offer WebBridge links in PubMed starting in January 2008, and it quickly became popular with our health sciences professors. These professors teach and encourage their students to use PubMed rather than Medline, which is offered through EBSCO and FirstSearch, because PubMed is what students will most likely use after they graduate.

Table 20.6 summarizes the type of resources that EWU PubMed users were most likely to click on in 2008 and 2009. Although the number of times users clicked on the WebBridge icon in PubMed increased almost fourfold from 2008 to 2009, the percentage of click-throughs to each type of resource did not appear to vary significantly. A third year of data is necessary to determine if there is a trend in the behavior of PubMed users at EWU (see Table 20.6).

EWU had only offered PubMed for two years at the time these data were compiled, but in those two years it had become a significant source of ILL requests. PubMed users were more likely to click-through to ILL than other WebBridge users, and they accounted for 11 percent of all ILL click-throughs in 2009.

EWU has not done an internal analysis of the cost of an ILL for an article, so we used the most recent figure we could find: a 2002 ARL estimate of $17.50 for the per-transaction cost of a filled "borrowing" ILL (combining monographs and periodicals) in research libraries (Jackson, 2004, p. 37). Using this figure, PubMed ILL requests cost us $4,147.50 in 2008 and $14,350.00 in 2009.

Table 20.6. PubMed Click-Throughs by Type of Target				
Click-Throughs	2008	2008	2009	2009
Open Access	81	10%	274	9%
Paid Subscriptions	342	42%	1333	43%
Interlibrary Loan	237	29%	820	26%
Fall-Back Links (No Full Text Offered)	157	19%	701	22%
Total	817	n/a	3128	n/a

It should be noted that these figures are top-end estimates. Not every click-through to ILL results in a loan request, so the real ILL costs that can be traced back to PubMed are probably somewhat less. But that does not diminish the fact that the "free" origin PubMed is a cost-generating, not cost-saving, resource at EWU.

Discussion

The Cost of "Free" Open Access Resources

A point to consider, which click-through statistics can shed some light on, is whether or not "free" resources are used enough to justify the work that is put into them. Open access is not really free when one considers the effort required to make them available through an OpenURL link resolver. In this case, EWU contracts with Serials Solutions for its journal coverage data file. The cost from Serials Solutions is determined by how many titles are included in the coverage file, so adding open access titles makes the coverage file more expensive. In addition to this direct cost, there are indirect labor costs, because a staff person must load the coverage data into the catalog, edit WebBridge to use the resource, test the resource, and monitor open access resources on an ongoing basis to make sure they continue to work correctly in WebBridge. These fees and labor costs would be the same if paid subscription journals were being added instead of open access journals. While a subscription-cost savings is realized from adding open access journals, there are costs to including open access journals in the library collection nonetheless.

At EWU, click-through data have shown that the percentage of click-throughs to open access is increasing yearly. This leads to two inferences. The first is that vendors are doing a better job of indexing open access articles. The second is that the number of open access articles is increasing. Open access articles are becoming more findable, and the greater variety means that it is more likely that an open access article will fit a user's needs. Users are being given more journal options and they are using them at an increasing rate. It is not possible to know if the students are choosing open access because it fits their information needs better than paid subscriptions, or if they are merely satisficing. Even if it is the latter, we are providing them with a usable option from the library, when they otherwise might have turned to Google or some other source outside of the library. While an analysis of the labor costs associated with adding and maintaining open access targets in WebBridge has not yet been done, the increasing availability and use of open access articles increases the library's confidence that it is worth the cost and that EWU should continue to offer linking to open access.

Unexpected Origins

One surprising thing in the data was the appearance of WorldCat Local and RefWorks at sixth and fourth, respectively, in the list of WebBridge origins used most often to click-through to open access (see Table 20.3, p. 314). WorldCat Local is a search and discovery interface that is used to combine local holdings information with that of the other members of the regional borrowing consortium. The WorldCat Local Search box is prominently located on the library's homepage, and users are encouraged to use it as a starting point. Although its primary purpose is as a discovery tool for books, videos, and other returnable materials, it contains citations to journal articles. It is configured to work with WebBridge and display the yellow "Check for Full Text" button in article citations (see Figure 20.1, p. 309). Users quickly discovered it, and while the click-through statistics for WorldCat Local are for September to December 2009 only, they are already greater than those for that of many other origins for that entire year. This was an unexpected result, but it demonstrates that efforts to familiarize users with the "Check for Full Text" button are working. The fact that WorldCat Local contains journal citations was not publicized, but users found the familiar yellow button in article citations and immediately began using it.

RefWorks, on the other hand, is an online bibliographic management system, not a database. Users can export an article's bibliographic information from an indexing/abstracting database to their RefWorks account for later use. WebBridge was configured to work with RefWorks, so that when bibliographic information is transferred to RefWorks, the yellow "Check for Full Text" button (see Figure 20.1, p. 309) appears in the stored citation in RefWorks. Users clicked on the yellow button enough times to make RefWorks the fourth largest source of click-throughs to open access in 2008 and 2009. Users appear to be exporting citations of interest to RefWorks as they search and then retrieving the full text of the articles via WebBridge from their saved citations later, in effect using WebBridge as an on-demand full-text retrieval tool in lieu of saving or printing a copy of the article when they first discover it in a database. So even though the volume of this kind of use of WebBridge was unexpected, it reinforces that EWU has been successful in informing and training its users about WebBridge and the "Check for Full Text" button.

Conclusion

Open access journals do get used, especially when the indexing of open access in the standard subscription-based indexing/abstracting services makes them more "findable." EWU's WebBridge click-through statistics clearly make the case that open access journals can be worth inclusion in an OpenURL link resolver. Also, PubMed and other "free" databases can be valuable resources to library users. In the case of EWU, PubMed quickly became a heavily used database origin once it was configured to work with WebBridge.

A full-text link was found to have been displayed 53 percent of the time in 2009. This figure was higher than expected based on previous experience. However, the authors deal primarily with the science and business professors where the collection is not as strong as that for other fields. Business and science journals also often embargo their content for the most recent 12 months, a time period that is of highest interest to these user communities.

When one takes into consideration the number of times the ILL link was clicked, users did not get full text or request an ILL 36.7 percent of the time. This figure was also higher than expected. It appears that the majority of users are unlikely to request an ILL. However, PubMed users quickly became a major source of ILL requests when the ILL link was added to the WebBridge results page. ILL expense was identified as one of the costs associated with a "free" database if a link resolver is used to offer links to ILL as well as to full-text resources.

Many libraries are already logging data from their OpenURL link resolvers, but have not used the data to gain insight into their users' behavior. Click-through statistics can provide information on this behavior, to learn if it is worthwhile to introduce (or continue) a service, and so that services and procedures can be adapted to better accommodate the way resources are being used. The data can also be used to investigate broad questions such as how a library's OpenURL link resolver is being used, and for more specific cases such as the impact of open access journals on the library. This work in analyzing EWU's users' interactions with free and open access academic materials is an example of how librarians can do data-driven analysis with information they already have. This analysis can better inform the decision-making process for librarians, especially administrators who need to make sometimes-difficult budget decisions respond better to statistics than to anecdotal evidence.

Acknowledgment

The authors would like to thank Nicholas Brown, Graphics Designer with the University Graphics office at Eastern Washington University, for his invaluable assistance with the figures in this chapter.

References

Gallagher, J., Bauer, K., & Dollar, D. M. (2005). Evidence-based librarianship: Utilizing data from all available sources to make judicious print cancellation decisions. *Library Collections, Acquisitions, & Technical Services, 29*(2), 169–179. doi:10.1016/j.lcats.2005.04.004.

Jackson, M. E. (2004). *Assessing ILL/DD services: New cost-effective alternatives.* Washington, DC: Association of Research Libraries.

Stengel, M. G. (2004). Using SFX to identify unexpressed user needs. *Collection Management, 29*(2), 7–14. doi:10.1300/J105v29n02_03.

Stowers, E., & Tucker, C. (2009). Using link resolver reports for collection management. *Serials Review, 35*(1), 28–34. doi:10.1016/j.serrev.2008.11.001.

Trainor, C., & Price, J. (2010a). Chapter 2: Improving the resolver menu: The most bang for your buck. *Library Technology Reports, 46*(7), 11–14.

Trainor, C., & Price, J. (2010b). Chapter 3: Digging into the data: Exposing the causes of resolver failure. *Library Technology Reports, 46*(7), 15–26.

Yi, H., & Herlihy, C. S. (2007). Assessment of the impact of an open-URL link resolver. *New Library World, 108*(7), 317–331. doi:10.1108/03074800710763617.

Virtual Tools and Attitude Adjustments to Improve Service

CHAPTER 21

LibAnswers: Improving Asynchronous Service

Lisa Campbell

Overview

In fall 2009, The University of Alabama Libraries (University Libraries) licensed and implemented LibAnswers, a web-based virtual reference (VR) system that pairs an internal knowledge base with a publicly accessible frequently asked questions (FAQ) database. LibAnswers enables libraries to build and maintain a database of questions and answers that can be used to improve response accuracy and reduce duplication of effort. It is one of several proprietary Knowledge Management Systems (KMS) which, at first glance, offer a more efficient and cost-effective means of managing VR transactions. This chapter examines one university library's use of the product as an alternative to traditional e-mail reference.

Background

Located in Tuscaloosa, The University of Alabama is a land grant institution with a 2009 enrollment of 28,807. The institution has 12 instructional schools that are served by five separate discipline-related libraries, collectively known as the University Libraries. Virtual reference services (VRS) in the University Libraries have changed significantly in a relatively short period of time. The University of Alabama was one of eight institutions that participated in the Association of Southeastern Research Libraries' Ask-a-Librarian consortium, a cooperative chat reference service that used Online Computer Library Center's (OCLC) QuestionPoint system before migrating to SirsiDynix's Docutek VRLplus software (Wright & Tu, 2010).

Following the consortium's dismantlement, the University Libraries implemented a local Ask-a-Librarian chat reference service, still using the VRLplus client. Due to ongoing software issues, low usage, and time and cost constraints, this local service was discontinued in July 2009. Its discontinuation marked the end of centrally coordinated synchronous VRS in the University Libraries. Each of the branches continued to offer asynchronous service through separate e-mail forms, and synchronous service through chat widgets maintained by individual reference librarians.

In August 2009, the Amelia Gayle Gorgas Library (Gorgas Library), the branch for humanities, social sciences, and government information, acquired two new commercial products for VR: Springshare's LibAnswers and Mosio's Text a Librarian. While licensing these products was largely the decision of one administrator, the choice was not illogical. The University Libraries already subscribed to LibGuides, Springshare's product for online subject and course guide creation. LibAnswers appeared to be a product that would have a familiar interface and integrate well with existing services. Both products were less expensive than their predecessors, and, being web-based, did not require local installation or updates.

Initially, the new services were managed separately from e-mail: one librarian answered all questions submitted to LibAnswers and Text a Librarian, while another librarian answered all questions sent through an e-mail form. Managing queries from three separate services created staffing and record-keeping challenges. The two-person staffing model did not take advantage of the Information Services Department's collective knowledge. In addition, the e-mail form and LibAnswers submission form were nearly identical, making the services more competitive than complementary. In order to streamline asynchronous VR in Gorgas Library, librarians replaced the e-mail form with a LibAnswers widget and canceled the Text a Librarian service in favor of Springshare's optional short message service (SMS) module.

Gorgas Library's LibAnswers Service: Basic Functions

LibAnswers is "a web 2.0 Q-and-A reference system and knowledge base builder offering SMS/TXTing and Twitter integration" (http://www.springshare.com/). Subscribing institutions are given a customizable homepage that provides access to the fully hosted system. The homepage functions as an FAQ that allows patrons to browse existing questions and submit new questions. Since August 2009, Gorgas Library has used LibAnswers to manage VR transactions and build a publicly accessible FAQ. The following is a summary of basic LibAnswers functions in the context of Gorgas Library's implementation.

Asking Questions

From the LibAnswers homepage (http://ask.lib.ua.edu/), users enter a question or key-words in a prominently placed search box. As the user types, an Auto-Suggest feature automatically searches the FAQ and displays recommended answers (see Figure 21.1). The user can either select a recommended answer to view it, or click the "Ask Us" button to submit a new question.

If the user's question matches a previously answered question, the system redirects the user to the appropriate response. If there is no direct match, the system directs the user to a question submission form that (1) displays any potential matches, (2) asks for additional details related to the question, and (3) asks for an e-mail address and answers to two demographic questions (see Figure 21.2). The form's questions and required fields are customizable. When users complete the form and click "Submit Your Question," they receive a confirmation message indicating they will receive a response by e-mail.

Figure 21.1. Auto-Suggest Recommending Answers

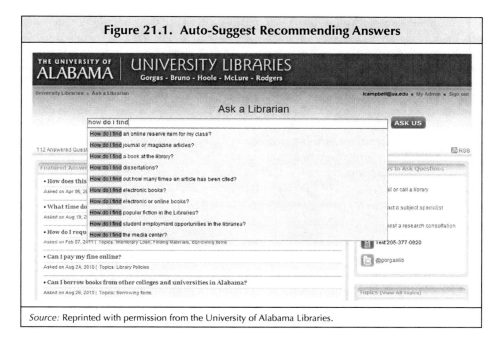

Source: Reprinted with permission from the University of Alabama Libraries.

Figure 21.2. Question Submission Form

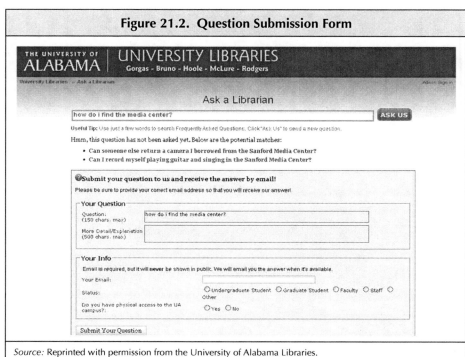

Source: Reprinted with permission from the University of Alabama Libraries.

LibAnswers provides additional ways for the users to ask their questions. Questions can be sent via SMS (an optional feature), Twitter, LibAnswers boxes embedded in LibGuides, or LibAnswers widgets embedded in webpages. A chat widget can be embedded in the LibAnswers homepage; however, questions sent to the chat widget will not register in the LibAnswers administrative console. Likewise, questions sent to a different free or proprietary SMS service will not appear in LibAnswers.

Browsing

Users can browse questions by topic category, keyword, popularity (view count), date, or librarian. While viewing responses, users can submit comments, view any embedded media, share the response through e-mail and a variety of social media, and view links to related questions, topics, or LibGuides (see Figure 21.3). Users can also create really simple syndication (RSS) feeds to keep track of new submissions to the FAQ.

Answering Questions

When a new question is submitted, notifications are sent to staff through e-mail, Google Talk, and browser notifications. The question then appears as "unanswered" in the administrative console (see Figure 21.4).

Librarians can use the administrative console to both answer new questions and modify existing answers. To answer a question, a staff member logs into the system and claims it. Claiming prevents other staff from sending duplicate responses. Once the

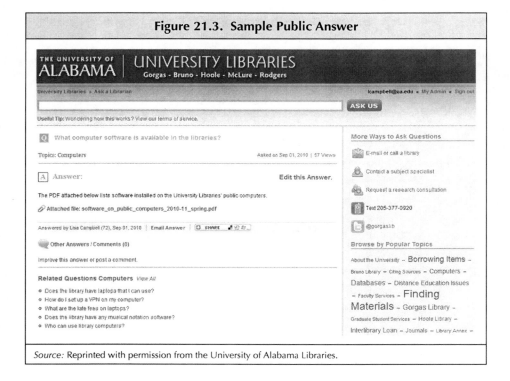

Figure 21.3. Sample Public Answer

Source: Reprinted with permission from the University of Alabama Libraries.

Figure 21.4. Sample Unanswered Question in Administrative Console

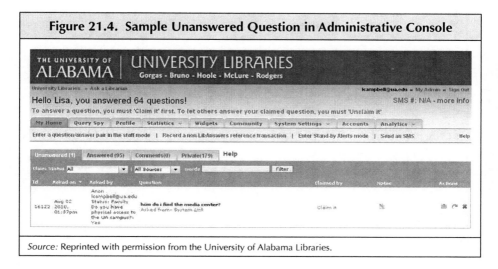

Source: Reprinted with permission from the University of Alabama Libraries.

question is claimed, the staff member can (1) answer it, (2) e-mail it to another LibAnswers account holder, (3) refer it to another library or campus department, or (4) transfer the question to another LibAnswers system. Staff can also add personal notes that will be visible to other account holders. The notes encourage collaboration and dissemination of information among staff.

Staff members use either a rich-text or plain-text editor to compose responses. The process is similar to composing an e-mail. Once an answer is composed, the answerer must choose whether to make the response public or private. Public answers, which appear in the FAQ, include the richest selection of optional content. Public answers can include topics and keywords, attached files and videos, and supplementary links to websites or related LibGuides. Private answers, which are saved in the internal knowledge base, are e-mailed to the user and can only include text and links. The question format largely determines what the answer can include; for instance, SMS messages are limited to 150 characters and, depending on the user's device, may not include working hyperlinks. Similarly, tweeted responses are limited to 140 characters.

Staff can also reuse an existing answer. Reusing an answer is fairly simple and only takes a few clicks. A Recommended Answers feature suggests answers to related questions from the FAQ, the knowledge base, and other subscribing institutions (see Figure 21.5). Staff can choose an answer to reuse it, or manually search the knowledge base for other responses. Gorgas Library encourages answer reuse because it reduces staff time spent answering questions and helps maintain answer consistency and accuracy.

Receiving Answers

When a response is sent, the user receives an e-mail that says, "Your question has been answered." The responding staff member is copied on the e-mail. This feature ensures that the user has a point of contact for follow-up. Users access public answers by clicking a link to the FAQ located in the body of the e-mail. Private answers appear as text within the e-mail. In Gorgas Library, all LibAnswers e-mails also include a link to a feedback

Figure 21.5. Recommended Answers Feature

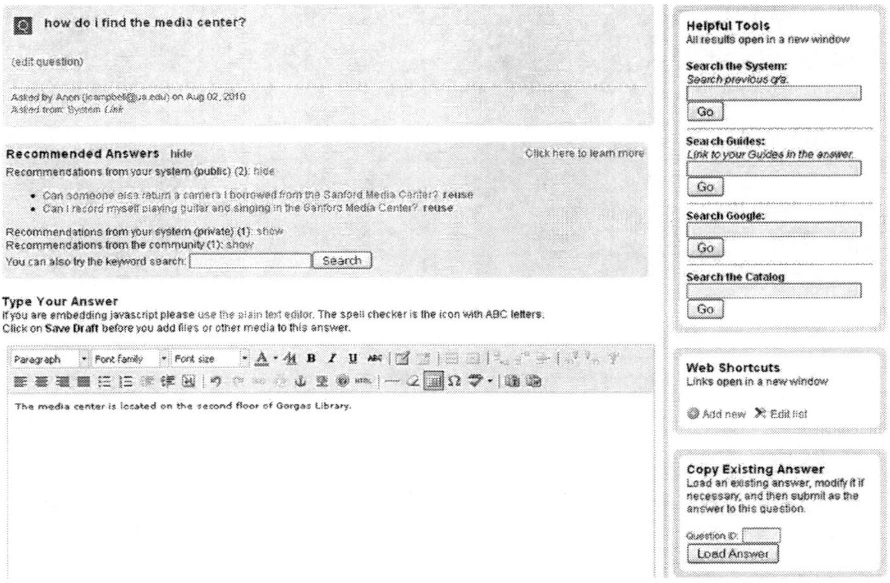

Source: Reprinted with permission from the University of Alabama Libraries.

form. SMS answers are sent to the user's mobile device, and Twitter replies are sent through Twitter (http://twitter.com/).

Building and Maintaining the Knowledge Base

By definition, an FAQ is "a logical, consistent, and efficient way of providing answers" (Wallace, Sassen, & Antonelli, 2009, p. 60). Because a brand-new LibAnswers system contains no questions, it is not very useful as an FAQ. Luckily, there is a staff entry mode that can be used to enter helpful question-and-answer pairs before the system is up and running. In Gorgas Library, popular library questions from internal training documents and departmental webpages were manually entered into the system.

Because questions are not stable entities, Gorgas Library puts significant effort into maintaining its knowledge base. Librarians regularly check the public FAQ for broken links and outdated content, making corrections as needed. While some institutions choose to make all their LibAnswers transactions public, Gorgas Library only publicizes questions that are frequently asked and relevant to more than one individual. As the FAQ grows in size and specificity, the less useful it becomes as a finding aid, and the more maintenance it requires.

Collecting Data

LibAnswers collects several types of statistics, including question counts that can be sorted by hour, day, month, staff member, turnaround time and more. The system also collects answers to demographic questions and counts the number of referrals to specific e-mail addresses.

LibAnswers makes it possible for librarians to see how users are both asking and viewing questions. Any time someone uses a LibAnswers search box and clicks "Ask Us" or a recommended answer, the system records the action. The Query Spy feature records how the user is accessing the FAQ (i.e., through the homepage, LibGuides, a widget, etc.), what search terms they are entering (keywords versus a natural language query), and whether or not their query was successfully submitted (see Figure 21.6). Staff can also use the Query Spy to see if the user was directed to an exact match or if they clicked on a potential match.

LibAnswers also collects patron data such as name (optional), e-mail address, and IP address. This information is never displayed publicly. Because e-mail addresses are saved in the system, staff members are able to reconnect with users if their answers need additions or corrections.

Benefits

LibAnswers is one of several commercial systems that capitalize on libraries' desires to increase the efficiency and cost-effectiveness of their VRS. Two conclusions have been drawn from the initial use of the product, as discussed in the following section.

LibAnswers: Cost-Effective and Efficient

LibAnswers is more cost-effective than Gorgas Library's traditional e-mail reference service, because it reduces staffing costs and the overall cost per question. This cost savings is achieved through several notable features. The FAQ gives users 24/7 access to popular information, providing a self-service option when staff members are unavailable. The

Figure 21.6. Query Spy

Time	Ip	Question Query	Result	Source
Aug 06, 12:32		What does it mean when I log in to ILLiad and it says I have been disavowed?	Direct match via auto-suggest	System
Aug 06, 09:29		how do i find the media center?	Question was submitted to the system	System
Aug 05, 16:29		Do you have old Crimson White issues in the stacks?	Direct match via auto-suggest	LibGuides
Aug 05, 11:04		The only thing special I can think of: Is there an unusual or quirky event tied to football? There was some reason why the Alabama-Auburn series was s	Question was submitted to the system	System
Aug 05, 10:44		How long can I keep a book?	Direct match via auto-suggest	System
Aug 02, 13:37		how do i find the media center?	Question was submitted to the system	System
Aug 01, 18:04		how do i download ebscohost?	Question was submitted to the system	System
Aug 01, 16:45		what does in process mean? (add)	Question not submitted!	System
Aug 01, 11:35		Where can I find reviews of the databases, for example, a review of JSTOR? Is there any where these are housed besides just doing a google search? (add)	Question not submitted!	System
Jul 31, 14:04		I've just graduated and joined the UA Alumni Assoc. How do I maintain library privileges?	Direct match via auto-suggest	System
Jul 31, 14:04		how do i say food in hungarian (add)	Question not submitted!	System
Jul 31, 14:03		how do say food in hungarian (add)	Question not submitted!	System

Source: Reprinted with permission from the University of Alabama Libraries.

Auto-Suggest feature directs users to exact or potential matches to their questions. LibAnswers' system of notifications also reduces the amount of staff time spent waiting for questions or checking for new submissions. As of April 2011, the most popular question in the system (*Is there a specific Distance Ed Librarian?*) has been viewed 162 times. Because the answer is available at the user's point of need, staff members spend less time repeating information. As usage of a particular question increases, the cost per question will continue to decrease.

LibAnswers also reduces staff time by simplifying the process of reusing responses. With the Gorgas Library e-mail reference service, reusing a response required searching e-mails, documents, or websites. These responses then needed to be copied, pasted, and edited into a new answer. The tediousness of this process can also be seen in Ralph's (2009) study of QuestionPoint's knowledge base. Ninety-six percent of survey respondents said they did not reuse responses, citing dislike of extra steps and mistrust in shared information. Because LibAnswers automatically searches the knowledge base and recommends responses, staff can reuse them without having to open a new window, application, or file.

In addition to simplifying key functions like question reuse, LibAnswers integrates processes like managing reference transactions, maintaining a knowledge base, and collecting statistics. Adopting the product has simplified Gorgas Library's work flow for asynchronous reference service. Patrons are not tied to one location or interface to ask their question, yet all questions are fed into a web-based administrative console that all participating staff members are able to access.

Finally, LibAnswers reduces the cost of implementation, maintenance, and training. Once the system was licensed, it required little time or technical expertise to implement. Springshare provides technical support that has been prompt and helpful. Because the LibAnswers work flow is similar to traditional e-mail reference and the interface is similar to LibGuides, it took very little time to train staff to use it. The FAQ and knowledge base have also been used to teach new hires about policies and institution-specific information.

LibAnswers: Builds Institutional Memory

With its former e-mail reference service, Gorgas Library retained little question-level data or patron information, and no information about turnaround times. As of April 2011, Gorgas Library has a public FAQ with 112 questions that have been viewed more than 3,000 times. It also has an internal knowledge base that contains an additional 641 questions. Thirty-six percent of the total questions had a turnaround time of ten minutes or less. Staff can browse these questions by date, topic, answerer, and turnaround time. They can reuse questions easily and post relevant answers or topics within their LibGuides. The knowledge base has helped Gorgas Library improve both reference training and provision of service. In one case, qualitative feedback indicated that users were displeased with the circulation question referral process. Based on this feedback, librarians amended the work flow. Gorgas Library has also used LibAnswers statistics to evaluate the effectiveness of the FAQ's content and interface. In the future, librarians hope to conduct additional usability testing and more in-depth analysis of the question/answer pairs.

Challenges

Despite its benefits, LibAnswers is not perfect. Some of the problems Gorgas Library encountered during its first year of LibAnswers use are described in this section.

Technical Difficulties

Occasionally, Springshare server outages and other technical problems interrupted access to the LibAnswers service. There were also cases in which publicly accessible questions disappeared from the administrative console. These issues, while frustrating, were resolved promptly by technical support.

Statistical Inaccuracies

LibAnswers has evolved considerably since Gorgas Library's initial implementation. The addition of new features caused minor statistical inaccuracies related to question counts and text messages. Other statistical inaccuracies were caused by librarians repeatedly testing or demonstrating the system during instruction sessions.

Lack of User Feedback

While LibAnswers enables users to leave comments, it does not have any built-in means of collecting user feedback. Though Gorgas Library links a feedback form to e-mailed LibAnswers responses, few users fill it out. Similar VR products give users the option to give feedback within the body of the answer using radio buttons, but LibAnswers currently does not have this option.

Service Integration Concerns

The LibAnswers Twitter integration functions poorly. While it is useful to have a record of tweeted questions, there is significant delay before tweets appear in the administrative console. In addition, any tweets that mention the linked Twitter account will appear in the administrative console, regardless of whether or not they contain questions. The majority of tweets mentioning Gorgas Library are from students discussing their location or study plans. These tweets must be deleted from the LibAnswers system to prevent statistical inaccuracies.

LibAnswers has worked well for Gorgas Library because it is the primary means of providing VR. While LibAnswers provides a central interface for managing many types of questions, it does not integrate everything. Libraries using separately managed chat and text message technologies may see fewer gains in efficiency, but they can still benefit greatly from the inexpensive system's asynchronous question work flow and rich statistical data.

Privacy Concerns

When Gorgas Library first started using LibAnswers, a patron requested that his or her question be removed from the public FAQ. It is important to note that some users may not want their questions displayed publicly, even if the questions are stripped of personal information. LibAnswers subscribers concerned about privacy can easily add a permission request to the question form; however, questions sent through Twitter, SMS, or certain widgets do not require users to complete this request form. Now, instead of posting FAQs verbatim, Gorgas Library manually enters rewritten versions in staff mode. Staff also created terms of service that include further clarification and a link to Springshare's privacy policy.

Practical Implications

Reference librarians use a variety of print and electronic documents to represent "need-to-know information" (Slater, 2006, p. 69). This information, however, is not always maintained, made public, or regularly used for knowledge retrieval. More often, it is disorganized, inconsistent, and "not structured in a way that lends itself to responding to specific questions" (Halperin, Eichler, Khanna & Dryer, 2006, p. 34). Consequently, reference librarians have looked to products like LibAnswers and other KMS as means to transform reference data into useful, easily accessed information.

Libraries have significant incentive to employ knowledge management (KM) for reference. An effective FAQ can promote self-service, reducing the number of staff hours spent answering repetitive questions, while still providing information at the user's point of need (Shaw & Spink, 2009; Jones, Kayongo, & Scofield, 2009). As noted earlier, FAQs and knowledge bases can also be used to train staff, support professional development, and build institutional memory (Slater, 2006; Anello & Bonfield, 2007). In addition, scholarly literature increasingly suggests asynchronous service supported by an FAQ database as a more cost-effective approach to VR (Shaw & Spink, 2009, p. 192).

Libraries are not new to KMS. A 2009 study found that more than 50 percent of 112 Association of Research Libraries (ARL) institutions had an FAQ on their website (Jones et al., 2009, p. 69). To create FAQs, libraries use various content management systems, programming languages, and open-source or proprietary systems. The choice of technology often depends more on time, money, technical expertise, and situation than efficacy. For example, the University of North Texas Libraries successfully implemented the FAQ knowledge base of Docutek's VRLplus software in 2005, but migrated to another tool after joining a regional consortium (Wallace et al., 2009). Similarly, The University of Alabama Libraries went through several commercial products before acquiring LibAnswers.

Vendors appear to be aware of the benefits of using KM for reference. Other VR systems that include KM features include OCLC's QuestionPoint (http://www.question point.org/) and IntelliResponse System Inc.'s IntelliResponse (http://www.intelli response.com/). While these solutions may seem attractive, not all libraries can afford them. Considering the speed of technological change, subscribing institutions should weigh the risks of becoming over-reliant on a vended product, especially when many charge extra for enhanced functionality or premium features.

Despite these concerns, LibAnswers' popularity has grown quickly. The University of Alabama was one of a handful of subscribing institutions in August 2009. Since then, the LibAnswers community has grown to more than 300 academic, public, and special libraries. While further research is needed to determine the impact of LibAnswers on VRS, Gorgas Library's initial experience has been positive.

References

Anello, K., & Bonfield, B. (2007). Providing reference service in our sleep: Using a FAQ database to guide users to the right sources. *Reference & User Services Quarterly*, 46(3), 28–33.

Halperin, M., Eichler, L., Khanna, D., & Dreyer, K. (2006). Just the FAQs, ma'am. *Journal of Business & Finance Librarianship, 12*(1), 33–40.

Jones, S., Kayongo, K., & Scofield, J. (2009). Ask us anytime: Creating a searchable FAQ using email and chat reference transcripts. *Internet Reference Services Quarterly, 14*(3), 67–81.

Ralph, L. (2009). If you build it they may not come: The case of QuestionPoint. *Electronic Journal of Academic and Special Librarianship, 10*(2). Retrieved November 15, 2010, from http://southernlibrarianship.icaap.org/content/v10n02/ralph_l01.html.

Shaw, K., & Spink, A. (2009). University library virtual reference services: Best practices and continuous improvement. *Australian Academic & Research Libraries, 40*(3), 192–205.

Slater, R. (2006). Reference desk notes: An online knowledge management system. *Internet Reference Services Quarterly, 11*(3), 69–83.

Wallace, R., Sassen, C., & Antonelli, M. (2009). Implementation of an authoritative FAQ database. *Texas Library Journal, 85*(2), 60–62.

Wright, A., & Tu, F. (2010). Expanding service and enhancing learning: Preliminary report on a novel virtual reference collaboration. In M. L. Radford & R. D. Lankes (Eds.), *Reference renaissance: Current and future trends* (pp. 183–202). New York: Neal-Schuman.

Additional Readings

Campbell, L. (2010). *List of related FAQ/KM technologies.* Retrieved April 4, 2011, from http://www.delicious.com/lisibit/faq.

Evans, G. (2011). LibAnswers. *The Charleston Advisor, 12*(4), 42–45.

## CHAPTER 22

It's Free, It's Interactive, and It's Available to All: Embracing Wikipedia at the Reference Desk and Beyond

Christy Zlatos

Overview

Whether you believe Wikipedia to be an unorthodox information source (Lim & Kwon, 2010) or the next big thing, the ease of use and functionality of the open web makes Wikipedia a potential game changer in the library and at the reference desk. Although few reference librarians are beginning their reference searches with Wikipedia at this time, some librarians are teaching it in information literacy sessions (Jennings, 2008) and many more are editing its entries to provide links to their digital holdings (Belden, 2008, Zentall & Cloutier, 2008; Lally & Dunford, 2007; Pressley & McCallum, 2008). This chapter provides an introduction to the tool, a review of the professional literature, which includes a call to librarians to become active in providing guidelines for Wikipedia use (Lim, 2009), an overview of the perils of using Wikipedia in original work, and advice to promote its optimal use.

Introduction

In this time of recession, library budgets across the United States are diminishing and the dwindling funds are resulting in real sacrifices in personnel, operations, and collections. Wikipedia, the free web-based collaborative encyclopedia, offers searchers free online content that by design offers constant improvement. Google search engine typically ranks Wikipedia articles at the top of results lists, making the online encyclopedia one of the most accessed websites extant (Alexa, n.d.) in a synergy which, according to Vaidhyanathan (2011), promotes the encyclopedia immeasurably, while enabling Google to avoid making judgments in controversial or emotionally charged topics. Because one academic has called Wikipedia potentially "the family encyclopedia of the twenty-first century" (Luyt & Tan, 2010, p. 720), librarians need to learn more about it in order to understand its issues and otherwise find ways to add this e-tool to their arsenal. Wikipedia is enabling countless people worldwide to be more knowledgeable and productive by endowing them with something librarians cherish: a verifiable means to look something up (Anderson, 2009a, p. 130). Although few reference librarians are adding searching Wikipedia into their professional repertoires at this time, some librarians are already teaching it in the information literacy classroom (Jennings, 2008) and others are taking advantage of its popularity by placing links to their e-collections within Wikipedia's articles (Belden, 2008; Zentall & Cloutier, 2008; Lally & Dunford, 2007).

In the ten short years of its existence, Wikipedia content has changed the nature of research for the general public by making encyclopedic information freely available to anyone with a browser and an Internet connection and by presenting a successful alternative publishing model based on the work of a cluster of volunteers without any top-down organizational structure (Lih, 2009, p. 82). Although Wikipedia definitely has improved the ease if not the quality of the research done by the general public overall (Weinberger, 2007; Anderson, 2009a; Vaidhyanathan, 2011), along with other social media sites, it is also changing the encyclopedia publishing business forever. With its web platform and low overhead, Wikipedia has matched or even bested some of its encyclopedia competitors that have had to adopt social media customs to remain viable. *Encyclopaedia Britannica* began taking suggestions from users in 2010 and Microsoft's Encarta was discontinued in 2009 (Anderson, 2009a).

Perhaps Wikipedia's greatest achievement is in assisting in the push for librarians to become less dependent on their library websites as they interact with their clientele in a variety of venues across their communities. Librarian reservations about Wikipedia traditionally have focused around its being a collaborative project in which its mutable, unsigned articles cannot be attributed to any one authority. Lim (2009), however, notes that with Wikipedia's popularity, librarian assistance in the creation of effective information literacy programs that include instruction in using this resource is sorely needed. As librarians enlarge their roles from that of information experts to that of information advocates by becoming more engaged in the knowledge creation in the world at large, some writers even envision the return of these librarians as "public" intellectuals (Bridges, 2008; Luyt, Ally, Low, & Ismail, 2010).

Wikipedia Description and Editorial Policies

Wikipedia's name is a combination of wiki, which is the Hawaiian word for quick, plus "pedia," from encyclopedia (http://en.wikipedia.org/wiki/Wikipedia:About). Anyone can edit Wikipedia, which is written anonymously by unpaid volunteers collaborating through the Internet. Although some of the volunteers are experts, many are not. Wikipedia articles range from undeveloped pieces, called stubs, to lengthy, more finished collaborations that reflect a neutral point of view (NPOV). Two salient points to remember are Wikipedia's great size and stature. In spring 2011, it contained more than 3.5 million articles by 667,571 contributors (http://en.wikipedia.org/wiki/Wikipedia: Size_of_Wikipedia). Alexa, the web ranking company, ranked Wikipedia seventh worldwide, behind Google, Facebook, YouTube, Yahoo!, Blogger.com, and Baidu.com, a Chinese-language search engine (http://www.alexa.com/).

A small number of the articles (to date 3,600 in April 2011 or approximately 1 in 1,000) have achieved "featured article" status as having passed stringent criteria and are designated with a small bronze star. In addition, portals in the lower right-hand portion of the articles help guide users through relevant content. A small number of these (to date 151 of 1,088 in April 2011 or approximately 1 in 7) are designated with bronze stars. Users are encouraged to pay attention to any or all qualitative tags at the top of articles that provide relevant clues about an article's quality (e.g., "This article needs additional citations for verification" or "This article may require clean up to meet Wikipedia's quality standards") (http://en.wikipedia.org/wiki/Wikipedia:Template_messages/Cleanup).

More substantial articles in Wikipedia have a consistent format that contains an introductory paragraph coupled with a clickable outline that provides an overview of a topic. Often a fact box on the right-hand side provides ready-reference facts such as birth and death dates for a person, or population for a place. All work on the articles is immediately made available for user consideration in Wikipedia's customary four-part wiki format that combines the article, a discussion forum (talk), an editing venue, and a history of the edits. Readers should explore these forums to judge the reliability of the writing.

Wikipedia's editorial policies are not petty or trivial but expansive, and meant to empower the editors. An expansion of pillar 5 (following) encourages editors to "be bold." Wikipedia's editorial policies are available over the website as the five pillars (http://en.wikipedia.org/wiki/Wikipedia:5P):

1. Wikipedia is an online encyclopedia.
2. Wikipedia has a neutral point of view.
3. Wikipedia is free content that anyone can edit and distribute.
4. Wikipedians should act in a respectful and civil manner.
5. Wikipedia does not have firm rules.

Jimmy Wales, the cofounder of Wikipedia, wants users to judge Wikipedia not by its contributors but by the quality of contributions. As a collaborative enterprise, Wales says articles have reached a NPOV when people stop changing them (Weinberger, 2007, p. 136). To the question of whether an NPOV is even possible in a digital world with infinite collaborating (or colliding) readers, Weinberger answers, "[Wikipedia] Socratically revels in being corrected" (p. 141).

Wikipedia is a global enterprise with 281 individual sites in most of the languages of the world, with many of the smaller versions struggling to survive. Although the English-language Wikipedia is by far the largest, there are also versions in German, French, Polish, Italian, Spanish, Japanese, Russian, and Dutch languages in descending order by size (http://meta.wikimedia.org/wiki/List_of_Wikipedias). Wikipedia receives its operating expenses from grants and donations. It received a major donation of $3 million over three years from the Sloan Foundation, the largest in its history, in 2008. At least presently, it can shun the cacophony of paid advertisements and pop-ups common to many websites on the Internet. These more traditional practices make the site stand out to many as an oasis on the Internet.

On Balance: Advantages and Disadvantages

Wikipedia utilizes all the functionality that modern information technology has to offer. If Stewart Brand said, "Information wants to be free," then Weinberger (2007) added "that it also wants to be miscellaneous" (p. 7). In the age of the Internet, inexpensive e-storage and lightning-fast processing speeds combine to make this site's unwieldy content quickly and easily searchable with an Internet connection. Whereas Wikipedia, by its very name, begs for comparison with other encyclopedias, Lih's (2009) definition of a global community of contributors "bound together by a passion of volunteering time, energy, and knowledge [to] put together the sum of all human knowledge so that others could have it for free—both as in freedom, and as in cost" (p. 3) seems a better fit, as it describes real people with Web 2.0 tools working together in the creation of something unique.

Early on, the unwieldy hive-produced work showed itself to be different and deserving of its own criteria for discussion that focused on currency and ease of use instead of the more traditional attributes of authority and reliability. Early critics Wallace and Van Fleet (2005) evaluated Wikipedia using Katz's six fundamental criteria for reference works (Katz, 2002, p. 27) and found it lacking. In their excellent critical review, these authors despaired that Wikipedia had no overarching structure and lacked authority, accountability, and an index—all while tying Wikipedia to such democratic institutions as public libraries. Calling it a "force for democratization," like the invention of movable type, the recording and broadcast media, and the Internet itself, they insisted that "the value of Wikipedia may lie entirely in the democratic circumstances under which its articles are created" (Wallace & Van Fleet, 2005, p. 102).

Dalby (2009) traces Wikipedia's genealogy as the heir of a three-prong progression of knowledge products that include the survey of knowledge, the dictionary, and the sourcebook. Further, both Dalby and Lih (2009) suggest that Wikipedia's use of volunteers in pursuit of a common project is not new. Unhappy with the popular dictionaries of Noah Webster and Samuel Johnson, the originators of the *Oxford English Dictionary* (*OED*) solicited English and American volunteers to comb through all the media of the day to inventory all the words in the English language, which were then written on slips and categorized into many pigeon holes and used to make a primitive pre-digital-age database. Both scholars view the *OED* as Wikipedia's closest parallel, because, although processed by hand, the quotations in any long *OED* word definition were submitted by many readers who remained anonymous when the publications of origin were cited (Dalby, 2009; Lih, 2009).

The open Internet and free licensing endow Wikipedia with other advantages as well. The content is freely available and, as such, offers researchers considerable advantage as it can be copied, adapted, attributed, and shared by anyone as they see fit in keeping with the Creative Commons guidelines (http://en.wikipedia.org/wiki/Wikipedia:Text_of_Creative_Commons_AttributionShareAlike_3.0_Unported_License). All changes in Wikipedia are dynamic, thus pushing the envelope and challenging anyone's definition of currency.

While Wikipedia's structure is designed to encourage anybody who sees anything amiss to edit or groom the articles, a small percentage of editors put in the most edits (http://en.wikipedia.org/wiki/Wikipedia:List_of_Wikipedians_by_number_of_edits) and, for Wikipedians, there does seem to be a gaming element to the edits. Although in 2005 Wallace and Van Fleet wrote that "the collaborative nature of the encyclopedia suggests that the primary audience may well be the collaborators themselves" (p. 102), McGrady (2009) shed some light on the community by revealing that "Wikipedia editors have functioned well as a community, having collaboratively developed a comprehensive set of social norms designed to place the project before any individual" and further pointed out that this ethic is called "gaming the system" (p. 1). Perhaps this might explain why many people put in what for some might be a 40-hour workweek editing an encyclopedia. For those who want the solidarity of a social community collaborating on a common project like the Library of Alexandria or the cathedrals of Europe, Wikipedia exemplifies one of the largest common projects in existence today.

Wikipedia is uneven in content, both in terms of the topics covered and the scope of the individual articles included. However, Wikipedians do not view this as a disadvantage because at some point everything gets revised. Instead, they acknowledge that their most formidable disadvantage is that Wikipedia's open contents are prone to vandalism. Among the well-publicized attempts include erroneous information inserted into the journalist John Seigenthaler's biography—that he was involved in the John F. Kennedy assassination; false quotations placed into composer Maurice Jarre's biography—that were picked up by several newspapers after his death; and an entirely bogus article titled the "Baldock Beer Disaster" that was featured briefly on Wikipedia's main page (Lindsey, 2010). Aware of this most formidable drawback, Jimmy Wales enacted countermeasures that included enforced registration and software "bots" to counteract it. Present-day vandals are caught by a four-pronged defense that includes incidental discovery, monitoring recent changes, watching edited pages, and employing bots that revert content back to previous form without human intervention. In some cases, the content is locked and marked with colored padlocks that indicate a level of protection (http://en.wikipedia.org/wiki/Vandalism_on_Wikipedia).

Not Quite Ready for Prime Time: Wikipedia in the Professional Literature

Although Wikipedians view their collaborative style as a distinct advantage that enables them to evaluate, refine, and capitalize on the voices of the many in the pursuit of knowledge production, as a source to cite, Wikipedia at the present time falls short in terms of being viable for the newsroom, the classroom, and the library (Shaw, 2008; Chen, 2010; Luyt et al., 2010). However, that does not mean that Wikipedia should be banished from these venues or that the many that consult Wikipedia, by searching directly or by choosing it as a browser search result, do not find it valuable. Using Wikipedia effectively requires more skepticism and critical thinking to compare, corroborate, and otherwise test the information. In addition, there is the idea that encyclopedias by themselves have never been sufficient information sources. To quote a truism from the literature that has possibly gone viral, "Encyclopedias are a great place to start with, but do not stop there!" (Farrelly, 2008; Fontichiaro & Harvey, 2010; Head & Eisenberg, 2010; Luyt et al., 2010).

In their large-scale study sample of Internet use at the Pew Internet and American Life Project, Zickuhr and Rainie (2011) reported that 53 percent of Internet users looked at Wikipedia in May 2010 (up from 36 percent in February 2007) and, interestingly, that in America it continues to be more popular among college-educated than among lesser-educated users, including high school graduates, and more popular with those who have broadband rather than dial-up connections. Regarding online activities, Zickuhr and Rainie revealed that using Wikipedia is more popular than instant messaging (IM) or rating a product, service, or person, but less popular than using social networking sites or watching videos over YouTube (2011).

Because little is known about how Wikipedia is used, the few use studies that have been done are particularly valuable. Chesney (2006) studied 55 academics regarding Wikipedia's credibility and revealed that experts considered this site's articles more credible than non-experts. Chen (2010) studied 201 academics and found that academic ranking and discipline is key to faculty attitudes regarding Wikipedia in teaching and research. Although the acceptance of Wikipedia is low at this time and many would not think of using it in their teaching and research, faculty with higher academic ranking and/or more online experience were also more comfortable with it.

Several usage studies with students also provide interesting results. Lim (2009) surveyed 134 students in an introductory journalism and mass communication course through an online questionnaire to explore undergraduate perceptions, uses of, and motivations for using Wikipedia based on social cognitive theory (SCT), a framework that focuses on how individuals acquire knowledge through their social encounters and interactions. Approximately one-third of the students reported using Wikipedia for quickly checking facts and finding background information in their academic work. They reported positive experiences with Wikipedia and that their expectations of the information quality were not high. Respondents' past experience with this site, their positive emotional states, and their disposition to believe the information they found, combined with an appreciation of Wikipedia's information utility (ease of use) all factored into reports of what constitutes a good experience. Because Wikipedia is a well-used tool among students, the researcher suggested that educators and librarians need to provide better guidelines for its use.

Lim and Kwon (2010) conducted a study of gender differences in information-seeking behavior using Wikipedia to reveal that its use was consistent with previous studies regarding gender. While both male and female students use the library's resources equally, in their study of 134 students, Lim and Kwon discovered that in using Wikipedia, male students were more likely than female students to discount the risks and embrace it more readily. Male students also received higher ratings in experiencing better outcome expectations from this site, more positive emotional states while using Wikipedia, a greater belief in the Wikipedia project, and more confidence in evaluating the information they found as well as in exploring the website itself. The researchers suggest that in doing so male students develop better information literacy skills and that educators and librarians could narrow the gender gap by encouraging female students to explore unorthodox resources like Wikipedia more strategically.

Head and Eisenberg (2010) conducted a survey of college students of six campuses to find out how and why students use Wikipedia while conducting course-related research. They found that students were far more likely to use it than not, and the use was higher for students in architecture, engineering, or the sciences. For student respondents, the greatest value may be Wikipedia's "ability to alleviate common frustrations students initially have with conducting research" (under "Why Wikipedia," para. 4). One participant called it "my presearch tool" (under "How Wikipedia fits into the research process," para. 5), and presearch was defined as the time when students initially explore and delineate topics.

Menchen-Trevino and Hargittai (2011) analyzed the searching behavior of a diverse group of 210 undergraduates to explore their use of Wikipedia. While noting that many college students have had access to the web from the time they were young and that students first face the responsibilities of adult life at this time, the authors suggested that these burgeoning life experiences also reflected an increased need for credible information. Menchen-Trevino and Hargittai revealed that few students fully understood the Wikipedia knowledge community, although most had some knowledge of how the site functions. Still, a few lacked such basic knowledge as the reality that anyone can edit the site. Although many students had been advised not to use Wikipedia in their academic pursuits, Menchen-Trevino and Hargittai discovered that students readily use it in their everyday lives.

Wikipedia has been framed as a polarized debate in the academic community where academic reputations are made on their knowledge productions (Luyt et al., 2010). Luyt and his collaborators analyzed the polarizing rhetoric that has appeared in several articles (Badke, 2008; Farrelly, 2008; Pressley & McCallum, 2008) before suggesting that the debate may indeed be a strategy to position one's own opinion as middle of the road— "a compromise that is usually in favor of Wikipedia as one tool in the arsenal of the reference librarian"—before concluding that "most librarians although cautious about using Wikipedia in their professional capacity, hold a range of generally positive attitudes towards the online encyclopedia, believing that it has a valid role in the information seeking of patrons today" (Luyt et al., 2010, pp. 57–58).

In order to provide evidence as to what practicing librarians might believe about the issue, Luyt and colleagues conducted a study of volunteers from the National Library Board of Singapore. In this qualitative study of the use of Wikipedia by practicing librarians, a selection of 26 librarians representing a cross-section of genders and work experiences were interviewed to reveal their use of Wikipedia by librarians in both their work and private life, and how librarians viewed Wikipedia's effects on their users (e.g., if Wikipedia was causing a change in how users viewed libraries and librarians).

Luyt and colleagues' (2010) findings are illuminating. While cautious about referring users to Wikipedia during the course of the workday, respondents not only were familiar with the site, but they used it outside of the workplace for the same reasons as their users: convenience, ease of use, and high visibility in browser search results. The key difference noted was that librarians through their training tend to look beyond the text toward resources they could maximize including keywords, definitions, citations, and external links. Luyt and colleagues' (2010) study ends optimistically as the researchers report that the majority of their respondents view Wikipedia favorably as both a means to elevate librarians' status in the community, because complex information needs still require librarian intervention, and as a medium of collaboration that holds a promise of increasing librarian credibility.

Although it would seem rare to see librarians beginning reference searches with Wikipedia or even including a Wikipedia link in a bibliography at this time, librarians are gaining experience with Wikipedia by editing it, by adding their holdings to it, and by teaching it as a part of information literacy (Belden, 2008; Jennings, 2008; Lally & Dunford, 2007; Pressley & McCallum, 2008; Zentall & Cloutier, 2008). Luyt and colleagues (2010) especially mention editing the reference work as a worthwhile activity that would promote the credibility of librarians. Other librarians, after realizing its impressive user statistics, are becoming editors after registering to add links in Wikipedia to their library's digital resources—notably Dreanna Belden at the University of North Texas (Belden, 2008), Lena Zentall and Camille Cloutier at the California Digital Library (Zentall & Cloutier, 2008), Ann Lally and Carolyn Dunford at the University of Washington (Lally & Dunford, 2007), and Lauren Pressley and Carolyn McCallum of Wake Forest University (Pressley & McCallum, 2008).

Jennings (2008) advocates that librarians use Wikipedia to teach information literacy and, in his excellent article, notes how a discussion of Wikipedia's attributes might fit within the frame of the Association of College and Research Libraries (ACRL) *Information Literacy Competency Standards for Higher Education* (Association of College and Research Libraries, 2000). Table 22.1 covers each of the five information literacy standards and uses Wikipedia to demonstrate each.

Use with Care: Perils of Cut-and-Paste for Wikipedia Content

Because pasting Wikipedia content into websites and print productions is very easy, care must always be taken to recommend using its text responsibly, so users understand its ethical use. In a recent study of student paper matches conducted during spring 2011, the plagiarism detection website Turnitin reported that Wikipedia was the most popular site on the Internet for matched content and that the site accounted for 7 percent of its total matches overall (Turnitin, 2011). The reasons for not citing Wikipedia content are numerous; some professors will not accept Wikipedia content, and citing this content may require more thought. The Turnitin authors, however, are optimistic that early instruction in information ethics will go a long way in reducing text that is copied without citations as students are beginning to approach the wealth of information available to them.

The perils of using Wikipedia in published research were never demonstrated more clearly than in Anderson's (2009b) book, *Free: The Future of a Radical Price*. Although Doris Kearns Goodwin and Stephen Ambrose are examples of two modern historians who received bad press for not properly citing their sources (Jennings, 2008), Anderson

Table 22.1. Using Wikipedia to Demonstrate the ACRL Information Literacy Competency Standards

	Standard	Application
1.	Determines the nature and extent of the information needed.	Use to understand a topic or idea.
2.	Accesses needed information effectively and efficiently.	Use to brainstorm keywords.
3.	Evaluates information and its sources critically.	Use as a starting point while explaining the limitations of encyclopedias as resources.
4.	Uses information effectively to accomplish a specific purpose.	Use to discuss different media to do specific things—notably wikis, knowledge of these will help students later in life.
5.	Understands many of the economic, legal, and social issues surrounding the use of information and uses information ethically and legally.	Use to discuss citing one's sources—Wikipedians cite sources in order to make their knowledge product credible.

Source: From Jennings, E. (2008). Using Wikipedia to teach information literacy. *College & Undergraduate Libraries*, 15(4), 432–437.

hit new heights in the press and the blogosphere when Jaquith (2009) of the *Virginia Quarterly Review* accused Anderson of plagiarizing substantial passages from Wikipedia in *Free*. Anderson's actions were not malicious in intention, but rather the result of adopting an "in-line" citation style for the book at the last minute that credited authored sources in the text rather than extensive footnoting when references to Wikipedia (without an author to credit) as well as a few authored sites were unceremoniously dropped. After freely admitting that his citation method was flawed in *Free* and that some of the historical background for the book (rather than the main ideas) came from Wikipedia, the author later published what became extensive notes and citations online for readers over his blog, *The Long Tail* (Anderson, 2009a).

In a dynamic online space, Jaquith (2009) carefully traced the questionable passages with their attributions on the VQRonline blog, lining up Anderson's text with the Wikipedia entries side-by-side with the offending parts bolded in yellow. In all, Jaquith revealed five questionable passages from Wikipedia. In explaining the considerable difficulties in citing online texts, Jaquith noted that Wikipedia presented a particular challenge because under Wikipedia's Creative Commons (CC) Attribution-Share Alike 3.0 license, Anderson would have been required to credit all the contributors, license his modifications with a similar CC license, note that the original work had been modified, and provide a link or the text of the license. Although easier to do in an online environment with hyperlinks than in the static print environment, Anderson decided to solve the problem in *Free* by avoiding the issue. Anderson spent 18 months crafting the work and stirred up controversy because scholars, including librarians, were outraged at what they viewed as the author's shoddy scholarship.

These actions, although shocking to librarians teaching information literacy classes, were not in the slightest bit illegal, but rather, as Vaidhyanathan (2009) notes in a *Publisher's Weekly* "Soapbox" editorial, violate "the norms of a reading community, not the law" (p. 132). Vaidhyanathan (2009) also asserts that the obsession with "plagiarism, originality, and copyright" has led us to conflate "the sin of borrowing passages with the crime of copyright infringement" that has driven us to become hypervigilant and run student papers through computer programs in order to assess their originality (p. 132). Wanting to see a lessening of what he termed the "gotcha" culture, Vaidhyanathan stressed that Anderson's mistakes were at the expense of the reading public who were deprived of additional information and, in general, the craft of writing rather than the work itself. He believes that Anderson's *Free* "revealed some of the most awkward truths about reading and writing in a digital environment" (p. 132), where ease of use and patchwriting combine to make it very easy-to-create text. The incident showed that scholarship is alive and well (in the world and over the web) and that readers still want to see the details in the notes.

Using Wikipedia's Gift: How Reference Librarians Can Embrace This Content

As this review of the literature has shown, library users are visiting Wikipedia regularly to satisfy their information needs, and most are doing it with an understanding of its collaborative style of authorship. Certainly peer pressure among colleagues would mitigate against starting reference searches with Wikipedia at this point in time when librarians have the whole panoply of reference works and subscription databases at their disposal. However, consulting Wikipedia publicly in those instances where the encyclopedia honestly might shed light on an inquiry will go a long way toward improving Wikipedia's reputation in the library.

Because it is hard for librarians to ignore the fact that Wikipedia is freely available to everyone with an Internet connection in many languages throughout the world, librarians need to appreciate its benefits by using it in order to develop an understanding of how it complements the knowledge landscape. In doing so, it is useful to note from the research that many people use Wikipedia for their "low stakes" rather than "high stakes" information needs (Menchen-Trevino & Hargittai, 2011) and as a very tentative and casual way to check something out, what Head and Eisenberg's (2010) students called "presearch" (gaining keywords and links before formally researching something). For colleagues who treat every reference encounter as a "high stakes" need for information, "presearching" with Wikipedia may come as an added new wrinkle that might hold a bonus.

Recognizing that some library users will not understand Wikipedia's collaborative editing (Menchen-Trevino & Hargittai, 2011), librarians should talk about it during the course of their reference encounters while demonstrating Wikipedia's wiki four-part structure. Although writers in the professional literature have suggested that Wikipedia's credibility issues make it more appropriate for the information literacy classroom rather than at the reference desk, Wikipedia offers reference librarians a great way to closely confer with users while exploring and discussing Wikipedia's credibility issues together. Reilly (2011) thinks of each part of the wiki's structure as a mirror rather than a window that is "multilayered and complex, requiring critical reflexivity" for productive consideration (Reilly, 2011, under "Abstract," para. 4). The quality of the conversation on the talk pages and the amount, dates, and types of edits to an article all provide clues to be used to assess an article's quality.

General encyclopedia content has never been sufficient in and of itself as the one quoted source in any reference inquiry or student paper, and Wikipedia should not become the exception. Especially in consideration of Wikipedia's collaborative authorship, information needs to be compared (with another information source) or, better yet, corroborated (with several information sources), a technique that Meola (2004) notes is "common in situations where the truth of information is in dispute, such as in journalism, witness testimony, or government intelligence work" (p. 341).

Wikipedia's strengths for use at a library's reference desk can only be assessed by the experience gained through using it, always noting the fact that its articles are in flux. Wikipedia's popularity, its ease of use, and its informal, not-quite-ready-but-needs-verification quality are persistent themes that appear throughout the articles. The advice consulted to write this article has been collected to produce Table 22.2.

Some authors believe that Wikipedia is emerging quickly to become as ubiquitous as browsers (Dalby, 2009; Weinberger, 2007). When that time comes, librarian inquiries about the results of user "presearching" as well as tentative Wikipedia searches with users to clarify their information needs may become the new standard features of reference sessions before getting into the more demanding bibliography that has always been the stock and trade of librarians. Until that time, reference librarians are invited to experience Wikipedia's gift: to search the site, to edit articles with the community, and/or add links

Table 22.2. Advice from the Professional Literature: When/When Not to Use Wikipedia	
When to Use Wikipedia	**When Not to Use Wikipedia/Caveats**
Use in the **first steps of a research process** [or] as a **last-ditch opportunity** for an overview, definitions, links, and keywords associated with esoteric terms (Luyt et al., 2010). Students call first steps **"presearch"** (Head & Eisenberg, 2010).	**Never use as a sole source** in any formal research inquiry without verification. Be sure to mention Wikipedia's style of collaborative, user-generated authorship and ways to investigate the links (references), conversation about the edits (talk), and history of the edits (Menchen-Trevino & Hargittai, 2011).
Use when there is a **need for convenience**, or as a first stop when working with a young, born digital patron who doesn't use or understand print resources (Luyt et al., 2010).	**Better for patrons' low stakes** rather than high-stakes needs for information (Menchen-Trevino and Hargittai, 2011).
Excellent source of **non-Western information** including the spellings and definitions of international words (Luyt et al., 2010).	Pay attention to **the possibility of bias** in "hot button" issues such as controversial and sensitive issues in Wikipedia as well as all reference works (Menchen-Trevino & Hargittai, 2011).
Excellent source of **world news** events within hours of occurrence such as the Tōhoku Earthquake and Tsunami of 2011; **sports coverage for international events** such as World Soccer or the Olympics; recent **world entertainment topics** as films, popular music, and television productions; and **worldwide popular culture**.	Better for events, sports, entertainment, and popular culture topics **that occurred more recently** than those topics that happened or were popular long ago. Users need to consider Wikipedia's short 10-year lifespan (Dalby, 2009).
Excellent source of information on **geographical locations** worldwide.	Because Wikipedians get unlimited space for writing, sometimes the information gets unwieldy and time-consuming to pick through (Dalby, 2009).
With caveats, excellent source of **biographical information** for world notables, particularly popular biography.	Understand that **biography has been a live area for self-serving edits and outright vandalism.** PR pros and congressional staffers have been known to edit their bosses' bios with glorified content, and the CIA and vandals have been known to have erroneously planted contents.

to their library's holdings to enrich the whole, and to teach others effective, efficient, and responsible ways to utilize the content.

Conclusion

This chapter examines Wikipedia at this point and time as a viable information resource and considers its use by reference librarians as a "not-quite-ready-for-prime time" resource. Because of its high ranking in browser search results and its ease of use, Wikipedia is emerging as an informal, tentative, and even playful way to glean useful intelligence about a topic.

The research studies into how Wikipedia is being used clearly show the need for librarian guidelines and support in its use. Studies that show Wikipedia was more favored by college-educated users than by high school graduates (Zickuhr & Rainie, 2011), more utilized by higher ranking faculty than lower ranking colleagues (Chen, 2010), more confidently used by male students than female students (Lim & Kwon, 2010), and more used by students in engineering, architecture, or the sciences than those in other subjects (Head & Eisenberg, 2010) are fascinating to consider and indicate areas for future librarian focus.

Librarians should realize a need to become better acquainted with this knowledge resource. By taking advantage of their users' Wikipedia searching and talking with them about its collaborative nature, by expanding reference encounters to include discussions of Wikipedia's four-part structure and responsible use of the content, and by conducting Wikipedia searches at the desk whenever relevant, reference librarians will begin to work the tool into the course of their routines. Why not take advantage of this resource as another free e-resource that can be leveraged in these difficult budget times to provide starting points and quick reference for low-stakes searches while cautioning users to verify information as appropriate? Is not this thus building their skill set for the future?

References

Alexa. (n.d.). Topsites: *The top 500 sites on the web*. Retrieved July 13, 2011, from http://www.alexa.com/topsites.

Anderson, C. (2009a). Corrections in the digital editions of *Free*. Retrieved July 13, 2011, from http://www.longtail.com/the_long_tail/2009/06/corrections-in-the-digital-editions-of-free.html.

Anderson, C. (2009b). *Free: The future of a radical price*. New York: Hyperion.

Association of College and Research Libraries. (2000). *Information literacy competency standards for higher education*. Chicago, IL: American Library Association. Retrieved July 13, 2011, from http://www.ala.org/ala/mgrps/divs/acrl/standards/informationliteracycompetency.cfm.

Badke, W. (2008). What to do with Wikipedia. *Online*, *32*(2), 48.

Belden, D. (2008). Harnessing social networks to connect with audiences: If you build it they will come 2.0? *Internet Reference Services Quarterly*, *13*(1), 99–111.

Bridges, K. (2008, March/April). Librarians and the attention economy. *Library Philosophy and Practice*. Retrieved July 13, 2011, from http://www.webpages.uidaho.edu/~mbolin/bridges3.pdf.

Chen, H. (2010). The perspectives of higher education faculty on Wikipedia. *The Electronic Library*, *28*(3), 361–373.

Chesney, T. (2006). An empirical examination of Wikipedia's credibility. *First Monday*, *11*(11). Retrieved July 13, 2011, from http:firstmonday.org/htbin/cgiwrap/bin/ojs/index.php/fm/article/view/1413/1331.

Dalby, A. (2009). *The world and Wikipedia: How we are editing reality*. Draycott, Somerset, England: Siduri Books.

Farrelly, M. (2008).Wiki-what? *Public Libraries*, *47*(4), 30–31.

Fontichiaro, K., & Harvey, C. (2010). How elementary is Wikipedia? *School Library Monthly*, *27*(2), 22–23.

Head, A., & Eisenberg, M. (2010). How today's college students use Wikipedia for course-related research. *First Monday*, *15*(3). Retrieved July 13, 2011, from http://firstmonday.org/htbin/cgiwrap/bin/ojs/index.php/fm/article/view/2830/2476.

Jaquith, W. (2009, June 23). Chris Anderson's *Free* contains apparent plagiarisms. Retrieved May 1, 2011, from http://www.vqronline.org/blog/2009/06/23/chris-anderson-free/.

Jennings, E. (2008). Using Wikipedia to teach information literacy. *College and Undergraduate Libraries*, *15*(4), 432–437.

Katz, W. (2002). *Introduction to reference work, volume 1: Basic information services* (8th ed.). Boston, MA: McGraw-Hill.

Lally, A., & Dunford, C. (2007). Using Wikipedia to extend digital collections. *D-Lib Magazine*, *13*(5–6). Retrieved May 1, 2011, from http://www.dlib.org/dlib/may07/lally/05lally.html.

Lih, A. (2009). *The Wikipedia Revolution: How a bunch of nobodies created the world's greatest encyclopedia*. New York: Hyperion.

Lim, S. (2009). How and why do students use Wikipedia? *Journal of the American Society for Information Science and Technology*, *60*(11), 2198–2202.

Lim, S., & Kwon, N. (2010). Gender differences in information behavior concerning Wikipedia, an unorthodox information source? *Library and Information Science Research*, *32*(3), 212–220.

Lindsey, D. (2010). Evaluating quality control of Wikipedia's feature articles. *First Monday*, *15*(4). Retrieved July 13, 2011, from http://firstmonday.org/htbin/cgiwrap/bin/ojs/index.php/fm/article/view/2721/2482.

Luyt, B., Ally, Y., Low, N., & Ismail, N. (2010). Librarian perception of Wikipedia: Threats or opportunities for librarianship? *Libri*, *60*(4), 57–64.

Luyt, B., & Tan, D. (2010). Improving Wikipedia's credibility: References and citations in a sample of history articles. *Journal of the American Society for Information Science and Technology*, *61*(4), 715–722.

McGrady, R. (2009). Gaming against the greater good. *First Monday*, *14*(2). Retrieved July 13, 2011, from http://firstmonday.org/htbin/cgiwrap/bin/ojs/index.php/fm/article/view/2215/2091.

Menchen-Trevino, E., & Hargittai, E. (2011). Young adults' credibility assessment of Wikipedia. *Information, Communication, & Society*, *14*(1), 24–51.

Meola, M. (2004). Chucking the checklist: A contextual approach to teaching undergraduates web-site evaluation. *portal: Libraries and the Academy*, *4*(3), 331–344.

Pressley, L., & McCallum, C. (2008). Putting the library in Wikipedia. *Online*, *32*(5), 39–42.

Reilly, C. (2011). Teaching Wikipedia as a mirrored technology. *First Monday*, *16*(1–3). Retrieved July 13, 2011, from http://firstmonday.org/htbin/cgiwrap/bin/ojs/index.php/fm/article/view/2824/2746.

Shaw, D. (2008, February/March). Wikipedia in the newsroom. *American Journalism Review*, *30*(1), 40–45.

Turnitin. (2011). *Plagiarism and the web myths and realities: An analytical study on where students find unoriginal content on the Internet*. Retrieved July 13, 2011, from http://pages.turnitin.com/PlagiarismandtheWebSEC.html.

Vaidhyanathan, S. (2009). Anderson's wiki-versy. *Publisher's Weekly*, *256*(26), 132.

Vaidhyanathan, S. (2011). *The Googlization of everything (and why we should worry)*. Berkeley, CA: University of California Press.

Wallace, D., & Van Fleet, C. (2005). The democratization of information? Wikipedia as a reference resource. *Reference and User Services Quarterly*, *45*(2), 100–103.

Weinberger, D. (2007). *Everything is miscellaneous: The power of the new digital disorder*. New York: Times Books.

Zentall, L., & Cloutier, C. (2008). The Calisphere Wikipedia project: Lessons learned. *CSLA Journal*, *32*(1), 27–29.

Zickuhr, K., & Rainie, L. (2011, January 13). *Wikipedia, past and present.* Washington, DC: Pew Research Center's Internet & Life Project. Retrieved July 13, 2011, from http://pewinternet .org/Reports/2011/Wikipedia.aspx.

CHAPTER 23

Addicted to Print:
Overcoming Book Lust in the Academic
Library Reference Collection

Mary Krautter

Overview

Traditional patterns of collection development for reference collections have changed radically as most reference sources have become available online. Transitioning reference collections from print to electronic is ongoing and necessary, but a number of factors must be taken into account. In managing a reference collection in the online environment, change is inevitable, and reference departments must deal with resistance to change from staff members in a positive manner. Decisions on the physical collection and space needs for users are strongly linked, with reductions in the traditional print collection potentially freeing up space that can be devoted to library users. Changing models of ownership of materials and budgeting readjustments are also essential factors in managing a reference collection that is increasingly online.

Introduction

Electronic journals, books, and reference materials have radically changed the way in which librarians provide reference service, and these new formats are also transforming collection development models. In the past, the ideal reference librarian was a variation on the stereotypical professorial "Sage on the Stage," a model reflected in the Katharine Hepburn character in the 1957 movie *Desk Set*, in which the librarian was the ultimate expert, the dispenser of all research knowledge. The quick and generally accurate provision of obscure knowledge is now most often provided through a Google search. Previously invaluable print directories of information such as addresses and phone numbers, if still published and purchased, are very rarely consulted, and many other types of ready-reference works have been superseded by online searches. The library reference desk is still a vital point of service, but the kinds of assistance that librarians now provide require very different types of resources than the print collections so carefully acquired in the past. Authoritative and reliable web-based subject encyclopedias now predominate in reference collection development. However, print resources and old models of collection building still have a certain allure. While public libraries with limited space may be comfortable with the idea of discarding reference books, in academic libraries, the past mission of making in-depth research possible through exhaustive holding of physical volumes can make contemplating needed changes more painful.

Around the middle of the past decade, titles in the professional literature were clearly reflecting the changing balance between print and electronic reference. In recent years, the death, or at least the terminal illness, of print reference has been almost universally acknowledged, but the change in attitudes and practices has been quite rapid. In 2005, the observation was made that "It is foolish to assume that online sources are on the verge of replacing all traditional reference sources; however, it is also foolish to deny the importance of the electronic format" (Puacz, 2005, p. 50). In the same year, it also was proposed that "serious consideration should be given to reallocating at least some of the library's reference budget from print sources to electronic sources" (Bradford, Costello, & Lenholt, 2005, p. 271). In the journal *Acquisitions Librarian*, the question was posed in the article title, "Are Research Libraries Favoring Electronic Access over Print?" with the conclusion, "The trend . . . is to cease receiving print versions of titles in lieu of electronic access" (Robbins, McCain, & Scrivener, 2006, p. 92). Additional questions were seen in article titles in 2008: "Are Reference Books Becoming an Endangered Species?" (Heintzelman, Moore, & Ward, 2008) and "Is Print Reference Dead?" (Polanka, 2008), with a 2009 article sounding a death knell: "Reference 2.0: The Future of Shrinking Print Reference Collections Seems Destined for the Web" (Hellyer, 2009). The authors of "Shelflessness as a Virtue: Preserving Serendipity in an Electronic Reference Collection" assume the predominance of e-reference and propose more effective organization of such sources (Ford, O'Hara, & Whiklo, 2009). What would have once been heresy for an academic library was stated emphatically by Barclay (2010): "The one certainty is that the continued over-my-dead body insistence that no books be removed from campus libraries is an unsustainable position that, sooner or later, must give way to new ways of managing and using academic libraries" (p. 54). Spiro and Henry (2010) pose the ultimate question in their article's title: "Can a New Research Library Be All-Digital?"

Recently, in weeding the library's storage facility, the author encountered a 700+-page bibliography on strawberries published in the mid-1970s. When it was published, such a title might have been very useful, but it is now difficult to imagine how such work would be more than very rarely, if ever, needed. Yet for an academic librarian, who for many years assumed that much of the prestige of a university library collection rested on volume counts, making the decision to discard this title gave momentary pause. This reaction was based on a quick flash of book lust, rather than any rational thought that the book might be needed by that dedicated scholar committed to researching the history of the strawberry and patient enough to wait for staff to retrieve it from the staff-only storage collection. Ruminating on changes in research titles and trends in libraries, a quick WorldCat search revealed 92,320 books in the database with publication dates from 1970–1979 and having the word "bibliography" in the title, while the same search for the dates 2000–2009 revealed only 15,883 WorldCat book titles. And, yes, the decision was made to weed that attractively bound title in pristine condition that had not circulated for at least 10 years, keeping in mind that the university in question has no agriculture program and that the library has limited space. Most similar decisions in this weeding project, which focused on titles in the LC classification of Z, were made more quickly and with less consideration; clearly, most bibliographies are not essential to modern research needs. The universe of publishing and scholarship has changed, and electronic models have made some materials superfluous. For the most part, librarians have embraced new models of research based on e-resources as society as a whole has embraced the electronic availability of information.

Numerous recent surveys have indicated that new purchases in reference departments are predominately electronic. In a survey of 133 public and academic libraries located in New York State, most respondents reported that in the past 5 years the size of their libraries' print reference collections had decreased (82.9 percent), while only 6.5 percent said that the reference collection size had increased (Kessler, 2010, p. 39). Another recent survey indicated that 77 percent of respondents were purchasing more or equal amounts of e-reference than print reference (Korah, Cassidy, Elmore, & Jerabek, 2009, p. 276). Singer's (2010) history of ready-reference collections reads almost like an elegy to the vanishing print collections—a nostalgic trip back to the past. As with any relatively rapid change, however, adjustments can be complex and difficult.

Along with the widespread and usually enthusiastic adoption of databases and e-journals, there is still a remnant of book lust in reference departments in this transitional phase. Most reference librarians embrace the progression that has transformed reference transactions from a provision of the ideal reference book to the provision of the perfect online source, but in many cases, reference librarians are developing new models of service while often grappling with previous models of reference collection building. Remnants of the past still linger as decisions are made on the fate of actual physical volumes. Some critical elements to consider in contemplating reference collections in this time of transition include the following: taking into account the human element as changes are made; determining the fate of print collections; examining library budgets and ensuring that they reflect current needs instead of historical patterns; and making wise purchasing decisions based on new publishing models.

The Human Element: Setting the Stage for Change

One consideration whenever change occurs is the reaction of individuals and sometimes the conflict created between those with differing attitudes. One normal human response to change is to cling to the old ways of doing things. However, others might embrace change quickly and display impatience toward those who are less fervent converts. The evidence is clear that librarians are purchasing and using e-reference sources, but the issue of the print collection can become a particular sticking point. The volumes are there in the reference area, and they are occasionally useful; the relative merits of keeping reference materials and discarding or at least moving them into circulating collections or storage facilities can become sources of debate. Revising budget patterns can be equally controversial, particularly if territoriality comes into play.

Conflict in viewing reference collections most often occurs when a radical change is viewed as an attack on the past. If a service or collection created in the past is viewed as old-fashioned and superfluous, then those who were instrumental in the creation process may feel that their previous efforts are not being respected or valued. The message can easily move from "change is wonderful" to "change is threatening."

Some debates are seen as a generational conflict, with older librarians valuing the reference collections they have created and used so well, and younger librarians becoming impatient with the slow rate of e-adoption. However, not all conflicts can be so easily categorized. Change can also be disconcerting to anyone comfortable with current routines. Both traditionalists and innovators need to view the transformation of existing collections and services necessitated by new types of reference materials as building on the past, not sweeping it away, with the continuing goal of providing needed information.

The types of changes necessitated by conversion to e-resources vary tremendously; changes in service models have been taking place over many years, but often changes in physical facilities and collections, budgeting patterns, and purchasing decisions have lagged behind, for a variety of reasons. Reactions to modifications in all of these areas may vary. As with any change, communication and consensus building are key elements— those who have a voice in the change process are much more likely to work productively and cooperatively in designing new systems.

Print Collections: What Do We Do with All the Books?

In viewing the reference area, deciding what to do with physical volumes can be one of the most vexing problems, and the area in which print addiction is most evident. Traditionally, librarians have a great fondness for physical books, even as they are using them less and less. Academic librarians are particularly prone to be strongly attached to print, having a traditional mission to build large and comprehensive collections. Inclusion in the Association of Research Libraries (ARL) group has traditionally been based to a large extent on the number of physical volumes held. Both public and academic librarians have been very proud of the reference collections built over the years and can relate stories of that perfect answer to a reference question coming from an obscure dusty volume. Librarians have nostalgia for those attractively bound volumes which served users so well, and in tight budget times, contemplating weeding materials that the library has spent many thousands of dollars accumulating can be particularly painful. The more attractive option of transferring these materials to library stacks is often difficult; many libraries are faced with a lack of space or insufficient technical services help to do the conversion or deal with backlogs. Funding for new buildings to house little-used materials has become a very hard sell, even on university campuses which have prided themselves on high-volume counts.

One of the impulses in terms of reference collections is to keep materials, if space is still available and budgets do not allow librarians to refashion existing space. Certainly, designing and implementing a careful and thorough weeding project is difficult and time-consuming, and ultimately, a somewhat unrewarding task (Singer, 2008). Radical transitions are often born of necessity during projects such as remodeling or moving to a new space, but discarding older materials can certainly affect how users ultimately view collections. In-depth descriptions of downsizing projects for particular collections, such as that of Delwiche and Bianchi (2006), note substantial benefits, including the discarding of dated materials, thus creating a collection in which useful materials became more visible and more attractive to users. Lee (2009) notes the difficulty of getting librarians to view weeding as a priority, but also talks about the improvement to the collection by removing outdated materials.

Librarians can be motivated to weed by developing a vision of user-centered space, replacing book-oriented space devoted to warehousing huge collections. As service models are transformed, the need for computers to access e-resources is clear. Librarians also need space to work with researchers who need assistance, and moving seldom-used volumes to create this needed space can help alleviate the withdrawal from print addiction. Weeding just to clean out space is not a strong motivation, but weeding to create a more modern learning commons model space that benefits library users can provide the needed impetus and can be very appealing to staff.

If decisions are made to weed or transfer volumes, whatever the motivation, these decisions need to be made based on usage data whenever possible. Making data-based decisions requires less agonizing and often requires less time than subjective title-by-title decisions. Kessler's (2010) study of New York libraries clearly reflects that reference collection weeding is not often based on use studies, but rather tends to be subjective. Only about 12 percent of reference departments conducted regular use studies, while fewer than 50 percent collected data by measuring reshelving of volumes. This study also showed that librarians acknowledge light use of print reference, with about 40 percent of those surveyed indicating that less than 20 percent of the reference collection was used in the past year. If data indicate that a book has not been used in several years, the decision to transfer to the stacks might be a simple one. Unfortunately, use of individual volumes in reference collections has often not been tracked. Tracking individual use of items used in house, particularly if these are not bar coded, can be an extremely time-consuming project, and realistically, at least a year's worth of data is needed to make good weeding decisions.

However, if a weeding project is a future possibility, some form of usage data is essential. If reference items are not currently counted, some method of tracking use of individual titles, even the very low-tech method of placing stick-on dots to volumes as they are reshelved, can make the process more palatable. The strongest resistance to moving reference materials out of proximity to the reference desk is likely to occur when no hard data about use are available. Even reshelving counts can be convincing—it is hard to argue that for the necessity of keeping all materials close at hand when such counts reveal that fewer than 10 percent are used in an individual year, as a study at Stetson University revealed (Bradford, 2005).

Even those who acknowledge the relatively low use of collections and are committed to discarding materials might suffer pangs of book lust. An alternative to consider if discarding materials is too painful would be offering print volumes to other libraries that might be unable to afford needed e-resources. If materials must be weeded, local recycling programs or alternatives such as Better World Books (http://www.betterworld books.com), which raises funds for literacy and has saved many millions of books from landfills, should be considered. The public relations nightmares that are possible when books are tossed in a dumpster should be clearly understood; members of the university community are often even more print addicted than librarians and will make known their outrage over discarded books, sometimes by contacting local media and even retrieving books from dumpsters, as happened during a Virginia Tech weeding project (Metz & Gray, 2005, p. 276).

Budgeting: Letting Go of OUR Money?

Potential changes in the physical reference collection can be obviously linked to print addiction. However, another form of adjustment to change is moving away from the assumption that a librarian's spending of an entire allocated budget indicates admirable performance. That sentiment is seen outside libraries, of course; many organizations have budgets based on the "use it or lose it" principle of financial management. This philosophy is one of the factors that has made the transformations of library budget patterns particularly difficult. Overall, the conversion of funds to e-resources is well under way. A 2009 survey revealed that 77 percent of academic reference librarians are buying more e-books than print and that those who bought more print tended to be from smaller academic libraries. The survey also collected data on how electronic titles are handled in the budget. Approximately 37 percent of respondents indicated that they were handled in the general reference budget, and 31 percent stated that they were part of the general institutional budget. An additional 15 percent said that there were specific budget lines in their respective institutions for the purchase of electronic reference books (Korah et al., 2009). Clearly, the commitment to purchasing e-reference materials has progressed more quickly than general agreement on how to budget funds for such purchases.

Older budgeting formats for academic libraries leaned heavily on budgets allocated by subject. Particularly during the 1970s and 1980s, there were numerous articles published detailing elaborate systems of budget allocation in university libraries, as reflected in Budd's (1991) "Allocation Formulas in the Literature: A Review" and Werking's (1988) "Allocating the Academic Library's Book Budget: Historical Perspectives and Current Reflections" (see also Casserly, 2008). In practice, collection development was often tied to the idea that bibliographers who were effective stewards of departmental budgets must spend all allocated funds, and the idea predominated that properly representing an academic area meant spending the allocated funds, thus indicating need and ensuring that budgets were maintained for future purchases. Budgets tended to be format and discipline based, and each department might have separate funds for monographs, serials, and continuations. Budgets were most often allocated historically; if the library budget was cut overall, then most often each subject budget was cut by an equal percentage. In academic libraries, budget models still often follow these patterns, and liaisons to academic departments go to battle on behalf of their subject areas. After all, liaisons work most directly with faculty and students and best understand their needs and should advocate on their behalf—a maxim still very often relied upon. As new formats, particularly interdisciplinary databases and e-journal packages, began to predominate, in many cases, new funds were created for new types of materials, but, frequently, previous allocations were not substantially reduced. However, addiction to past spending patterns and territoriality should be reviewed as carefully as addiction to print resources. A budget crisis might be needed to trigger a careful examination of spending patterns, but maintaining previous patterns out of habit, loyalty, or lethargy does not serve collections well.

In the past, reference budgets were viewed in much the same way as subject budgets, with good management being equated with expending all available funds. Toward the end of a budgeting cycle, reference departmental reminders would go out asking for suggested purchases, and those tendencies often continue. However, currently, electronic reference materials are often available in large subject packages, such as those provided by Oxford, Gale, and Credo, which replace the print materials that might have been purchased individually in the past. Reference budgets should be rigorously examined to determine that the most efficient use of increasingly limited funds is being made.

As head of the Reference Department at the University of North Carolina at Greensboro (UNCG), the author has tried to carefully consider actual needs of the reference collection as well as look at the value of the materials acquired. In the past three years, prompted initially by library-wide budget cuts, the department has been examining holdings in such areas as reference continuations, and has shifted funds from the reference monograph budget to support databases in specific subject areas. From the 2007–2008 fiscal year to 2009–2010, the overall reference budget allocation has been reduced by 33 percent, and percentage of funds spent on print sources in 2009–2010 was only 39 percent of the smaller total budget, as opposed to 78 percent expended on print sources in 2007–2008. During the 2010–2011 fiscal year, these trends had accelerated, and the final budget expenditures for print were even lower. The percentage of funds spent on e-resources is becoming more appropriately aligned with current needs. The decision was also made to voluntarily transfer some funds from reference to support materials paid for from a central database fund, a move away from the old territorial model of expending funds in order to ensure future levels of funding.

In a similar move, when reference continuations were reviewed in the summer of 2009, as a response to an overall budget reduction for the library, approximately 66 percent of the budget was cut, well in excess of the requested reduction of 10 to 20 percent. Changes included cancellations and reductions in the frequency of some reference materials. Some of the print materials cut were duplicated by electronic formats, but without a careful review, purchases of these might have continued. Additional cuts for print reference sources will and should continue, based on their relatively low use and the needs of users. Voluntarily reducing funding has required a change in the way in which budgets are viewed, emphasizing the overall needs of the collection, as opposed to maintaining the budget for the reference department at an unnecessarily high level.

For all reference collections, other budget factors can greatly change the way in which materials are provided and funds are expended. In many states, the existence of a statewide virtual library has long been a critical factor, since often such virtual collections provide valuable reference resources. Funding models vary from state to state, but clearly smaller public and academic libraries have greatly increased the electronic resources available to their users. Recent trends indicate that library budgets are being slashed. In *Library Journal*'s annual budget 2010 survey, 72 percent of respondents reported experiencing budget cuts (Kelley, 2011, p. 28). Academic libraries are facing similar situations. Drake (2010) reported on a survey that found 85 percent of libraries expected flat or decreased budgets in 2011, and noted, "Libraries are dealing with the declines in budgets by reducing acquisitions of books, journals, databases, and other information products and services" (p. 19). Clearly, in this economic climate, sources of electronic information will be vulnerable in coming years, but even more clearly, duplication of materials in print and electronic formats is not a responsible use of limited funds.

Publishing Models: Just Tell Me What It Costs!

For that portion of the reference budget still devoted to individual electronic reference titles, additional complexities abound in making purchasing decisions. Sources that restrict printing and downloading capabilities can quickly become frustrating for librarians and users and reduce the value of the sources. Searching individual words and terms throughout e-reference sources should be efficient and easy; a virtual index is most often far better than the old print versions. To maximize use and to facilitate locating titles, catalog records are essential for individual titles, and if vendors provide high-quality records, large packages of titles can be downloaded into the online catalog quickly and easily. As more libraries add discovery tools such as Summon from SerialsSolutions (http://www.serialssolutions.com/summon/) or Ebsco's Discovery Service (http://www .ebscohost.com/discovery/), the ability to retrieve reference works through these is crucial in more seamlessly integrating such sources into the research process. All of these factors enter into purchasing decisions.

Previously, when print predominated, materials were purchased and left on the shelves, unless withdrawn when newer editions were purchased or if the information became hopelessly outdated. Budget cuts might mean no new editions were bought, but older materials were still available and in some cases, still served the needed purpose. However, currently venerable works such as the *Oxford English Dictionary* (http:// www.oed.com/) are accessed electronically, and there is no guarantee that a budget cut will not completely eliminate access. Decisions about weeding print volumes can be more difficult when factoring in this uncertainty.

One of the adjustments in purchasing reference materials stems from new publishing models, including subscriptions to encyclopedias and data sets that are continuously updated. Subscription fees often include invaluable updates, and perhaps are not that different from purchasing print supplements, but in almost all cases, this model is more expensive than previous print sources. Older reference materials with static statistical tables are far inferior to resources that allow users to create their own customized tables, and the value added through such features can be substantial—and is reflected in pricing. Another of the variations for electronic access is that prices can also be different depending on the size of the population served; this pricing structure has existed long enough now that it is taken for granted, but is yet another complicating factor. With older print sources, the largest libraries paid the same prices as did the smallest. Costs for publishing and shipping a dictionary did not vary based on the size of the library, but electronic access costs will vary for publishers; larger populations require that systems can be accessed by a larger number of simultaneous users. For smaller libraries, such a pricing model can be a bonus. For larger collections, reference sources that offer lower prices for smaller numbers of simultaneous users provide one possible method of controlling costs.

One vexing current problem in managing the reference budget is the need to obtain price quotes. Some publishers clearly advertise prices in ads and on websites, but others invite the librarian to e-mail for a tailored quote, thus making purchasing decisions more time-consuming. As with buying a car, this individualized pricing model might lend itself to speculating on whether or not the best deal is being offered. Can prices be negotiated? Sometimes, particularly for large packages of titles, substantial price discounts are available, but negotiating for individual titles is also time-consuming and might offer little return. Librarians need to become more adept at wheeling and dealing for electronic products and deciding when such attempts might be productive, and many acquisitions and reference librarians are mastering the art of seeking out the best possible prices.

While it is clear that data on the use of print volumes are needed in weeding projects, maintaining and analyzing usage data for electronic sources is even more important. In both cases, objective models of collecting data must often still be analyzed in subjective ways. With electronic sources, the need to pay subscription fees every year means that potentially the decision to keep a reference source is reviewed every year. Print continuations and frequently updated reference tools were other forms of subscriptions that might be reviewed and ultimately canceled in the past, but usage data were more difficult to collect systematically. Price-per-use data may be possible to calculate with either print or e-resources, but a strict adherence to keeping only the cheapest titles is not possible. Considerations for covering particular subject disciplines and the relative costs of materials in different disciplines must also be taken into account. A business resource might cost substantially more per use than a humanities volume, in either print or electronic version, and for an individual library, the potential audience for a particular source will play an essential role in its value.

However, some new publishing models often are so different from the old that determining value becomes very complex. If funds are broken down into separate categories for reference materials and databases, determining whether an individual electronic product should be called a database for budgeting purposes is one of the complexities of working within a fairly traditional budget structure. Recently, the Reference Department at UNCG purchased a print encyclopedia, which offered free online access for one year. This product was paid for out of the reference monograph budget, but a decision will have to be made about future access, potentially subscribing to this subject encyclopedia as part of an online system that offers several different resources. In the library's budgeting system, such products have traditionally been treated as databases, but should the library continue to do so? For this particular product, there are enhancements to the online version and updates that might be valuable if the subscription is renewed at the end of a year, in addition to adding new electronic access to other resources, although in this subject area, the majority of information is not of a type that will change or become outdated very quickly. If budget reductions occur, print access continues, making it less likely that the library will subscribe to the electronic access when the "free" access expires.

For certain types of reference sources, publishers now frequently offer purchase versus subscription pricing models, although electronic purchase agreements normally also include some type of maintenance fee to continue the electronic access. An individual subject encyclopedia, particularly a multivolume work, might be offered as a subscription, sometimes with updates available at varying intervals, but libraries can also choose a much higher purchase price for permanent access to the material. What is the break-even point at which purchasing an electronic source is a better decision than subscribing? Countless factors can enter in, including the availability of end-of-year money—again, the budgeting philosophy of "use it or lose it. " Expected tight future budgets might also argue for a purchase model, but in viewing overall budget needs, subscribing to a product provides the flexibility of analyzing use, taking into account changes in programs, and allowing future savings through cancellations if use of a source is not as extensive as expected. That option might seem attractive, but canceling even a seldom-used electronic resource can create negative reactions from library staff and faculty members.

Vendor-provided data may vary significantly in how usage is tracked, making it difficult to compare different products. At UNCG, a three-person team of which the author is a member as head of reference makes decisions on databases, both recommending purchases and cutting resources when necessary. Usage data is carefully examined and provided to all other librarians for their consideration and feedback, but this group is also aware of drawbacks. The usage data is most often compared based on "click-throughs" from the database page since this is a consistent way to determine how often databases are viewed. The library is unable to track titles accessed from the online catalog in the same way, and also has not tried to compare the type or duration of use. Some vendors do provide such information, but in such varying formats that tracking across systems is very difficult. Of course, this usage data is only one factor in the decision-making process, but it is a valuable one.

Service Implications

Ultimately, a little book lust is not a bad thing, as long as it is in the best interest of service. Despite the longtime availability of *Statistical Abstract of the United States* (http://www.census.gov/compendia/statab/) and the *Occupational Outlook Handbook* (http://www.bls.gov/oco/) online, the author still prefers the print versions for ease of use and browsability, and for both these titles, the budget implications are insignificant. Citation guides are still among the heavily used print resources, and are kept within easy reach at the main reference service point in the UNCG library, since none of those most heavily used are available as online subscription products, with the exception of the *Chicago Manual of Style* (http://www.chicagomanualofstyle.org/home.html). When answering questions on citations at the reference desk, the author often uses the print style guides at the reference desk, but often refers users, particularly those who visit through the chat service, to the library's two page guides for different citation styles and sources such as OWL at Purdue Online Writing Lab (http://owl.english.purdue.edu/owl/search.php), which offer extensive examples of different citations. Realizing the value offered by many print resources is an important component of offering the best possible service.

Part of the transition to e-reference includes improvements in how these collections are organized. Libraries struggle with improved organization. Library catalogs still make call number arrangements possible, but browsing using this feature, or even the existence of such a feature, is likely something that would never occur to a library user who might find the notion of browsing the shelves perfectly natural. One suggestion has been to create a different model of organizing e-reference sources to enable users to find them more successfully (Ford et al., 2009). Almost all academic libraries provide subject guides, with many using the increasingly popular LibGuides (http://www.springshare.com/libguides/) system, but there is no question that library users often have difficulty in locating information and that librarians need to continue to find more effective methods of searching and organizing the electronic products being acquired.

Looking Toward the Future

As current budgets and publishing models are examined, librarians need to consider general publishing trends and reader preferences. When e-reference books were initially introduced, there was a fear among librarians that users would resist these formats. However, in the past few years, it has become clear that they are quite comfortable with online resources (although in doing research papers, the difficulty of citing such sources still causes student frustrations). The comfort level of the general public with e-books is now quite clear as their popularity is accelerating rapidly, based on the sales of Kindle, Nook, and the appeal of the iPad as an e-book reader. Prior to the introduction of the Kindle, numerous e-book readers were introduced over a period of years, with overall lukewarm reviews and poor sales. However, the Kindle has proven to be a game changer, particularly with the announcement that the Kindle format has now overtaken the hardcover format in terms of Amazon sales (Li, 2010), and Amazon's assertion that the Kindle reader has been its top-selling single item for the past two years (Gonsalves, 2010), Indicating even stronger sales is the announcement in June 2011 that Amazon is on track to sell about three times as many Kindles in 2011 as were sold in 2010 (Coutts, 2011). It is hard to predict exactly how these formats will be used in libraries, because of ongoing issues with copyright, or what effect use will have on library services. Certainly the growing popularity of downloadable audiobooks indicates that library users might be an enthusiastic audience for downloadable e-books that can be accessed through e-book readers. This trend also implies that reference resources will need to be accessible in ways that are constantly changing.

While reference departments are transforming themselves and moving away from print addiction, there is no patented formula for just what mix of printed books, electronic sources, budgets, and space will best meet the needs of users of reference materials. Each library will need to continually seek the right mixture for its group of users and adjust as technology and scholarship evolve. Flexibility in building collections will help to align budgets and services with continual and inevitable changes. Professional book lust may linger in some regards, but reference librarians are adapting as they make the changes necessary to provide the best possible services in an online world.

References

Barclay, D. A. (2010). The myth of browsing. *American Libraries, 41*(6/7), 52–54.

Bradford, J. T. (2005). What's coming off the shelves? A reference use study analyzing print reference sources used in a university library. *The Journal of Academic Librarianship, 31*(6), 546–558.

Bradford, J. T., Costello, B., & Lenholt, R. (2005). Reference service in the digital age: An analysis of sources used to answer reference questions. *The Journal of Academic Librarianship, 31*(3), 263–272.

Budd, J. M. (1991). Allocation formulas in the literature: A review. *Library Acquisitions: Practice & Theory, 15*(1), 95–107.

Casserly, M. F. (2008). Research in academic library collection management. In M. L. Radford & P. Snelson (Eds.), *Academic library research: Perspectives and current trends* (pp. 82–137). Chicago: ACRL.

Coutts, A. (2011, June 7). Kindle sales will be 10 percent of Amazon's business in 2010, says Citi analyst. *Digital Trends*. Retrieved June 18, 2011, from http://www.digitaltrends.com/mobile/kindle-sales-will-be-10-percent-of-amazons-business-in-2012-says-citi-analyst/.

Delwiche, F. A., &. Bianchi, N. A. (2006). Transformation of a print reference collection. *Medical Reference Services Quarterly, 25*(2), 21–29.

Drake, M. A. (2010). Academic library challenges. *Searcher, 18*(9), 16–21, 52–53.

Ford, L., O'Hara, L. H., & Whiklo, J. (2009). Shelflessness as a virtue: Preserving serendipity in an electronic reference collection. *Journal of Electronic Resources Librarianship, 21*(3/4), 251–262.

Gonsalves, A. (2010, July 29). Amazon launches $139 Kindle. *InformationWeek*. Retrieved June 17, 2011, from http://www.informationweek.com/news/software/web_services/showArticle .jhtml?articleID=226300291.

Heintzelman, N., Moore, C., & Ward, J. (2008). Are reference books becoming an endangered species: Results of a yearlong study of reference book usage at the Winter Park Public Library. *Public Libraries, 47*(5), 60–64.

Hellyer, P. (2009). Reference 2.0: The future of shrinking print reference collections seems destined for the Web. *AALL Spectrum, 13*(5), 24–27.

Kelley, M. (2011). "Bottoming out?" *Library Journal, 136*(1), 28–31.

Kessler, J. (2010). Print reference collections in New York State: Report of a survey. *Journal of the Library Administration & Management Section, 6*(2), 32–44. Retrieved from http://www .nyla.org/uploads/LAMS/1304701202_JLAMS_09_10V6N2.pdf.

Korah, A., Cassidy, E., Elmore, E., & Jerabek, A. (2009). Off the shelf: Trends in the purchase and use of electronic books. *Journal of Electronic Resources Librarianship, 21*(3/4), 263–278.

Lee, M. (2009). Weeding is not just for gardeners: A case study on weeding a reference collection. *Community & Junior College Libraries, 15*(3), 129–135.

Li, S. (2010, July 20). Amazon.com says it's selling 80% more downloaded books than hardcovers. *Los Angeles Times Online*. Retrieved June 17, 2011, from http://articles.latimes.com/2010/jul/ 20/business/la-fi-amazon-kindle-20100720.

Metz, P. & Gray, C. (2005). Public relations and library weeding. *The Journal of Academic Librarianship, 31*(3), 273–279.

Polanka, S. (2008). Is print reference dead? *Booklist, 104*(9/10), 127.

Puacz, J. H. (2005). Electronic vs. print reference sources in public library collections. *Reference Librarian, 44*(91/92), 39–51.

Robbins, S., McCain, C., & Scrivener, L. (2006). The changing format of reference collections: Are research libraries favoring electronic access over print? *Acquisitions Librarian, 18*(35/36), 75–95.

Singer, C. A. (2008). Weeding gone wild: Planning and implementing a review of the reference collection. *Reference & User Services Quarterly, 47*(3), 256–264.

Singer, C. A. (2010). Ready reference collections: A history. *Reference & User Services Quarterly, 49*(3), 253–264.

Spiro, L. & Henry, G. (2010). Can a new research library be all-digital? In *The idea of order: Transforming research collections for 21st century scholarship* (pp. 5–80). CLIR Publication, No. 147. Washington, DC: Council on Library and Information Resources. Retrieved June 17, 2011, from http://www.clir.org/pubs/abstract/pub147abst.html.

Werking, R. H. (1988). Allocating the academic library's book budget: Historical perspectives and current reflections. *Journal of Academic Librarianship, 14*(3), 140–144.

About the Editor
and Contributors

Marie L. Radford, PhD, is Associate Professor at Rutgers, the State University of New Jersey, School of Communication & Information, BA (English), College of New Jersey; MSLS, Syracuse University, New York; PhD (Communication, Information, and Library Studies), Rutgers University. Research interests include qualitative methods, virtual reference, interpersonal communication, cultural studies, and librarian stereotypes. Recent books include *Reference Renaissance: Current and Future Trends* (with R. David Lankes, Neal-Schuman, 2010) and *Conducting the Reference Interview* (with Catherine Sheldrick Ross and Kirsti Nilsen, Neal-Schuman, 2009). She is Co-PI of an IMLS Grant: "Seeking Synchronicity: Evaluating Virtual Reference Services from User, Non-User, and Librarian Perspectives" (IMLS, 2005–2008). She directs the web-based Virtual Reference Bibliography (http://vrbib.rutgers.edu/). Radford received the 2010 Isadore Gilbert Mudge Award for distinguished contributions to reference librarianship from the American Library Association, Reference and User Services Association.

* * *

Beth Avery is Head of Collection Development at the University of North Texas (UNT). Previously, she was Head of Research and Instruction at UNT, Western State College Library Director, Lamar University Library Director, and Head of Science and Technology Libraries at Colorado State University. She has been interested in virtual reference since serving on the Pathfinder Regional Library System VR task force and the Colorado State Library Collaborative Virtual Reference Committee, Steering Committee. She participated in the pilot project for My Info Quest. For the past two years she has been researching user satisfaction with virtual reference. She received a BA in Education from the College of William and Mary, and a master's and Certificate of Advanced Study from Drexel University.

Susan Beatty is Head of Learning Commons at the Taylor Family Digital Library, University of Calgary, Canada. She has extensive experience in managing excellent customer service in both academic and public libraries. Her main responsibility is coordinating the delivery of reference service and technical support in the new Learning Commons. It is her belief that the best service within Learning Commons is provided through collaboration with other academic units. Susan has presented at various international conferences in Hong Kong, New Zealand, United States, England, and Scotland.

Steven J. Bell is Associate University Librarian for Research and Instructional Services at Temple University. He writes and speaks about academic librarianship, learning technologies, design thinking, user experience, and library management. Steven is a co-founder of the Blended Librarian's Online Learning Community on the Learning

Times Network and has participated in numerous virtual presentations. He blogs at Kept-Up Academic Librarian, ACRLog, and Designing Better Libraries, a blog about design thinking and library user experiences. His weekly column "From the Bell Tower" appears at Library Journal's Academic Newswire. He is co-author of the book "Academic Librarianship by Design." Bell is currently serving as the vice-president/president-elect for the Association of College & Research Libraries (ACRL). For additional information or links to Bell's projects, point your browser to http://stevenbell.info or to his blog, *Designing Better Libraries*, at http://dbl.lishost.org.

Jay Bhatt is Reference Librarian for Engineering at Drexel University's W.W. Hagerty Library, and has been since joining in December 1997. He received his MLIS and MS in Electrical and Computer Engineering from Drexel University, and his MS in Education from the University of Pennsylvania. His interest areas include collection development in engineering, outreach to faculty and students, teaching engineering information-seeking skills to faculty and students, and exploring how Web 2.0 can be used for increasing information awareness among students and learning about how it is changing today's scholarly communication. Jay loves mentoring and working with students and is actively involved with the Engineering Libraries Division of the American Society for Engineering Education. In 2010, he received the Homer I. Bernhardt Distinguished Service Award from the Engineering Libraries Division of the American Society for Engineering Education. He is the 2003 recipient of Drexel University's Harold Myers Distinguished Service Award.

Karen Biglin is Faculty Librarian at Scottsdale Community College, and has been an academic librarian since 1978. Her experience includes working at both the university and college levels, where she has taught countless classes in face-to-face and online formats. She has been providing face-to-face reference services for all 33 years of her career. She holds an MLS from the University of Arizona and an MA from California State University, Dominguez Hills. While serving on the Assessment Steering Committee at her college, she attended the Harvard Graduate School of Education's Workshop on Assessment in Higher Education, as well as the Higher Learning Commission's Academy for Assessment of Student Learning. Karen served as chair of her college's Writing Assessment Committee. She has always been interested in improving library services and decided to use her experience with assessment and reference to develop a method to evaluate VRS.

Wayne Bivens-Tatum is Philosophy and Religion Librarian at the Princeton University Library, where he provides general and specialized reference and instruction, develops and manages the philosophy and religion collections, and acts as liaison to the departments of Philosophy and Religion. He has graduate degrees in English and Library and Information Science from the University of Illinois. He has taught writing seminars on political philosophy in the Princeton Writing Program and arts and humanities librarianship courses for the University of Illinois Graduate School of Library and Information Science. He has given numerous workshops on search technologies to New Jersey librarians, and writes frequently about issues in reference, instruction, collection development, technology, and higher education on his blog, *Academic Librarian*. He's currently working on a book about the relationship between libraries and the project of Enlightenment.

Elizabeth Brodak is Library Director at Tomlinson Library on the Mesa State College Campus in Grand Junction, Colorado. She has been a librarian in special and academic libraries, beginning her career as the Assistant Command Reference Librarian for USARV (United States Army Vietnam) 1971–1972; her transition to academic librarianship was made through WCAHEC (Western Colorado Area Health Education Center, an academic medical library). At Mesa State she had been Reference Librarian and Head of Public Services before taking over as director. Her love of reference and interest in breaking down access barriers for students led to involvement in virtual reference. She received a BA degree from Carthage College in Kenosha Wisconsin and a MLS from the University of Hawaii in Honolulu.

Christopher C. Brown is Associate Professor, Reference Technology Integration Librarian, and Government Documents Coordinator at the University of Denver, Penrose Library. He is a frequent presenter on online access issues relating to depository collections including tracking click-throughs to online documents through the online catalog. His recent article in *College & Research Libraries* (2011) surveys user click-throughs to government documents in the University of Denver online catalog over a six-year period. He often consults with libraries concerning retooling of depository libraries for the digital age, implementation of click-through technologies, and technology solutions for adding online content to the local catalog. For the past 12 years, Chris has taught various courses at the University of Denver's Library and Information Science program, including Reference, Internet Reference and Research, Information Access and Retrieval, and Government Publications.

Lisa Campbell is Digital Learning Services Librarian at the University of Michigan. Previously, Lisa was Information Services Librarian for The University of Alabama's Amelia Gayle Gorgas Library in Tuscaloosa, Alabama, where she worked with reference, instruction, outreach, and emerging technologies. Lisa also once served in Public Services at the University of Pittsburgh. She holds an MLIS from the University of Pittsburgh and a BFA in cello performance from Carnegie Mellon University. Lisa is an active member of the American Library Association and the Association of College and Research Libraries. She is a regular reviewer for *Library Journal*, a 2011 ALA Emerging Leader, and a 2011 ACRL Immersion Program (Teacher Track) participant.

Emily K. Chan has a BA in Biological Sciences from Grinnell College in Grinnell, Iowa. Her MLIS is from San José State University. She is currently a liaison librarian at San José State University's King Library in San José, California. Previously, she was Assistant Professor, Sciences Librarian at the University of the Pacific in Stockton, California. Her research interests include instructional pedagogy, information literacy, and health sciences librarianship.

Leo Clougherty is Head of the Sciences Library at the University of Iowa. His responsibilities include administration of the Sciences Library, supervision of the Education and Outreach Librarian and several library assistant staff, and collection management and liaison activities with the faculty in the departments of Biology, Chemistry, Geoscience, Mathematics, and Statistics and Actuarial Sciences. His interests include needs assessment, new models for collections and outreach, and scholarly communication. Prior to his present position, he was Head of five distinct branch libraries at the University of Iowa and the Reference and Instruction Librarian and AHEC Coordinator at UAMS in Little Rock. He has been President of the Arkansas Library Association and President of the Iowa Chapter of ACRL. He has a BS in Geoscience from the University of Wisconsin-Whitewater and an MLS from the University of Wisconsin-Milwaukee.

Claudette Cloutier is Director of Science and Engineering in Libraries and Cultural Resources at the University of Calgary and is also Interim Program Director for the Taylor Family Digital Library. She has more than 15 years' experience as a science librarian and has earned her MLIS. In her role as Librarian for Geology and Geophysics, Engineering and Northern Studies, she is interested in understanding the nature of the interactions that academic librarians have with their research communities and the impact that these interactions have on researcher-librarian collaborations.

Lynn Silipigni Connaway, PhD, is Senior Research Scientist at OCLC Research. Her PhD is in Library and Information Science (LIS) from the University of Wisconsin-Madison. She was Visiting Researcher at the University of Sheffield, and completed several U.K. projects funded by JISC (Joint Information Systems Committee) to investigate users' behaviors, including virtual research (VR) environments and digital repositories. She is collaborating with JISC and the University of Oxford to study digital visitors and residents. She is coauthor of the fifth edition of *Basic Research Methods for Librarians* (Libraries Unlimited, 2010). Connaway was co-PI of two IMLS-funded projects, one evaluating sustainability and relevance of VR services, and one studying the information-seeking behaviors of faculty, graduate students, and undergraduates. Previously she was Vice President of Research and Library Systems at NetLibrary, director of the Library and Information Services Department at the University of Denver, and on the faculty of the Library and Informational Science program at the University of Missouri, Columbia.

Memo Cordova is Assistant Professor/Librarian at Boise State University's Albertsons Library, Idaho, and serves as liaison and collection manager to the Modern Languages & Literatures, Bilingual Education, Basque Studies, Philosophy, Psychology, and Anthropology departments. Memo has worked in private, public, and academic libraries. His research interests include the intersection of Web 2.0 in education, libraries, and everyday life. His writings and presentations can be found at http://works.bepress.com/memo_cordova/. Memo received his MLIS in 2003 from the University of Washington's iSchool and has been an active blogging member of the Special Projects Library Action Team (SPLAT) since 2006. He blogs at http://bit.ly/m3moSPLAT and tweets at http://twitter.com/#!/m3mo.

Jean Costello is a passionate library advocate and activist who champions citizen involvement in the future of the library. In this spirit, she spent two years blogging as "The Radical Patron." Her controversial article in *Library Journal*, "Why I Don't Use Libraries for Reference Anymore," generated a firestorm of debate. Jean was a speaker at *Library Journal*'s virtual e-book summit and a plenary panelist at the 2010 Reference Renaissance Conference. In March 2011, she outlined her vision for building "a new Alexandria" in a colloquium presentation at the University of Toronto's iSchool titled "The Transcendental Library and Disruption from Within."

Sara Davidson is Head of User Communication and Instruction at the University of California, Merced, and holds an MLIS degree from the University of British Columbia (UBC). She enjoys teaching students and faculty how to take advantage of library resources, working with campus partners to create library initiatives in support of effective first-year experiences, and collaborating with UC librarians to establish shared services. She is actively involved in assessment of library instruction and services. Recently, she co-authored an article titled "Inside the iPod, Outside the Classroom" for *Reference Services Review.*

Karen Docherty is Virtual Reference Coordinator for the Maricopa County Community College District serving the Phoenix, Arizona, metropolitan area. She manages all aspects of the District's ten-college Ask a Librarian service, which includes both 24/7 chat and Txt a Librarian. In collaboration with the District's Ask a Librarian committee, she leads the effort to assess their virtual reference service. In addition to her interests in assessment, her professional interests include promoting reference services and implementing cooperative projects of all types. After earning her MA in Library and Information Studies from the University of Wisconsin-Madison in 1995, she worked as a librarian in Australia, Canada, and the United States. Her range of library experience includes working as Reference Librarian, Electronic Resources Librarian, and Administrator, primarily in academic libraries with an emphasis on multi-college and consortial settings. Karen also teaches several online, for-credit library courses.

Patrick Farrell is Digital Resources Librarian at the Jefferson County Public Library in Colorado, where his work includes subscription databases and online resources, web content strategy, digitization projects, and emerging technologies. Patrick staffs Ask-Colorado, Colorado's statewide virtual reference cooperative, and is a former member and co-chair of the AskColorado/AskAcademic Quality Assurance Subcommittee. Patrick also runs Jeffco Stories, a community-based oral history project. He holds an MA in English from Temple University and a MS in Library and Information Science from the University of Illinois at Urbana-Champaign.

Carrie Forbes is Associate Professor and Instruction Coordinator and Reference Librarian at the University of Denver, Penrose Library. Her work involves integrating research skills instruction into the university's academic programs. She also serves as the subject specialist to History, Education, University College, the Women's College, and the Writing Program. Her research interests include research and writing collaborations, online learning, and the application of emerging technologies to library instruction. Carrie's recent publications and presentations include a book chapter on integrating discipline-based library instruction into the curriculum in *Research within the Disciplines: Foundations for Reference and Library Instruction*, a co-authored article in *Reference Services Review* on Penrose Library's Research Center, and a presentation at the 2009 Internet Librarian International Conference on using the Google Custom Search Engine with LibGuides.

Julie Fronmueller is Outreach Librarian at Colorado State University–Pueblo and is responsible for planning events and programs for the campus and greater Pueblo communities. She is also the liaison to the Hasan School of Business. Julie earned her

MLIS at Louisiana State University, Baton Rouge, and her MBA at Boise State University. Previously, she worked at a small public library in Central New York and university libraries in California and Louisiana. She is currently concentrating her research efforts on the subject of incorporating local history and culture into library programming and exhibits.

Colbe Galston is Business and Reference Librarian for Douglas County (Colorado) Libraries, Parker branch. She graduated from the University of Denver with a MLIS in 2005. She received her BA in English and Spanish from Tulane University. Throughout her career with Douglas County Libraries, Colbe has worked on several outreach and business initiatives including BizInfo, the DCL business research service, the Community Reference Project and embedded librarianship with the Parker Downtown Development Council. She is Chair of the Colorado Association of Libraries Business Services Interest Group.

Patrick Griffis is Business Librarian for the University Libraries, at the University of Nevada, Las Vegas. In his position of Business Librarian, he serves as the liaison librarian to UNLV's College of Business and provides outreach services to the business community in the Las Vegas area. Mr. Griffis holds a BS in Business Administration from the University of Southern California and earned his MLIS from the University of North Texas.

Elizabeth Kelsen Huber is Adult Services Department Head at the Highlands Ranch Library, one of seven libraries in the Douglas County (Colorado) Libraries district. In this capacity, she supervises a staff of professional and paraprofessional staff, maintains a vibrant collection and focuses on community outreach and engagement. She joined the Douglas County Libraries staff in 2006 as Program & Outreach Coordinator. In this position, she supported district-wide programming, including the development of an evaluative structure that improved program quality and increased program attendance. She was also responsible for coordinating major events and fundraisers. She serves as Chair of the Colorado Association of Libraries Leadership Development Committee, which coordinates a statewide Leadership Institute. She has a BS in Broadcast Journalism from University of Colorado-Boulder and a MLS from Emporia State University.

Nancy Huling is Division Head of Reference and Research Services, in the University of Washington Libraries. She has held positions at the State University of New York, Binghamton, and the University of California, Riverside. She obtained a BA in English and master's degrees in Library Science and History. Nancy has been active in the Reference and User Services Association (RUSA) of ALA, serving as President in 2003–2004. She is the Chair of the OCLC QuestionPoint User Group, and a member of the QuestionPoint 24/7 Cooperative Advisory Board. She is the author (with Nancy L. Baker) of *A Research Guide for Undergraduate Students: English and American Literature* (6th edition, 2006). In 2009, Nancy received the Isadore Gilbert Mudge Award, which recognizes distinguished contributions to reference librarianship, and she was selected as the University of Washington's 2011 Distinguished Librarian. She is a part-time lecturer in the UW Information School, and teaches Principles of Information Services.

Katherine Johnson is Adult Services Librarian at the Highlands Ranch Library, a regional branch of Douglas County Libraries system in Colorado, and has been since

2004. She has served the Douglas County Libraries for 18 years, having started as a shelver at the Philip S. Miller branch in Castle Rock, Colorado, during high school. After obtaining a BAS degree with a concentration in Psychology at Fort Lewis College, Katherine began her professional career as a Library Assistant II at Philip S. Miller in 1997. She was promoted to branch Assistant Circulation Supervisor in 1998. While working in this capacity, she earned a MLIS degree from Emporia State University's School of Library & Information Management at its Denver location. Katherine's passions include contributing to the Community Reference Project for Douglas County Libraries, working with patrons, and conducting research.

Kris Johnson is Virtual Reference Consultant for the State Library of Colorado and the AskColorado/AskAcademic Coordinator. She has lived and worked in Colorado since July 2006. Prior to this, she worked for 15 years in academic libraries across the Western United States, most recently as a tenured Information Literacy Librarian at California State University, Chico. Kris holds a MLIS from the University of Texas at Austin and a BA in Music from Montana State University, Bozeman.

Mary Wilkins Jordan is Assistant Professor at Simmons College Graduate School of Library and Information Science. Her teaching and research areas revolve around effective administration of libraries. Her teaching focus at Simmons College is Management, Reference, and the Internship classes. Prior to entering academia, she worked as a public library director and administrator, and was an attorney. She has a BA in Psychology and a BS in Political Science from Quincy University (Quincy, Illinois), a JD from Case Western Reserve University School of Law (Cleveland, Ohio), a MLIS from the University of Wisconsin–Milwaukee (Milwaukee, Wisconsin), and is finishing a PhD in Library Science from the University of North Carolina–Chapel Hill (Chapel Hill, North Carolina).

Mary Kickham-Samy is a reference librarian at Macomb Community College in Warren, Michigan. She received her MLIS at Wayne State University in Detroit in 2000. Previously, in 1975, she earned a master's in Teaching English as a Foreign Language at the American University in Cairo, Egypt. Currently, Mary is working on her dissertation for a doctoral degree in instructional design and technology at Old Dominion University in Norfolk, Virginia. Active in the Michigan Virtual Reference Collaborative, she coedits a training newsletter called "The Research Help Now Training Newsletter." She is also the training coordinator for the collaborative. Her research interests include discourse analysis of virtual reference transcripts and applying what is known about cognitive load theory to instruction in information literacy.

Rebekah Kilzer is Technology Partnerships Librarian and Manager of Partnership Program Development at the Drexel University Libraries as well as an adjunct professor at Drexel's iSchool, the College of Information Science and Technology where she teaches cataloging and metadata courses for the graduate program. She earned her MS in Library Science and Information Systems from Drexel University. In addition to her current position, she has also held positions at The Ohio State University Libraries and at OCLC. Her professional interests include the evolving technological landscape in the library environment, including changes in metadata and system standards, and how users are affected by these changes. In addition to articles on these topics, she has most recently coedited a book on user research as a part of the eXtensible Catalog project at the University of Rochester Libraries titled *Scholarly Practice, Participatory Design and the eXtensible Catalog* (ARCL, 2011). She lives in Philadelphia.

Lorrie A. Knight has a BA in Political Science from the University of Texas at Austin and a MLIS from Louisiana State University. She is currently Professor, Reference and Instruction Librarian at the University of the Pacific in Stockton, California. Prior to her time at Pacific, Lorrie worked at Connecticut College and the Louisiana State Legislature. Lorrie has published articles in *Reference Services Review* and the *Journal of Academic Librarianship*. Her research interests focus on the assessment of information literacy and library instruction in general.

Kari A. Kozak is Sciences Education and Outreach Librarian at the University of Iowa. She coordinates education and outreach activities for the Sciences Library, including reference, exhibits, instructional, and access services in the disciplines of physics and astronomy, chemistry, biological sciences, geosciences, and mathematical sciences and serves as liaison to the physics and astronomy department. She holds a bachelor's degree in Meteorology and Environmental Studies from Iowa State University, and a master's degree in Library Science from the University of North Carolina–Chapel Hill. Before joining the University of Iowa in November 2008, she worked at Texas A & M University as a Science & Engineering Librarian.

Mary Krautter is Head of Reference and Instructional Services at the University of North Carolina at Greensboro Libraries, a position she has held since 2007. Previously, she was Director of Interdisciplinary Information Literacy and held several other positions in public services at the University of Kentucky. She received her MLS from the University of North Carolina at Chapel Hill and also holds MA and BA degrees in English from Virginia Tech. Her research interests include integrating information literacy into the higher education curriculum and changing patterns of collection management for reference collections. She is currently co-editing a book on entrepreneurial librarians scheduled to be published by McFarland in 2012. She serves as Treasurer of the North Carolina Chapter of Special Libraries Association and on the Board of Directors for BOOKMARKS Book Festival, based in Winston-Salem, North Carolina.

Jamie LaRue is the director of the Douglas County Libraries, headquartered in Castle Rock, Colorado, and has been since 1990. He is the author of *The New Inquisition: Understanding and Managing Intellectual Freedom Challenges*, and has written a weekly newspaper column for more than 23 years. He was Colorado Librarian of the Year in 1998, the Castle Rock Chamber of Commerce's 2003 Business Person of the Year, and in 2007 won the Julie J. Boucher Award for Intellectual Freedom.

Kristen Laughlin is a librarian at Red Rocks Community College in Lakewood, Colorado. She is interested in electronic resource management, serving distance students, and creating a great user experience for in-person as well as remote users of the library. She has worked previously at Jones International University as Library Technology Coordinator, and as an After-Hours Librarian for AskColorado/AskAcademic, Colorado's virtual reference cooperative. Kristen began volunteering with AskColorado/AskAcademic in 2008 as a student intern, while pursuing her MLIS online at the University of Alabama. She has a BA in literature from Juniata College, and has also worked at the Denver Public Library. Before she was a librarian, Kristen worked as a GED teacher and a scientist.

Amy Long is Patron Services Department Head for Castle Pines Library in Douglas County (Colorado), a 2,300-square-foot store-front library with a highly used popular collection. Amy started at Douglas County in 2004 as a Library Assistant II in circulation before moving into the IT department as frontline technical support and later, a supervisor. While in IT, she was instrumental in the installation, support, and training for the Automated Materials Handling systems. She received her MLS degree from Southern Connecticut State University's online program in 2007 and was promoted to Department Head in 2009. Amy is passionate about the future of libraries and loves working on any project that will help public libraries to be relevant long into the future.

Sidney Lowe is Head of the Research and Information Department for the University Libraries, at the University of Nevada, Las Vegas. She is responsible for administering the reference services provided at Lied Library. Sidney also manages the Libraries' government information resources, and serves as a subject liaison librarian for political science. She earned her MLIS from the University of North Texas. Sidney holds a BA in Sociology from the University of California, Santa Barbara, and also a master's degree in Public Administration from the University of Nevada, Las Vegas.

Paul M. Mascareñas is Reference Librarian at Adams State College Nielsen Library and came to librarianship via painting a cataloging librarian's house. A former co-owner of Used to be a Tree Booksellers, Paul is interested in reading, literature, and books. He began to learn the way of the librarian while working as an interlibrary loan assistant at Nielsen Library. Able to surround himself with books and help share information with the masses, Paul graduated with his MLS degree from Emporia State University in 2009. Paul is co-chair of the Colorado Virtual Reference Quality Assurance Committee (CVRQA) for Ask Colorado/Academic. He is also a member of the Colorado Association of Libraries Leadership Institute (CALLI). He is perpetually interested in learning how to make reference desk services transferrable to places other than the reference desk. You can sometimes read what is on his mind at https://blogs.adams.edu/library.

Erin McCaffrey is Digital Systems Librarian, Associate Professor, at Regis University in Denver, Colorado. Previously, she was Distance Learning Librarian at Regis University and Assistant Instruction Coordinator at DePaul University. Her research interests are in human-computer interaction and interactive media. She has experience in web-based library services, system administration, distance learning, and reference and instruction. She coordinates the library's chat reference service and is a past chair of the Association of Jesuit Colleges and Universities (AJCU) Virtual Reference steering committee. Erin received her BA degree from DePaul University, with a major in Psychology, and earned her MLIS degree from Dominican University.

Larry Milliken is Liaison Librarian for the Humanities and Social Sciences at Drexel University. He received his MLIS in 2002 from Rutgers, the State University of New

Jersey. Prior to becoming a librarian he earned an MA in Medieval Studies from Fordham University and was a doctoral student in Medieval European History at the City University of New York's Graduate School and University Center. Before coming to Drexel, he was Assistant Professor and Coordinator for Information Literacy at Neumann College (now Neumann University) and had been Assistant Librarian for the Sciences at St. Peter's College. His research interests alternate between Library and Information Science and History and include librarian involvement with digital humanities projects, collaborations with History faculty in the education of Engineering undergraduates, medieval visual culture, and early contacts between the medieval West and the Mongol Empire.

Doris Munson is Systems/Reference Librarian at Eastern Washington University. Her primary responsibilities are the maintenance of the library's Millennium integrated library system and the supervision of the library's systems unit. She maintains WebBridge and participates in the administration of other online systems such as ILLiad, CONTENTdm, and EZProxy. In addition to her systems responsibilities, Doris also does reference and instruction and is the library's subject specialist for the university's science and engineering programs. Doris holds an MLS from the University of Washington and BS in Animal Science from Oregon State University.

Justin Otto is Social Sciences Librarian at Eastern Washington University. He is a reference and instruction librarian who liaisons with the university's social sciences programs as well as provides reference services for government documents. Previously, he was Economics Librarian at Emory University. His research interests include information literacy with regard to data and statistics, and methods for data-driven analysis of library services. Justin holds an MLIS from the University of Washington, and both an MA and BA in Economics from Washington State University. He is active in the ALA Government Documents Round Table (GODORT), and has served as a member of the Federal Depository Library Program's Depository Library Council to the Public Printer of the United States.

Sylvia Owens is Library Services Reference Facilitator at Austin Community College, where she has been employed for the past four years as a Reference Librarian/Assistant Professor. Within this capacity, she collaborates within the department to facilitate communication regarding reference services throughout the Austin Community College district on uniform policies, procedures, and training. Sylvia coordinates and evaluates the operation of virtual reference chat services and teaches information literacy classes. She is also a cooperative virtual reference representative for AskAcademic. Sylvia received her MLS from the University of North Texas and her BSE from Eastern Illinois University.

Amy Sieving is Systems/Technical Services Librarian at the Wilkinson Public Library in Telluride, Colorado. She has experience working in both reference and cataloging and has worked in both departments during the five years she has been at WPL. A graduate of Boston University, Amy received her BA in Biology and spent several years working as a wildlife biologist. She earned her MLIS in 2009 through the online program at the University of Southern Mississippi, where her research focused on cataloging and optimizing OPAC usability. Amy is excited to learn about the world of systems librarianship as well as staffing AskColorado, Colorado's statewide virtual reference cooperative.

Karen Sobel is Research and Instruction Librarian and Assistant Professor at the University of Colorado Denver. Her library also serves Metropolitan State College of Denver and the Community College of Denver. She works extensively with the campus's freshman composition and first-year experience programs. Karen holds a BA in English from Penn State University and master's degrees in Library Science and English from the University of North Carolina at Chapel Hill.

Amy VanScoy is a doctoral candidate at the School of Information and Library Science at the University of North Carolina at Chapel Hill. Her research focuses on the practitioner beliefs of reference and information services professionals. Her dissertation research, "Exploring the Meaning of Reference Work for Librarians in Academic Research Libraries" was awarded the Jesse H. Shera Award in 2011 for the Support of Dissertation Research and the Eugene Garfield Doctoral Dissertation Fellowship. VanScoy's 12-year career as an academic reference librarian began at North Carolina State University Libraries where she was Librarian for Undergraduate Research. She later held two management positions at NCSU Libraries, Assistant Head and Associate Head of Research & Information Services. In these positions, she shared responsibility for managing reference and digital reference services, coordinated reference staff training and assessment of user instruction, and had significant supervisory responsibilities. A frequent presenter at national and local conferences, VanScoy has published in the areas of digital reference, diversity, and undergraduate instruction.

Robin E. Veal is a candidate for her EdD with a focus in Higher Education Leadership at Saint Mary's University of Minnesota. She has worked as an Academic Librarian at Capella University and Saint Mary's University of Minnesota. Robin holds an MLIS from Dominican University. Her research interests include virtual reference, adult learners, and library anxiety.

Amy Vecchione is Assistant Professor/Librarian at Albertsons Library, Boise State University, Idaho. As liaison to the Departments of Chemistry, Biochemistry, Biology, and Raptor Studies, she teaches science information literacy and also develops collections in those areas. On the Boise State campus, she is a part of the mLearning Scholars Community helping to bring mobile technology tools into the classroom. Amy also serves as an active leader in the Idaho Library Association. You can find more of her scholarly and creative works at the website http://works.bepress.com/amy_vecchione/.

Andrew Walsh is Academic Librarian at the University of Huddersfield, where his main role involves subject liaison for the schools of Education and Professional Development and Music, Humanities, and Media. Andrew is particularly interested in information literacy, the use of active learning within library sessions, the application of mobile technologies within the library environment, and taking advantage of appropriate Web 2.0 technologies to make his life easier (@andywalsh999 on Twitter). Over recent years, he has delivered conference papers and published articles on information literacy, active learning and mobile learning in libraries, and has cowritten a book on active learning tips for librarians. Most of his recent publications and talks can be found via the University of Huddersfield repository (http://bit.ly/lilacAW). Andrew is an active researcher practitioner, including studying part-time for an information literacy-related PhD at the University of Huddersfield.

Shaye White is Virtual Librarian for the Pioneer Library System in Oklahoma, which serves Cleveland, McClain, and Pottawatomie Counties. She is part of a team that manages the library system's Internet presence. This includes websites, social networking sites, online catalog, databases, OverDrive audiobook and e-book collection, and Info Quest text reference questions. The Pioneer Library System can be found at http://www.just soyouknow.us or http://www.facebook.com/pioneerlibrarysystem. She also trains staff members, works as a cataloger, and performs library outreach in the community. Her professional interests include improving the user experience and understanding digital material consumption and usage. Shaye attended the University of Oklahoma in Norman, where she earned a BA in Information Science in 2007 and an MA of Library and Information Studies in 2009.

Christy Zlatos is currently on the reference team at Washington State University. She received her MSLS degree from the University of Illinois. She has worked at academic reference desks at the University of Southern Indiana, Auburn University (where she was Wikipedia founder Jimmy Wales' librarian in 1986), Northeastern University, and Washington State University.

Peter A. Zuber is Engineering Librarian at Brigham Young University, Utah. Apart from collection responsibilities, he has helped evaluate and implement virtual reference services and comanaged the redesign of the library's website with the integration of a new federated search engine. As Chair of the library's Research Behavior Group and User Studies and Assessment Team, he worked with librarians to discover user preferences and habits and how they impact current library services and tools. Published papers include topics such as search engine constraints, open access, institutional repositories, and remote services. Before joining the university, he was Director of Imaging and Process Engineering for T/R Systems in Atlanta. He holds 29 patents in the areas of electrophotographic engine design, color theory, and digital image processing. He received his MLIS from the University of Southern Mississippi and his master's in Imaging Science and Engineering from the Rochester Institute of Technology in New York.

Index

Page numbers followed by the letter "f" indicate figures and those followed by the letter "t" indicate tables.

CPSIA information can be obtained at www.ICGtesting.com
Printed in the USA
LVOW070910020512

280000LV00005B/2/P